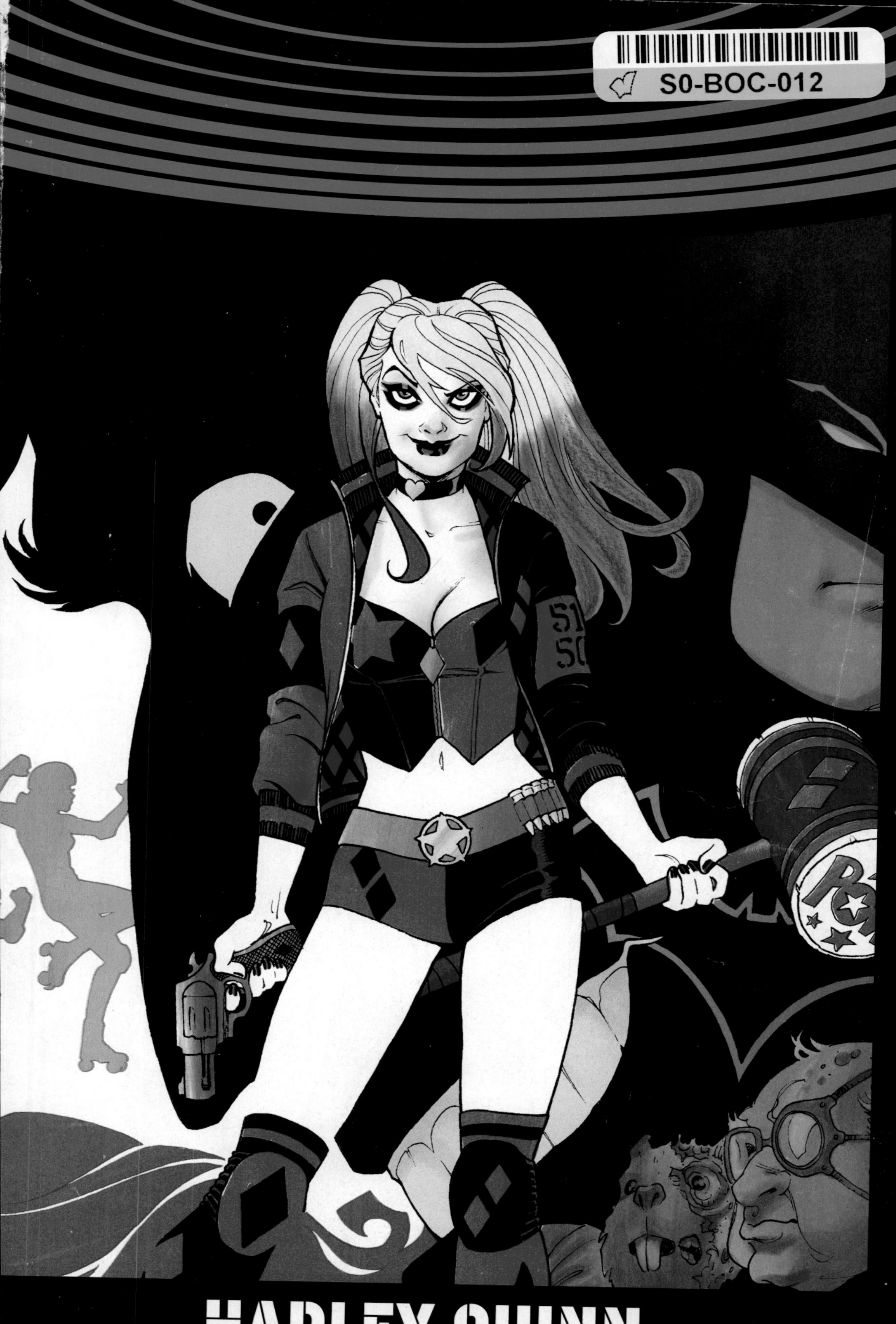
51
50

HARLEY QUINN

VOL.1 DIE LAUGHING

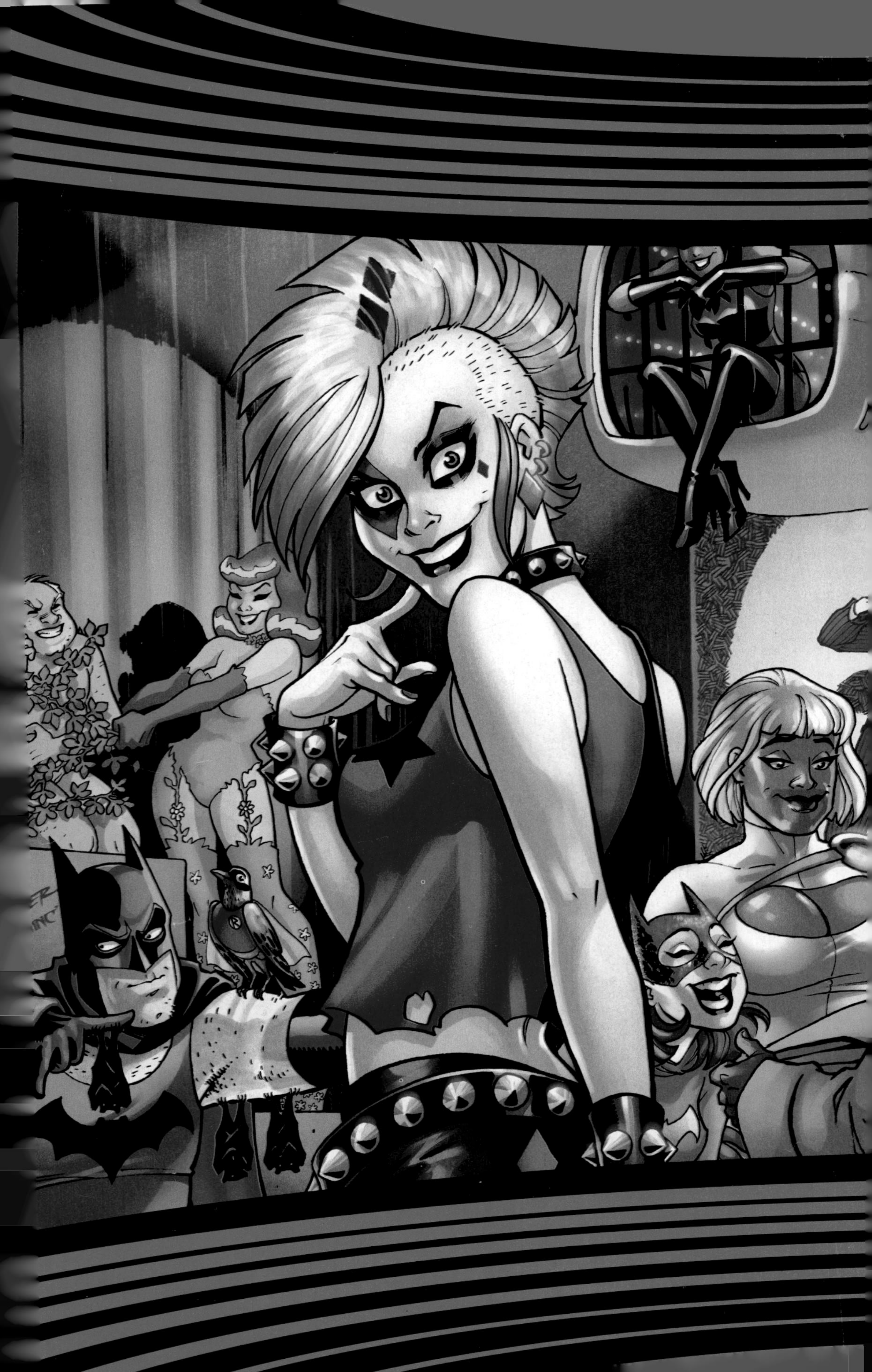

HARLEY QUINN
VOL.1 DIE LAUGHING

AMANDA CONNER
JIMMY PALMIOTTI
writers

JOHN TIMMS * CHAD HARDIN * BRET BLEVINS
JOSEPH MICHAEL LINSNER * JILL THOMPSON
artists

ALEX SINCLAIR
HI-FI * JILL THOMPSON
colorists

DAVE SHARPE
letterer

AMANDA CONNER and ALEX SINCLAIR
original series and collection cover artists

HARLEY QUINN created by **PAUL DINI** and **BRUCE TIMM**

CHRIS CONROY EDITOR - ORIGINAL SERIES * **DAVE WIELGOSZ** ASSISTANT EDITOR - ORIGINAL SERIES * **JEB WOODARD** GROUP EDITOR - COLLECTED EDITIONS
ROBIN WILDMAN EDITOR - COLLECTED EDITION * **STEVE COOK** DESIGN DIRECTOR - BOOKS * **MONIQUE GRUSPE** Publication Design

BOB HARRAS Senior VP - Editor-in-Chief, DC Comics

DIANE NELSON President * **DAN DiDIO** Publisher * **JIM LEE** Publisher * **GEOFF JOHNS** President & Chief Creative Officer
AMIT DESAI Executive VP - Business & Marketing Strategy, Direct to Consumer & Global Franchise Management * **SAM ADES** Senior VP - Direct to Consumer
BOBBIE CHASE VP - Talent Development * **MARK CHIARELLO** Senior VP - Art, Design & Collected Editions
JOHN CUNNINGHAM Senior VP - Sales & Trade Marketing * **ANNE DePIES** Senior VP - Business Strategy, Finance & Administration
DON FALLETTI VP - Manufacturing Operations * **LAWRENCE GANEM** VP - Editorial Administration & Talent Relations
ALISON GILL Senior VP - Manufacturing & Operations * **HANK KANALZ** Senior VP - Editorial Strategy & Administration
JAY KOGAN VP - Legal Affairs * **THOMAS LOFTUS** VP - Business Affairs
JACK MAHAN VP - Business Affairs * **NICK J. NAPOLITANO** VP - Manufacturing Administration
EDDIE SCANNELL VP - Consumer Marketing * **COURTNEY SIMMONS** Senior VP - Publicity & Communications
JIM (SKI) SOKOLOWSKI VP - Comic Book Specialty Sales & Trade Marketing * **NANCY SPEARS** VP - Mass, Book, Digital Sales & Trade Marketing

HARLEY QUINN VOL. 1: DIE LAUGHING

DC Comics, 2900 West Alameda Ave., Burbank, CA 91505. Printed by LSC Communications, Salem, VA, USA. 2/10/17.
First Printing. ISBN: 978-1-4012-6831-2

Library of Congress Cataloging-in-Publication Data is available.

PEFC Certified
Printed on paper from sustainably managed forests, controlled sources
PEFC
PEFC/29-31-337
www.pefc.org

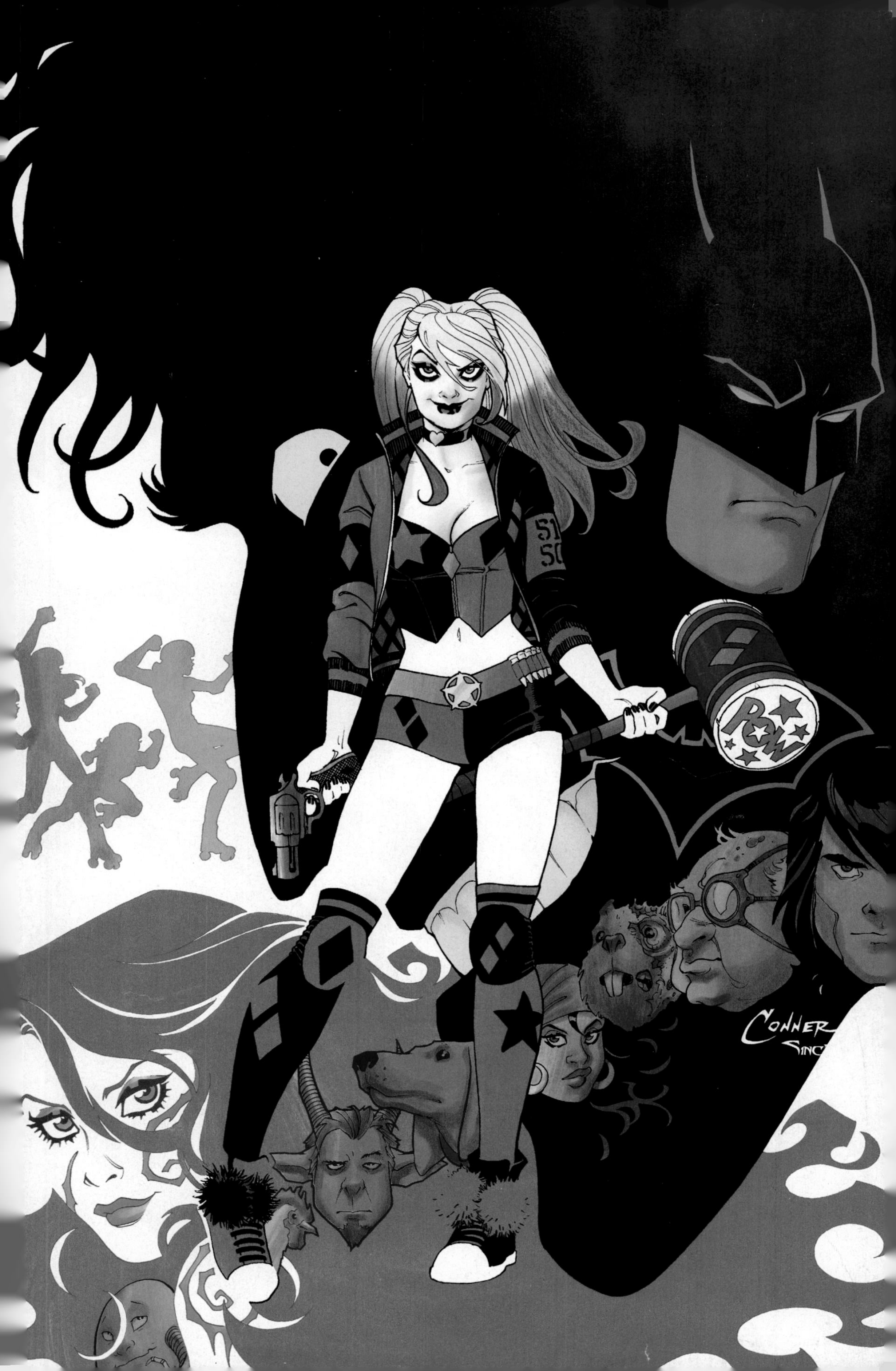

51
50
POW
CONNER

DIE LAUGHING PART 1: AFTERBIRTH

AMANDA CONNER and JIMMY PALMIOTTI writers ∗ CHAD HARDIN artist
ALEX SINCLAIR colorist ∗ DAVE SHARPE letterer

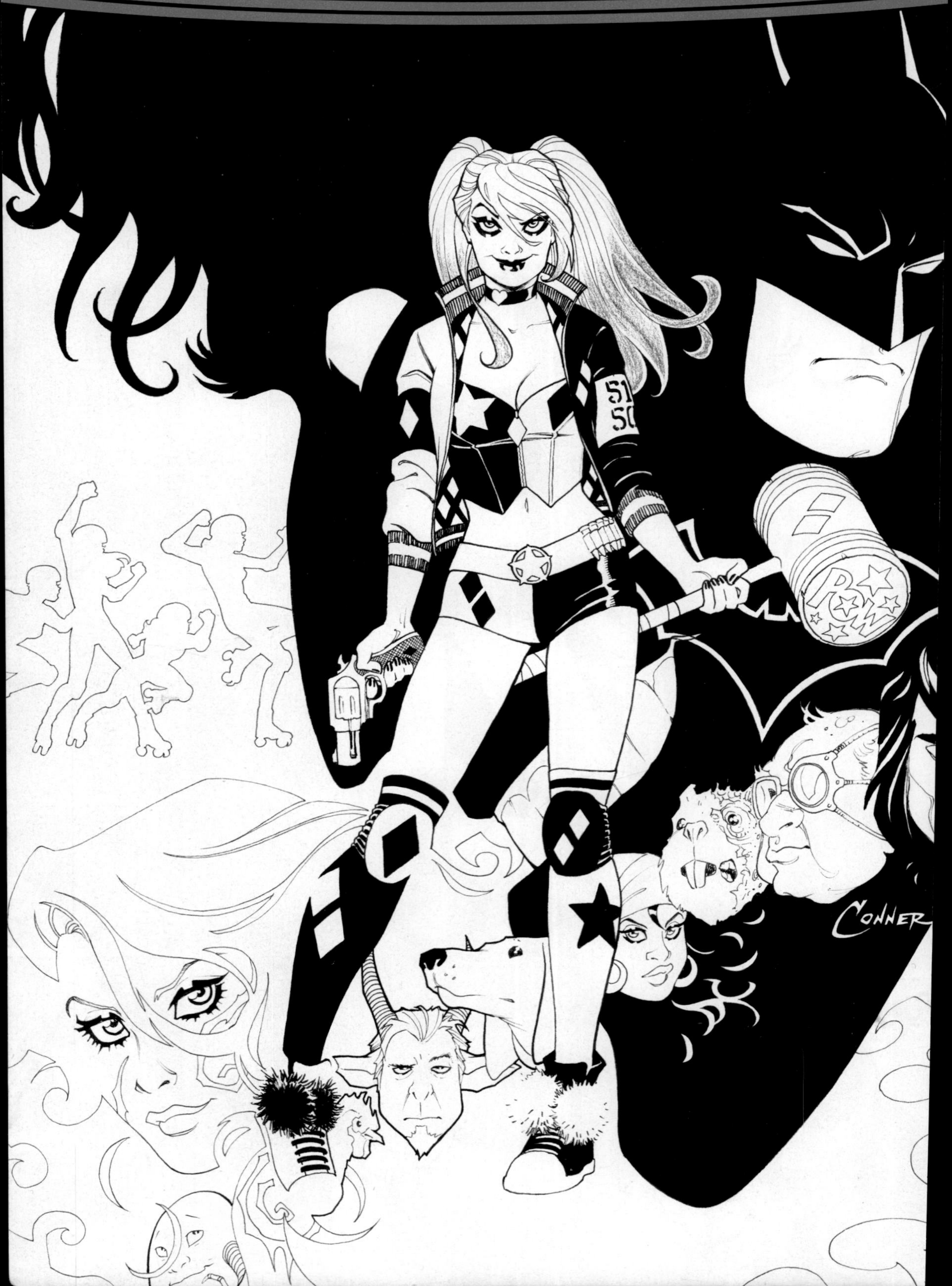
51
50
CONNER

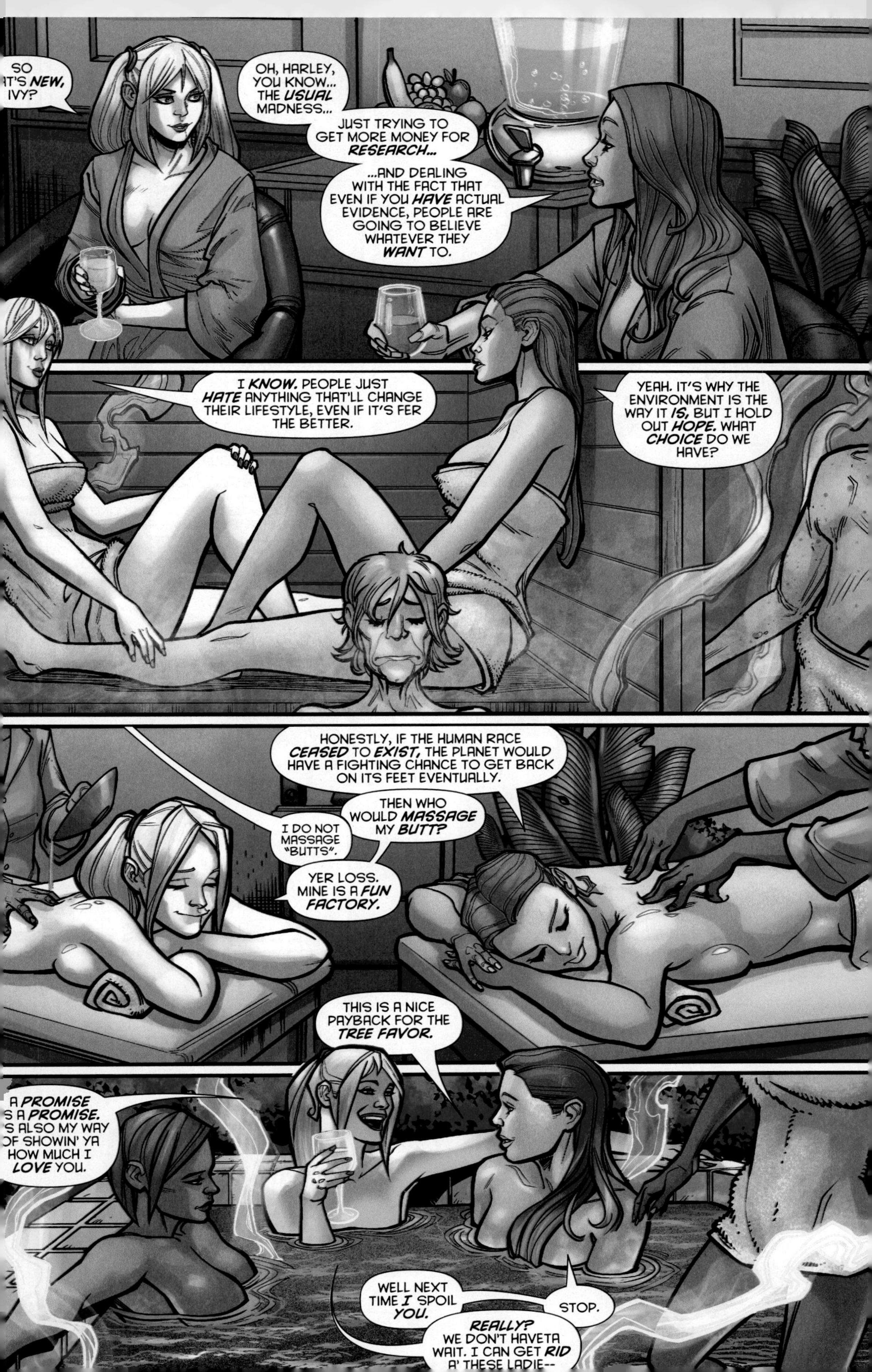
SO AT'S NEW, IVY?
OH, HARLEY, YOU KNOW... THE USUAL MADNESS...
JUST TRYING TO GET MORE MONEY FOR RESEARCH...
...AND DEALING WITH THE FACT THAT EVEN IF YOU HAVE ACTUAL EVIDENCE, PEOPLE ARE GOING TO BELIEVE WHATEVER THEY WANT TO.
I KNOW. PEOPLE JUST HATE ANYTHING THAT'LL CHANGE THEIR LIFESTYLE, EVEN IF IT'S FER THE BETTER.
YEAH. IT'S WHY THE ENVIRONMENT IS THE WAY IT IS, BUT I HOLD OUT HOPE. WHAT CHOICE DO WE HAVE?
HONESTLY, IF THE HUMAN RACE CEASED TO EXIST, THE PLANET WOULD HAVE A FIGHTING CHANCE TO GET BACK ON ITS FEET EVENTUALLY.
THEN WHO WOULD MASSAGE MY BUTT?
I DO NOT MASSAGE "BUTTS".
YER LOSS. MINE IS A FUN FACTORY.
THIS IS A NICE PAYBACK FOR THE TREE FAVOR.
A PROMISE S A PROMISE. S ALSO MY WAY OF SHOWIN' YA HOW MUCH I LOVE YOU.
WELL NEXT TIME I SPOIL YOU.
STOP.
REALLY? WE DON'T HAVETA WAIT. I CAN GET RID A' THESE LADIE--

HOT PEPPER FACIAL, HUH?

YOU'RE GOING TO LOVE IT.

OUCH.

STOP BEING SUCH A BABY.

OUCH!

SO, HOW'S OWNING A BUSINESS *AND* TWO BUILDINGS GOING?

UGHH. NON-STOP SUPERVISION.

AN' THE *BILLS*...

HAVING THE GANG AN' TONY TAKE CARE A' THINGS REALLY HELPS.

LATER TODAY I'M BRINGIN' IN *TWO NEW* HELPERS TA MY GROUP.

OH. *THAT* SHOULDN'T COMPLICATE THINGS.

NO, REALLY! IT'LL KEEP MY SCHEDULE AT THE *SENIOR HOME* OPEN, AN' GIMME MORE SPA TIME WITH MY *FAVORITE DANDELIONESS*.

YEAH. I *LOVE* BEING SPOILED LIKE THIS.

RED, THEN BLACK...EVERY OTHER NAIL, PLEASE.

I HAVE TO DO THIS MORE OFTEN FOR *SURE*.

IT'S *GOOD* TO SEE YOU SURROUND YOURSELF W[ITH] *WONDERFUL* PEOPLE. WE *ALL* NEED THAT IN THIS L[IFE].

THEN *WHY NOT* MOVE IN? *SERIOUSLY!* I GOT A *BIG BE[D]* AN' *PLENTY A' ROOM*, AN' *PLENT[Y]* A' *CUTE PETS* AN'...

OH, SWEETHEART, THAT WILL COMPLICATE YOUR LIFE EVEN *MORE* THAN IT ALREADY *IS*.

609

WELL, IF YA CHANGE YER MIND, I'M *HERE*. *ALWAYS*.

I'LL BE BACK IN *THREE DAYS*. WE CAN TALK SOME *MORE*.

LOVE YOU.

LOVE YOU *BACK*.

GOTHAM

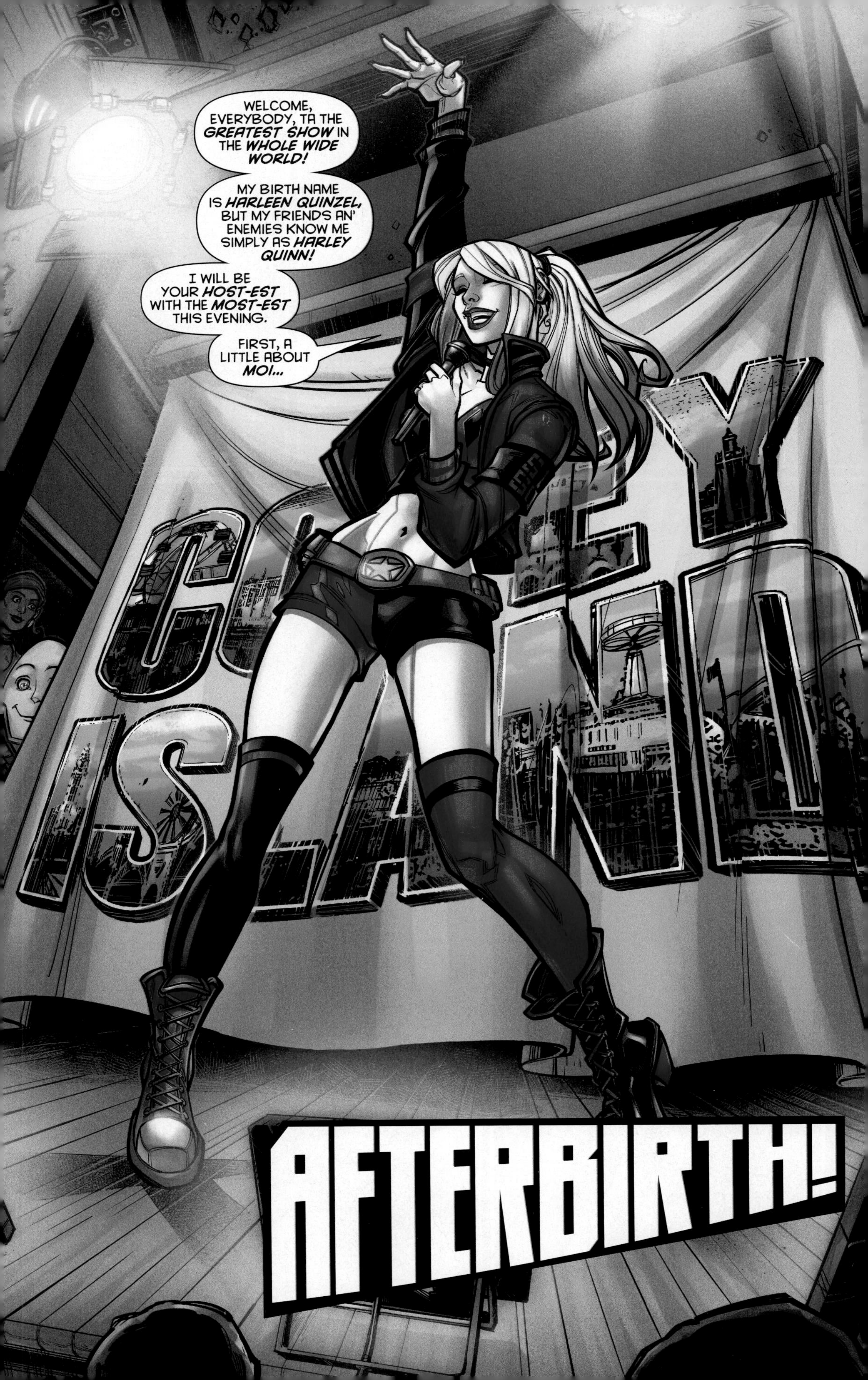

WELCOME, EVERYBODY, TA THE GREATEST SHOW IN THE WHOLE WIDE WORLD!
MY BIRTH NAME IS HARLEEN QUINZEL, BUT MY FRIENDS AN' ENEMIES KNOW ME SIMPLY AS HARLEY QUINN!
I WILL BE YOUR HOST-EST WITH THE MOST-EST THIS EVENING.
FIRST, A LITTLE ABOUT MOI...
AFTERBIRTH!

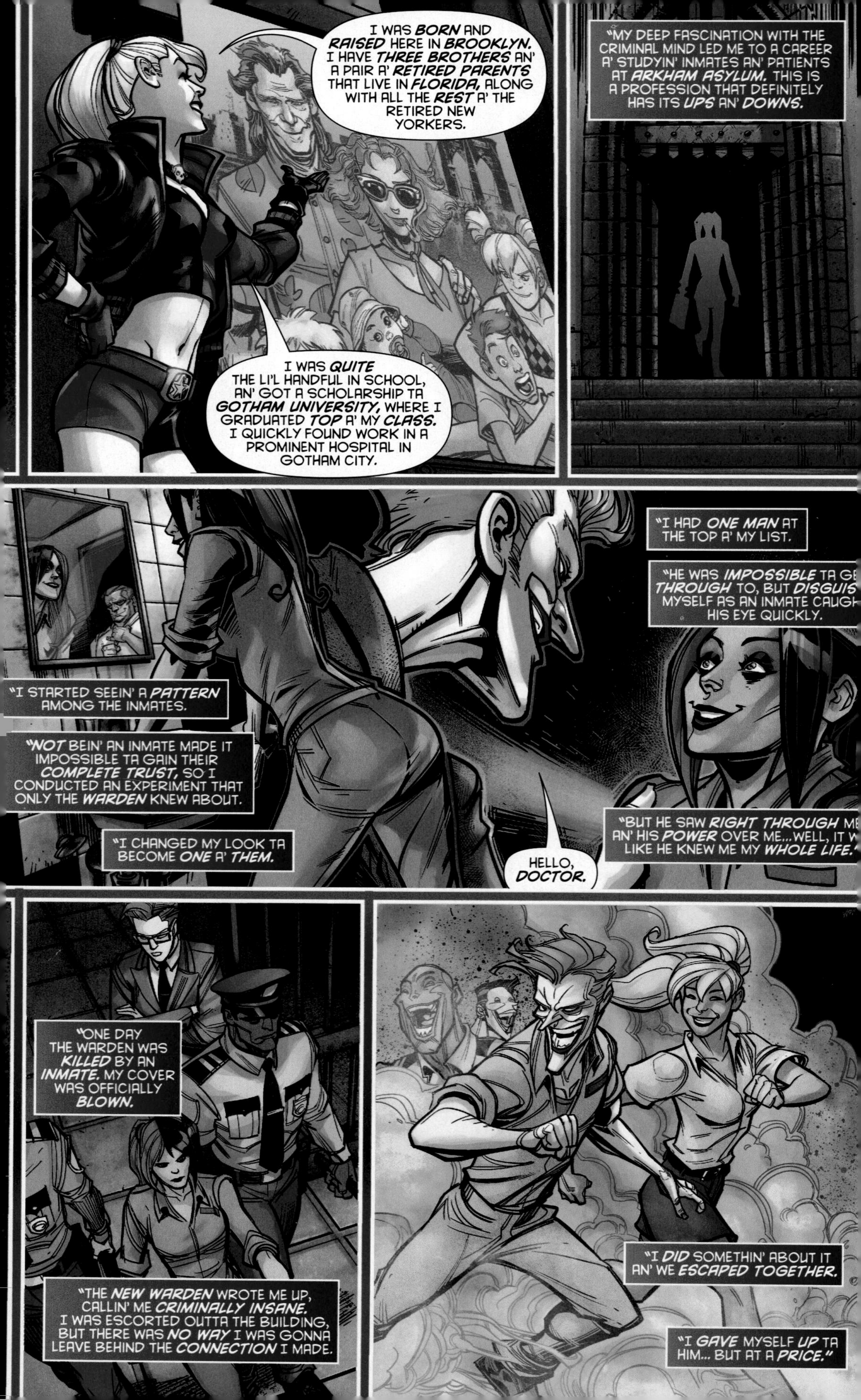
I WAS BORN AND RAISED HERE IN BROOKLYN. I HAVE THREE BROTHERS AN' A PAIR A' RETIRED PARENTS THAT LIVE IN FLORIDA, ALONG WITH ALL THE REST A' THE RETIRED NEW YORKERS.
I WAS QUITE THE LI'L HANDFUL IN SCHOOL, AN' GOT A SCHOLARSHIP TA GOTHAM UNIVERSITY, WHERE I GRADUATED TOP A' MY CLASS. I QUICKLY FOUND WORK IN A PROMINENT HOSPITAL IN GOTHAM CITY.
"MY DEEP FASCINATION WITH THE CRIMINAL MIND LED ME TO A CAREER A' STUDYIN' INMATES AN' PATIENTS AT ARKHAM ASYLUM. THIS IS A PROFESSION THAT DEFINITELY HAS ITS UPS AN' DOWNS.
"I STARTED SEEIN' A PATTERN AMONG THE INMATES.
"NOT BEIN' AN INMATE MADE IT IMPOSSIBLE TA GAIN THEIR COMPLETE TRUST, SO I CONDUCTED AN EXPERIMENT THAT ONLY THE WARDEN KNEW ABOUT.
"I CHANGED MY LOOK TA BECOME ONE A' THEM.
"I HAD ONE MAN AT THE TOP A' MY LIST.
"HE WAS IMPOSSIBLE TA GE THROUGH TO, BUT DISGUIS MYSELF AS AN INMATE CAUGH HIS EYE QUICKLY.
HELLO, DOCTOR.
"BUT HE SAW RIGHT THROUGH ME AN' HIS POWER OVER ME...WELL, IT W LIKE HE KNEW ME MY WHOLE LIFE."
"ONE DAY THE WARDEN WAS KILLED BY AN INMATE. MY COVER WAS OFFICIALLY BLOWN.
"THE NEW WARDEN WROTE ME UP, CALLIN' ME CRIMINALLY INSANE. I WAS ESCORTED OUTTA THE BUILDING, BUT THERE WAS NO WAY I WAS GONNA LEAVE BEHIND THE CONNECTION I MADE.
"I DID SOMETHIN' ABOUT IT AN' WE ESCAPED TOGETHER.
"I GAVE MYSELF UP TA HIM... BUT AT A PRICE."

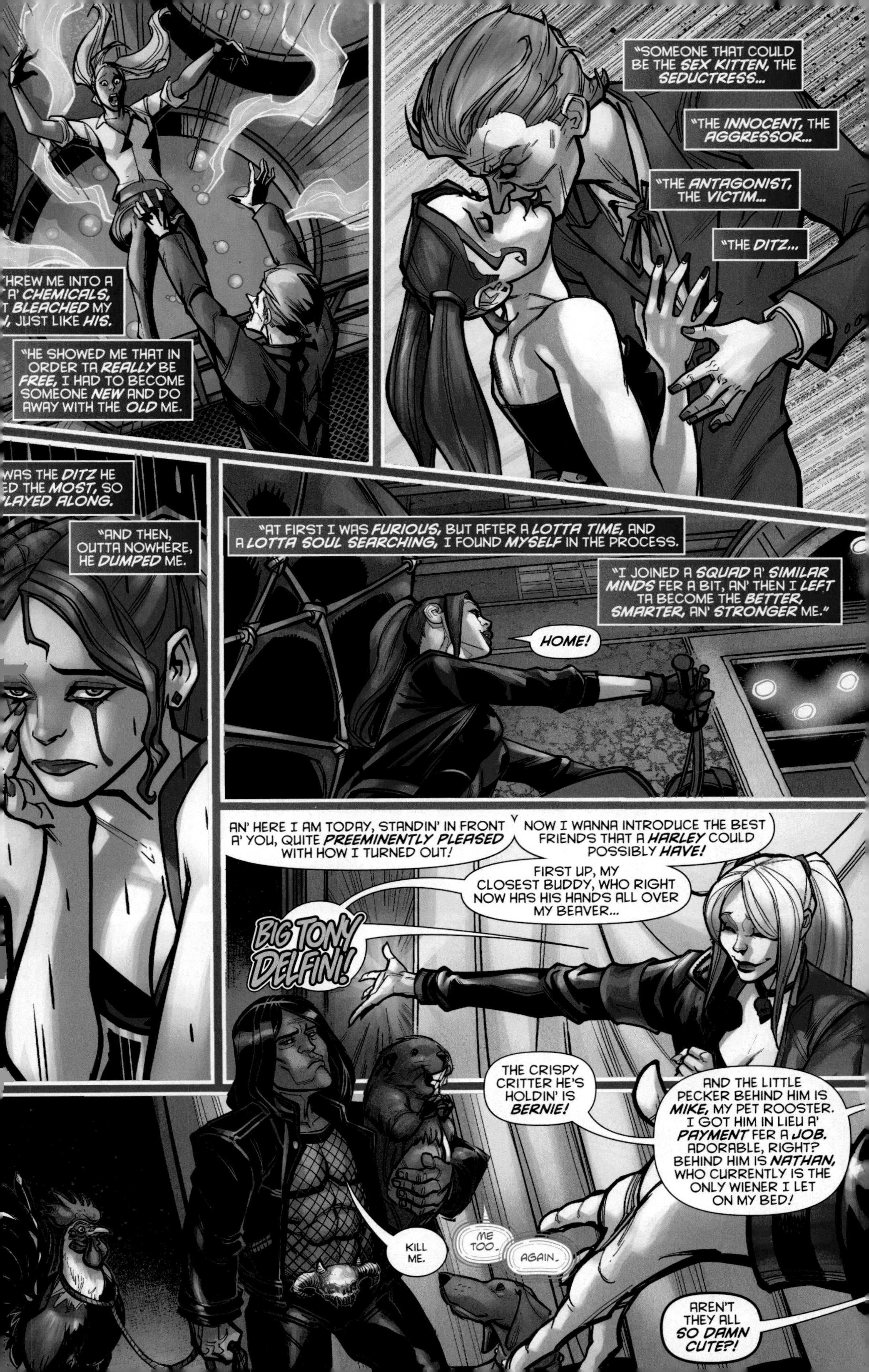

"THREW ME INTO A ... A' CHEMICALS, ... BLEACHED MY ..., JUST LIKE HIS.
"HE SHOWED ME THAT IN ORDER TA REALLY BE FREE, I HAD TO BECOME SOMEONE NEW AND DO AWAY WITH THE OLD ME.
"SOMEONE THAT COULD BE THE SEX KITTEN, THE SEDUCTRESS...
"THE INNOCENT, THE AGGRESSOR...
"THE ANTAGONIST, THE VICTIM...
"THE DITZ...
...WAS THE DITZ HE ...ED THE MOST, SO ...PLAYED ALONG.
"AND THEN, OUTTA NOWHERE, HE DUMPED ME.
"AT FIRST I WAS FURIOUS, BUT AFTER A LOTTA TIME, AND A LOTTA SOUL SEARCHING, I FOUND MYSELF IN THE PROCESS.
"I JOINED A SQUAD A' SIMILAR MINDS FER A BIT, AN' THEN I LEFT TA BECOME THE BETTER, SMARTER, AN' STRONGER ME."
HOME!
AN' HERE I AM TODAY, STANDIN' IN FRONT A' YOU, QUITE PREEMINENTLY PLEASED WITH HOW I TURNED OUT!
NOW I WANNA INTRODUCE THE BEST FRIENDS THAT A HARLEY COULD POSSIBLY HAVE!
FIRST UP, MY CLOSEST BUDDY, WHO RIGHT NOW HAS HIS HANDS ALL OVER MY BEAVER...
BIG TONY DELFINI!
THE CRISPY CRITTER HE'S HOLDIN' IS BERNIE!
AND THE LITTLE PECKER BEHIND HIM IS MIKE, MY PET ROOSTER. I GOT HIM IN LIEU A' PAYMENT FER A JOB. ADORABLE, RIGHT? BEHIND HIM IS NATHAN, WHO CURRENTLY IS THE ONLY WIENER I LET ON MY BED!
KILL ME.
ME TOO.
AGAIN.
AREN'T THEY ALL SO DAMN CUTE?!

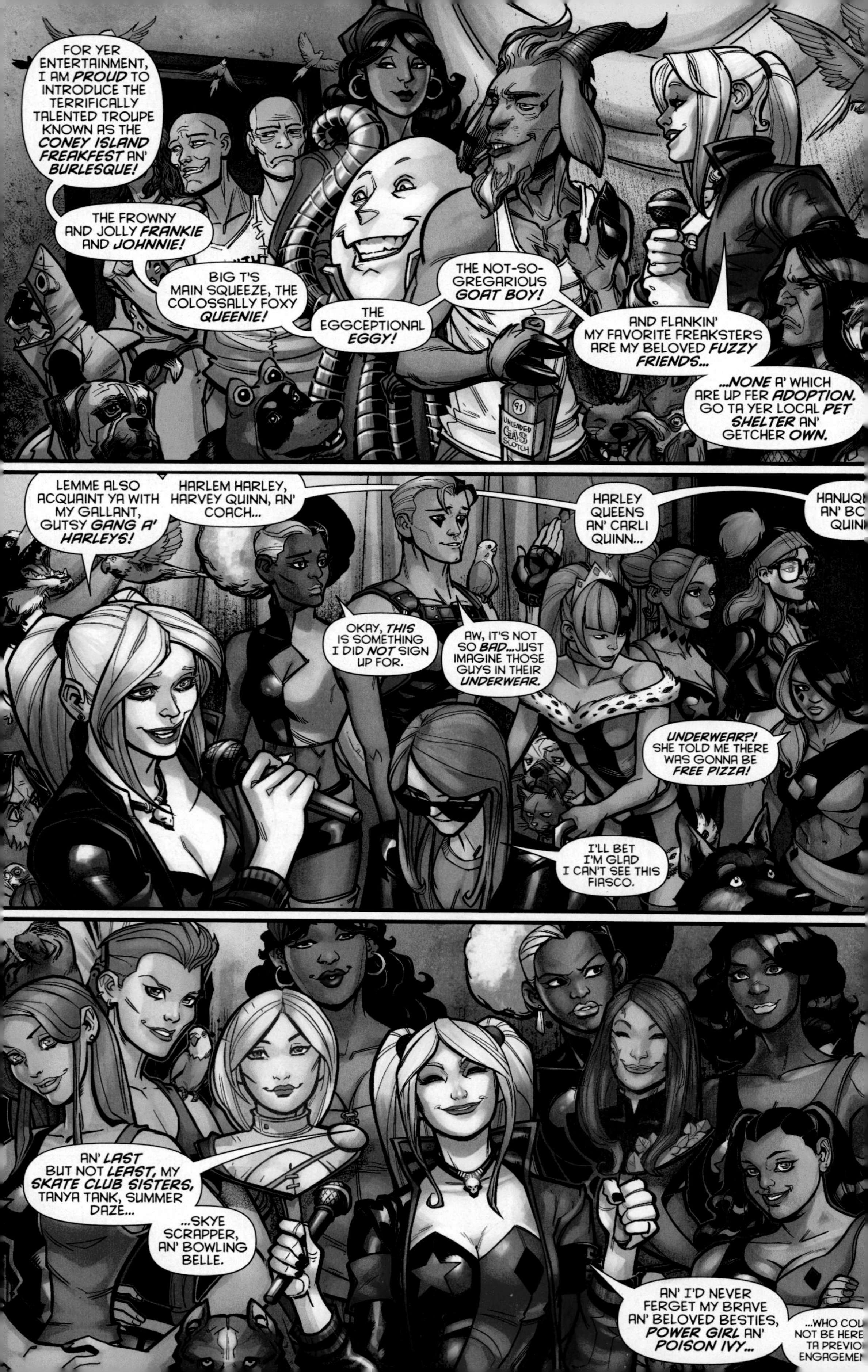
FOR YER ENTERTAINMENT, I AM PROUD TO INTRODUCE THE TERRIFICALLY TALENTED TROUPE KNOWN AS THE CONEY ISLAND FREAKFEST AN' BURLESQUE!
THE FROWNY AND JOLLY FRANKIE AND JOHNNIE!
BIG T'S MAIN SQUEEZE, THE COLOSSALLY FOXY QUEENIE!
THE EGGCEPTIONAL EGGY!
THE NOT-SO-GREGARIOUS GOAT BOY!
AND FLANKIN' MY FAVORITE FREAKSTERS ARE MY BELOVED FUZZY FRIENDS...
...NONE A' WHICH ARE UP FER ADOPTION. GO TA YER LOCAL PET SHELTER AN' GETCHER OWN.
91 UNLEADED GAS SCOTCH
LEMME ALSO ACQUAINT YA WITH MY GALLANT, GUTSY GANG A' HARLEYS!
HARLEM HARLEY, HARVEY QUINN, AN' COACH...
HARLEY QUEENS AN' CARLI QUINN...
HANUQ
AN' BO
QUINN
OKAY, THIS IS SOMETHING I DID NOT SIGN UP FOR.
AW, IT'S NOT SO BAD...JUST IMAGINE THOSE GUYS IN THEIR UNDERWEAR.
UNDERWEAR?! SHE TOLD ME THERE WAS GONNA BE FREE PIZZA!
I'LL BET I'M GLAD I CAN'T SEE THIS FIASCO.
AN' LAST BUT NOT LEAST, MY SKATE CLUB SISTERS, TANYA TANK, SUMMER DAZE...
...SKYE SCRAPPER, AN' BOWLING BELLE.
AN' I'D NEVER FERGET MY BRAVE AN' BELOVED BESTIES, POWER GIRL AN' POISON IVY...
...WHO COU
NOT BE HERE
TA PREVIO
ENGAGEMEN

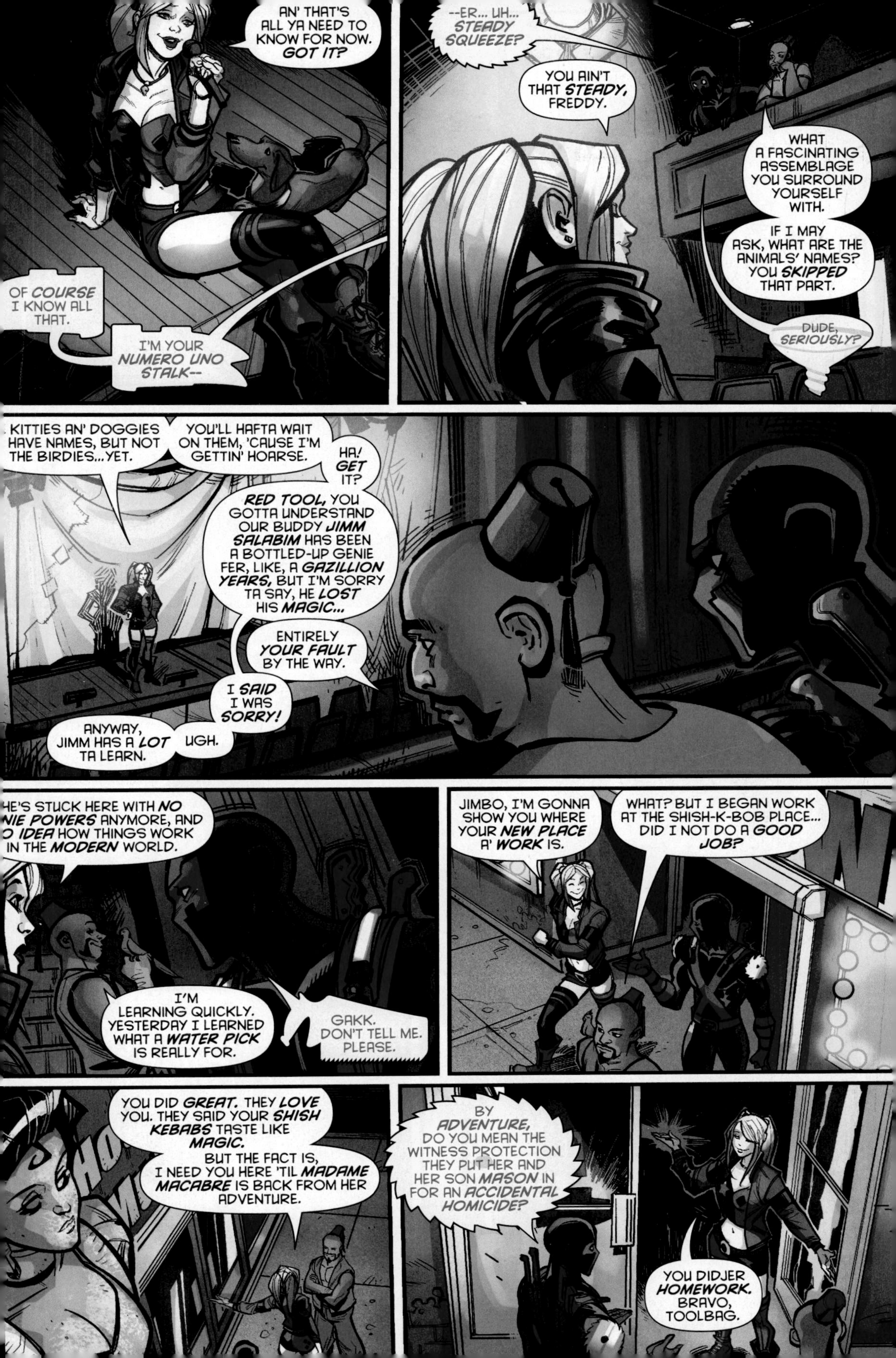
AN' THAT'S ALL YA NEED TO KNOW FOR NOW. GOT IT?
OF COURSE I KNOW ALL THAT.
I'M YOUR NUMERO UNO STALK--
--ER... UH... STEADY SQUEEZE?
YOU AIN'T THAT STEADY, FREDDY.
WHAT A FASCINATING ASSEMBLAGE YOU SURROUND YOURSELF WITH.
IF I MAY ASK, WHAT ARE THE ANIMALS' NAMES? YOU SKIPPED THAT PART.
DUDE, SERIOUSLY?
KITTIES AN' DOGGIES HAVE NAMES, BUT NOT THE BIRDIES...YET.
YOU'LL HAFTA WAIT ON THEM, 'CAUSE I'M GETTIN' HOARSE.
HA! GET IT?
RED TOOL, YOU GOTTA UNDERSTAND OUR BUDDY JIMM SALABIM HAS BEEN A BOTTLED-UP GENIE FER, LIKE, A GAZILLION YEARS, BUT I'M SORRY TA SAY, HE LOST HIS MAGIC...
ENTIRELY YOUR FAULT BY THE WAY.
I SAID I WAS SORRY!
ANYWAY, JIMM HAS A LOT TA LEARN.
UGH.
HE'S STUCK HERE WITH NO NIE POWERS ANYMORE, AND O IDEA HOW THINGS WORK IN THE MODERN WORLD.
I'M LEARNING QUICKLY. YESTERDAY I LEARNED WHAT A WATER PICK IS REALLY FOR.
GAKK. DON'T TELL ME. PLEASE.
JIMBO, I'M GONNA SHOW YOU WHERE YOUR NEW PLACE A' WORK IS.
WHAT? BUT I BEGAN WORK AT THE SHISH-K-BOB PLACE... DID I NOT DO A GOOD JOB?
YOU DID GREAT. THEY LOVE YOU. THEY SAID YOUR SHISH KEBABS TASTE LIKE MAGIC.
BUT THE FACT IS, I NEED YOU HERE 'TIL MADAME MACABRE IS BACK FROM HER ADVENTURE.
BY ADVENTURE, DO YOU MEAN THE WITNESS PROTECTION THEY PUT HER AND HER SON MASON IN FOR AN ACCIDENTAL HOMICIDE?
YOU DIDJER HOMEWORK. BRAVO, TOOLBAG.

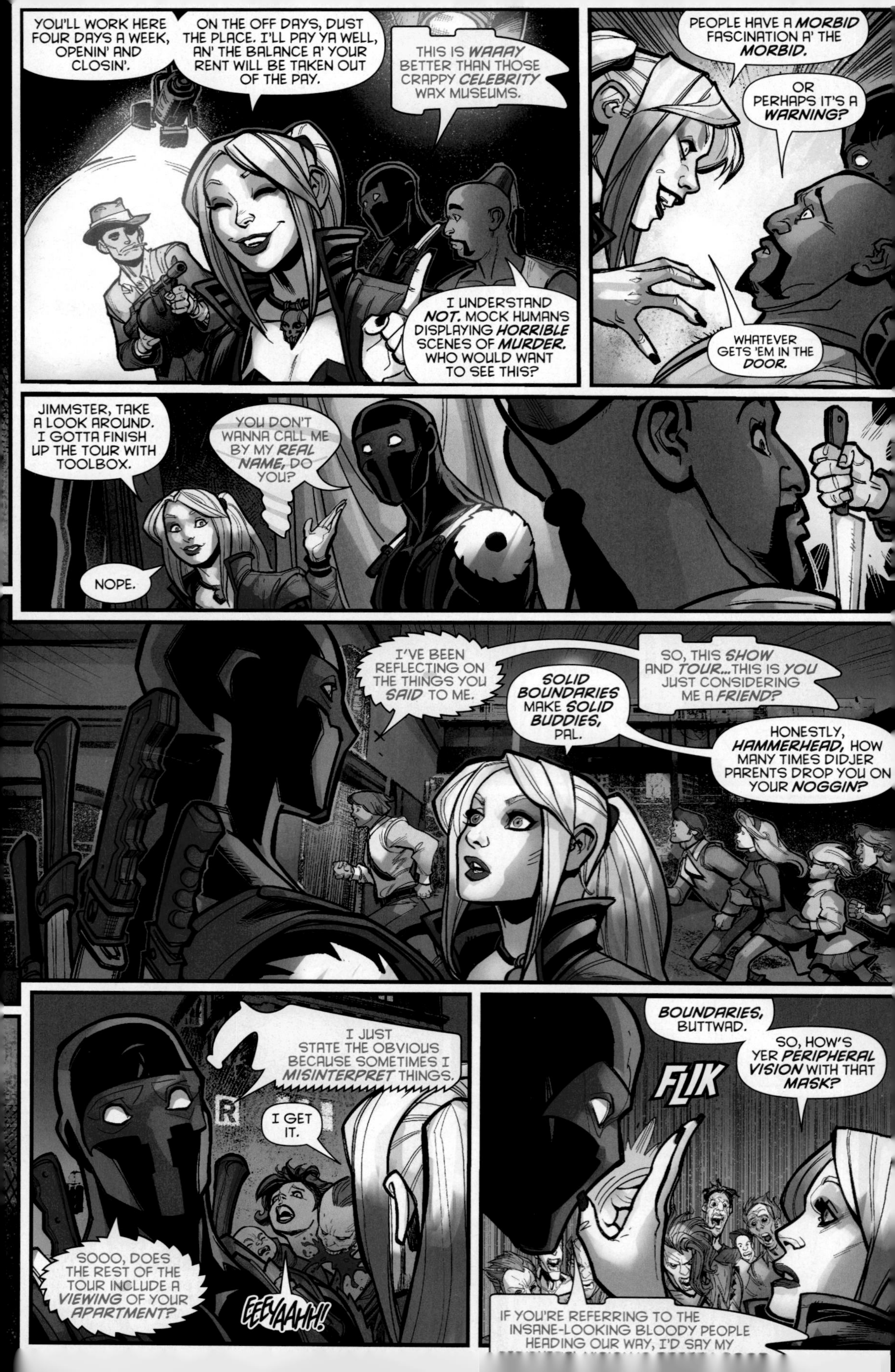

YOU'LL WORK HERE FOUR DAYS A WEEK, OPENIN' AND CLOSIN'.
ON THE OFF DAYS, DUST THE PLACE. I'LL PAY YA WELL, AN' THE BALANCE A' YOUR RENT WILL BE TAKEN OUT OF THE PAY.
THIS IS WAAAY BETTER THAN THOSE CRAPPY CELEBRITY WAX MUSEUMS.
I UNDERSTAND NOT. MOCK HUMANS DISPLAYING HORRIBLE SCENES OF MURDER. WHO WOULD WANT TO SEE THIS?
PEOPLE HAVE A MORBID FASCINATION A' THE MORBID.
OR PERHAPS IT'S A WARNING?
WHATEVER GETS 'EM IN THE DOOR.
JIMMSTER, TAKE A LOOK AROUND. I GOTTA FINISH UP THE TOUR WITH TOOLBOX.
YOU DON'T WANNA CALL ME BY MY REAL NAME, DO YOU?
NOPE.
I'VE BEEN REFLECTING ON THE THINGS YOU SAID TO ME.
SOLID BOUNDARIES MAKE SOLID BUDDIES, PAL.
SO, THIS SHOW AND TOUR...THIS IS YOU JUST CONSIDERING ME A FRIEND?
HONESTLY, HAMMERHEAD, HOW MANY TIMES DIDJER PARENTS DROP YOU ON YOUR NOGGIN?
I JUST STATE THE OBVIOUS BECAUSE SOMETIMES I MISINTERPRET THINGS.
I GET IT.
SOOO, DOES THE REST OF THE TOUR INCLUDE A VIEWING OF YOUR APARTMENT?
EEEYAAHH!
BOUNDARIES, BUTTWAD.
FLIK
SO, HOW'S YER PERIPHERAL VISION WITH THAT MASK?
IF YOU'RE REFERRING TO THE INSANE-LOOKING BLOODY PEOPLE HEADING OUR WAY, I'D SAY MY

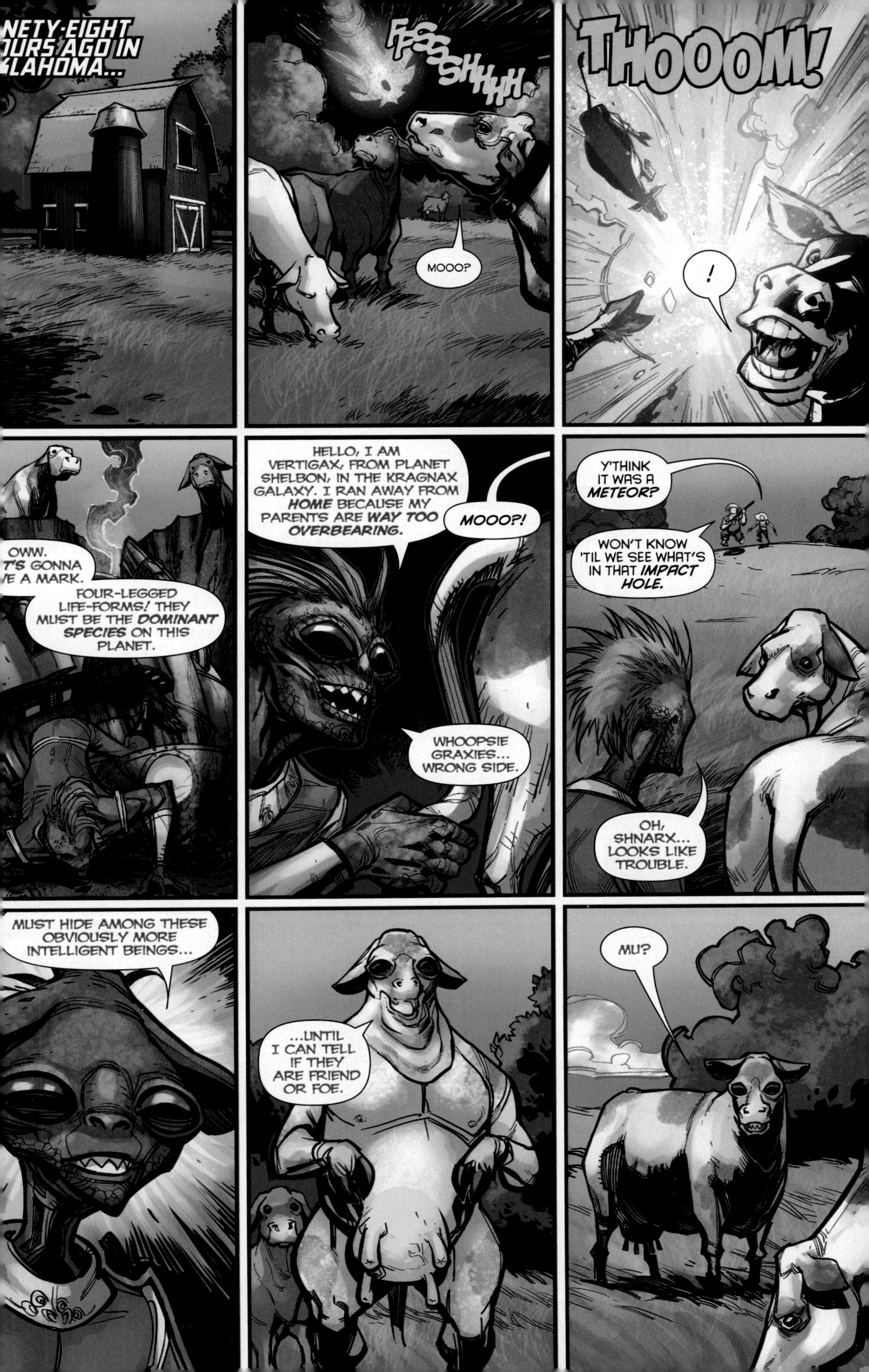
NETY-EIGHT
OURS AGO IN
LAHOMA...
FSSSHHHH
MOOO?
THOOOM!
!
OWW.
T'S GONNA
E A MARK.
FOUR-LEGGED LIFE-FORMS! THEY MUST BE THE DOMINANT SPECIES ON THIS PLANET.
HELLO, I AM VERTIGAX, FROM PLANET SHELBON, IN THE KRAGNAX GALAXY. I RAN AWAY FROM HOME BECAUSE MY PARENTS ARE WAY TOO OVERBEARING.
MOOO?!
WHOOPSIE GRAXIES... WRONG SIDE.
Y'THINK IT WAS A METEOR?
WON'T KNOW 'TIL WE SEE WHAT'S IN THAT IMPACT HOLE.
OH, SHNARX... LOOKS LIKE TROUBLE.
MUST HIDE AMONG THESE OBVIOUSLY MORE INTELLIGENT BEINGS...
...UNTIL I CAN TELL IF THEY ARE FRIEND OR FOE.
MU?

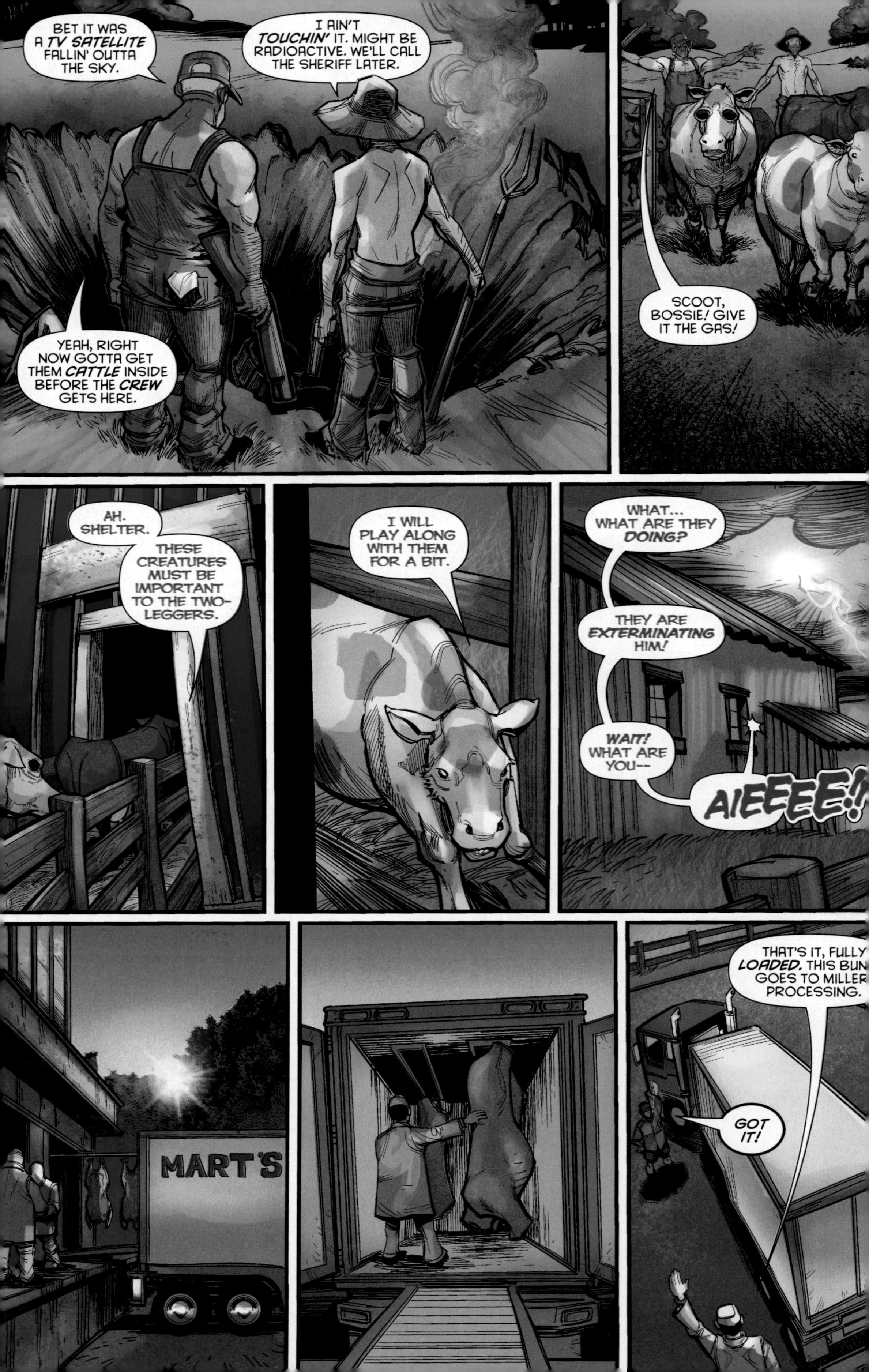
BET IT WAS A TV SATELLITE FALLIN' OUTTA THE SKY.
I AIN'T TOUCHIN' IT. MIGHT BE RADIOACTIVE. WE'LL CALL THE SHERIFF LATER.
YEAH, RIGHT NOW GOTTA GET THEM CATTLE INSIDE BEFORE THE CREW GETS HERE.
SCOOT, BOSSIE! GIVE IT THE GAS!
AH. SHELTER.
THESE CREATURES MUST BE IMPORTANT TO THE TWO-LEGGERS.
I WILL PLAY ALONG WITH THEM FOR A BIT.
WHAT... WHAT ARE THEY DOING?
THEY ARE EXTERMINATING HIM!
WAIT! WHAT ARE YOU--
AIEEEEE!!
MART'S
THAT'S IT, FULLY LOADED. THIS BUN GOES TO MILLER PROCESSING.
GOT IT!

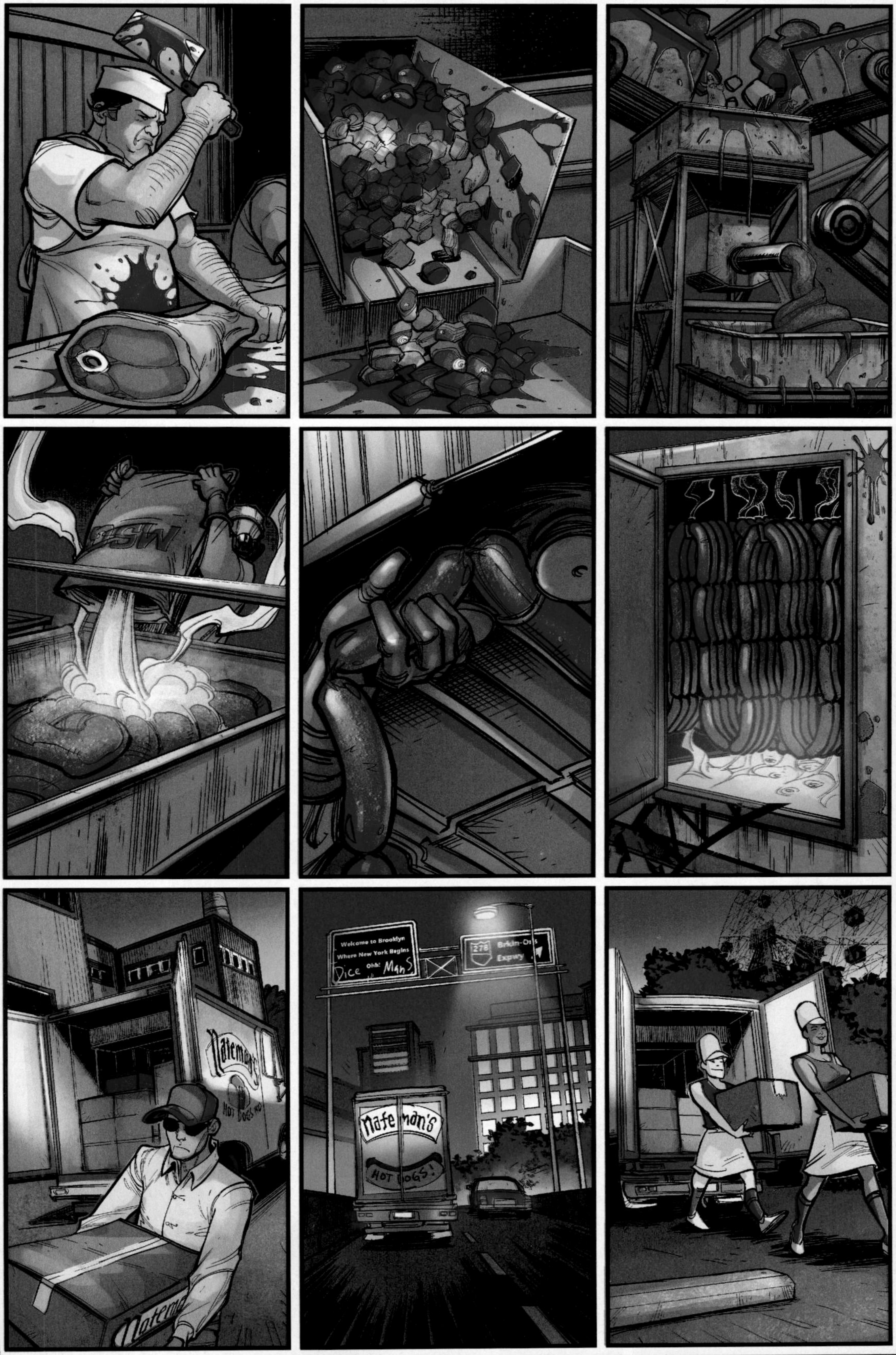
DSW
Nateman's
HOT DOGS
Welcome to Brooklyn
Where New York Begins
Dice Ohh! ManS
278
Expwy
Nateman's
HOT DOGS!

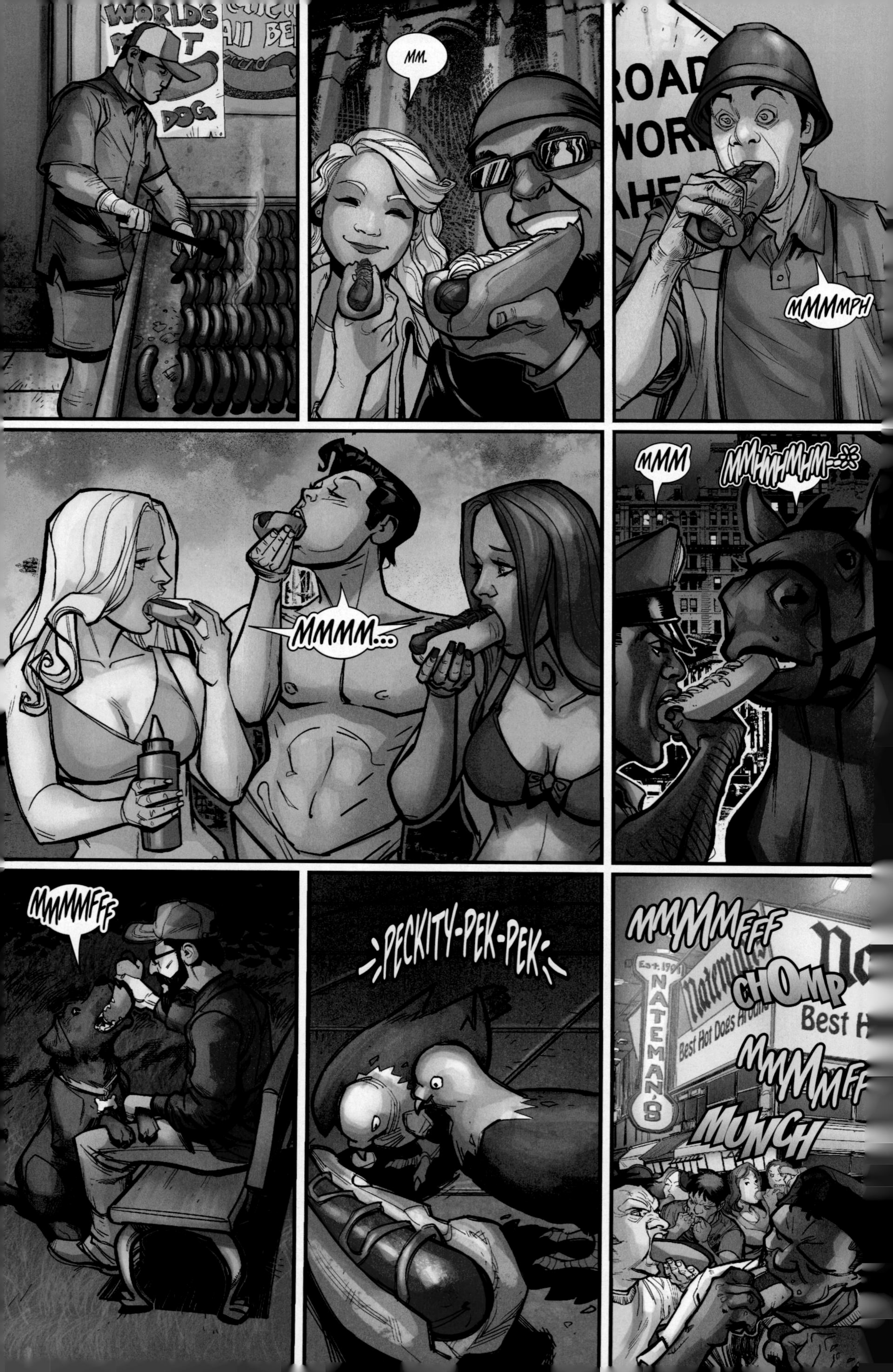
WORLD'S
DOG
MM.
ROAD
WOR
AHE
MMMMPH
MMMM...
MMM
MMMMMHMM--
MMMMFFF
PECKITY-PEK-PEK
MMMMFFF
Est. 1900
NATEMAN'S
Nateman's
Best Hot Dogs Around
CHOMP
Best H
MMMMFF
MUNCH

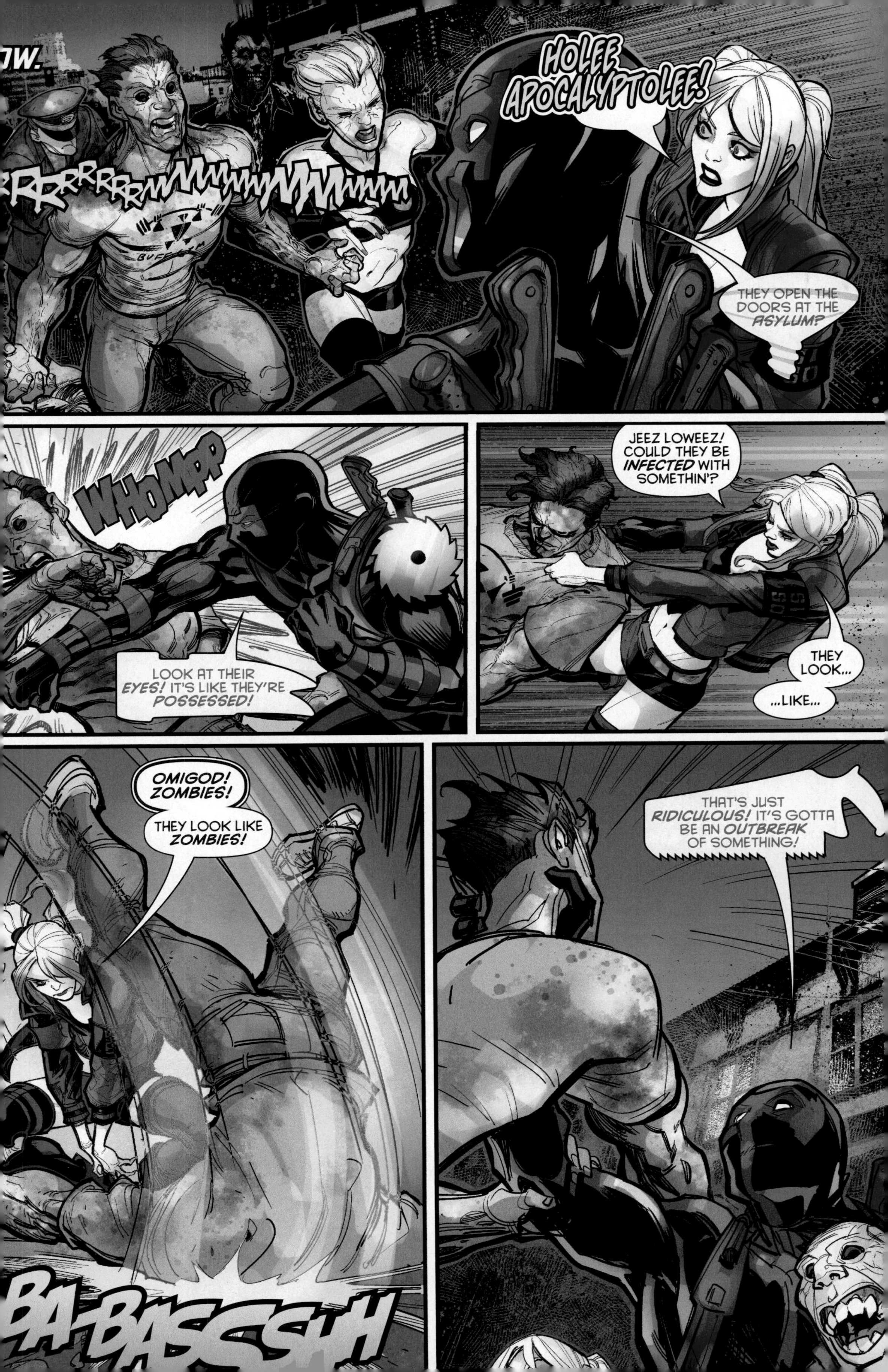
OW.
RRRRRRRRWWWWWWWWWWWWW
HOLEE APOCALYPTOLEE!
THEY OPEN THE DOORS AT THE ASYLUM?
WHOMPP
LOOK AT THEIR EYES! IT'S LIKE THEY'RE POSSESSED!
JEEZ LOWEEZ! COULD THEY BE INFECTED WITH SOMETHIN'?
THEY LOOK...
...LIKE...
OMIGOD! ZOMBIES!
THEY LOOK LIKE ZOMBIES!
BA-BASSSH
THAT'S JUST RIDICULOUS! IT'S GOTTA BE AN OUTBREAK OF SOMETHING!

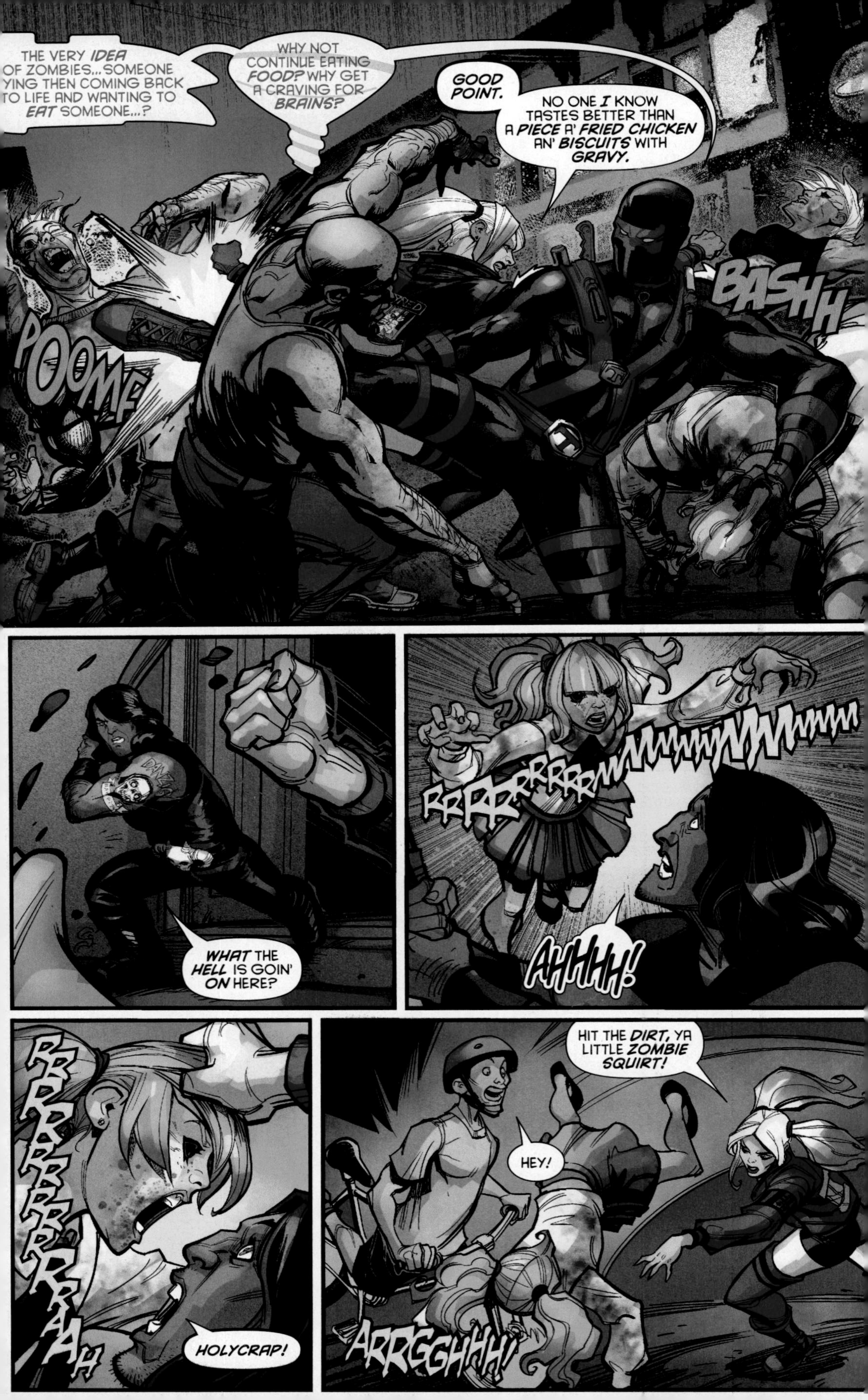
THE VERY IDEA OF ZOMBIES...SOMEONE DYING THEN COMING BACK TO LIFE AND WANTING TO EAT SOMEONE...?
WHY NOT CONTINUE EATING FOOD? WHY GET A CRAVING FOR BRAINS?
GOOD POINT.
NO ONE I KNOW TASTES BETTER THAN A PIECE A' FRIED CHICKEN AN' BISCUITS WITH GRAVY.
POOMF
BASHH
WHAT THE HELL IS GOIN' ON HERE?
RRRRRRRRRRWWWWWWWWW
AHHHH!
RRRRRRRRRRAAH
HOLYCRAP!
HIT THE DIRT, YA LITTLE ZOMBIE SQUIRT!
HEY!
ARRGGHHH!

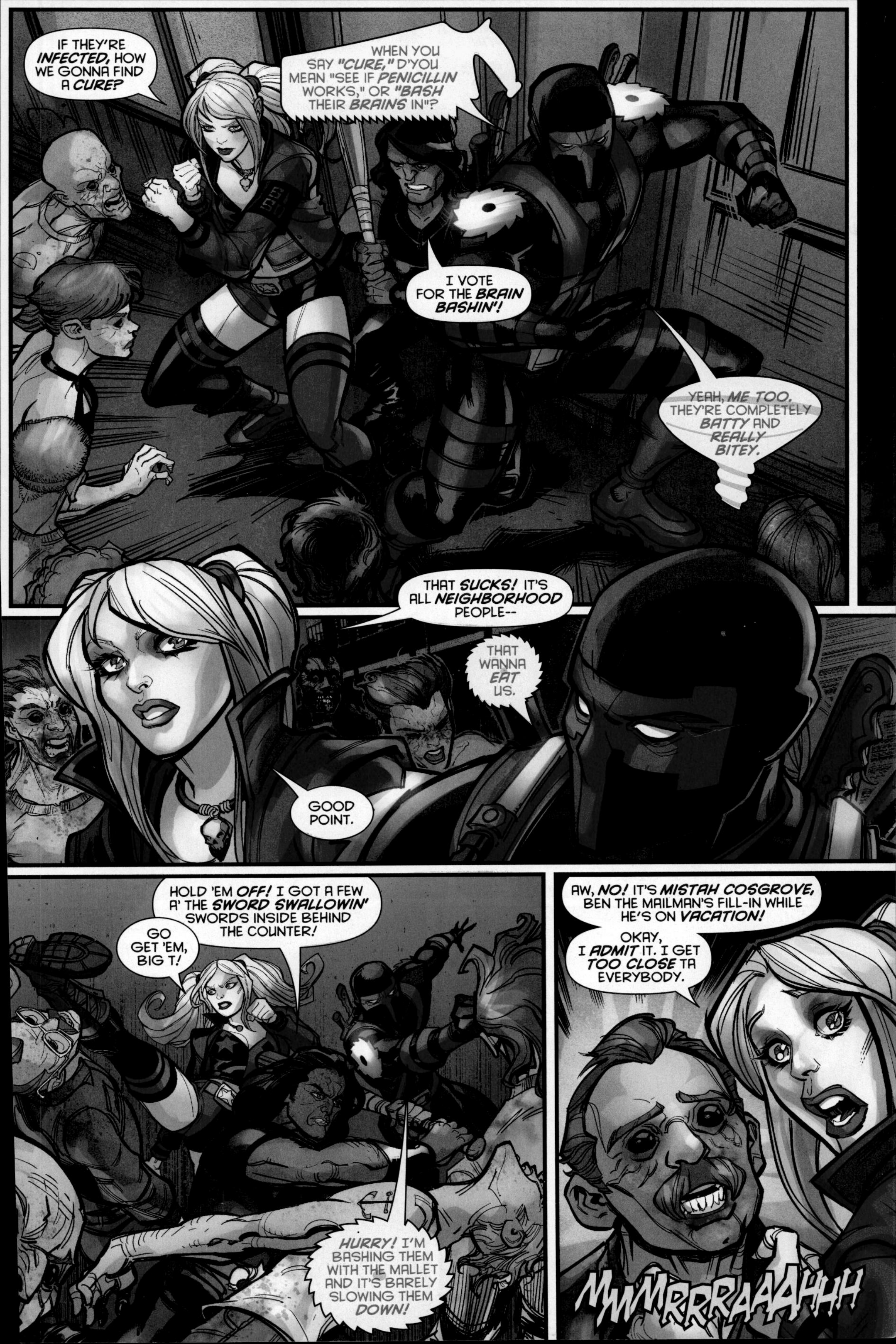

IF THEY'RE INFECTED, HOW WE GONNA FIND A CURE?
WHEN YOU SAY "CURE," D'YOU MEAN "SEE IF PENICILLIN WORKS," OR "BASH THEIR BRAINS IN"?
I VOTE FOR THE BRAIN BASHIN'!
YEAH, ME TOO. THEY'RE COMPLETELY BATTY AND REALLY BITEY.
THAT SUCKS! IT'S ALL NEIGHBORHOOD PEOPLE--
THAT WANNA EAT US.
GOOD POINT.
HOLD 'EM OFF! I GOT A FEW A' THE SWORD SWALLOWIN' SWORDS INSIDE BEHIND THE COUNTER!
GO GET 'EM, BIG T!
HURRY! I'M BASHING THEM WITH THE MALLET AND IT'S BARELY SLOWING THEM DOWN!
AW, NO! IT'S MISTAH COSGROVE, BEN THE MAILMAN'S FILL-IN WHILE HE'S ON VACATION!
OKAY, I ADMIT IT. I GET TOO CLOSE TA EVERYBODY.
MMMRRRAAAHHH

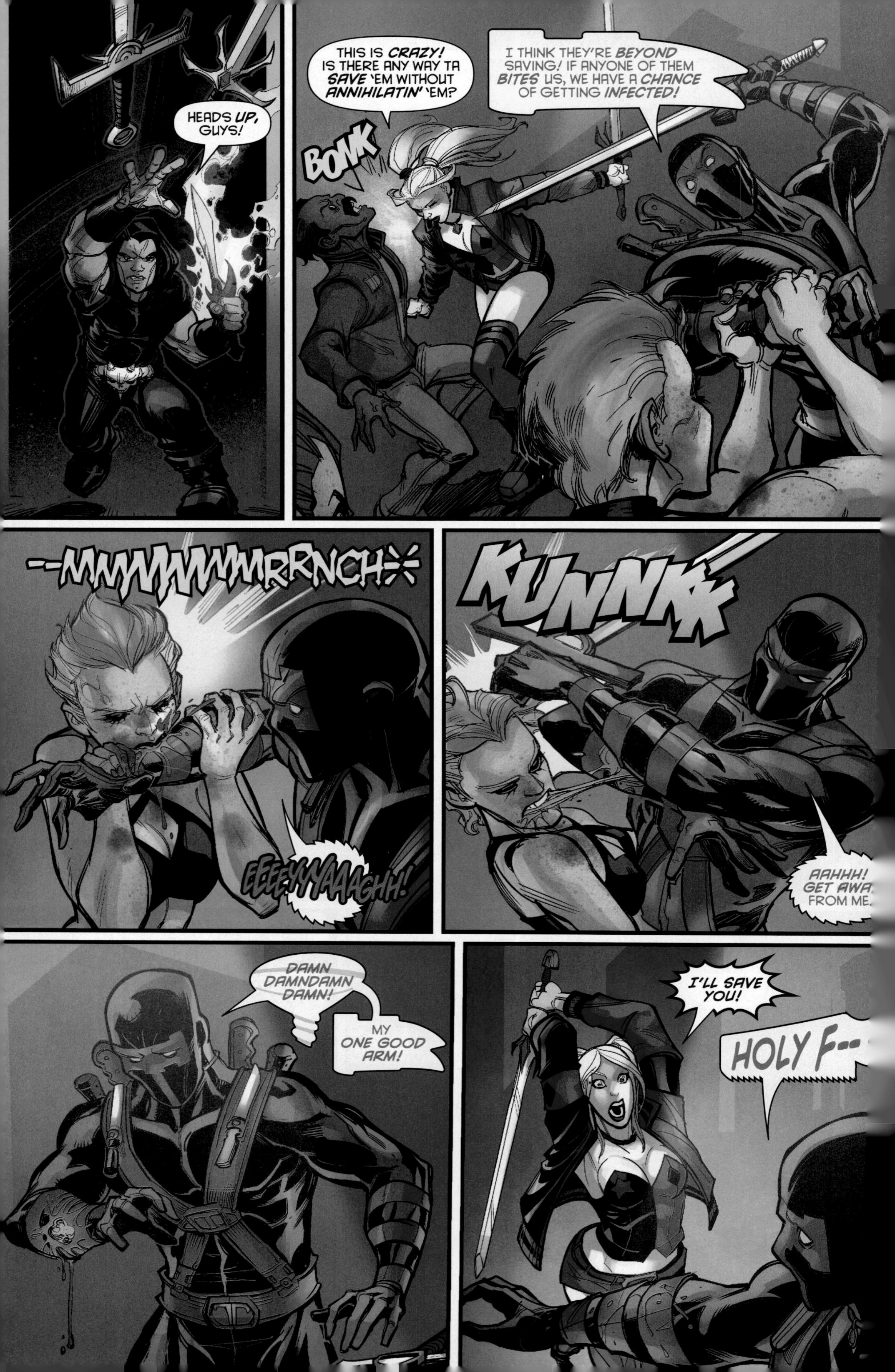
HEADS UP, GUYS!
THIS IS CRAZY! IS THERE ANY WAY TA SAVE 'EM WITHOUT ANNIHILATIN' 'EM?
I THINK THEY'RE BEYOND SAVING! IF ANYONE OF THEM BITES US, WE HAVE A CHANCE OF GETTING INFECTED!
BONK
--MNYMMMMRRNCH
EEEEYYYAAAGHH!
KUNNKK
AAHHH! GET AWA FROM ME
DAMN DAMNDAMN DAMN!
MY ONE GOOD ARM!
I'LL SAVE YOU!
HOLY F--

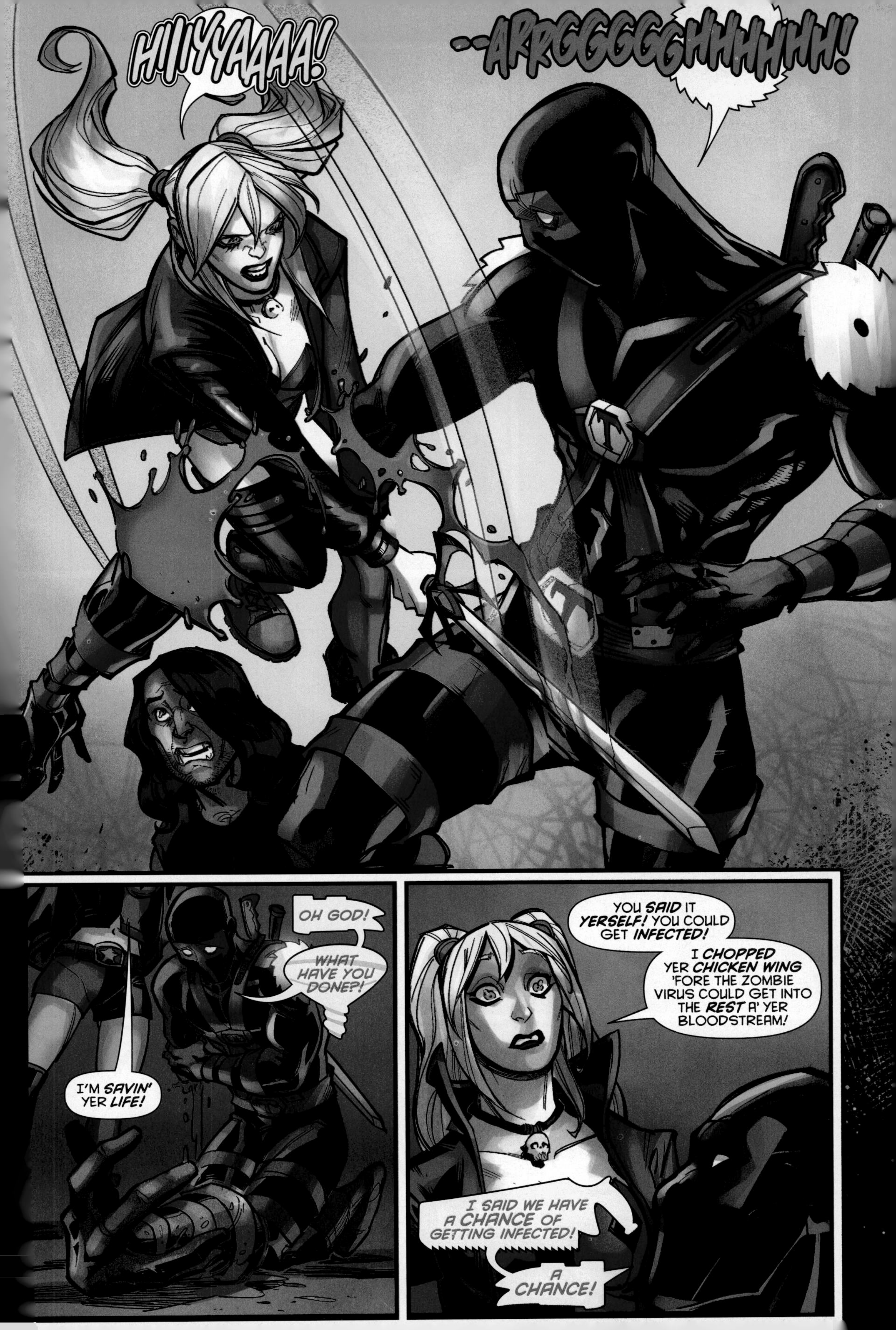
HIIIYYAAAA!
--ARRGGGGGHHHHHHH!
OH GOD!
WHAT HAVE YOU DONE?!
I'M SAVIN' YER LIFE!
YOU SAID IT YERSELF! YOU COULD GET INFECTED!
I CHOPPED YER CHICKEN WING 'FORE THE ZOMBIE VIRUS COULD GET INTO THE REST A' YER BLOODSTREAM!
I SAID WE HAVE A CHANCE OF GETTING INFECTED!
A CHANCE!

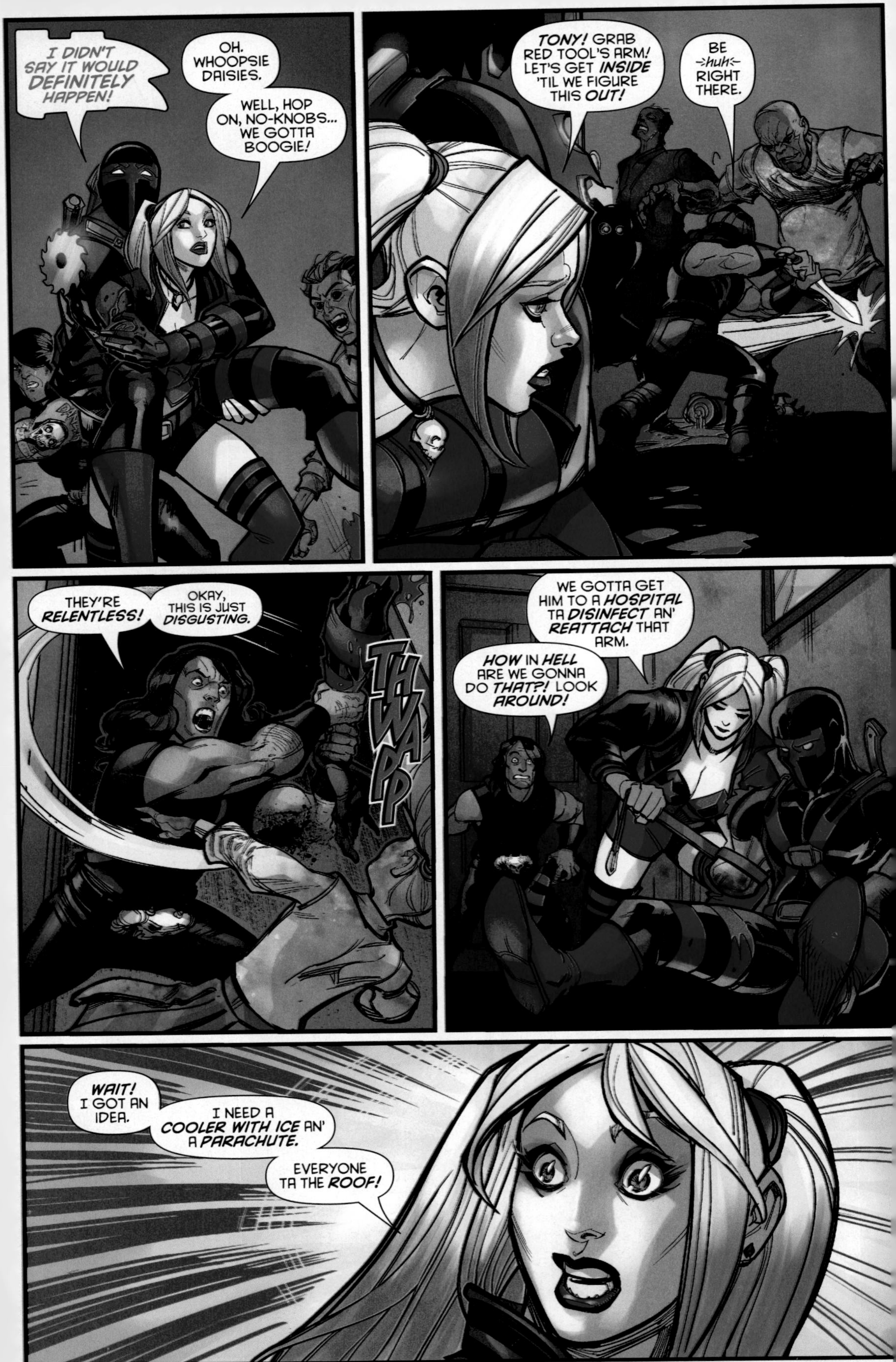
I DIDN'T SAY IT WOULD DEFINITELY HAPPEN!
OH. WHOOPSIE DAISIES.
WELL, HOP ON, NO-KNOBS... WE GOTTA BOOGIE!
TONY! GRAB RED TOOL'S ARM! LET'S GET INSIDE 'TIL WE FIGURE THIS OUT!
BE -huh- RIGHT THERE.
THEY'RE RELENTLESS!
OKAY, THIS IS JUST DISGUSTING.
THWAPP
WE GOTTA GET HIM TO A HOSPITAL TA DISINFECT AN' REATTACH THAT ARM.
HOW IN HELL ARE WE GONNA DO THAT?! LOOK AROUND!
WAIT! I GOT AN IDEA.
I NEED A COOLER WITH ICE AN' A PARACHUTE.
EVERYONE TA THE ROOF!

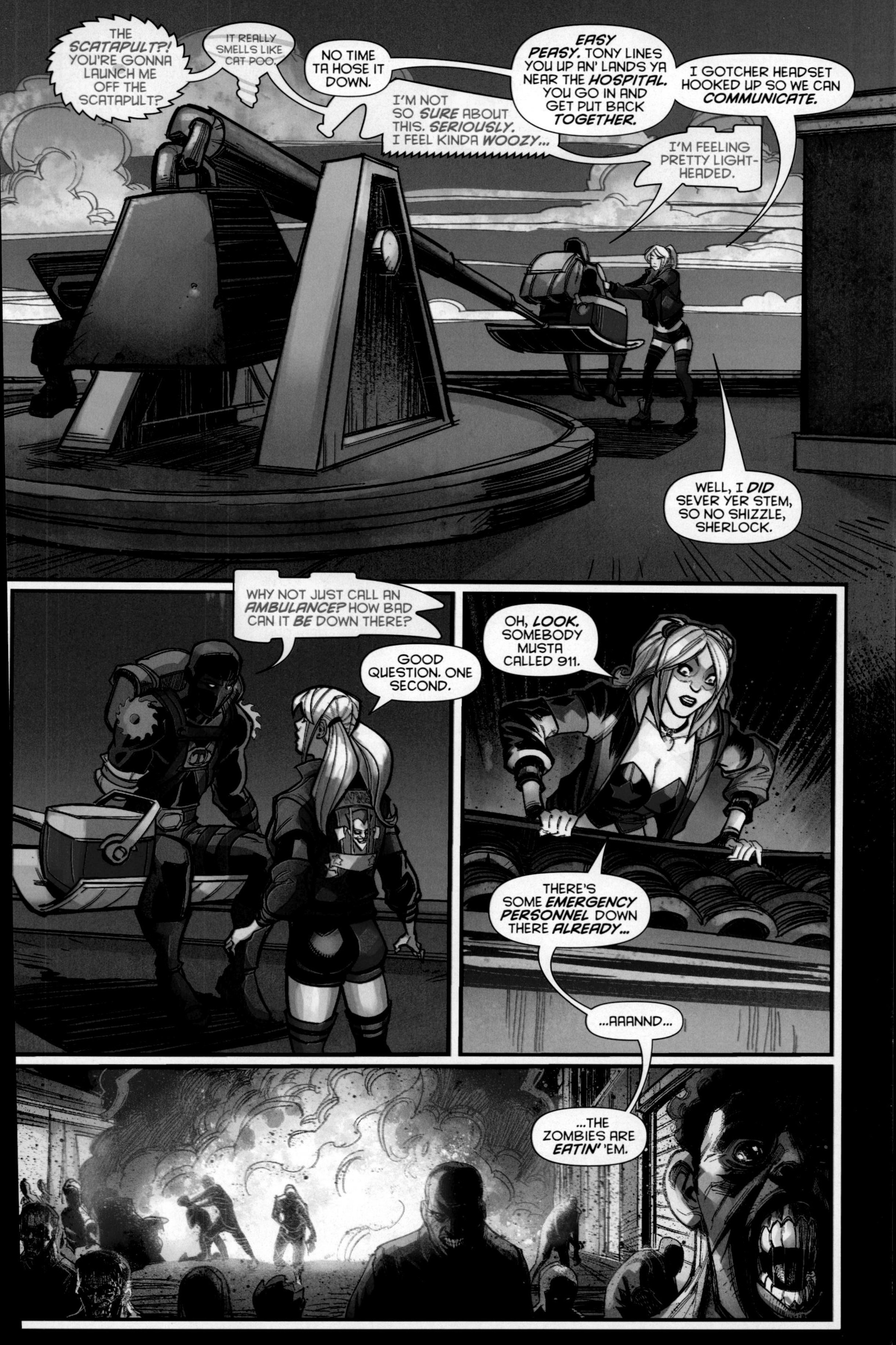

THE SCATAPULT?! YOU'RE GONNA LAUNCH ME OFF THE SCATAPULT?
IT REALLY SMELLS LIKE CAT POO.
NO TIME TA HOSE IT DOWN.
I'M NOT SO SURE ABOUT THIS. SERIOUSLY. I FEEL KINDA WOOZY...
EASY PEASY. TONY LINES YOU UP AN' LANDS YA NEAR THE HOSPITAL. YOU GO IN AND GET PUT BACK TOGETHER.
I GOTCHER HEADSET HOOKED UP SO WE CAN COMMUNICATE.
I'M FEELING PRETTY LIGHT-HEADED.
WELL, I DID SEVER YER STEM, SO NO SHIZZLE, SHERLOCK.
WHY NOT JUST CALL AN AMBULANCE? HOW BAD CAN IT BE DOWN THERE?
GOOD QUESTION. ONE SECOND.
OH, LOOK. SOMEBODY MUSTA CALLED 911.
THERE'S SOME EMERGENCY PERSONNEL DOWN THERE ALREADY...
...AAAAND...
...THE ZOMBIES ARE EATIN' 'EM.

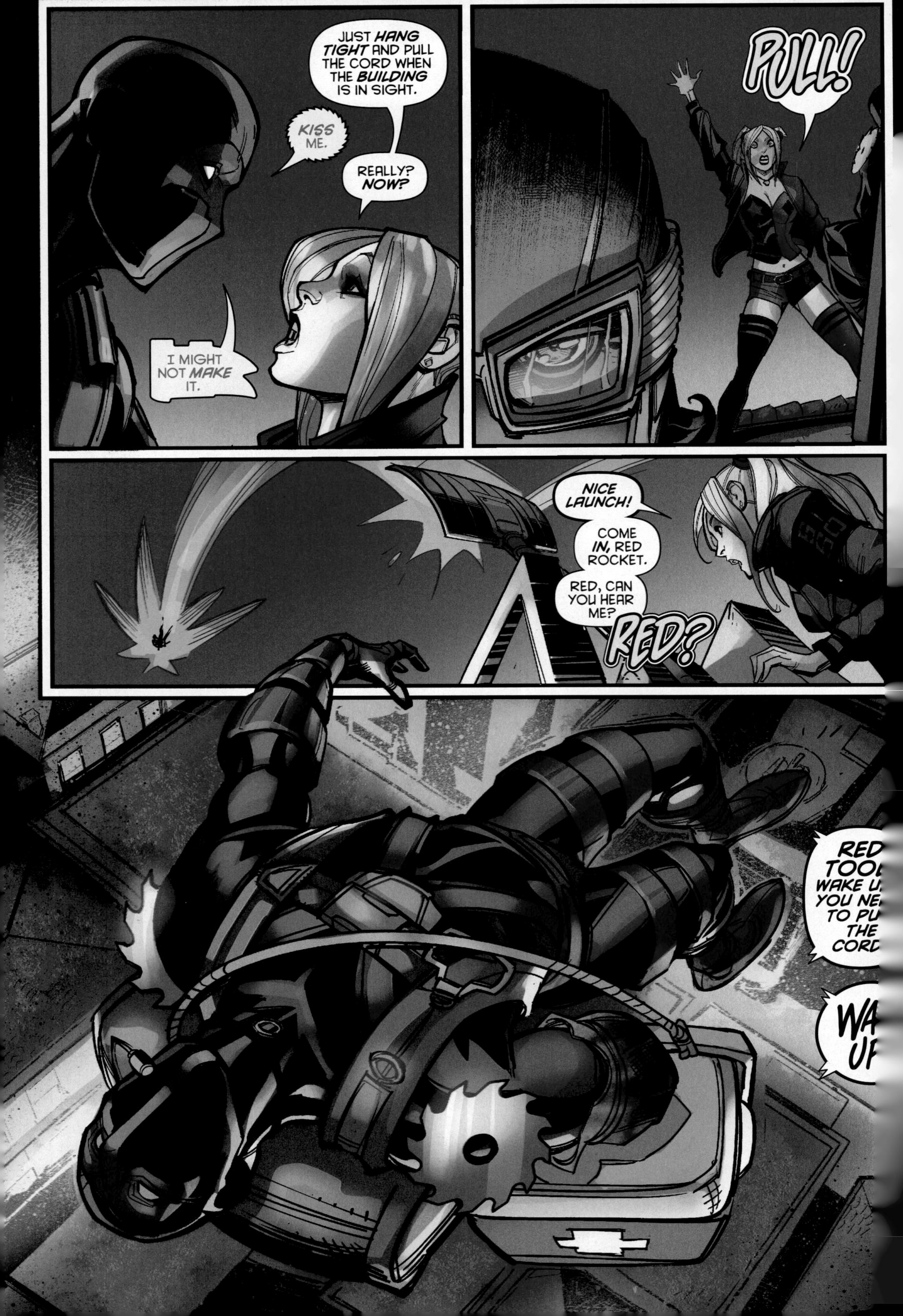
JUST HANG TIGHT AND PULL THE CORD WHEN THE BUILDING IS IN SIGHT.
KISS ME.
REALLY? NOW?
I MIGHT NOT MAKE IT.
PULL!
NICE LAUNCH!
COME IN, RED ROCKET.
RED, CAN YOU HEAR ME?
RED?

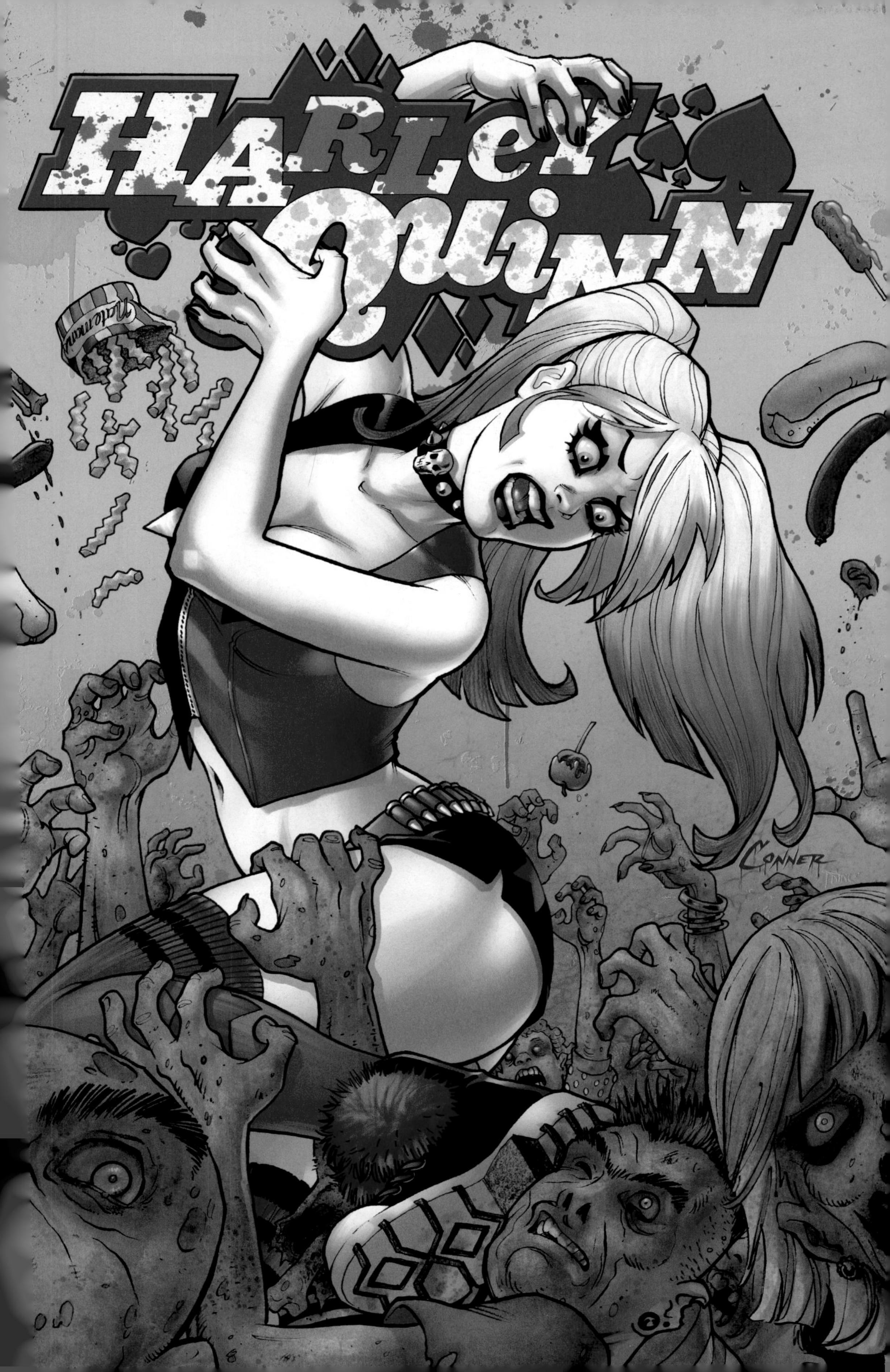
HARLEY QUINN
CONNER

DIE LAUGHING PART 2: THE CONEY ISLAND OF THE DAMNED

JIMMY PALMIOTTI and AMANDA CONNER writers * BRET BLEVINS layouts
CHAD HARDIN (p. 1-10) and JOHN TIMMS (p. 11-20) finishes * ALEX SINCLAIR colorist * DAVE SHARPE letterer

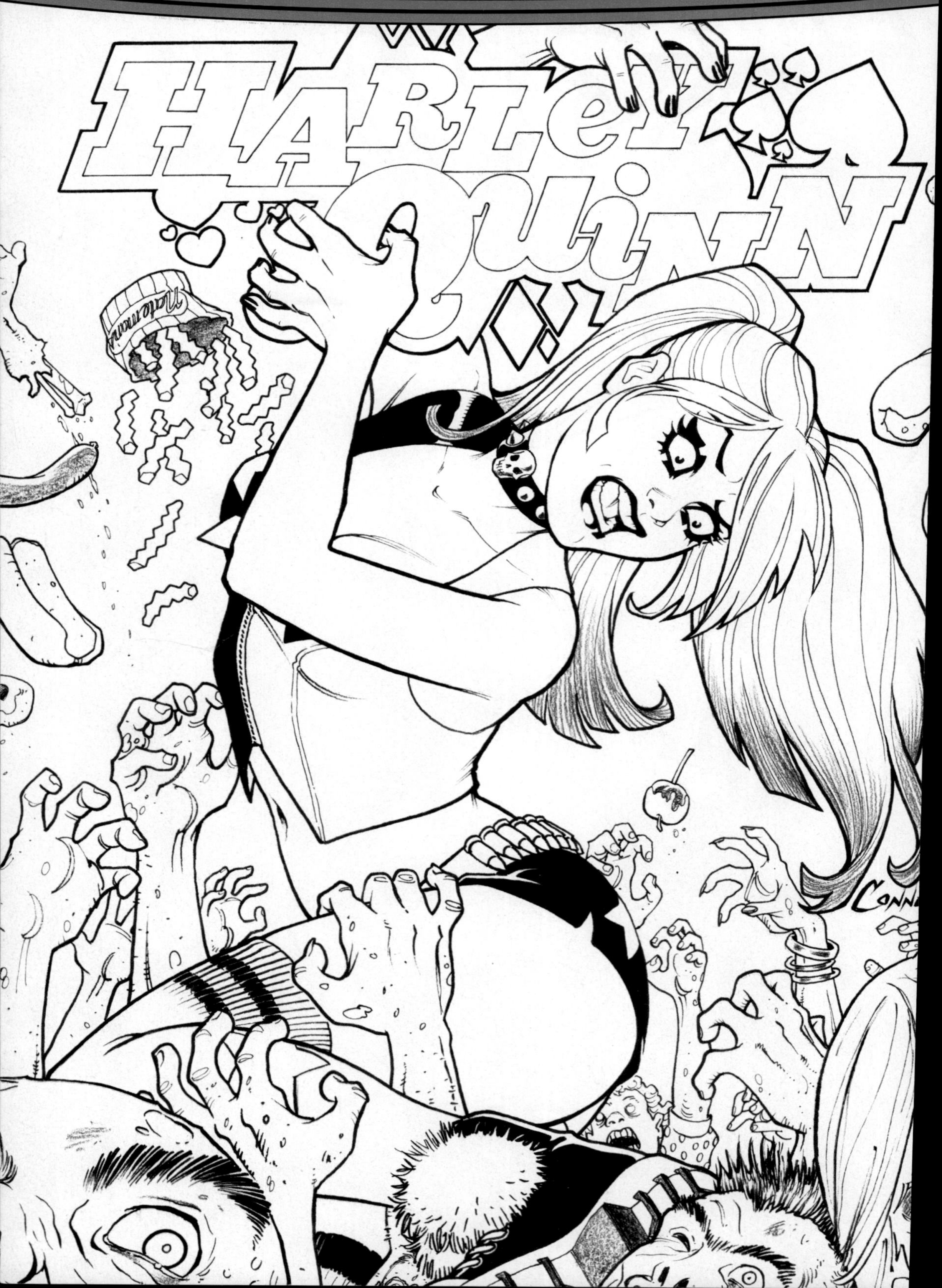
HARLEY QUINN

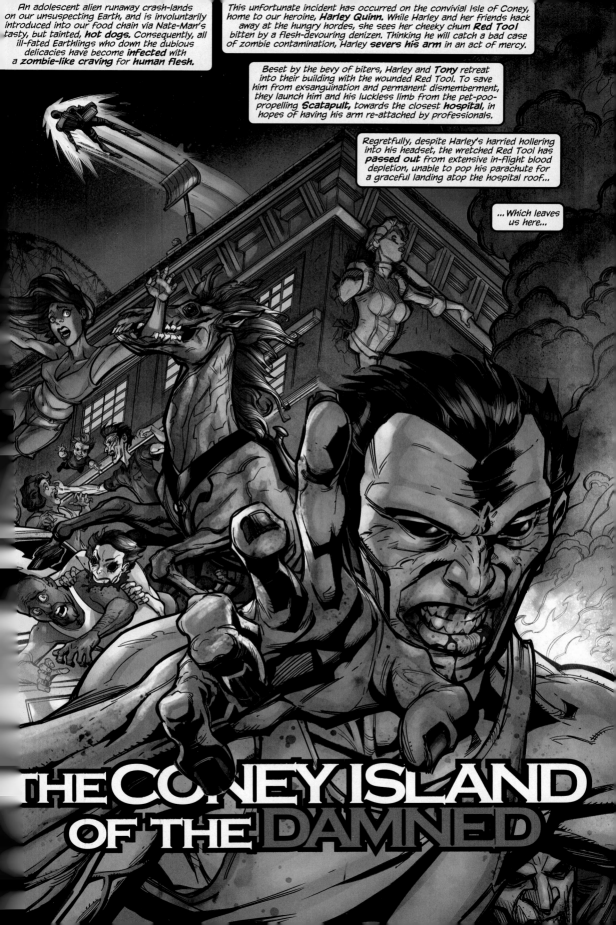

An adolescent alien runaway crash-lands on our unsuspecting Earth, and is involuntarily introduced into our food chain via Nate-Man's tasty, but tainted, **hot dogs**. Consequently, all ill-fated Earthlings who down the dubious delicacies have become **infected** with a **zombie-like craving** for **human flesh**.

This unfortunate incident has occurred on the convivial Isle of Coney, home to our heroine, **Harley Quinn**. While Harley and her friends hack away at the hungry hordes, she sees her cheeky chum **Red Tool** bitten by a flesh-devouring denizen. Thinking he will catch a bad case of zombie contamination, Harley **severs his arm** in an act of mercy.

Beset by the bevy of biters, Harley and **Tony** retreat into their building with the wounded Red Tool. To save him from exsanguination and permanent dismemberment, they launch him and his luckless limb from the pet-poo-propelling **Scatapult**, towards the closest **hospital**, in hopes of having his arm re-attached by professionals.

Regretfully, despite Harley's harried hollering into his headset, the wretched Red Tool has **passed out** from extensive in-flight blood depletion, unable to pop his parachute for a graceful landing atop the hospital roof...

...Which leaves us here...

THE CONEY ISLAND OF THE DAMNED

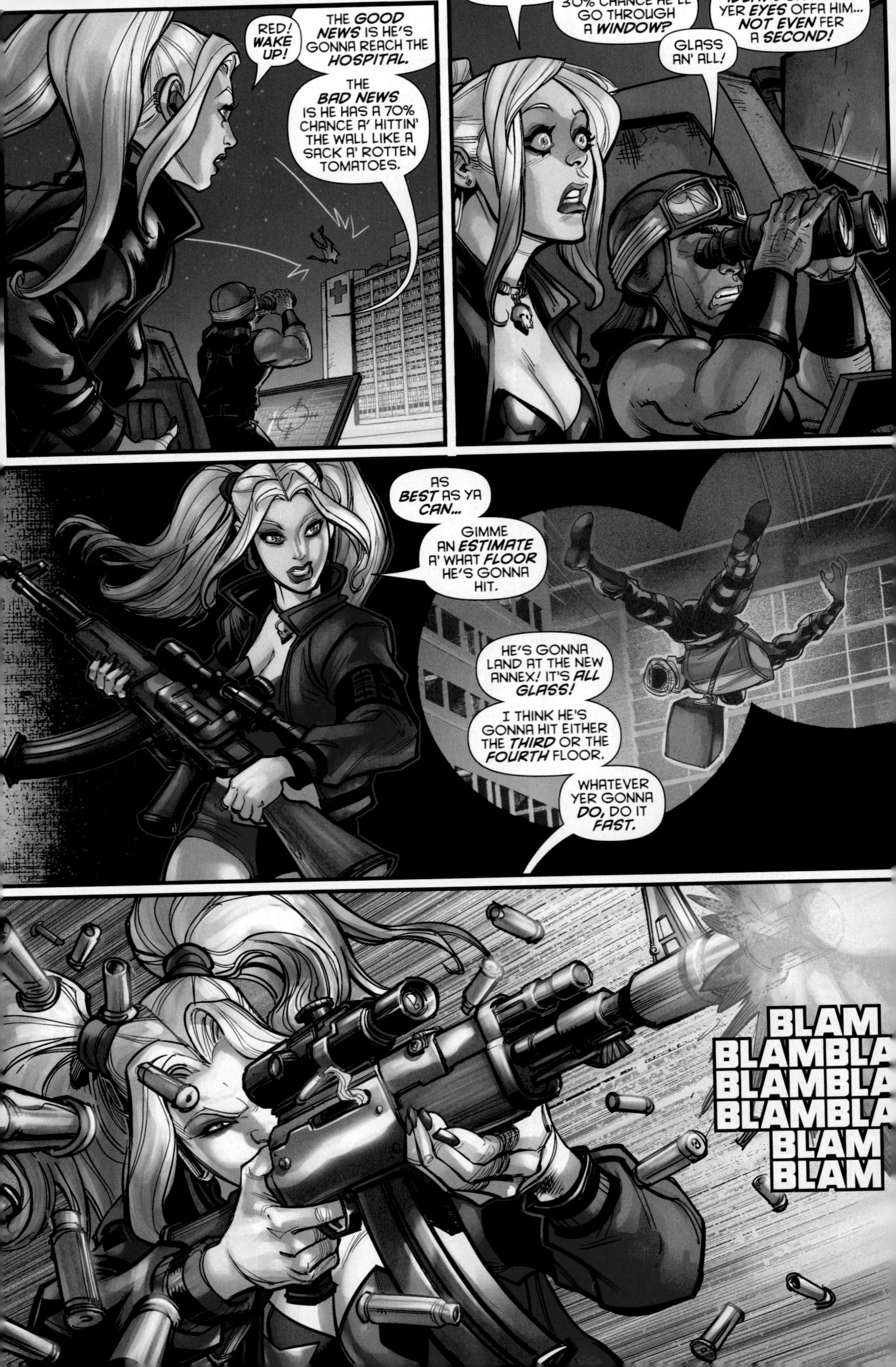
RED! WAKE UP!
THE GOOD NEWS IS HE'S GONNA REACH THE HOSPITAL.
THE BAD NEWS IS HE HAS A 70% CHANCE A' HITTIN' THE WALL LIKE A SACK A' ROTTEN TOMATOES.
30% CHANCE HE'LL GO THROUGH A WINDOW?
GLASS AN' ALL!
IDEA! DON'T TAKE YER EYES OFFA HIM... NOT EVEN FER A SECOND!
AS BEST AS YA CAN...
GIMME AN ESTIMATE A' WHAT FLOOR HE'S GONNA HIT.
HE'S GONNA LAND AT THE NEW ANNEX! IT'S ALL GLASS!
I THINK HE'S GONNA HIT EITHER THE THIRD OR THE FOURTH FLOOR.
WHATEVER YER GONNA DO, DO IT FAST.
BLAM BLAMBLA BLAMBLA BLAMBLA BLAM BLAM

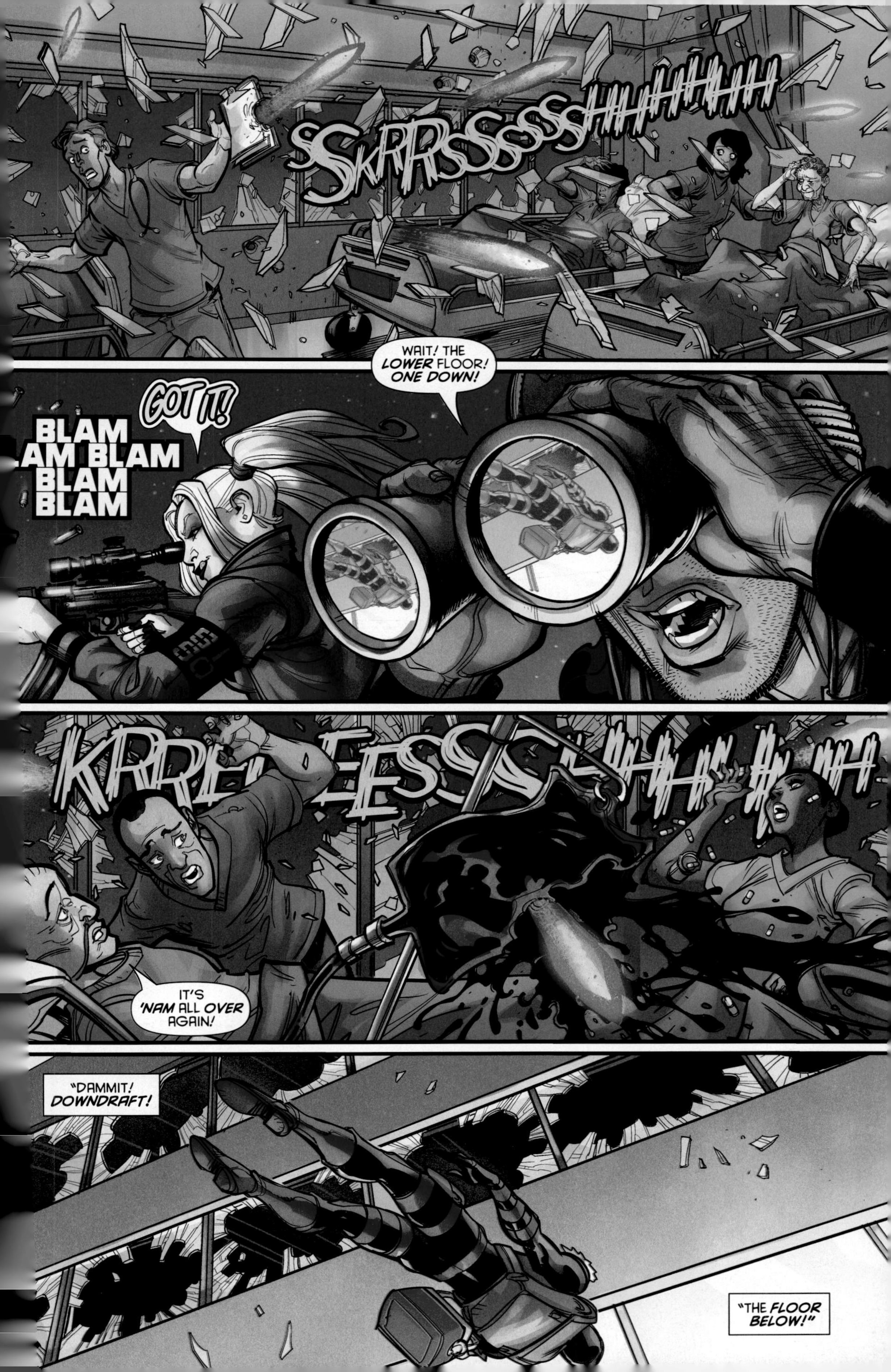

SKRRSSSSSHHHHHHHH
WAIT! THE LOWER FLOOR! ONE DOWN!
GOT IT!
BLAM AM BLAM BLAM BLAM
KRREEESSSSHHHHHH
IT'S 'NAM ALL OVER AGAIN!
"DAMMIT! DOWNDRAFT!
"THE FLOOR BELOW!"

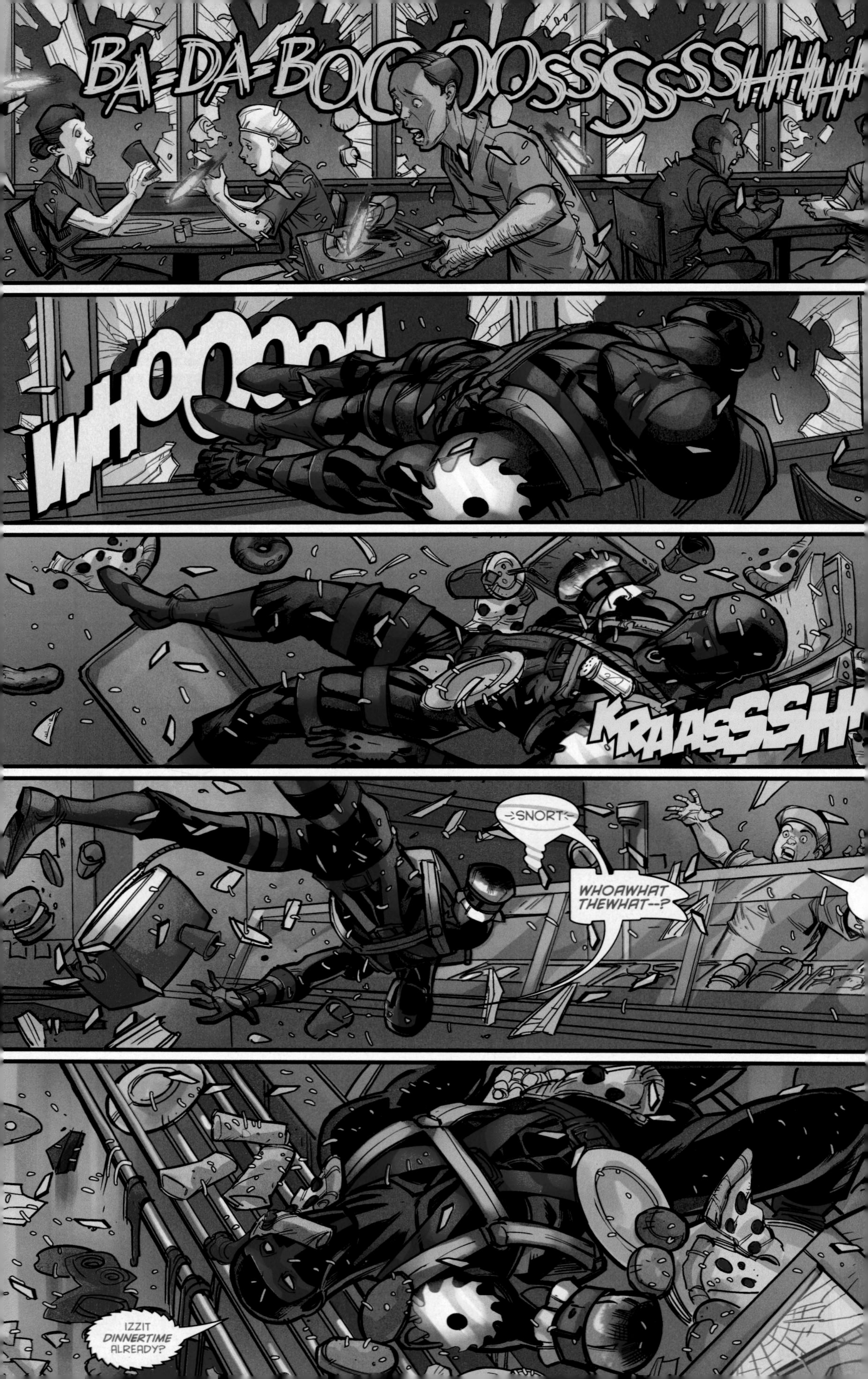
BA-DA-BOOOOOSSSSSSHHHH
WHOOOOM
KRAASSSH
-SNORT-
WHOAWHAT THEWHAT--?
IZZIT DINNERTIME ALREADY?

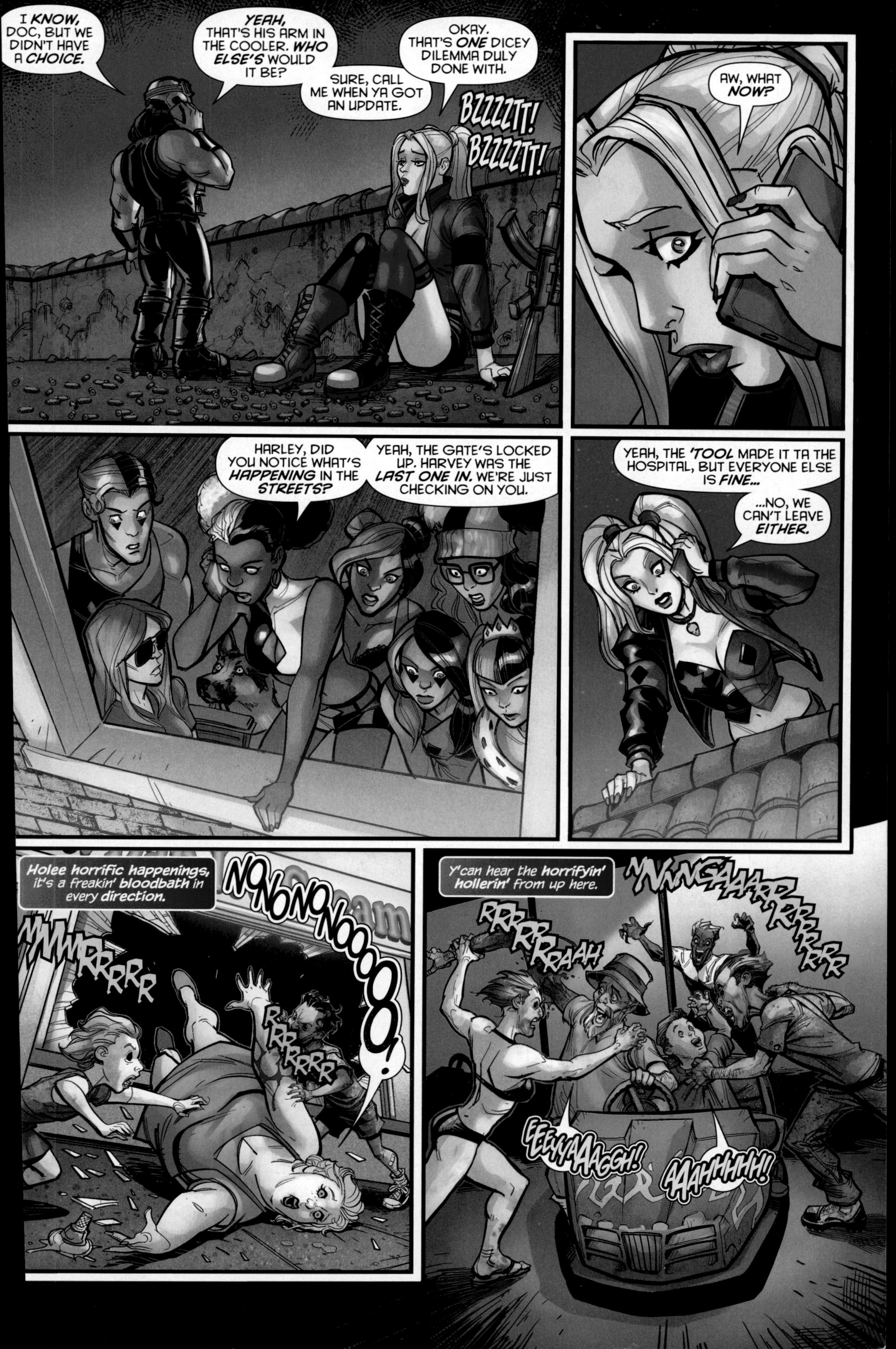
I KNOW, DOC, BUT WE DIDN'T HAVE A CHOICE.
YEAH, THAT'S HIS ARM IN THE COOLER. WHO ELSE'S WOULD IT BE?
SURE, CALL ME WHEN YA GOT AN UPDATE.
OKAY. THAT'S ONE DICEY DILEMMA DULY DONE WITH.
BZZZZZTT! BZZZZZTT!
AW, WHAT NOW?
HARLEY, DID YOU NOTICE WHAT'S HAPPENING IN THE STREETS?
YEAH, THE GATE'S LOCKED UP. HARVEY WAS THE LAST ONE IN. WE'RE JUST CHECKING ON YOU.
YEAH, THE 'TOOL MADE IT TA THE HOSPITAL, BUT EVERYONE ELSE IS FINE...
...NO, WE CAN'T LEAVE EITHER.
Holee horrific happenings, it's a freakin' bloodbath in every direction.
NONONONOOOOOO!
MWRRRRR
RRRRRR
Y'can hear the horrifyin' hollerin' from up here.
NNNGAAARRRRRRRR
RRRRRRAAH
EEEYYAAAAGGH!
AAAHHHHH!

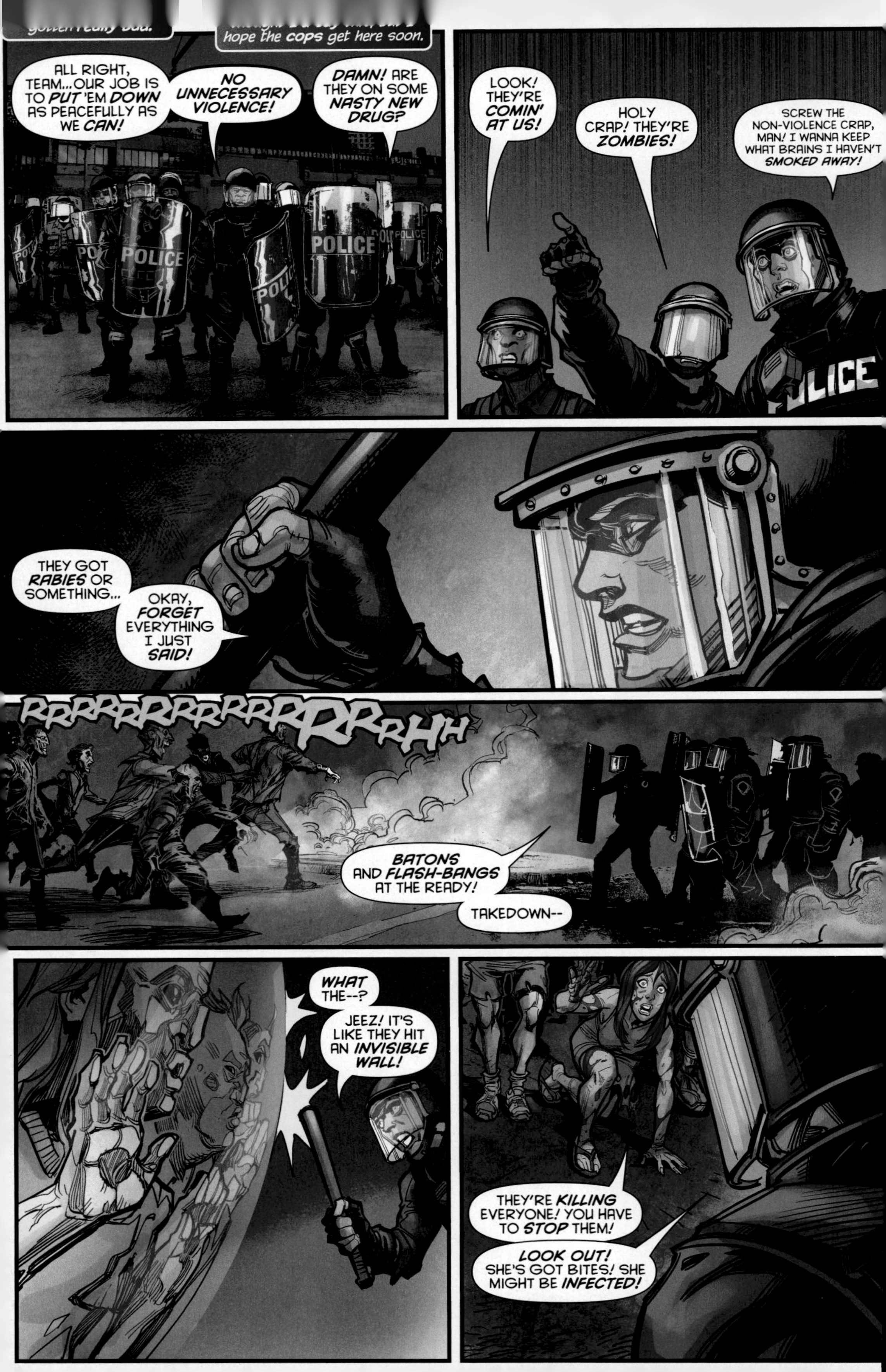

gotten really bad.
hope the cops get here soon.
ALL RIGHT, TEAM... OUR JOB IS TO PUT 'EM DOWN AS PEACEFULLY AS WE CAN!
NO UNNECESSARY VIOLENCE!
DAMN! ARE THEY ON SOME NASTY NEW DRUG?
LOOK! THEY'RE COMIN' AT US!
HOLY CRAP! THEY'RE ZOMBIES!
SCREW THE NON-VIOLENCE CRAP, MAN! I WANNA KEEP WHAT BRAINS I HAVEN'T SMOKED AWAY!
POLICE
THEY GOT RABIES OR SOMETHING...
OKAY, FORGET EVERYTHING I JUST SAID!
RRRRRRRRRRRRRRRRRRRRRRHH
BATONS AND FLASH-BANGS AT THE READY!
TAKEDOWN--
WHAT THE--?
JEEZ! IT'S LIKE THEY HIT AN INVISIBLE WALL!
THEY'RE KILLING EVERYONE! YOU HAVE TO STOP THEM!
LOOK OUT! SHE'S GOT BITES! SHE MIGHT BE INFECTED!

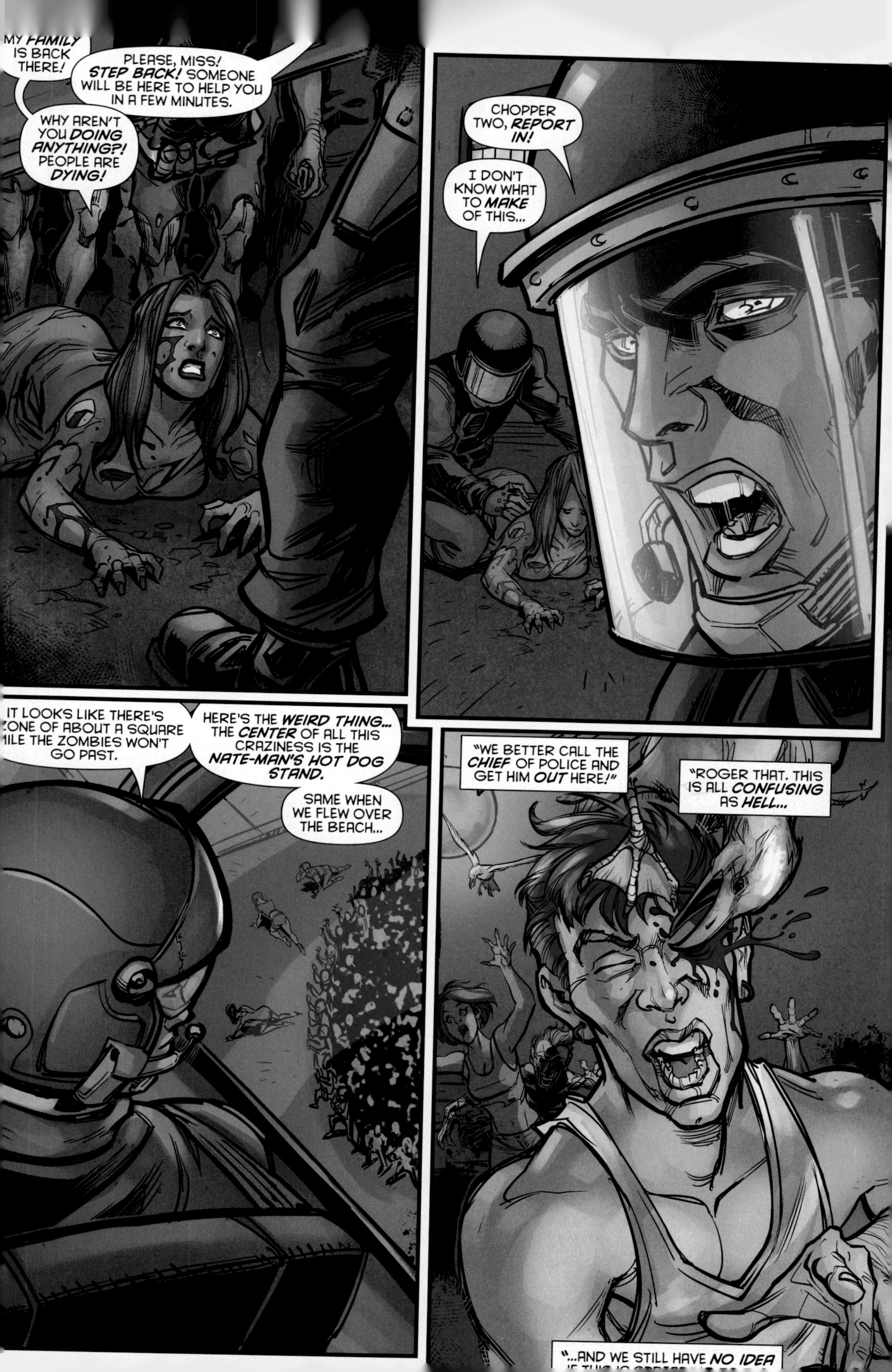
MY FAMILY IS BACK THERE!
PLEASE, MISS! STEP BACK! SOMEONE WILL BE HERE TO HELP YOU IN A FEW MINUTES.
WHY AREN'T YOU DOING ANYTHING?! PEOPLE ARE DYING!
CHOPPER TWO, REPORT IN!
I DON'T KNOW WHAT TO MAKE OF THIS...
IT LOOKS LIKE THERE'S ZONE OF ABOUT A SQUARE ILE THE ZOMBIES WON'T GO PAST.
HERE'S THE WEIRD THING... THE CENTER OF ALL THIS CRAZINESS IS THE NATE-MAN'S HOT DOG STAND.
SAME WHEN WE FLEW OVER THE BEACH...
"WE BETTER CALL THE CHIEF OF POLICE AND GET HIM OUT HERE!"
"ROGER THAT. THIS IS ALL CONFUSING AS HELL...
"...AND WE STILL HAVE NO IDEA

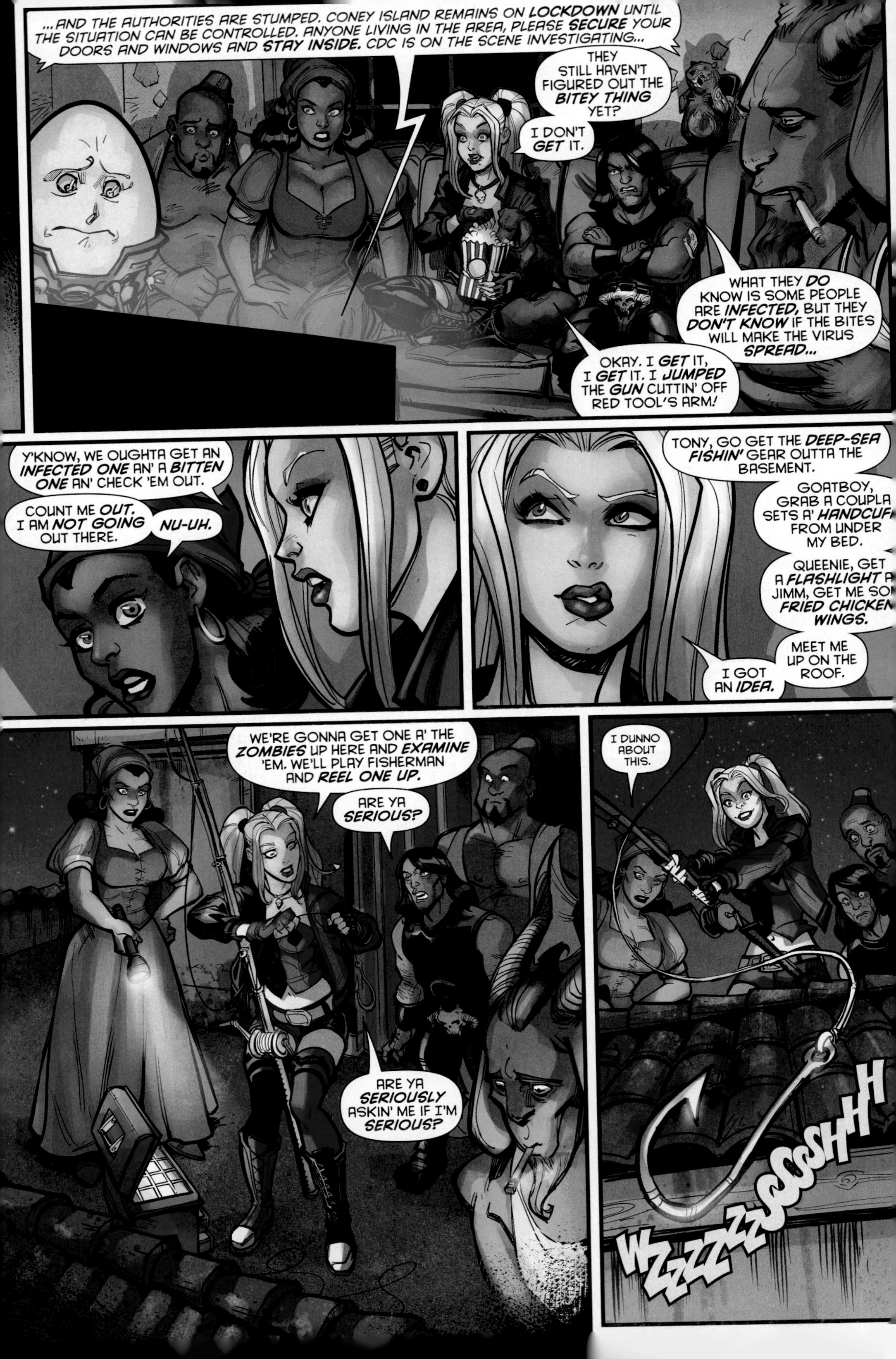
...AND THE AUTHORITIES ARE STUMPED. CONEY ISLAND REMAINS ON LOCKDOWN UNTIL THE SITUATION CAN BE CONTROLLED. ANYONE LIVING IN THE AREA, PLEASE SECURE YOUR DOORS AND WINDOWS AND STAY INSIDE. CDC IS ON THE SCENE INVESTIGATING...
THEY STILL HAVEN'T FIGURED OUT THE BITEY THING YET?
I DON'T GET IT.
WHAT THEY DO KNOW IS SOME PEOPLE ARE INFECTED, BUT THEY DON'T KNOW IF THE BITES WILL MAKE THE VIRUS SPREAD...
OKAY. I GET IT, I GET IT. I JUMPED THE GUN CUTTIN' OFF RED TOOL'S ARM!
Y'KNOW, WE OUGHTA GET AN INFECTED ONE AN' A BITTEN ONE AN' CHECK 'EM OUT.
COUNT ME OUT. I AM NOT GOING OUT THERE.
NU-UH.
TONY, GO GET THE DEEP-SEA FISHIN' GEAR OUTTA THE BASEMENT.
GOATBOY, GRAB A COUPLA SETS A' HANDCUFF FROM UNDER MY BED.
QUEENIE, GET A FLASHLIGHT A JIMM, GET ME SO FRIED CHICKEN WINGS.
I GOT AN IDEA.
MEET ME UP ON THE ROOF.
WE'RE GONNA GET ONE A' THE ZOMBIES UP HERE AND EXAMINE 'EM. WE'LL PLAY FISHERMAN AND REEL ONE UP.
ARE YA SERIOUS?
ARE YA SERIOUSLY ASKIN' ME IF I'M SERIOUS?
I DUNNO ABOUT THIS.
WZZZZZZZSSSHHH

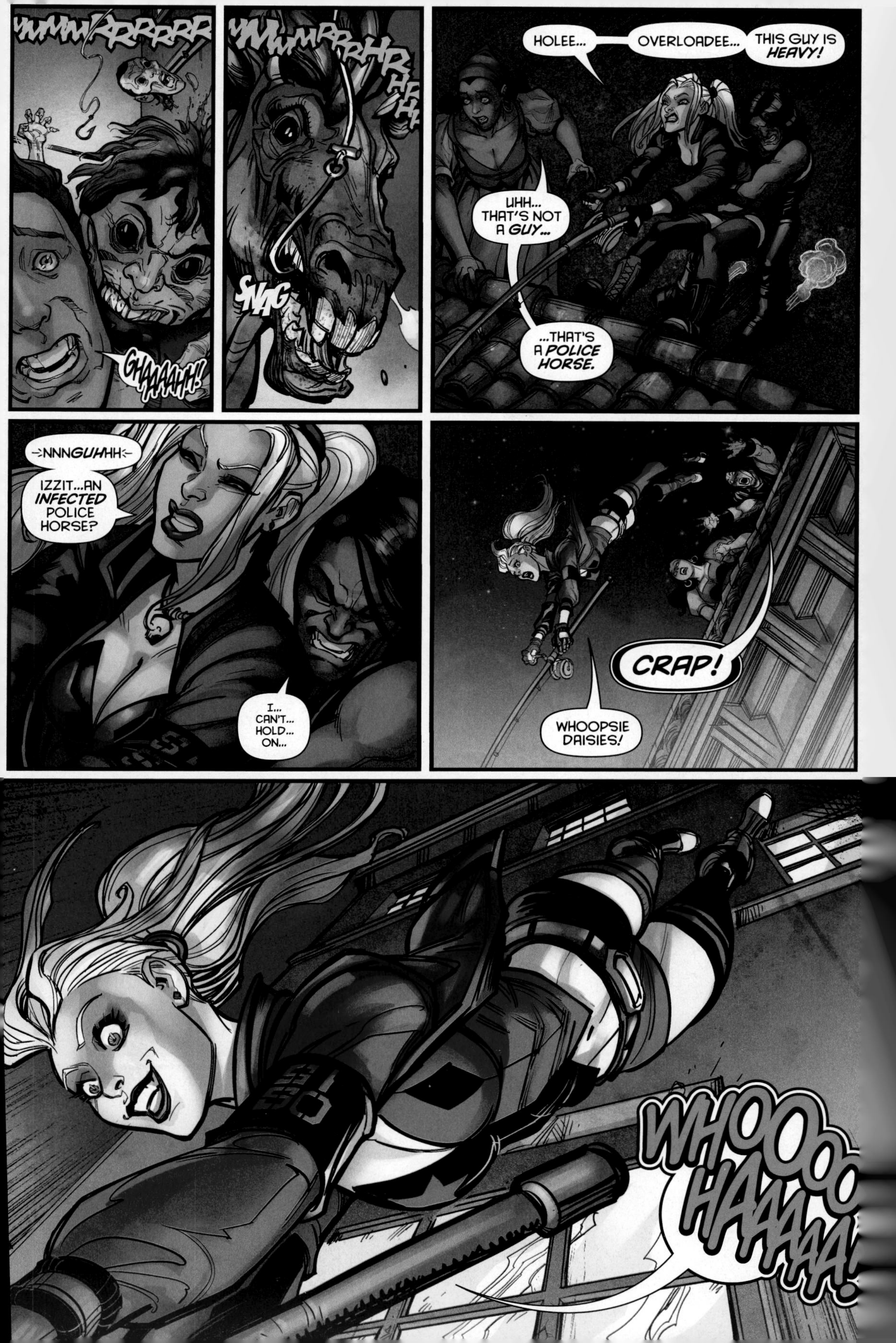

WMMMKRRRRRR
WMMMRRRHRHH
GHAAAAHH!
SNAG
HOLEE...
OVERLOADEE...
THIS GUY IS HEAVY!
UHH... THAT'S NOT A GUY...
...THAT'S A POLICE HORSE.
NNNGUHHH
IZZIT...AN INFECTED POLICE HORSE?
I... CAN'T... HOLD... ON...
CRAP!
WHOOPSIE DAISIES!
WHOOoo HAAAAA!

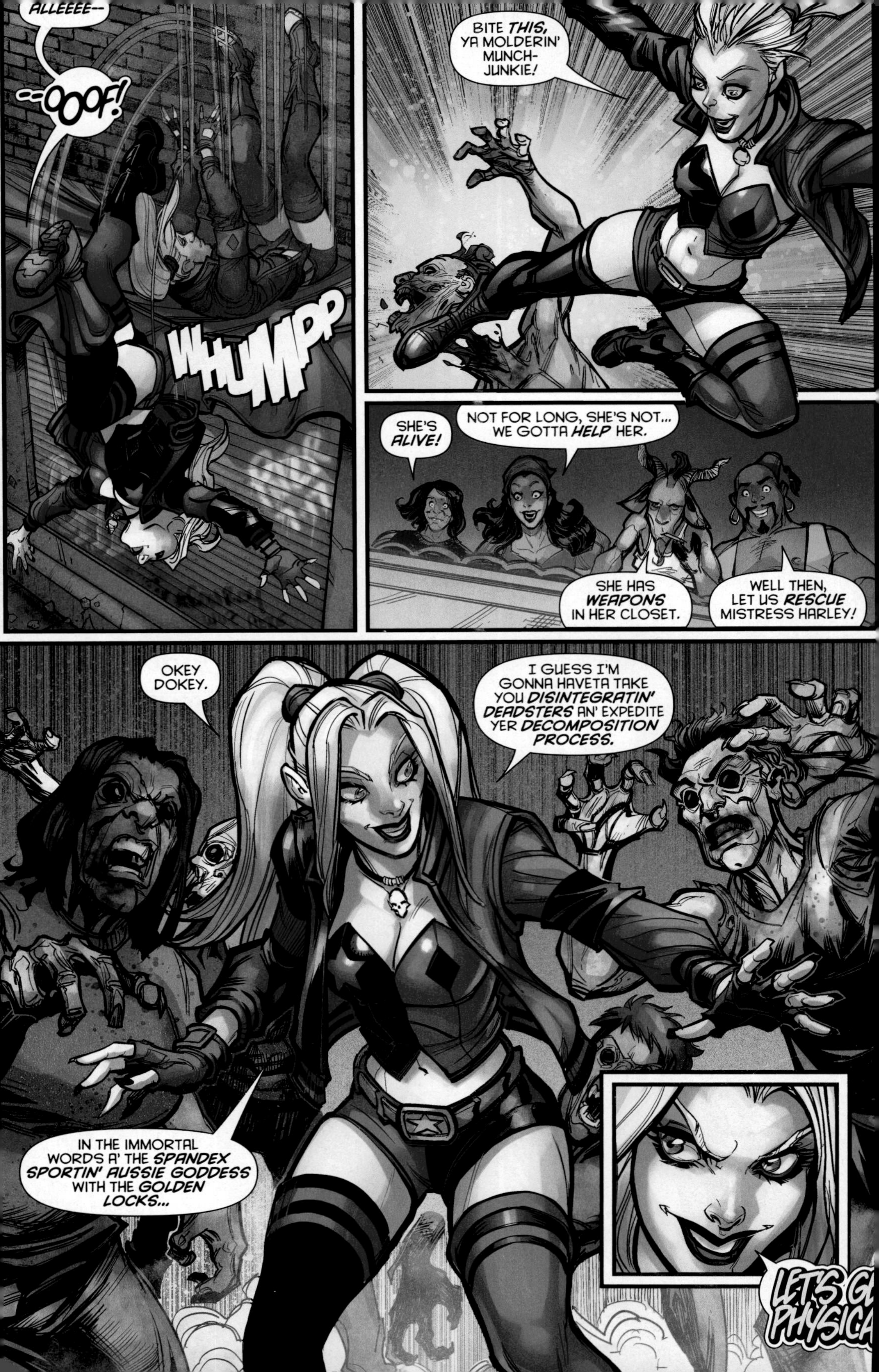

ALLEEEE--
--OOOF!
WHUMPP
BITE THIS, YA MOLDERIN' MUNCH-JUNKIE!
SHE'S ALIVE!
NOT FOR LONG, SHE'S NOT... WE GOTTA HELP HER.
SHE HAS WEAPONS IN HER CLOSET.
WELL THEN, LET US RESCUE MISTRESS HARLEY!
OKEY DOKEY.
I GUESS I'M GONNA HAVETA TAKE YOU DISINTEGRATIN' DEADSTERS AN' EXPEDITE YER DECOMPOSITION PROCESS.
IN THE IMMORTAL WORDS A' THE SPANDEX SPORTIN' AUSSIE GODDESS WITH THE GOLDEN LOCKS...

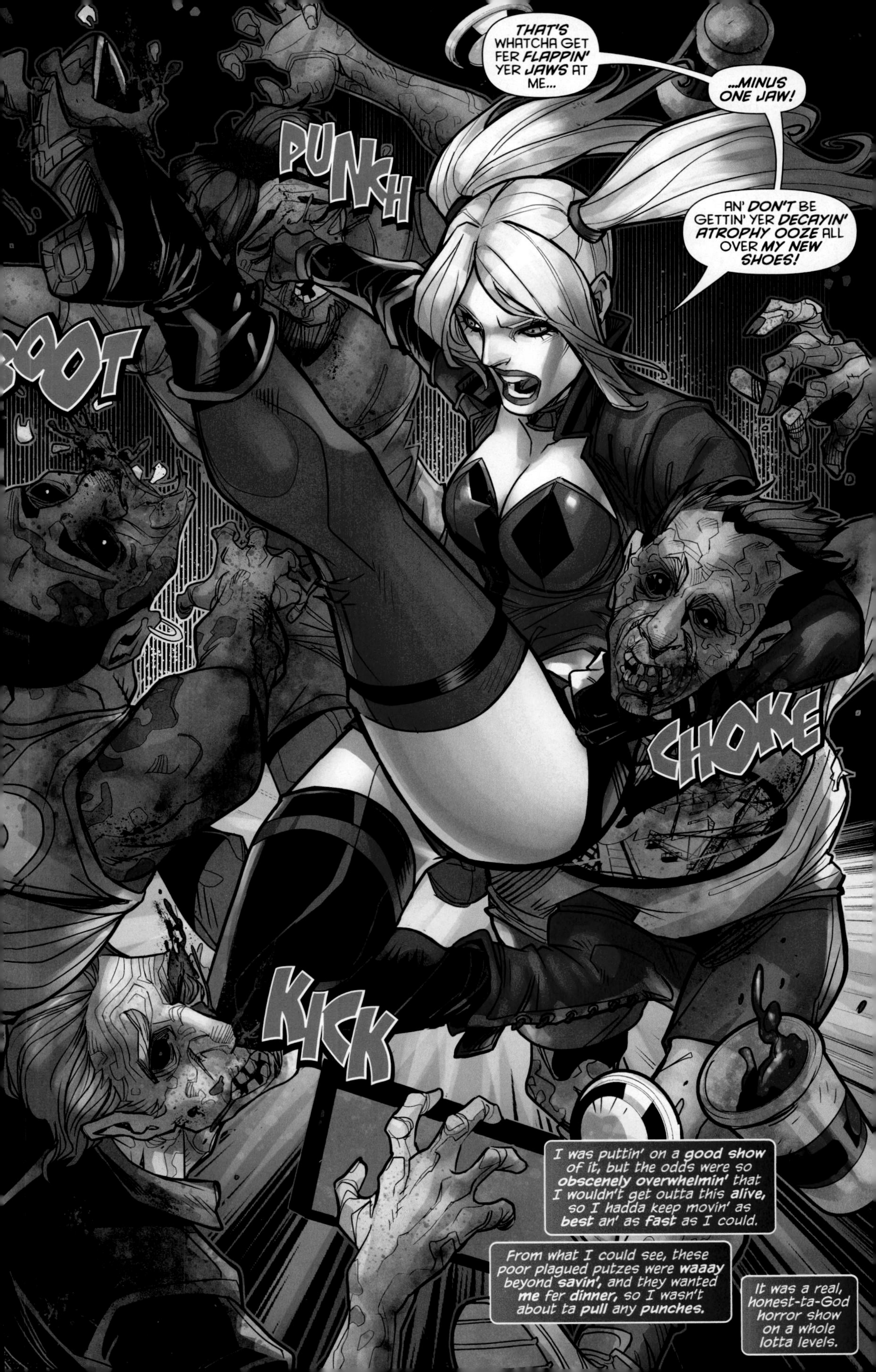
THAT'S WHATCHA GET FER FLAPPIN' YER JAWS AT ME...
...MINUS ONE JAW!
PUNKH
AN' DON'T BE GETTIN' YER DECAYIN' ATROPHY OOZE ALL OVER MY NEW SHOES!
CHOKE
KICK
I was puttin' on a good show of it, but the odds were so obscenely overwhelmin' that I wouldn't get outta this alive, so I hadda keep movin' as best an' as fast as I could.
From what I could see, these poor plagued putzes were waaay beyond savin', and they wanted me fer dinner, so I wasn't about ta pull any punches.
It was a real, honest-ta-God horror show on a whole lotta levels.

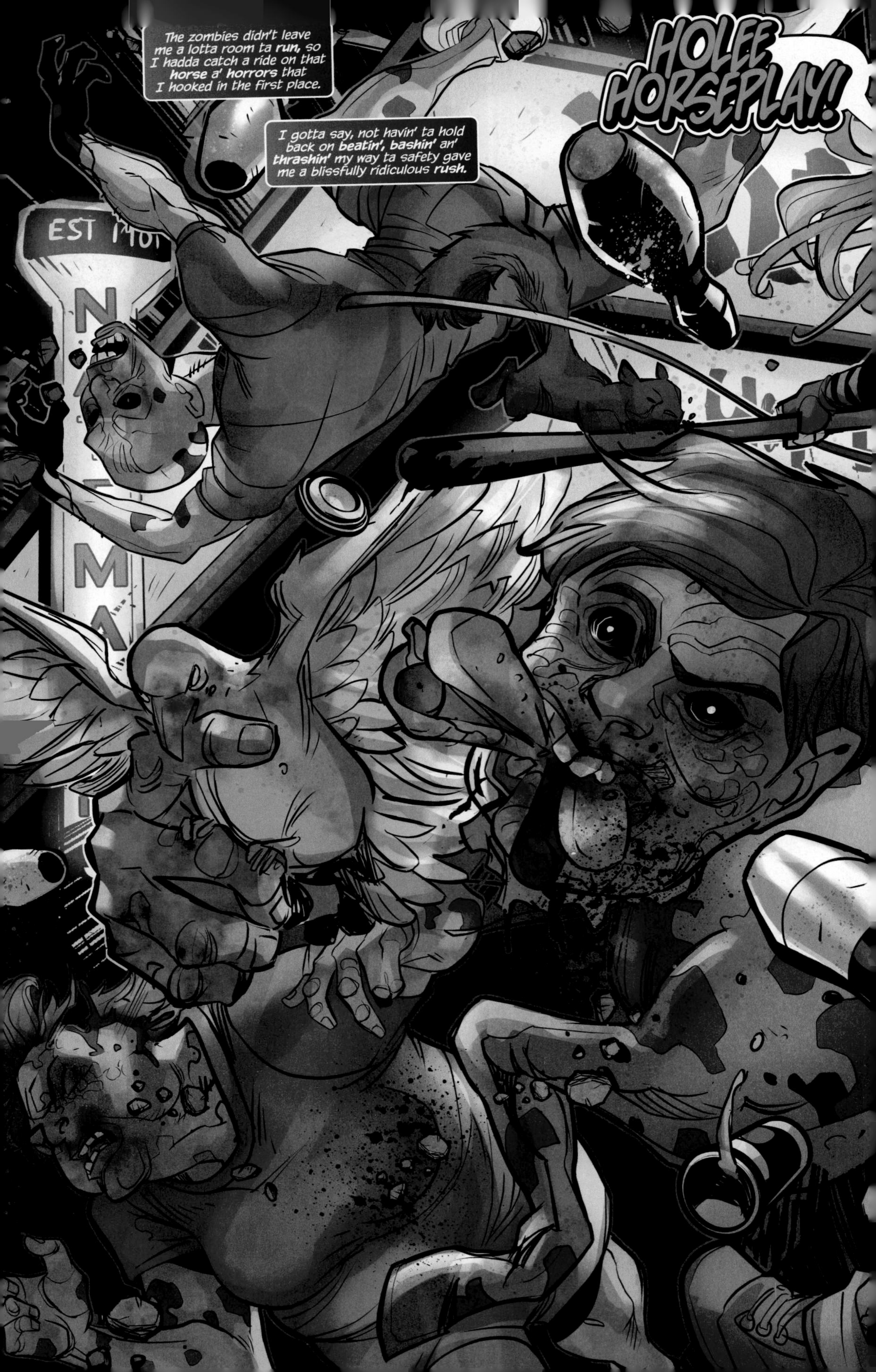
The zombies didn't leave me a lotta room ta run, so I hadda catch a ride on that horse a' horrors that I hooked in the first place.
HOLEE HORSEPLAY!
I gotta say, not havin' ta hold back on beatin', bashin' an' thrashin' my way ta safety gave me a blissfully ridiculous rush.
EST 1901

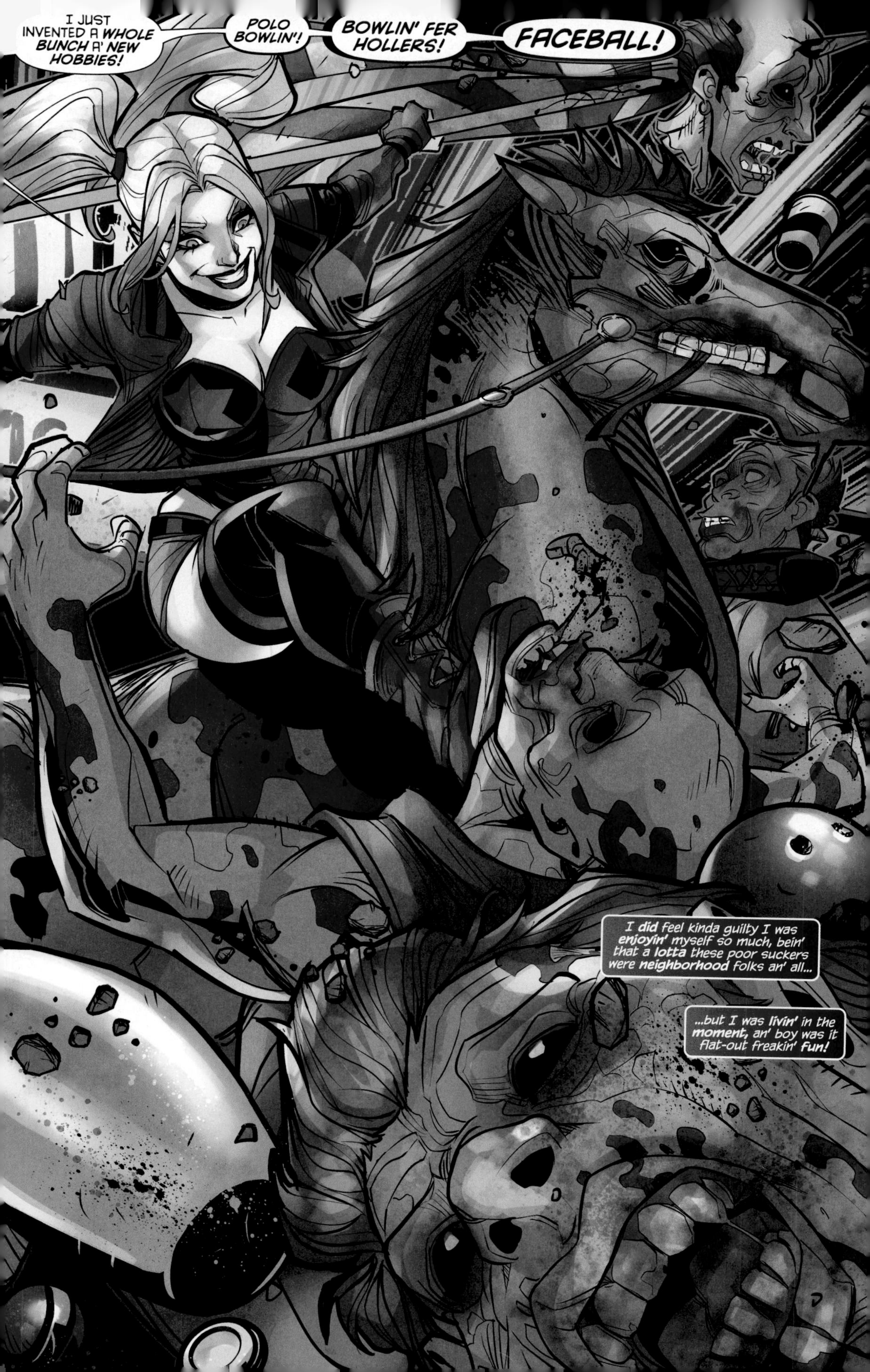
I JUST INVENTED A WHOLE BUNCH A' NEW HOBBIES!
POLO BOWLIN'!
BOWLIN' FER HOLLERS!
FACEBALL!
I did feel kinda guilty I was enjoyin' myself so much, bein' that a lotta these poor suckers were neighborhood folks an' all...
...but I was livin' in the moment, an' boy was it flat-out freakin' fun!

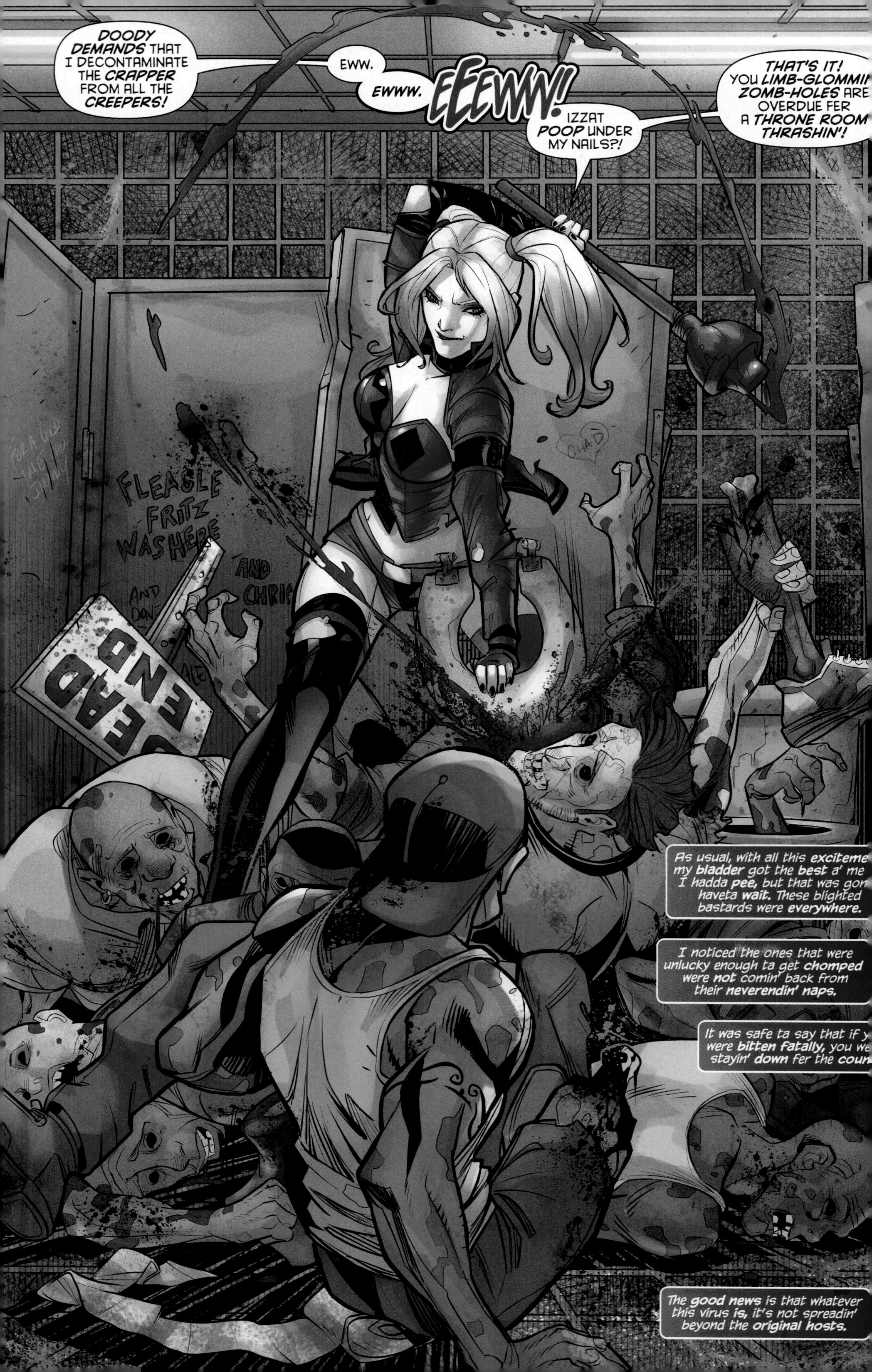
DOODY DEMANDS THAT I DECONTAMINATE THE CRAPPER FROM ALL THE CREEPERS!
EWW.
EWWW.
EEEWW!
IZZAT POOP UNDER MY NAILS?!
THAT'S IT! YOU LIMB-GLOMMIN ZOMB-HOLES ARE OVERDUE FER A THRONE ROOM THRASHIN'!
FLEAGLE FRITZ WAS HERE
AND DAN
AND CHRIS
DEAD END
CHAD
As usual, with all this exciteme my bladder got the best a' me I hadda pee, but that was gon haveta wait. These blighted bastards were everywhere.
I noticed the ones that were unlucky enough ta get chomped were not comin' back from their neverendin' naps.
It was safe ta say that if y were bitten fatally, you we stayin' down fer the cou
The good news is that whatever this virus is, it's not spreadin' beyond the original hosts.

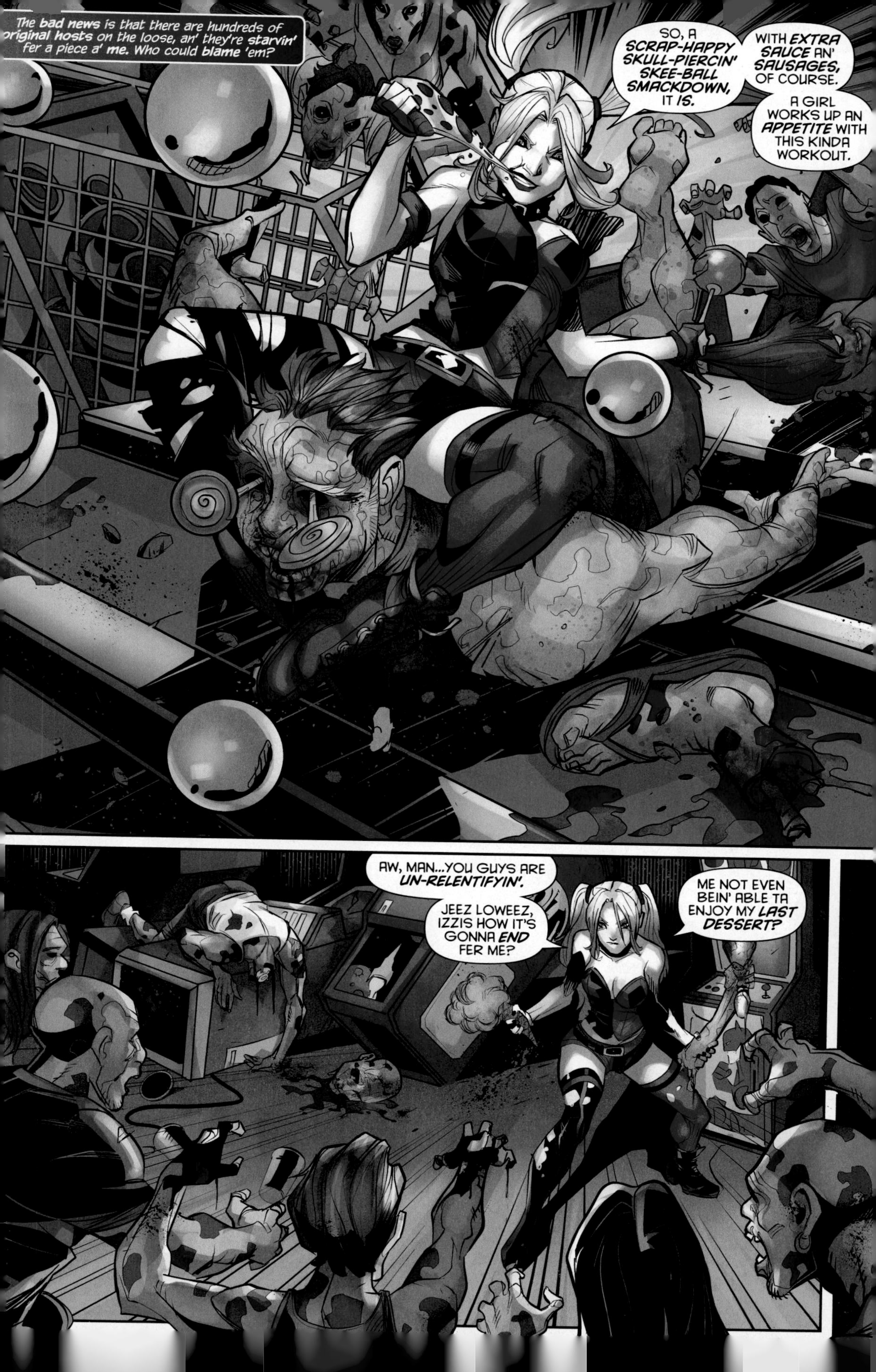
The bad news is that there are hundreds of original hosts on the loose, an' they're starvin' fer a piece a' me. Who could blame 'em?
SO, A SCRAP-HAPPY SKULL-PIERCIN' SKEE-BALL SMACKDOWN, IT IS.
WITH EXTRA SAUCE AN' SAUSAGES, OF COURSE.
A GIRL WORKS UP AN APPETITE WITH THIS KINDA WORKOUT.
AW, MAN...YOU GUYS ARE UN-RELENTIFYIN'.
JEEZ LOWEEZ, IZZIS HOW IT'S GONNA END FER ME?
ME NOT EVEN BEIN' ABLE TA ENJOY MY LAST DESSERT?

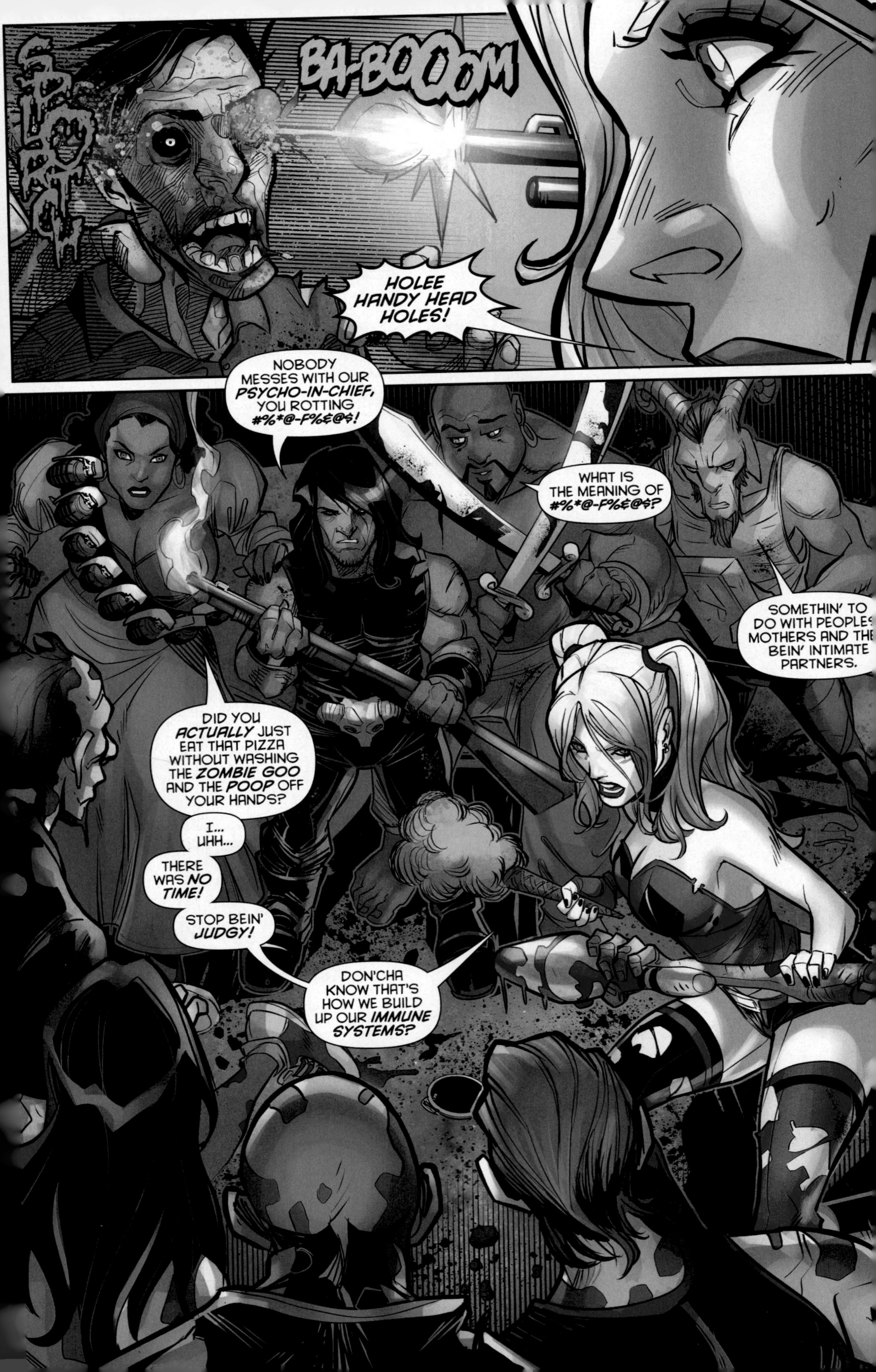
SPLORTCH
BA-BOOOOM
HOLEE HANDY HEAD HOLES!
NOBODY MESSES WITH OUR PSYCHO-IN-CHIEF, YOU ROTTING #%*@-F%£@$!
WHAT IS THE MEANING OF #%*@-F%£@$?
SOMETHIN' TO DO WITH PEOPLES MOTHERS AND THE BEIN' INTIMATE PARTNERS.
DID YOU ACTUALLY JUST EAT THAT PIZZA WITHOUT WASHING THE ZOMBIE GOO AND THE POOP OFF YOUR HANDS?
I... UHH...
THERE WAS NO TIME!
STOP BEIN' JUDGY!
DON'CHA KNOW THAT'S HOW WE BUILD UP OUR IMMUNE SYSTEMS?

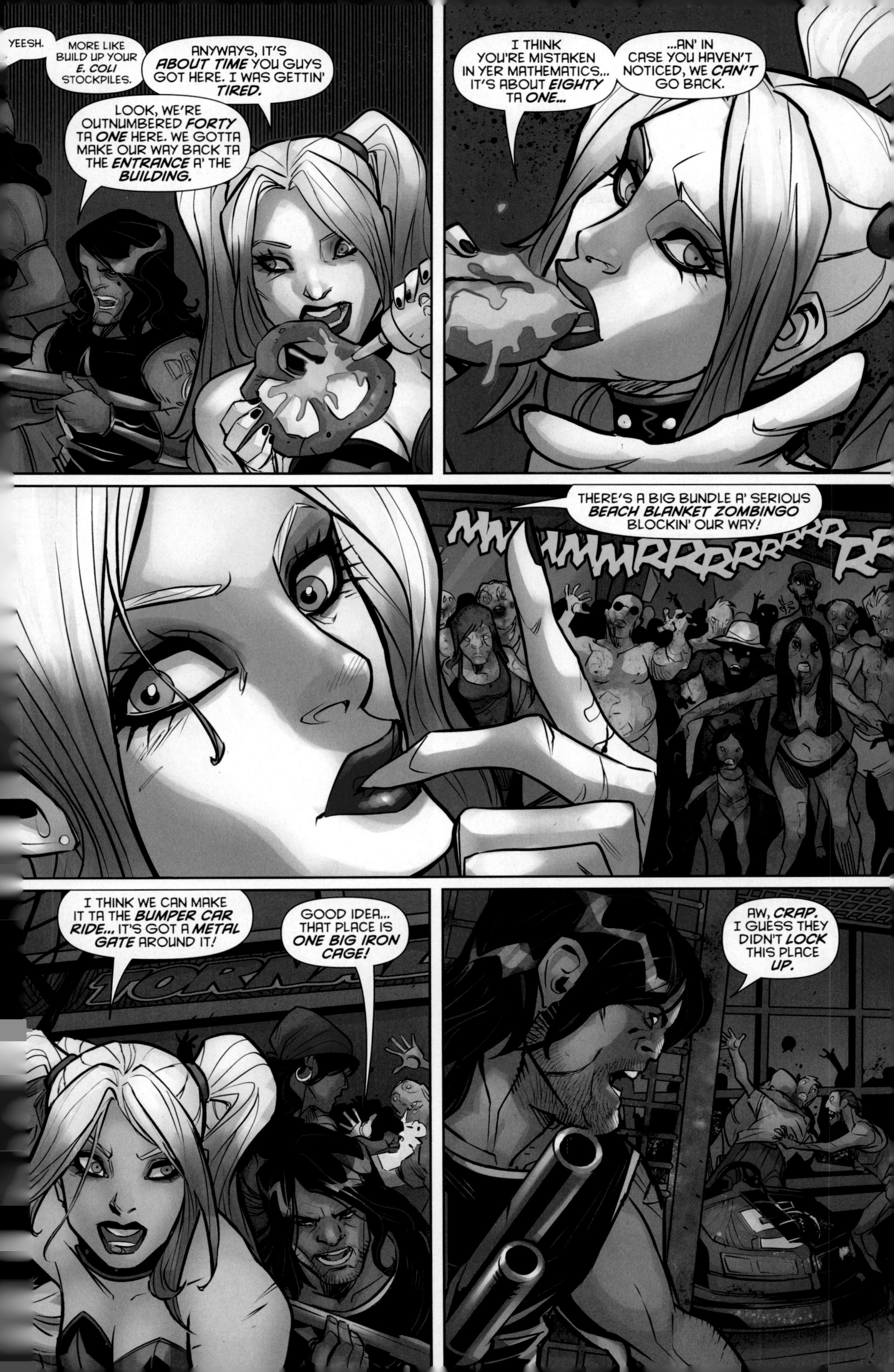
YEESH.
MORE LIKE BUILD UP YOUR E. COLI STOCKPILES.
ANYWAYS, IT'S ABOUT TIME YOU GUYS GOT HERE. I WAS GETTIN' TIRED.
LOOK, WE'RE OUTNUMBERED FORTY TA ONE HERE. WE GOTTA MAKE OUR WAY BACK TA THE ENTRANCE A' THE BUILDING.
I THINK YOU'RE MISTAKEN IN YER MATHEMATICS... IT'S ABOUT EIGHTY TA ONE...
...AN' IN CASE YOU HAVEN'T NOTICED, WE CAN'T GO BACK.
THERE'S A BIG BUNDLE A' SERIOUS BEACH BLANKET ZOMBINGO BLOCKIN' OUR WAY!
MMMMMMRRRRRRRRRRR
I THINK WE CAN MAKE IT TA THE BUMPER CAR RIDE... IT'S GOT A METAL GATE AROUND IT!
GOOD IDEA... THAT PLACE IS ONE BIG IRON CAGE!
AW, CRAP. I GUESS THEY DIDN'T LOCK THIS PLACE UP.

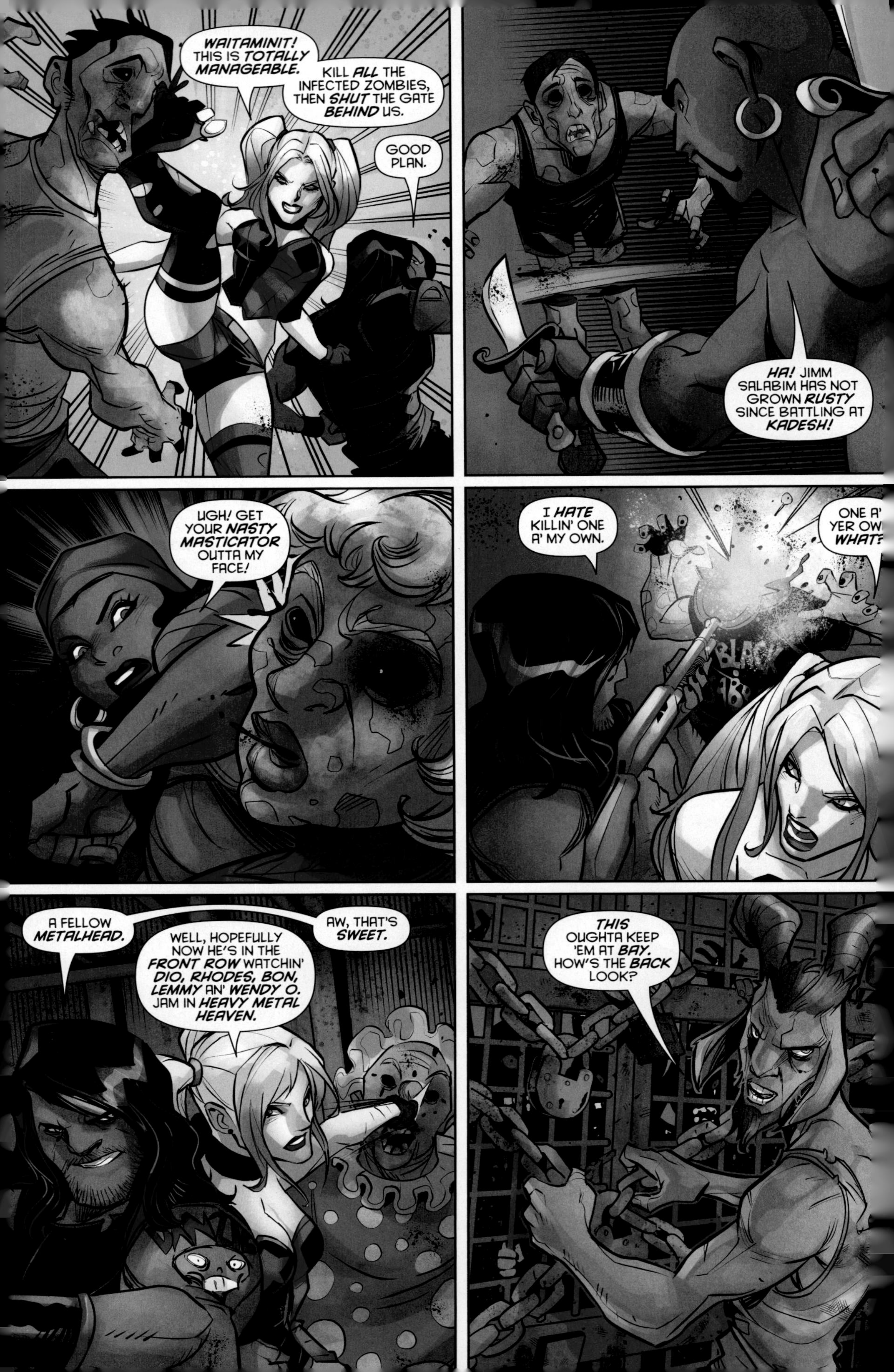
WAITAMINIT! THIS IS TOTALLY MANAGEABLE.
KILL ALL THE INFECTED ZOMBIES, THEN SHUT THE GATE BEHIND US.
GOOD PLAN.
HA! JIMM SALABIM HAS NOT GROWN RUSTY SINCE BATTLING AT KADESH!
UGH! GET YOUR NASTY MASTICATOR OUTTA MY FACE!
I HATE KILLIN' ONE A' MY OWN.
ONE A' YER OW WHAT?
A FELLOW METALHEAD.
WELL, HOPEFULLY NOW HE'S IN THE FRONT ROW WATCHIN' DIO, RHODES, BON, LEMMY AN' WENDY O. JAM IN HEAVY METAL HEAVEN.
AW, THAT'S SWEET.
THIS OUGHTA KEEP 'EM AT BAY. HOW'S THE BACK LOOK?

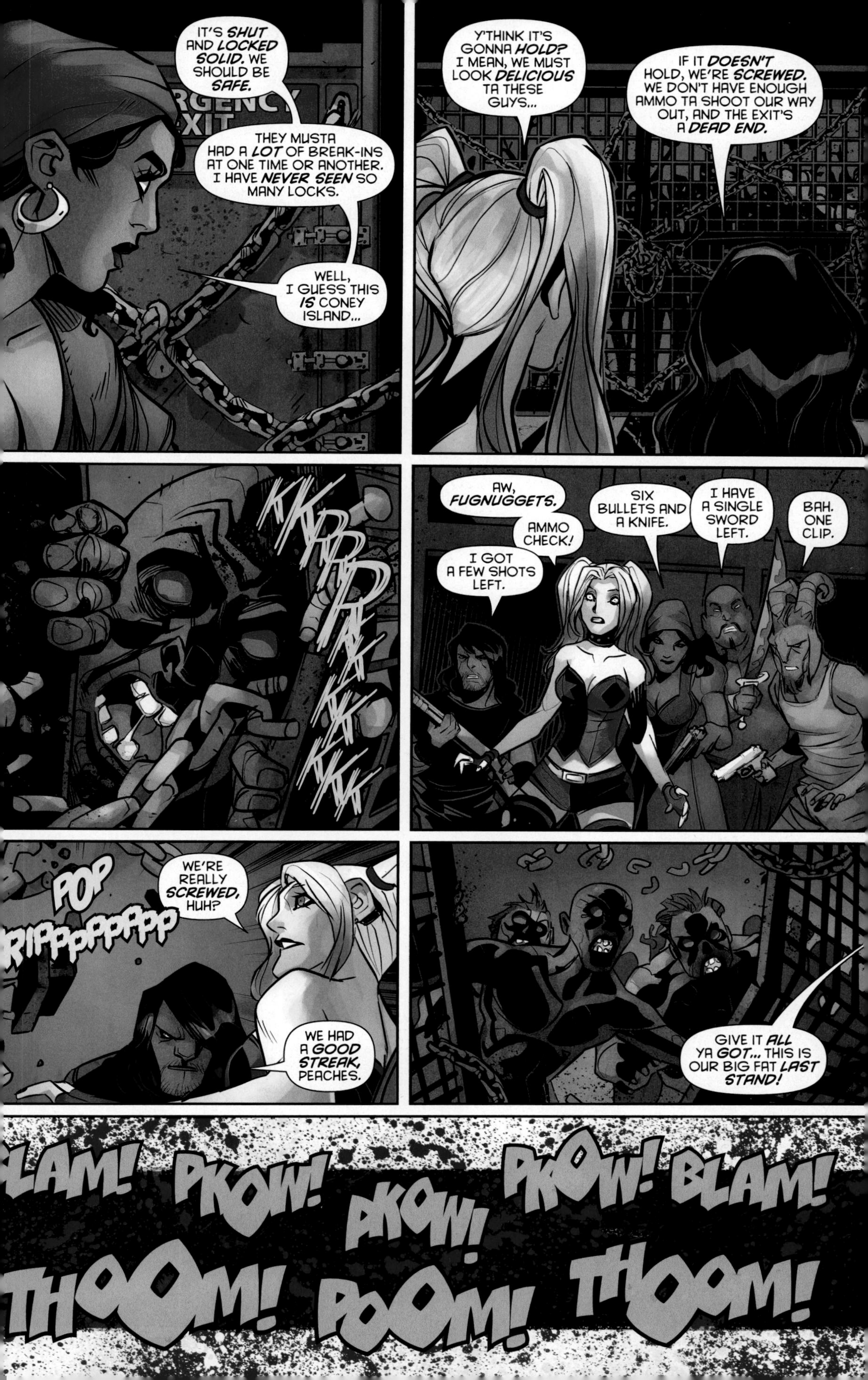
IT'S SHUT AND LOCKED SOLID. WE SHOULD BE SAFE.
THEY MUSTA HAD A LOT OF BREAK-INS AT ONE TIME OR ANOTHER. I HAVE NEVER SEEN SO MANY LOCKS.
WELL, I GUESS THIS IS CONEY ISLAND...
Y'THINK IT'S GONNA HOLD? I MEAN, WE MUST LOOK DELICIOUS TA THESE GUYS...
IF IT DOESN'T HOLD, WE'RE SCREWED. WE DON'T HAVE ENOUGH AMMO TA SHOOT OUR WAY OUT, AND THE EXIT'S A DEAD END.
KKRRRRKKKKK
AW, FUGNUGGETS.
AMMO CHECK!
I GOT A FEW SHOTS LEFT.
SIX BULLETS AND A KNIFE.
I HAVE A SINGLE SWORD LEFT.
BAH. ONE CLIP.
POP
RIPPPPPPPP
WE'RE REALLY SCREWED, HUH?
WE HAD A GOOD STREAK, PEACHES.
GIVE IT ALL YA GOT... THIS IS OUR BIG FAT LAST STAND!
BLAM! PKOW! PKOW! PKOW! BLAM!
THOOM! POOM! THOOM!

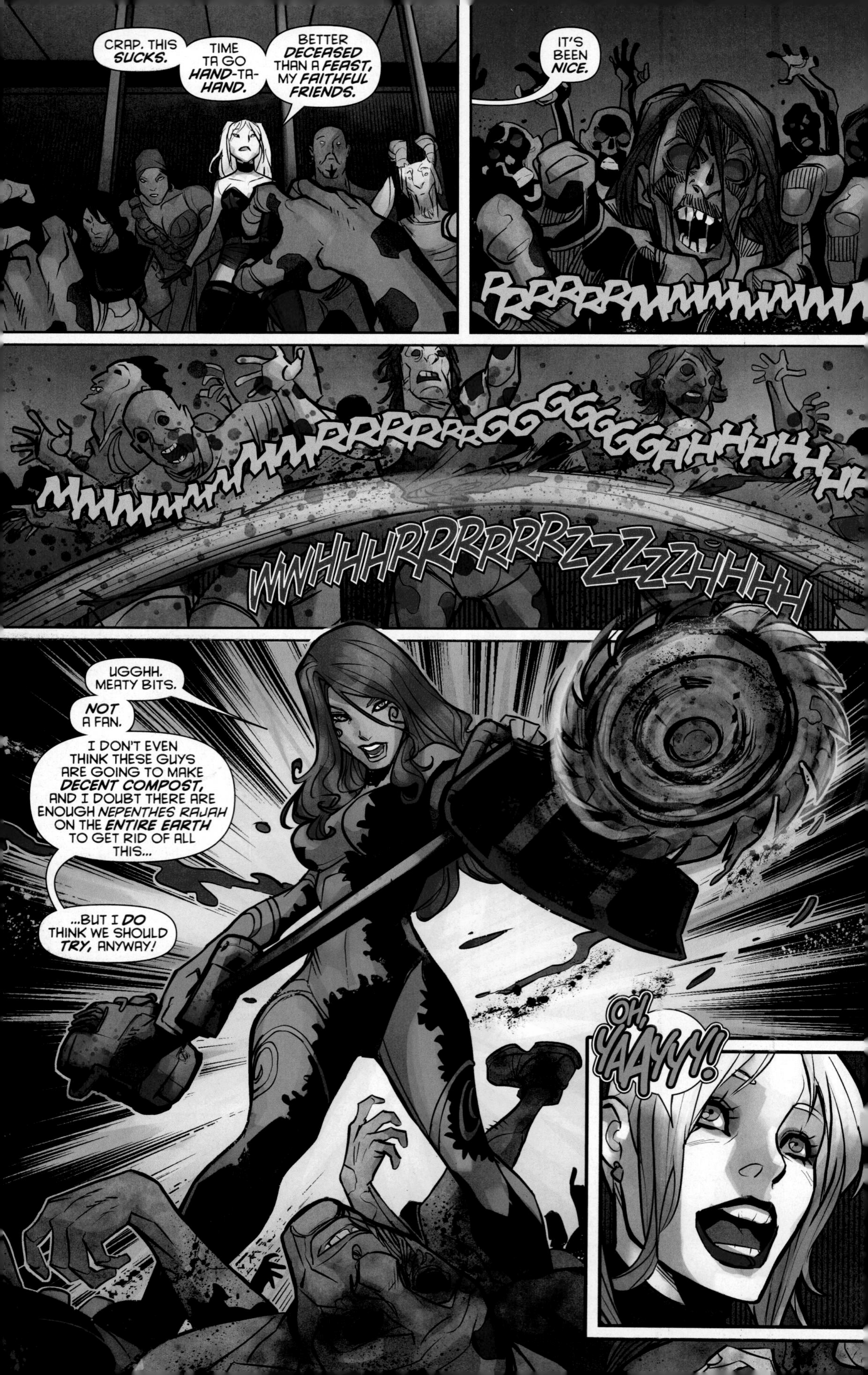
CRAP. THIS SUCKS.
TIME TA GO HAND-TA-HAND.
BETTER DECEASED THAN A FEAST, MY FAITHFUL FRIENDS.
IT'S BEEN NICE.
RRRRRRAAAAHHHHAAAA
MMMMMMMMMRRRRRRRGGGGGGGHHHHHHH
WWHHHRRRRRRRZZZZZHHHHH
UGGHH. MEATY BITS.
NOT A FAN.
I DON'T EVEN THINK THESE GUYS ARE GOING TO MAKE DECENT COMPOST, AND I DOUBT THERE ARE ENOUGH NEPENTHES RAJAH ON THE ENTIRE EARTH TO GET RID OF ALL THIS...
...BUT I DO THINK WE SHOULD TRY, ANYWAY!
OH, YAAYYY!

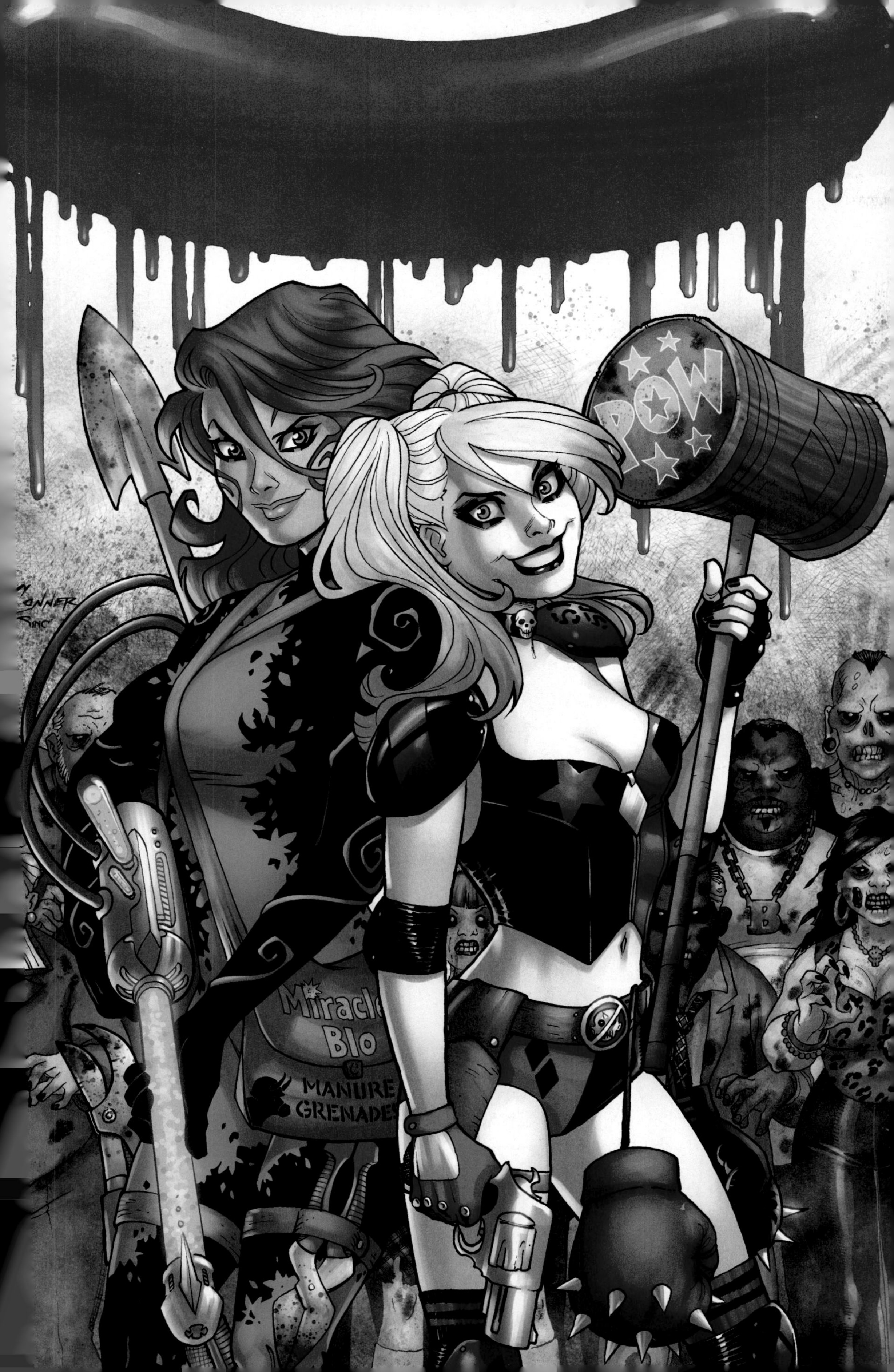
POW
Miracle Blo
MANURE GRENADES

DIE LAUGHING PART 3: GOIN' FOR TAKEOUT

AMANDA CONNER and JIMMY PALMIOTTI writers * BRET BLEVINS layouts
CHAD HARDIN (p. 1-10) & JOHN TIMMS (p. 11-20) finishes * ALEX SINCLAIR with HI-FI colorists * DAVE SHARPE letterer

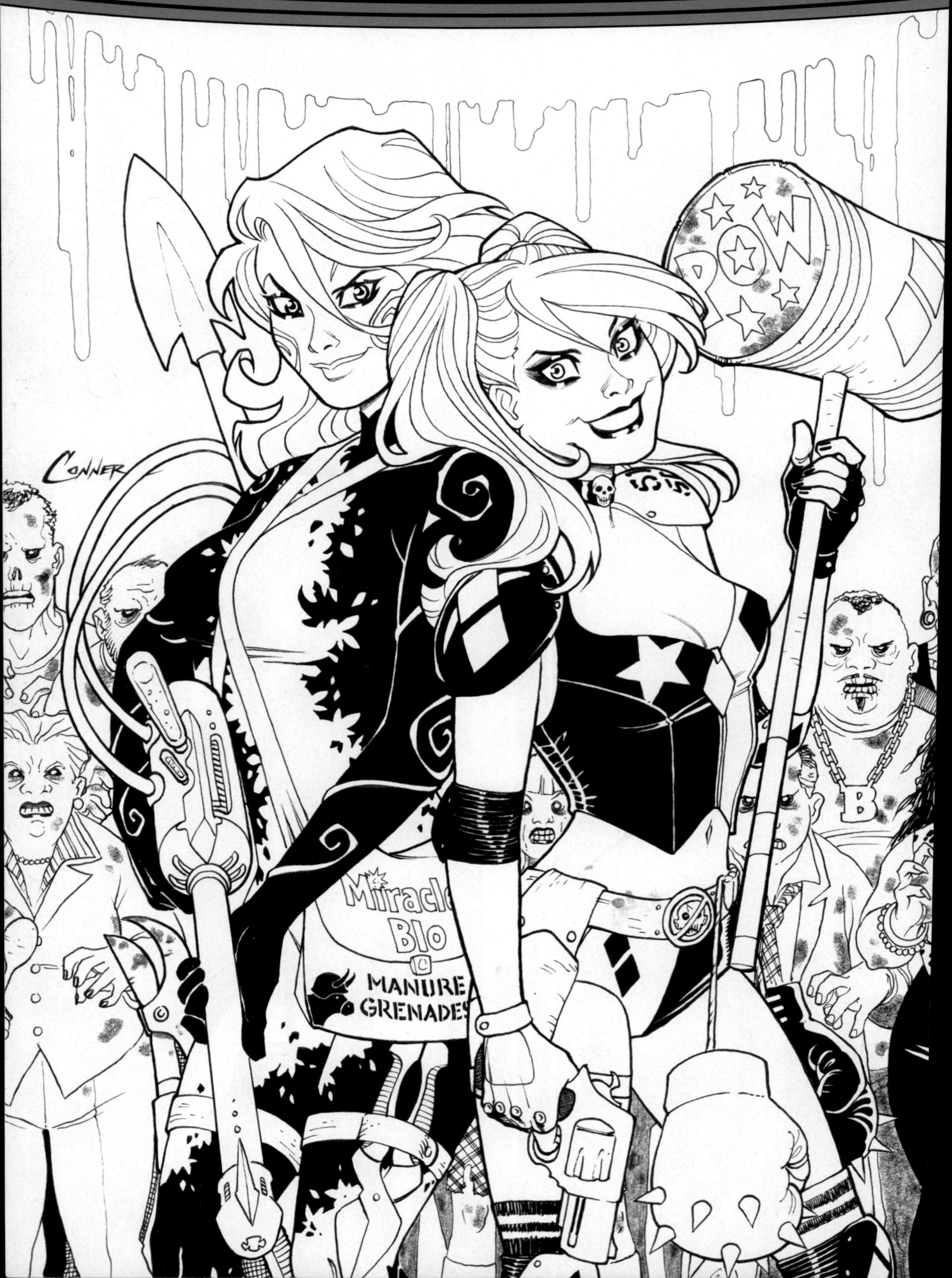
CONNER
POW
Miracle Blo
MANURE GRENADES
B

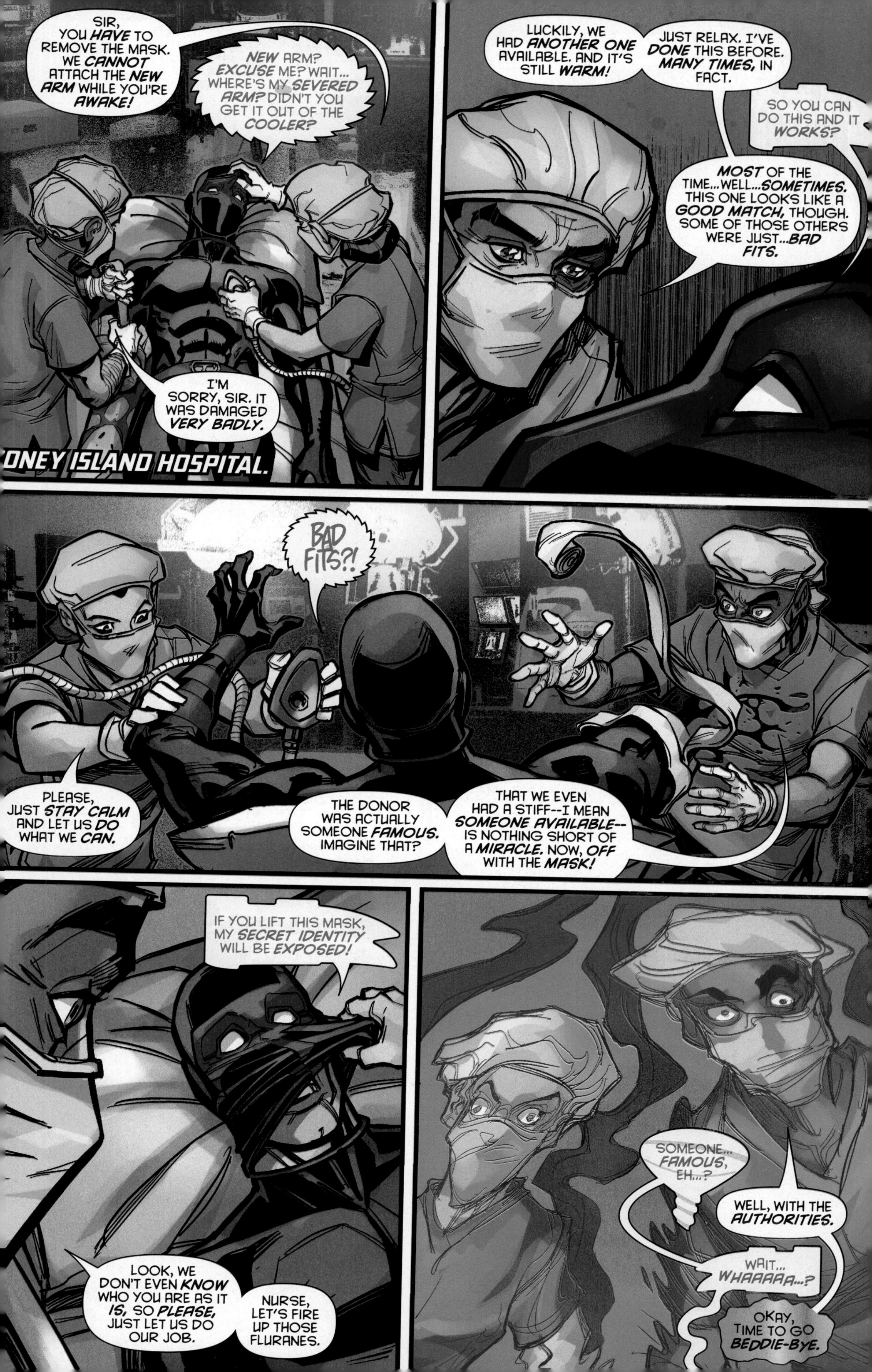

ONEY ISLAND HOSPITAL.
SIR, YOU HAVE TO REMOVE THE MASK. WE CANNOT ATTACH THE NEW ARM WHILE YOU'RE AWAKE!
NEW ARM? EXCUSE ME? WAIT... WHERE'S MY SEVERED ARM? DIDN'T YOU GET IT OUT OF THE COOLER?
I'M SORRY, SIR. IT WAS DAMAGED VERY BADLY.
LUCKILY, WE HAD ANOTHER ONE AVAILABLE. AND IT'S STILL WARM!
JUST RELAX. I'VE DONE THIS BEFORE. MANY TIMES, IN FACT.
SO YOU CAN DO THIS AND IT WORKS?
MOST OF THE TIME...WELL...SOMETIMES. THIS ONE LOOKS LIKE A GOOD MATCH, THOUGH. SOME OF THOSE OTHERS WERE JUST...BAD FITS.
BAD FITS?!
PLEASE, JUST STAY CALM AND LET US DO WHAT WE CAN.
THE DONOR WAS ACTUALLY SOMEONE FAMOUS. IMAGINE THAT?
THAT WE EVEN HAD A STIFF--I MEAN SOMEONE AVAILABLE-- IS NOTHING SHORT OF A MIRACLE. NOW, OFF WITH THE MASK!
IF YOU LIFT THIS MASK, MY SECRET IDENTITY WILL BE EXPOSED!
LOOK, WE DON'T EVEN KNOW WHO YOU ARE AS IT IS, SO PLEASE, JUST LET US DO OUR JOB.
NURSE, LET'S FIRE UP THOSE FLURANES.
SOMEONE... FAMOUS, EH...?
WELL, WITH THE AUTHORITIES.
WAIT... WHAAAAA...?
OKAY, TIME TO GO BEDDIE-BYE.

MEANWHILE, ON PLANET ZHELBON... IN A GALAXY VERY FAR, FAR AWAY.

THAT KID.

I DON'T SEE HIS SHIP. HE *BETTER* NOT HAVE LEFT OUR *GALAXY* AGAIN!

YOU WOULD *THINK* AFTER LAST TIME HE WOULD HAVE *LEARNED* HIS *LESSON.*

DARLING, I'M *SO* WORRIED ABOUT VERTIGAX. HE SAID HE WAS STAYING OVER AT HIS FRIEND *FROOZAX'S* HOUSE, BUT I CONTACTED HIS MATRIARCHAL PROGENITOR AND SHE SAID HE WAS *NEVER OVER* THERE.

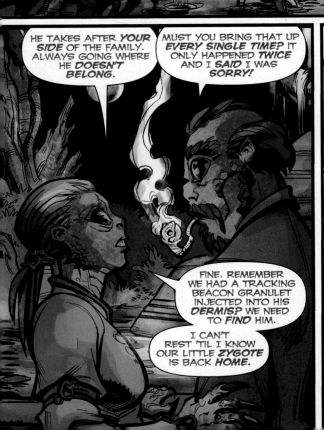

HE TAKES AFTER *YOUR SIDE* OF THE FAMILY. ALWAYS GOING WHERE HE *DOESN'T BELONG.*

MUST YOU BRING THAT UP *EVERY SINGLE TIME?* IT ONLY HAPPENED *TWICE* AND I *SAID* I WAS SORRY!

FINE. REMEMBER WE HAD A TRACKING BEACON GRANULET INJECTED INTO HIS *DERMIS?* WE NEED TO *FIND* HIM.

I CAN'T REST 'TIL I KNOW OUR LITTLE *ZYGOTE* IS BACK *HOME.*

DON'T WORRY YOUR PRETTY LITTLE *PEDICELLARIAE,* DEAR. WE'LL GET THE SHIP AND GO *FIND* HIM.

I'M SURE HE'S *SAFE* AND *SOUND...* I BET HE'S SOMEWHERE OUT THERE MAKING NEW FRIENDS.

THAT'S TRUE. HE *DOES* HAVE AN *INFECTIOUS PERSONALITY.*

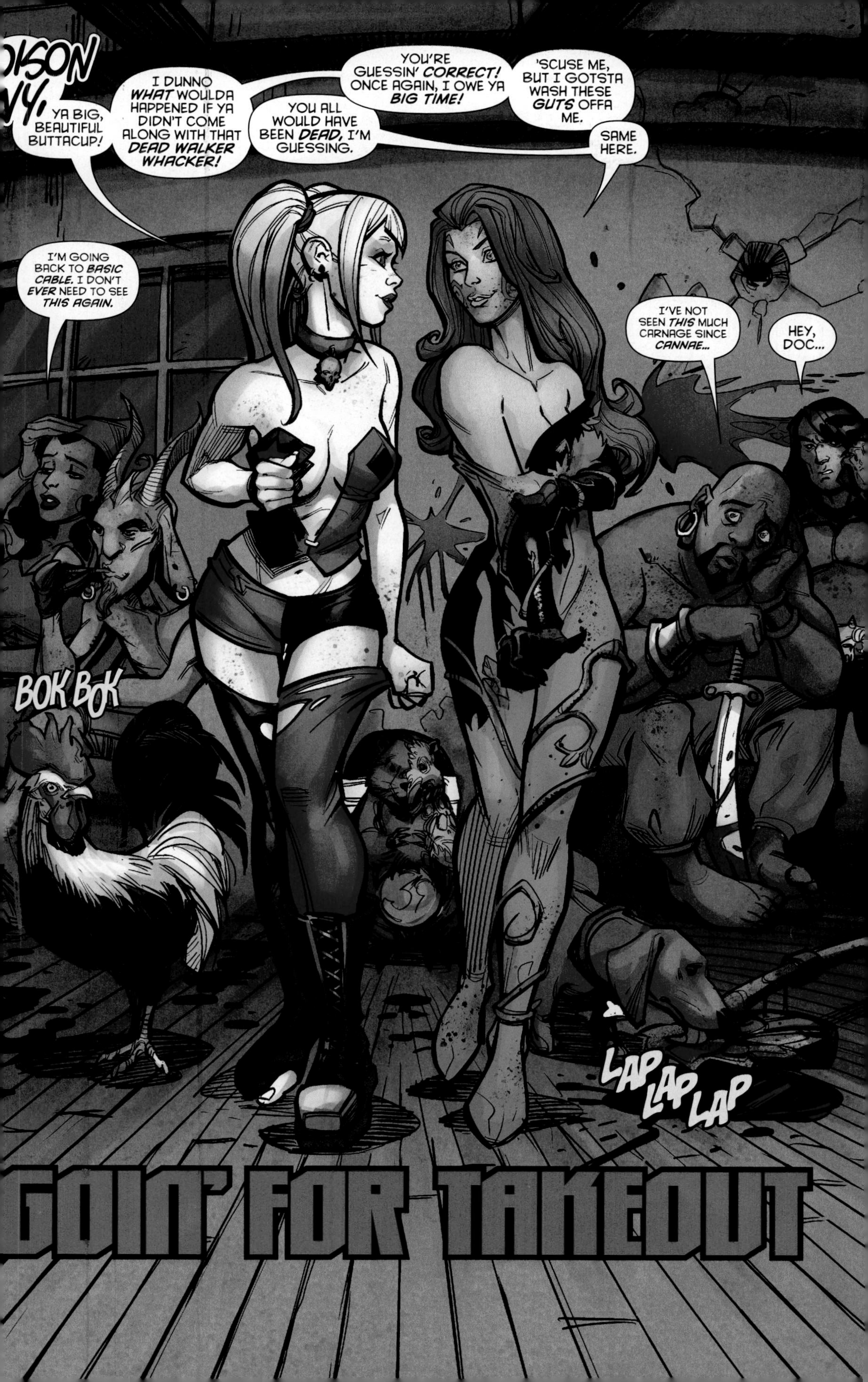

OISON
VY,
YA BIG, BEAUTIFUL BUTTACUP!
I DUNNO WHAT WOULDA HAPPENED IF YA DIDN'T COME ALONG WITH THAT DEAD WALKER WHACKER!
YOU ALL WOULD HAVE BEEN DEAD, I'M GUESSING.
YOU'RE GUESSIN' CORRECT! ONCE AGAIN, I OWE YA BIG TIME!
'SCUSE ME, BUT I GOTSTA WASH THESE GUTS OFFA ME.
SAME HERE.
I'M GOING BACK TO BASIC CABLE. I DON'T EVER NEED TO SEE THIS AGAIN.
I'VE NOT SEEN THIS MUCH CARNAGE SINCE CANNAE...
HEY, DOC...
BOK BOK
LAP LAP LAP
GOIN' FOR TAKEOUT

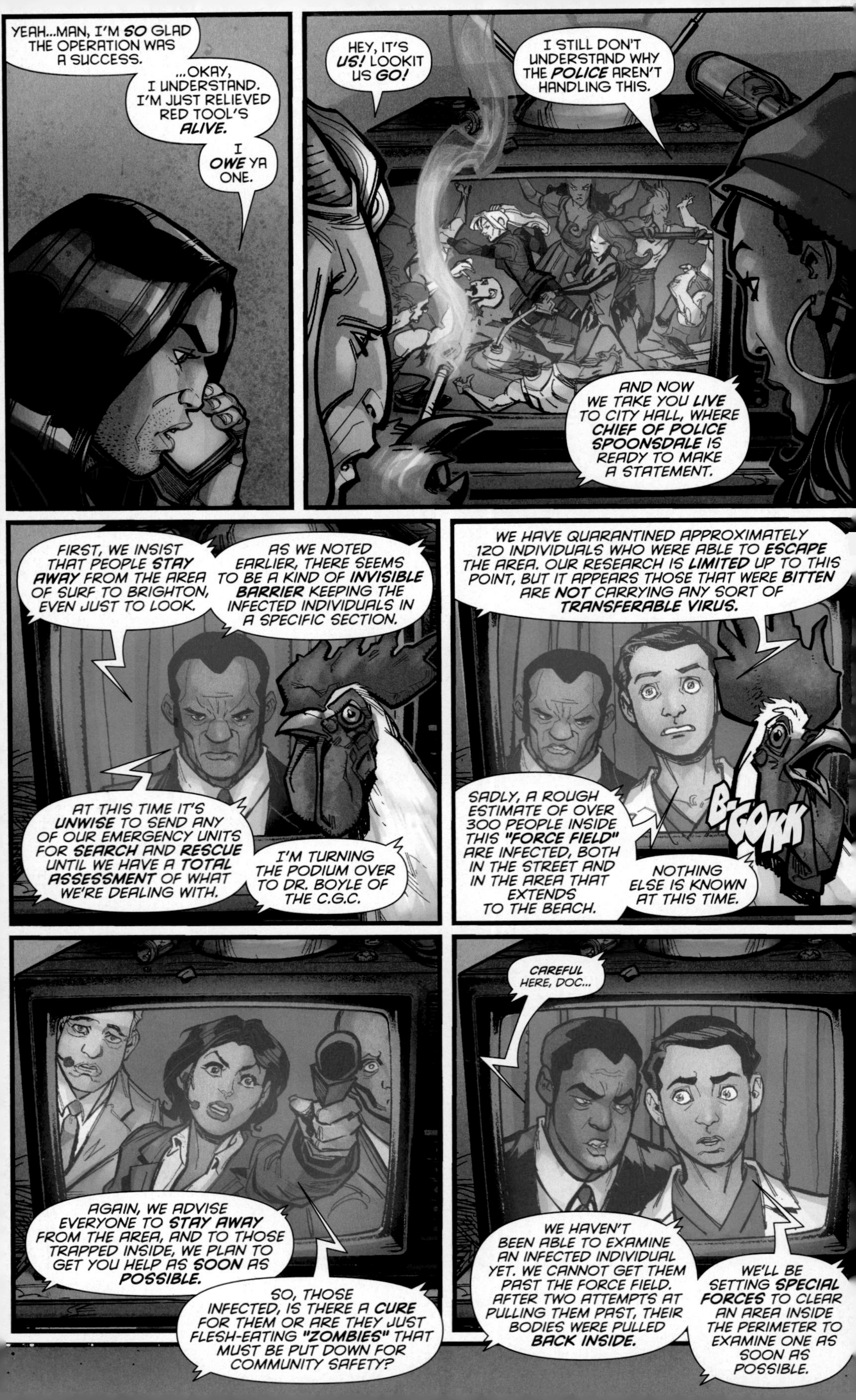
YEAH...MAN, I'M SO GLAD THE OPERATION WAS A SUCCESS.
...OKAY, I UNDERSTAND. I'M JUST RELIEVED RED TOOL'S ALIVE.
I OWE YA ONE.
HEY, IT'S US! LOOKIT US GO!
I STILL DON'T UNDERSTAND WHY THE POLICE AREN'T HANDLING THIS.
AND NOW WE TAKE YOU LIVE TO CITY HALL, WHERE CHIEF OF POLICE SPOONSDALE IS READY TO MAKE A STATEMENT.
FIRST, WE INSIST THAT PEOPLE STAY AWAY FROM THE AREA OF SURF TO BRIGHTON, EVEN JUST TO LOOK.
AS WE NOTED EARLIER, THERE SEEMS TO BE A KIND OF INVISIBLE BARRIER KEEPING THE INFECTED INDIVIDUALS IN A SPECIFIC SECTION.
AT THIS TIME IT'S UNWISE TO SEND ANY OF OUR EMERGENCY UNITS FOR SEARCH AND RESCUE UNTIL WE HAVE A TOTAL ASSESSMENT OF WHAT WE'RE DEALING WITH.
I'M TURNING THE PODIUM OVER TO DR. BOYLE OF THE C.G.C.
WE HAVE QUARANTINED APPROXIMATELY 120 INDIVIDUALS WHO WERE ABLE TO ESCAPE THE AREA. OUR RESEARCH IS LIMITED UP TO THIS POINT, BUT IT APPEARS THOSE THAT WERE BITTEN ARE NOT CARRYING ANY SORT OF TRANSFERABLE VIRUS.
SADLY, A ROUGH ESTIMATE OF OVER 300 PEOPLE INSIDE THIS "FORCE FIELD" ARE INFECTED, BOTH IN THE STREET AND IN THE AREA THAT EXTENDS TO THE BEACH.
NOTHING ELSE IS KNOWN AT THIS TIME.
B-GOKK
AGAIN, WE ADVISE EVERYONE TO STAY AWAY FROM THE AREA, AND TO THOSE TRAPPED INSIDE, WE PLAN TO GET YOU HELP AS SOON AS POSSIBLE.
SO, THOSE INFECTED, IS THERE A CURE FOR THEM OR ARE THEY JUST FLESH-EATING "ZOMBIES" THAT MUST BE PUT DOWN FOR COMMUNITY SAFETY?
CAREFUL HERE, DOC...
WE HAVEN'T BEEN ABLE TO EXAMINE AN INFECTED INDIVIDUAL YET. WE CANNOT GET THEM PAST THE FORCE FIELD. AFTER TWO ATTEMPTS AT PULLING THEM PAST, THEIR BODIES WERE PULLED BACK INSIDE.
WE'LL BE SETTING SPECIAL FORCES TO CLEAR AN AREA INSIDE THE PERIMETER TO EXAMINE ONE AS SOON AS POSSIBLE.

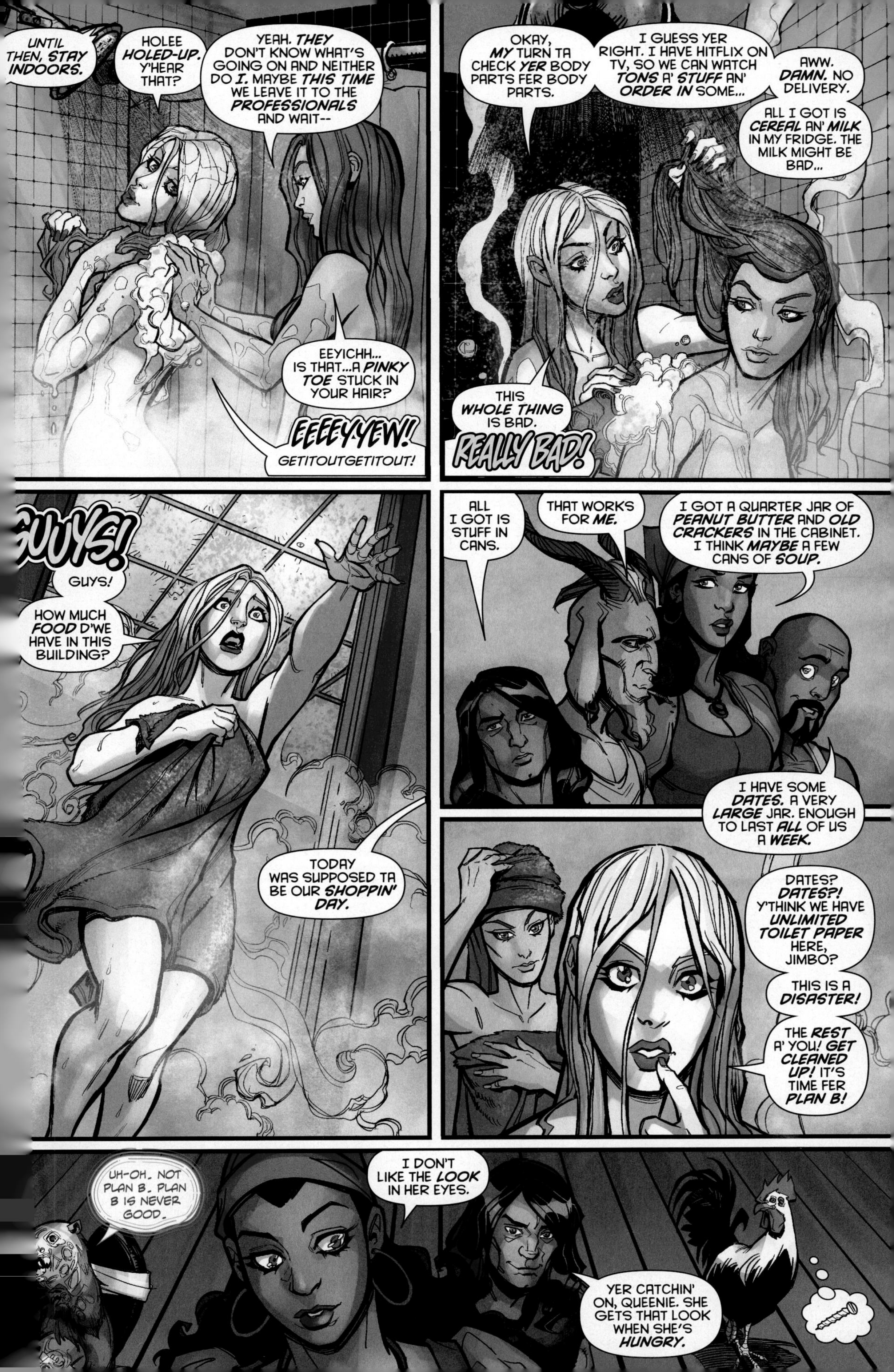
UNTIL THEN, STAY INDOORS.
HOLEE HOLED-UP. Y'HEAR THAT?
YEAH. THEY DON'T KNOW WHAT'S GOING ON AND NEITHER DO I. MAYBE THIS TIME WE LEAVE IT TO THE PROFESSIONALS AND WAIT--
EEYICHH... IS THAT...A PINKY TOE STUCK IN YOUR HAIR?
EEEEYYEW!
GETITOUTGETITOUT!
OKAY, MY TURN TA CHECK YER BODY PARTS FER BODY PARTS.
I GUESS YER RIGHT. I HAVE HITFLIX ON TV, SO WE CAN WATCH TONS A' STUFF AN' ORDER IN SOME...
AWW. DAMN. NO DELIVERY.
ALL I GOT IS CEREAL AN' MILK IN MY FRIDGE. THE MILK MIGHT BE BAD...
THIS WHOLE THING IS BAD.
REALLY BAD!
GUUYS!
GUYS!
HOW MUCH FOOD D'WE HAVE IN THIS BUILDING?
TODAY WAS SUPPOSED TA BE OUR SHOPPIN' DAY.
ALL I GOT IS STUFF IN CANS.
THAT WORKS FOR ME.
I GOT A QUARTER JAR OF PEANUT BUTTER AND OLD CRACKERS IN THE CABINET. I THINK MAYBE A FEW CANS OF SOUP.
I HAVE SOME DATES. A VERY LARGE JAR. ENOUGH TO LAST ALL OF US A WEEK.
DATES? DATES?! Y'THINK WE HAVE UNLIMITED TOILET PAPER HERE, JIMBO?
THIS IS A DISASTER!
THE REST A' YOU! GET CLEANED UP! IT'S TIME FER PLAN B!
UH-OH. NOT PLAN B. PLAN B IS NEVER GOOD.
I DON'T LIKE THE LOOK IN HER EYES.
YER CATCHIN' ON, QUEENIE. SHE GETS THAT LOOK WHEN SHE'S HUNGRY.

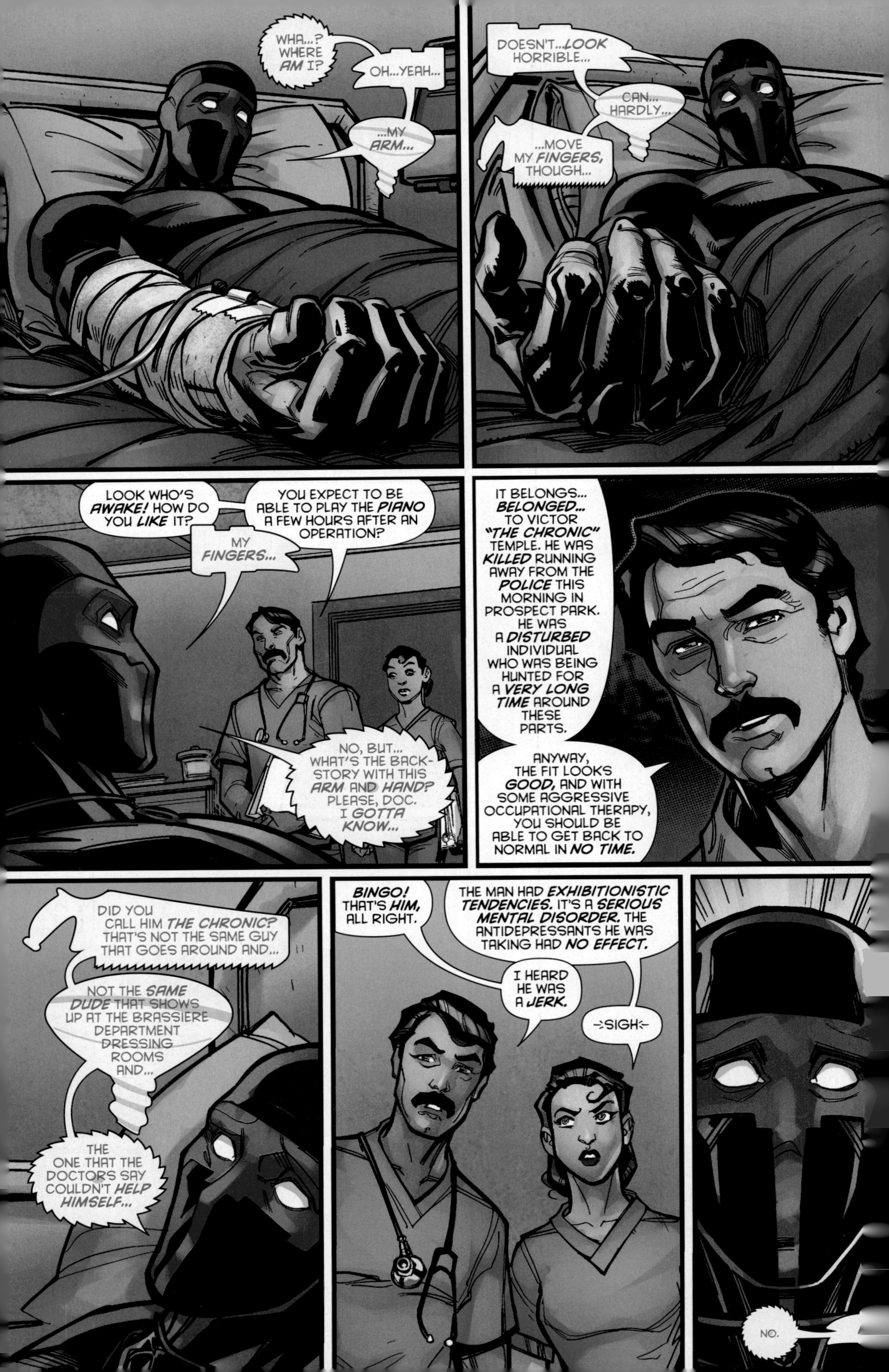
WHA...? WHERE AM I?
OH...YEAH...
...MY ARM...
DOESN'T...LOOK HORRIBLE...
CAN... HARDLY...
...MOVE MY FINGERS, THOUGH...
LOOK WHO'S AWAKE! HOW DO YOU LIKE IT?
MY FINGERS...
YOU EXPECT TO BE ABLE TO PLAY THE PIANO A FEW HOURS AFTER AN OPERATION?
NO, BUT... WHAT'S THE BACK-STORY WITH THIS ARM AND HAND? PLEASE, DOC. I GOTTA KNOW...
IT BELONGS... BELONGED... TO VICTOR "THE CHRONIC" TEMPLE. HE WAS KILLED RUNNING AWAY FROM THE POLICE THIS MORNING IN PROSPECT PARK. HE WAS A DISTURBED INDIVIDUAL WHO WAS BEING HUNTED FOR A VERY LONG TIME AROUND THESE PARTS.
ANYWAY, THE FIT LOOKS GOOD, AND WITH SOME AGGRESSIVE OCCUPATIONAL THERAPY, YOU SHOULD BE ABLE TO GET BACK TO NORMAL IN NO TIME.
DID YOU CALL HIM THE CHRONIC? THAT'S NOT THE SAME GUY THAT GOES AROUND AND...
NOT THE SAME DUDE THAT SHOWS UP AT THE BRASSIERE DEPARTMENT DRESSING ROOMS AND...
THE ONE THAT THE DOCTORS SAY COULDN'T HELP HIMSELF...
BINGO! THAT'S HIM, ALL RIGHT.
THE MAN HAD EXHIBITIONISTIC TENDENCIES. IT'S A SERIOUS MENTAL DISORDER. THE ANTIDEPRESSANTS HE WAS TAKING HAD NO EFFECT.
I HEARD HE WAS A JERK.
-SIGH-
NO.

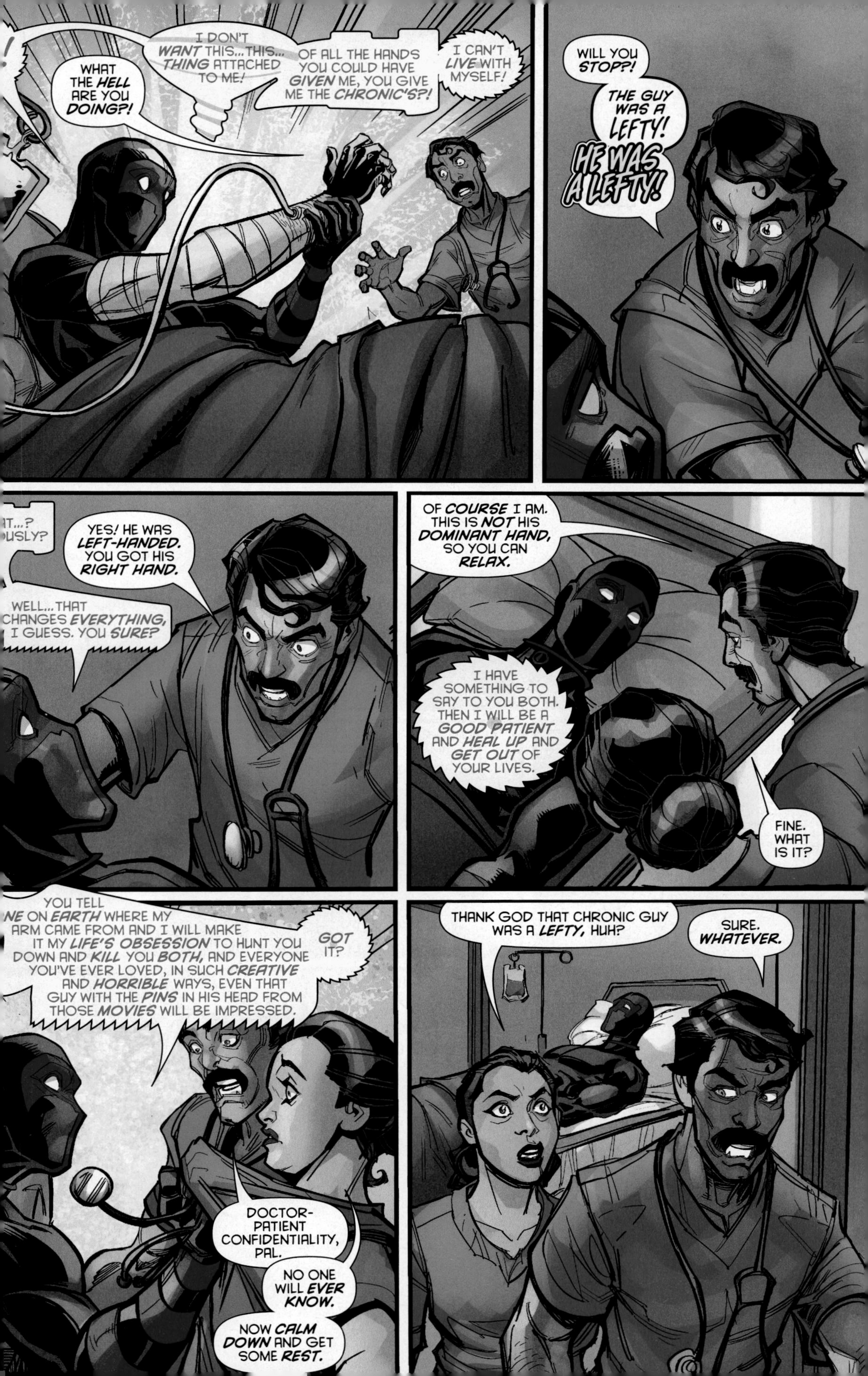

WHAT THE HELL ARE YOU DOING?!
I DON'T WANT THIS... THIS... THING ATTACHED TO ME!
OF ALL THE HANDS YOU COULD HAVE GIVEN ME, YOU GIVE ME THE CHRONIC'S?!
I CAN'T LIVE WITH MYSELF!
WILL YOU STOP?!
THE GUY WAS A LEFTY!
HE WAS A LEFTY!
YES! HE WAS LEFT-HANDED. YOU GOT HIS RIGHT HAND.
WELL... THAT CHANGES EVERYTHING, I GUESS. YOU SURE?
OF COURSE I AM. THIS IS NOT HIS DOMINANT HAND, SO YOU CAN RELAX.
I HAVE SOMETHING TO SAY TO YOU BOTH. THEN I WILL BE A GOOD PATIENT AND HEAL UP AND GET OUT OF YOUR LIVES.
FINE. WHAT IS IT?
YOU TELL NE ON EARTH WHERE MY ARM CAME FROM AND I WILL MAKE IT MY LIFE'S OBSESSION TO HUNT YOU DOWN AND KILL YOU BOTH, AND EVERYONE YOU'VE EVER LOVED, IN SUCH CREATIVE AND HORRIBLE WAYS, EVEN THAT GUY WITH THE PINS IN HIS HEAD FROM THOSE MOVIES WILL BE IMPRESSED.
GOT IT?
DOCTOR-PATIENT CONFIDENTIALITY, PAL.
NO ONE WILL EVER KNOW.
NOW CALM DOWN AND GET SOME REST.
THANK GOD THAT CHRONIC GUY WAS A LEFTY, HUH?
SURE. WHATEVER.

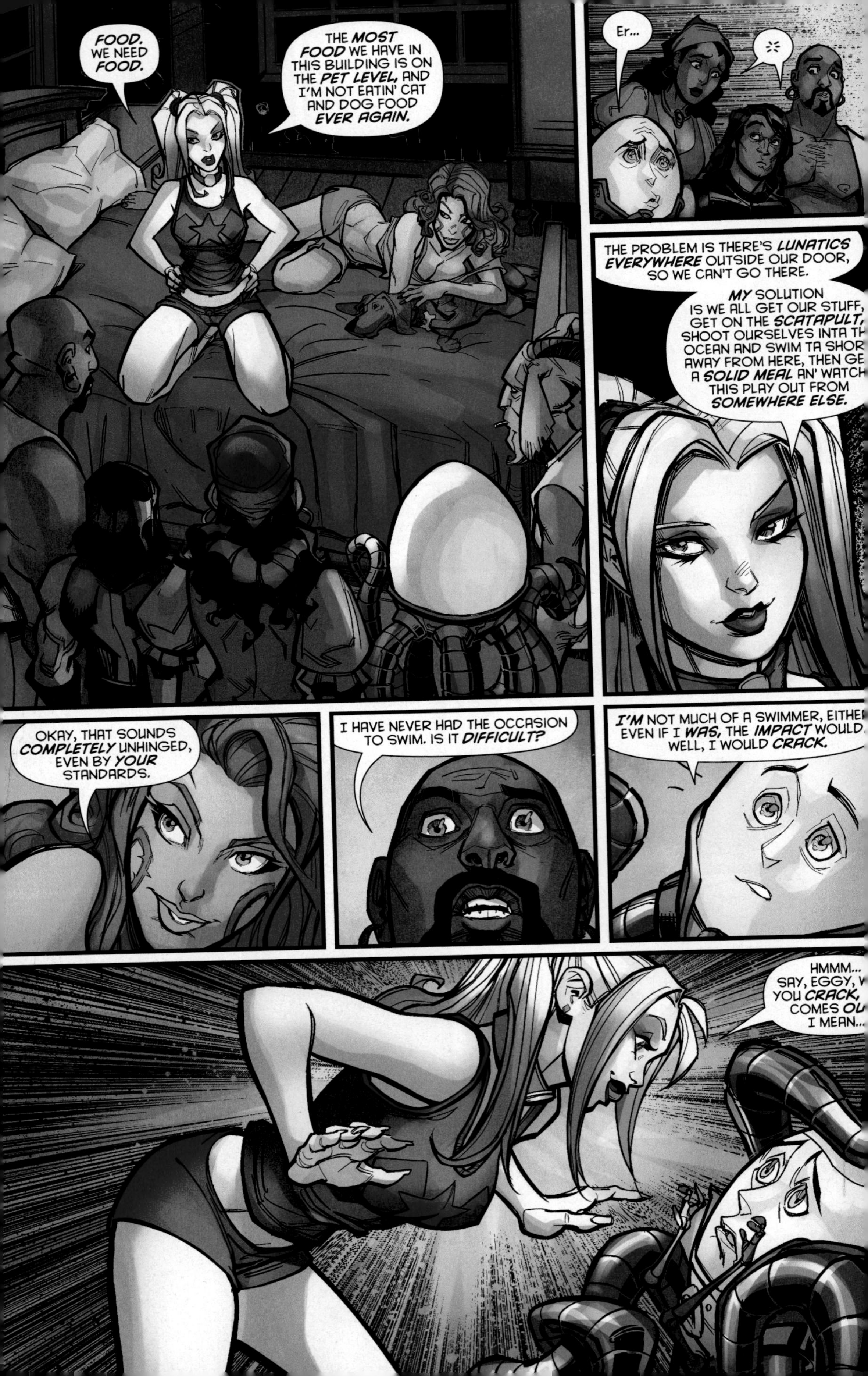
FOOD. WE NEED FOOD.
THE MOST FOOD WE HAVE IN THIS BUILDING IS ON THE PET LEVEL, AND I'M NOT EATIN' CAT AND DOG FOOD EVER AGAIN.
Er...
THE PROBLEM IS THERE'S LUNATICS EVERYWHERE OUTSIDE OUR DOOR, SO WE CAN'T GO THERE.
MY SOLUTION IS WE ALL GET OUR STUFF, GET ON THE SCATAPULT, SHOOT OURSELVES INTA TH OCEAN AND SWIM TA SHOR AWAY FROM HERE, THEN GE A SOLID MEAL AN' WATCH THIS PLAY OUT FROM SOMEWHERE ELSE.
OKAY, THAT SOUNDS COMPLETELY UNHINGED, EVEN BY YOUR STANDARDS.
I HAVE NEVER HAD THE OCCASION TO SWIM. IS IT DIFFICULT?
I'M NOT MUCH OF A SWIMMER, EITHE EVEN IF I WAS, THE IMPACT WOULD WELL, I WOULD CRACK.
HMMM... SAY, EGGY, W YOU CRACK, COMES OU I MEAN...

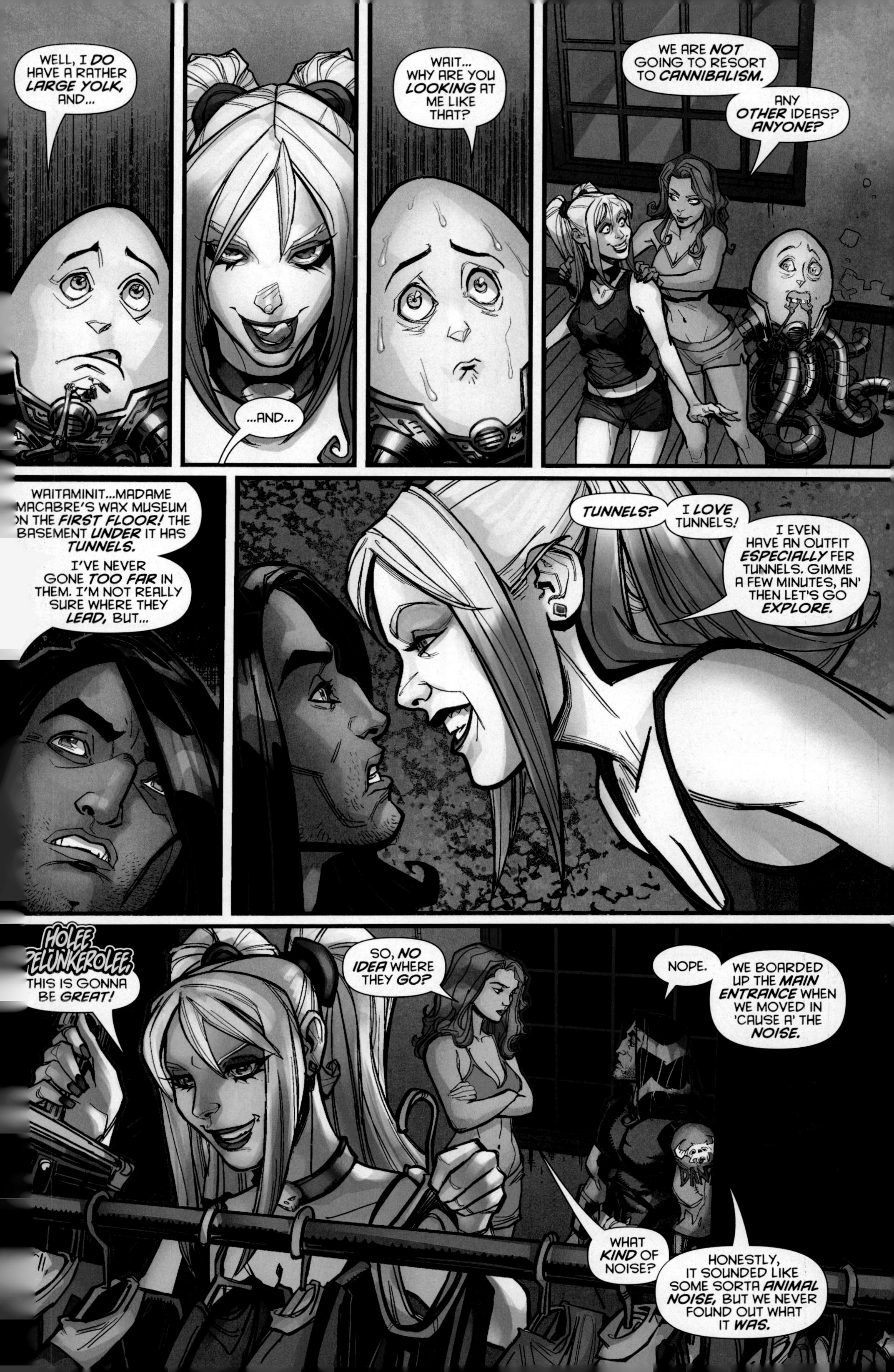
WELL, I DO HAVE A RATHER LARGE YOLK, AND...
...AND...
WAIT... WHY ARE YOU LOOKING AT ME LIKE THAT?
WE ARE NOT GOING TO RESORT TO CANNIBALISM.
ANY OTHER IDEAS? ANYONE?
WAITAMINIT...MADAME MACABRE'S WAX MUSEUM ON THE FIRST FLOOR! THE BASEMENT UNDER IT HAS TUNNELS.
I'VE NEVER GONE TOO FAR IN THEM. I'M NOT REALLY SURE WHERE THEY LEAD, BUT...
TUNNELS?
I LOVE TUNNELS!
I EVEN HAVE AN OUTFIT ESPECIALLY FER TUNNELS. GIMME A FEW MINUTES, AN' THEN LET'S GO EXPLORE.
HOLEE SPELUNKEROLEE, THIS IS GONNA BE GREAT!
SO, NO IDEA WHERE THEY GO?
NOPE.
WE BOARDED UP THE MAIN ENTRANCE WHEN WE MOVED IN 'CAUSE A' THE NOISE.
WHAT KIND OF NOISE?
HONESTLY, IT SOUNDED LIKE SOME SORTA ANIMAL NOISE, BUT WE NEVER FOUND OUT WHAT IT WAS.

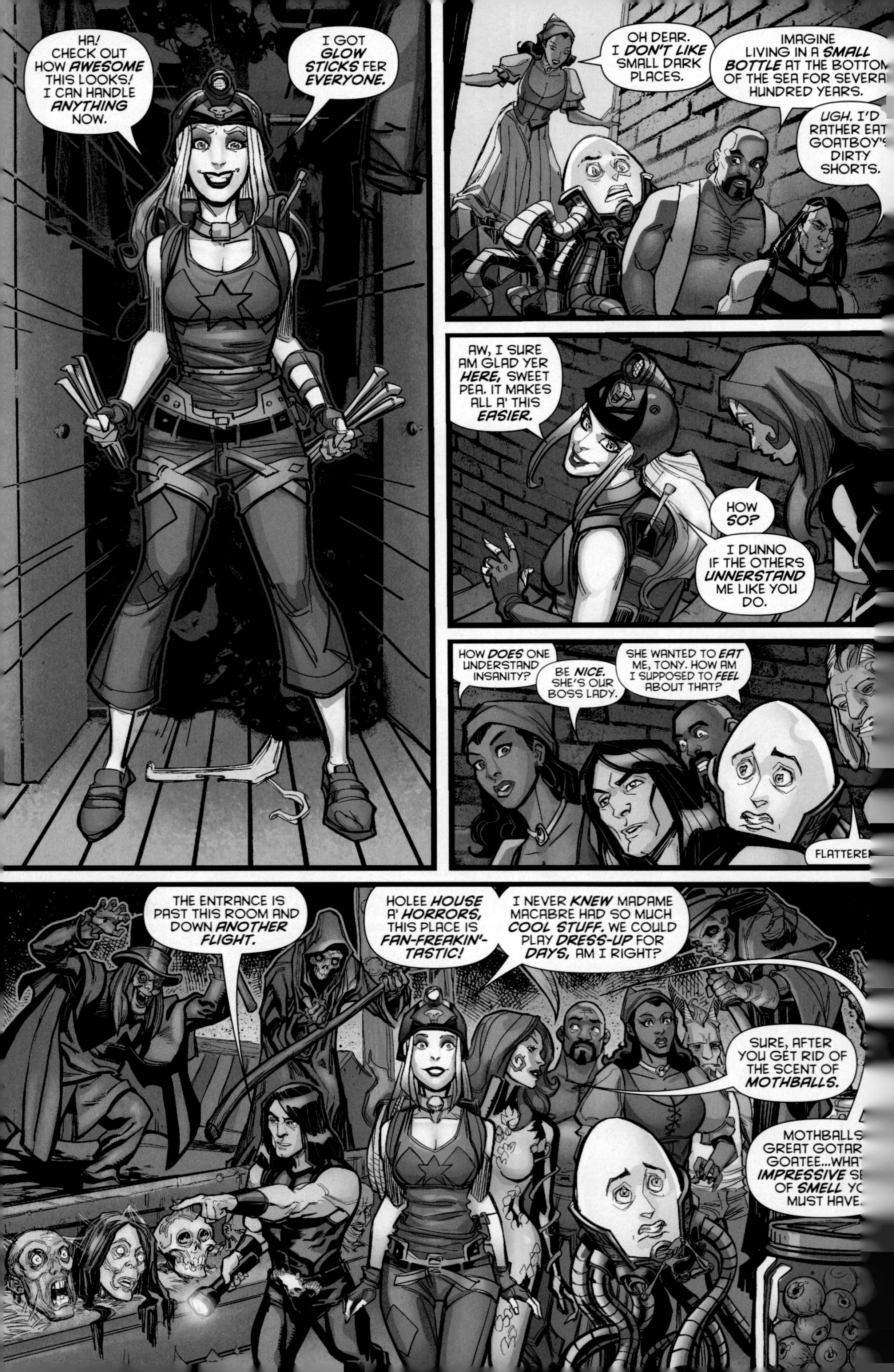
HA! CHECK OUT HOW AWESOME THIS LOOKS! I CAN HANDLE ANYTHING NOW.
I GOT GLOW STICKS FER EVERYONE.
OH DEAR. I DON'T LIKE SMALL DARK PLACES.
IMAGINE LIVING IN A SMALL BOTTLE AT THE BOTTOM OF THE SEA FOR SEVERA HUNDRED YEARS.
UGH. I'D RATHER EAT GOATBOY'S DIRTY SHORTS.
AW, I SURE AM GLAD YER HERE, SWEET PEA. IT MAKES ALL A' THIS EASIER.
HOW SO?
I DUNNO IF THE OTHERS UNNERSTAND ME LIKE YOU DO.
HOW DOES ONE UNDERSTAND INSANITY?
BE NICE. SHE'S OUR BOSS LADY.
SHE WANTED TO EAT ME, TONY. HOW AM I SUPPOSED TO FEEL ABOUT THAT?
FLATTERE
THE ENTRANCE IS PAST THIS ROOM AND DOWN ANOTHER FLIGHT.
HOLEE HOUSE A' HORRORS, THIS PLACE IS FAN-FREAKIN'-TASTIC!
I NEVER KNEW MADAME MACABRE HAD SO MUCH COOL STUFF. WE COULD PLAY DRESS-UP FOR DAYS, AM I RIGHT?
SURE, AFTER YOU GET RID OF THE SCENT OF MOTHBALLS.
MOTHBALLS GREAT GOTAR GOATEE...WHAT IMPRESSIVE SE OF SMELL YO MUST HAVE.

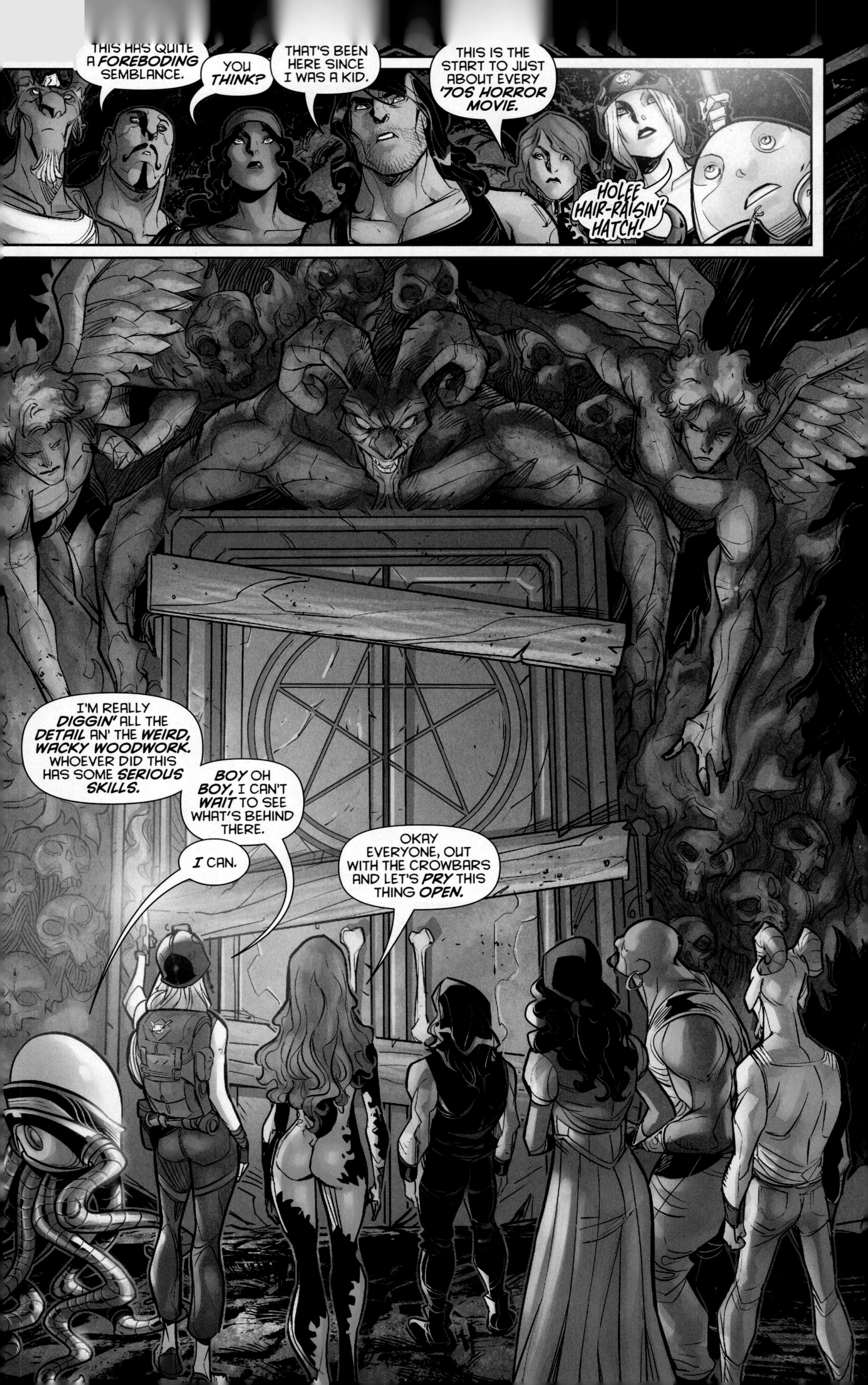
THIS HAS QUITE A FOREBODING SEMBLANCE.
YOU THINK?
THAT'S BEEN HERE SINCE I WAS A KID.
THIS IS THE START TO JUST ABOUT EVERY '70S HORROR MOVIE.
HOLEE HAIR-RAISIN' HATCH!
I'M REALLY DIGGIN' ALL THE DETAIL AN' THE WEIRD, WACKY WOODWORK. WHOEVER DID THIS HAS SOME SERIOUS SKILLS.
BOY OH BOY, I CAN'T WAIT TO SEE WHAT'S BEHIND THERE.
I CAN.
OKAY EVERYONE, OUT WITH THE CROWBARS AND LET'S PRY THIS THING OPEN.

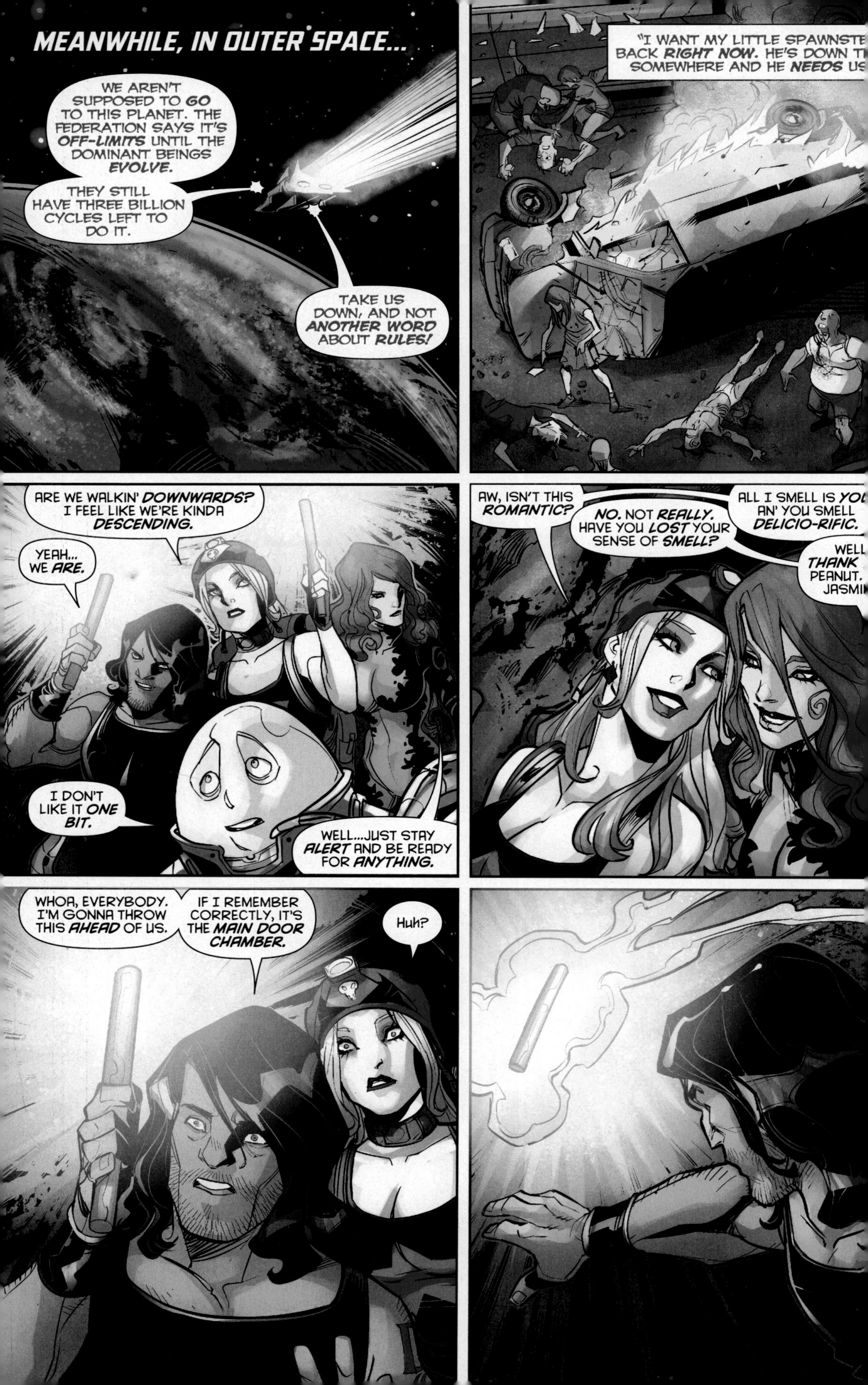
MEANWHILE, IN OUTER SPACE...
WE AREN'T SUPPOSED TO GO TO THIS PLANET. THE FEDERATION SAYS IT'S OFF-LIMITS UNTIL THE DOMINANT BEINGS EVOLVE.
THEY STILL HAVE THREE BILLION CYCLES LEFT TO DO IT.
TAKE US DOWN, AND NOT ANOTHER WORD ABOUT RULES!
"I WANT MY LITTLE SPAWNSTE
BACK RIGHT NOW. HE'S DOWN T
SOMEWHERE AND HE NEEDS US
ARE WE WALKIN' DOWNWARDS? I FEEL LIKE WE'RE KINDA DESCENDING.
YEAH... WE ARE.
I DON'T LIKE IT ONE BIT.
WELL...JUST STAY ALERT AND BE READY FOR ANYTHING.
AW, ISN'T THIS ROMANTIC?
NO. NOT REALLY. HAVE YOU LOST YOUR SENSE OF SMELL?
ALL I SMELL IS YO
AN' YOU SMELL DELICIO-RIFIC.
WELL
THANK
PEANUT.
JASMI
WHOA, EVERYBODY. I'M GONNA THROW THIS AHEAD OF US.
IF I REMEMBER CORRECTLY, IT'S THE MAIN DOOR CHAMBER.
Huh?

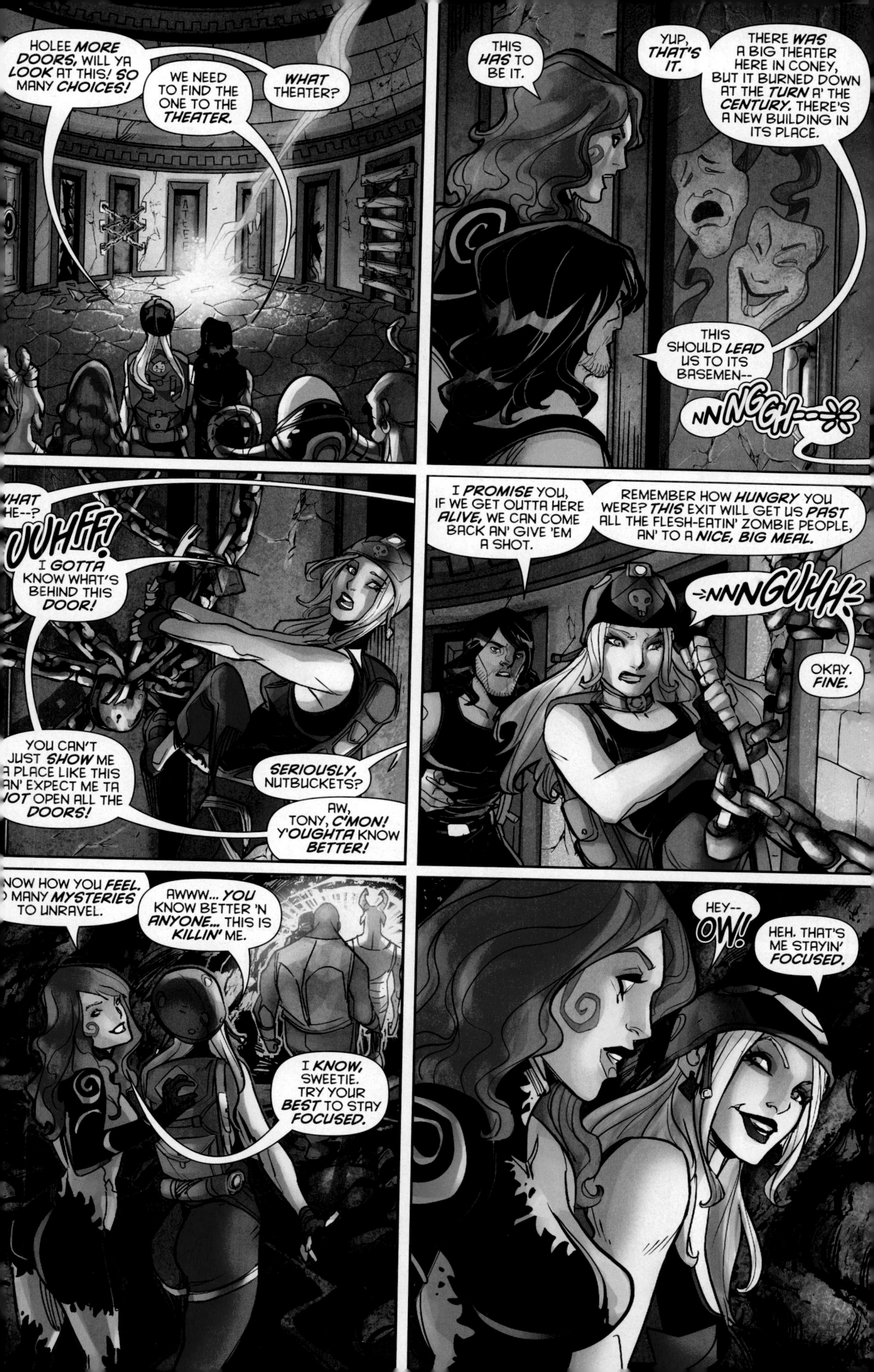
HOLEE MORE DOORS, WILL YA LOOK AT THIS! SO MANY CHOICES!
WE NEED TO FIND THE ONE TO THE THEATER.
WHAT THEATER?
THIS HAS TO BE IT.
YUP, THAT'S IT.
THERE WAS A BIG THEATER HERE IN CONEY, BUT IT BURNED DOWN AT THE TURN A' THE CENTURY. THERE'S A NEW BUILDING IN ITS PLACE.
THIS SHOULD LEAD US TO ITS BASEMEN--
NNNGGH--
WHAT HE--?
UUHFF!
I GOTTA KNOW WHAT'S BEHIND THIS DOOR!
YOU CAN'T JUST SHOW ME A PLACE LIKE THIS AN' EXPECT ME TA NOT OPEN ALL THE DOORS!
SERIOUSLY, NUTBUCKETS?
AW, TONY, C'MON! Y'OUGHTA KNOW BETTER!
I PROMISE YOU, IF WE GET OUTTA HERE ALIVE, WE CAN COME BACK AN' GIVE 'EM A SHOT.
REMEMBER HOW HUNGRY YOU WERE? THIS EXIT WILL GET US PAST ALL THE FLESH-EATIN' ZOMBIE PEOPLE, AN' TO A NICE, BIG MEAL.
NNNGUHH
OKAY. FINE.
NOW HOW YOU FEEL. SO MANY MYSTERIES TO UNRAVEL.
AWWW... YOU KNOW BETTER 'N ANYONE... THIS IS KILLIN' ME.
I KNOW, SWEETIE. TRY YOUR BEST TO STAY FOCUSED.
HEY-- OW!
HEH. THAT'S ME STAYIN' FOCUSED.

KER-SLAMMM!

UHFF! HERE WE GO!

SHOOooofs!

SHOES AS FAR AS YER PEEPERS CAN SEE.

HMM. I WONDER IF THEY HAVE ANY BOOTS?

LADIES, CAN WE FOCUS?

I AM, ON A PAIR A' JIMMY CHOOS IN MY SIZE ABOUT TEN FEET UP!

MINE!

MINEMINE MINEMINEMINE MINEMINE!

HEY, PEACHES-- OOOFF!

AWW, IT WAS MEANT TA BE.

HELLOOO, DARLINGS.

MMMMRRRRRRRGHH

UH-OH-- AW, CRAP. WE GOT COMPANY.

AN' IT AIN'T THE "BRING OUT THE DIP AN' CHIPS" KINDA COMPANY, EITHER.

EVERYONE BACK INTO THE TUNNEL!

YOU HEARD 'ER!

SKRGGH

EVERYBODY RELAX! I GOT THIS!

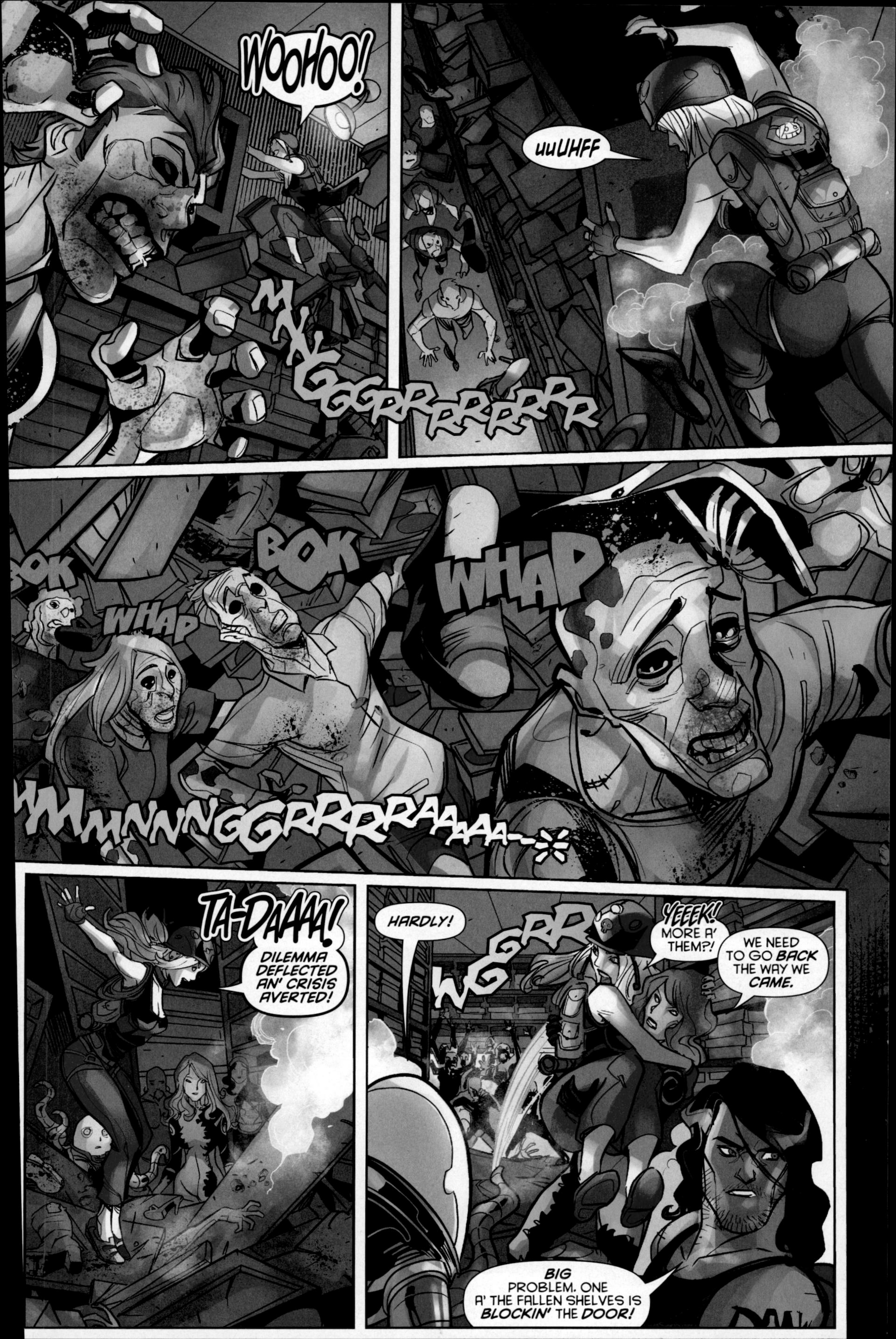
WOOHOO!
MNNGGGRRRRRRRR
uuUHFF
BOK
BOK
WHAP
WHAP
MMMNNNGGRRRRAAAAA--*
TA-DAAAA!
DILEMMA DEFLECTED AN' CRISIS AVERTED!
HARDLY!
WGGRR
YEEEK! MORE A' THEM?!
WE NEED TO GO BACK THE WAY WE CAME.
BIG PROBLEM. ONE A' THE FALLEN SHELVES IS BLOCKIN' THE DOOR!

BLRRRR...

GNYAAAHH

I DON'T *UNDERSTAND*. I'M GETTING A READING THAT HE'S ALL OVER *HERE*... AND *THERE*...LIKE *HUNDREDS* OF READINGS AT *ONCE*.

THERE *MUST* BE SOMETHING *WRONG*.

EEEEEEEE

SOK

OHDEAR OHDEAR OHDEAR

HIT 'EM *HARD!*

GAKK

STAB

BAFF

THEY'RE *MESSIN'* UP MY *BEAUTIFUL* SHOES WITH THEIR *BLOODY* FACES!

NO...NOTHING *WRONG*...IT'S SHOWING *HUNDREDS* OF *PIECES* OF HIM *EVERYWHERE!*

WAS HE...*IS* HE...

IT SEEMS THESE *SAVAGES* RIPPED HIM TO *SHREDS!*

OH *NO!*

KIK

CHOK

FINE!

RUIN MY NEW SHOES, YA *WALKIN'* WADS A' WASTE!

I GOT AN *UNLIMITED* SUPPLY A' *STILETTOS* TA STICK *RIGHT* UP YER STINKHOLES!

THERE'S *MORE* WHERE THESE CAME FROM!

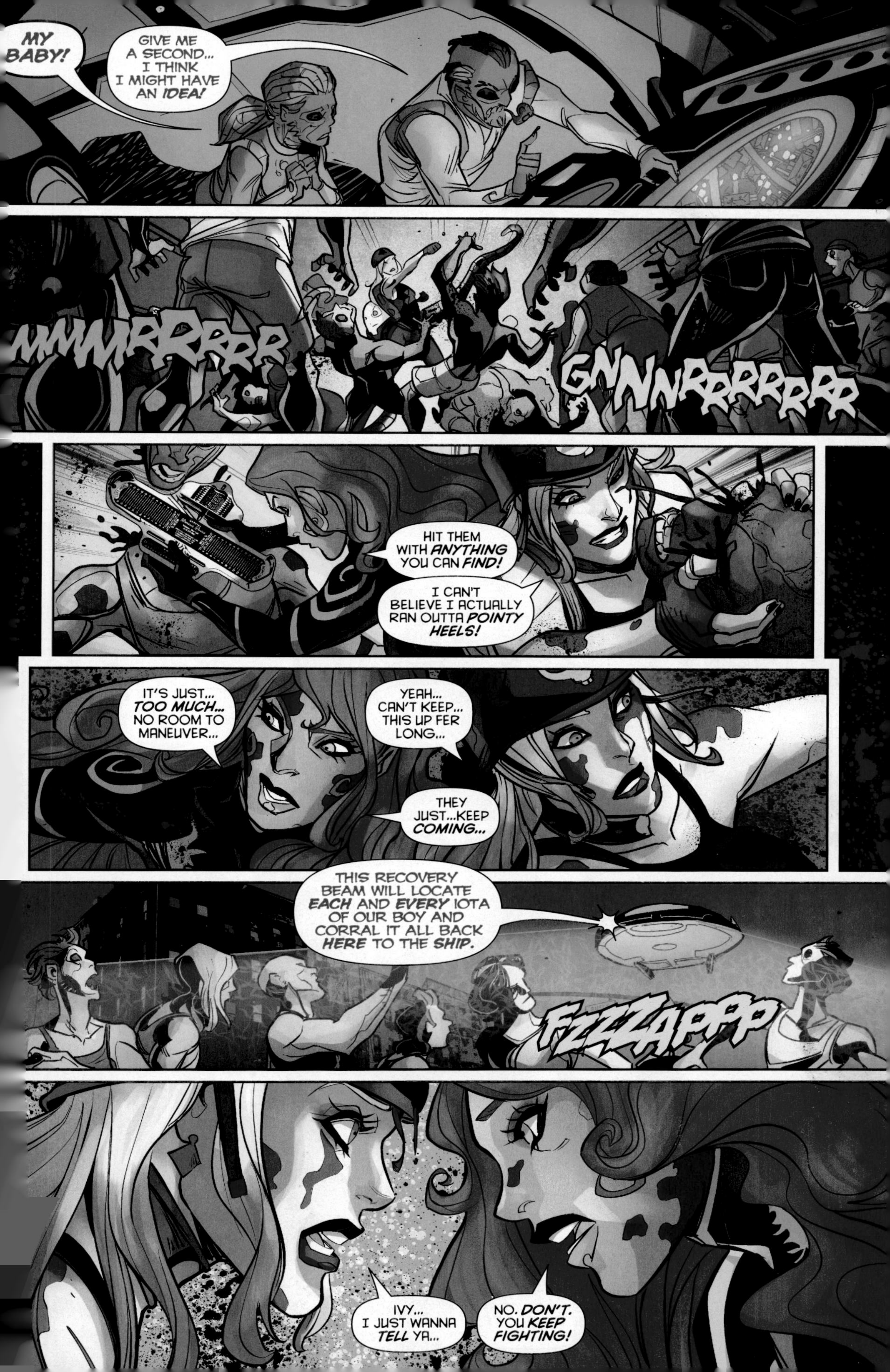
MY BABY!
GIVE ME A SECOND... I THINK I MIGHT HAVE AN IDEA!
NNNNRRRRRR
GNNNRRRRRRRR
HIT THEM WITH ANYTHING YOU CAN FIND!
I CAN'T BELIEVE I ACTUALLY RAN OUTTA POINTY HEELS!
IT'S JUST... TOO MUCH... NO ROOM TO MANEUVER...
YEAH... CAN'T KEEP... THIS UP FER LONG...
THEY JUST...KEEP COMING...
THIS RECOVERY BEAM WILL LOCATE EACH AND EVERY IOTA OF OUR BOY AND CORRAL IT ALL BACK HERE TO THE SHIP.
FZZZAPPP
IVY... I JUST WANNA TELL YA...
NO. DON'T. YOU KEEP FIGHTING!

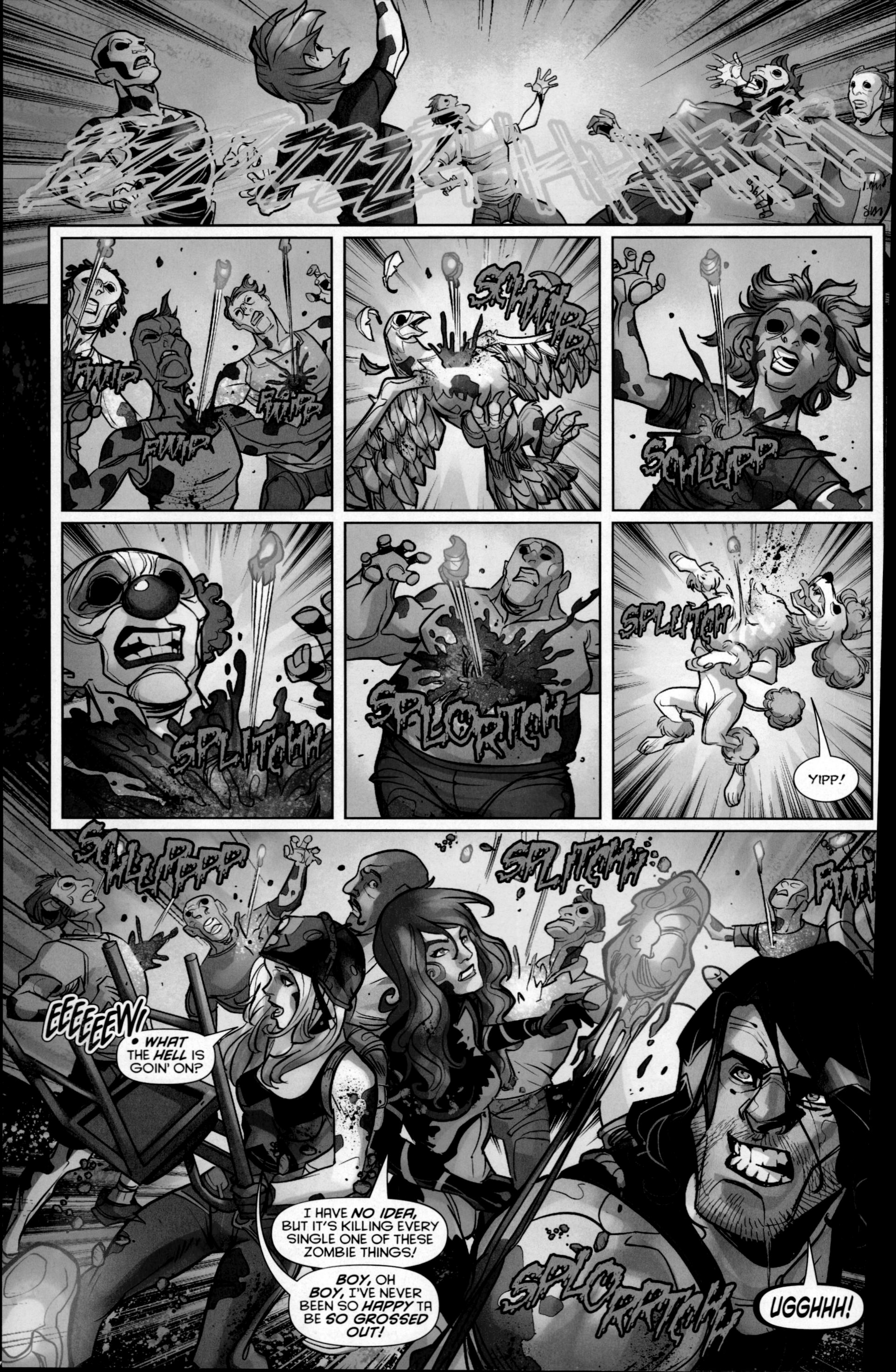
FWIP
FWIP
FWIP
SCHHHRP
SCHLUPP
SPLITCHH
SPLORTCH
SPLUTCH
YIPP!
SCHLURPP
SPLITCHH
EEEEEEEW!
WHAT THE HELL IS GOIN' ON?
I HAVE NO IDEA, BUT IT'S KILLING EVERY SINGLE ONE OF THESE ZOMBIE THINGS!
BOY, OH BOY, I'VE NEVER BEEN SO HAPPY TA BE SO GROSSED OUT!
SPLORRTCH
UGGHHH!

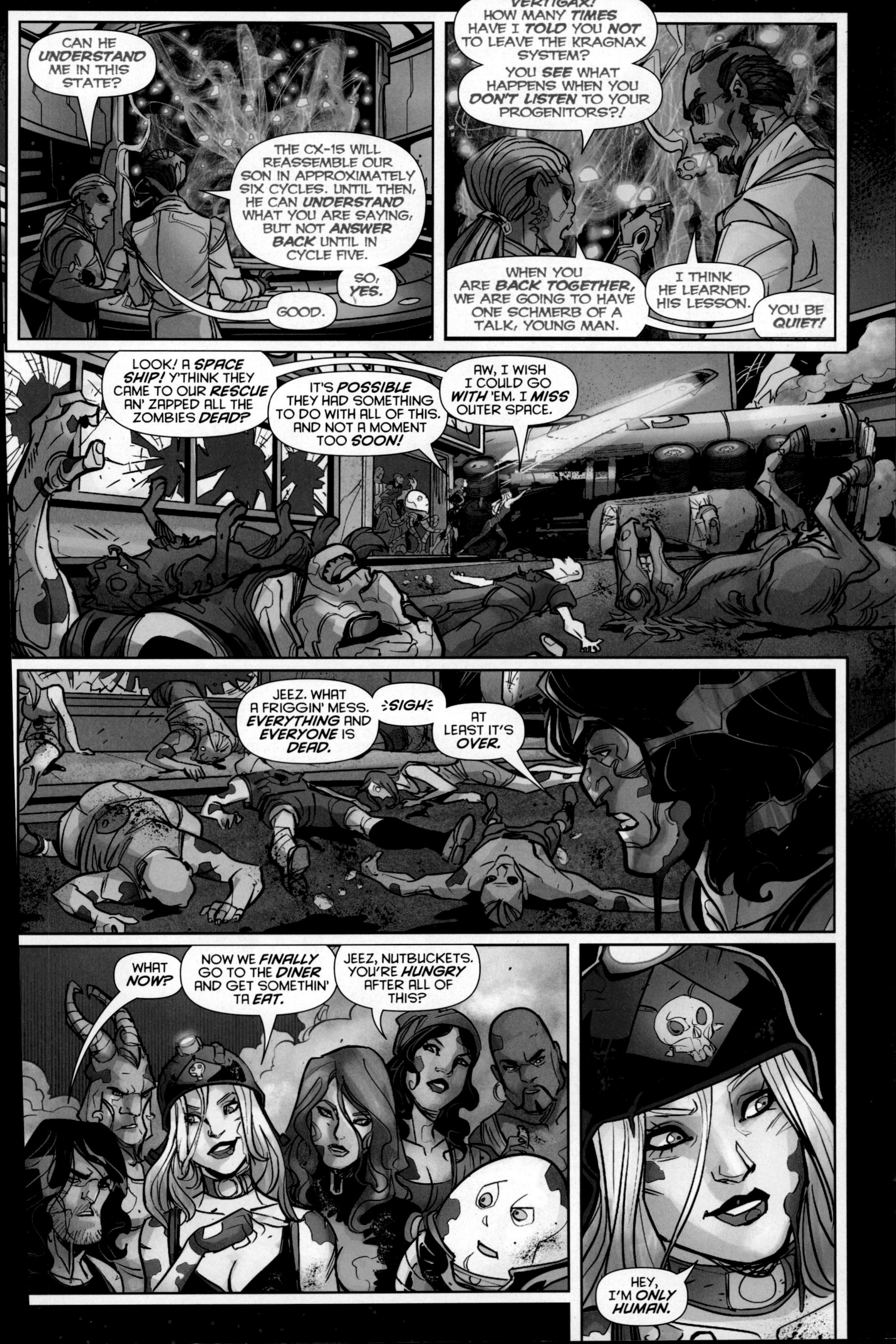
CAN HE UNDERSTAND ME IN THIS STATE?
THE CX-15 WILL REASSEMBLE OUR SON IN APPROXIMATELY SIX CYCLES. UNTIL THEN, HE CAN UNDERSTAND WHAT YOU ARE SAYING, BUT NOT ANSWER BACK UNTIL IN CYCLE FIVE.
SO, YES.
GOOD.
VERTIGAX! HOW MANY TIMES HAVE I TOLD YOU NOT TO LEAVE THE KRAGNAX SYSTEM?
YOU SEE WHAT HAPPENS WHEN YOU DON'T LISTEN TO YOUR PROGENITORS?!
WHEN YOU ARE BACK TOGETHER, WE ARE GOING TO HAVE ONE SCHMERB OF A TALK, YOUNG MAN.
I THINK HE LEARNED HIS LESSON.
YOU BE QUIET!
LOOK! A SPACE SHIP! Y'THINK THEY CAME TO OUR RESCUE AN' ZAPPED ALL THE ZOMBIES DEAD?
IT'S POSSIBLE THEY HAD SOMETHING TO DO WITH ALL OF THIS. AND NOT A MOMENT TOO SOON!
AW, I WISH I COULD GO WITH 'EM. I MISS OUTER SPACE.
JEEZ. WHAT A FRIGGIN' MESS. EVERYTHING AND EVERYONE IS DEAD.
:SIGH:
AT LEAST IT'S OVER.
WHAT NOW?
NOW WE FINALLY GO TO THE DINER AND GET SOMETHIN' TA EAT.
JEEZ, NUTBUCKETS. YOU'RE HUNGRY AFTER ALL OF THIS?
HEY, I'M ONLY HUMAN.

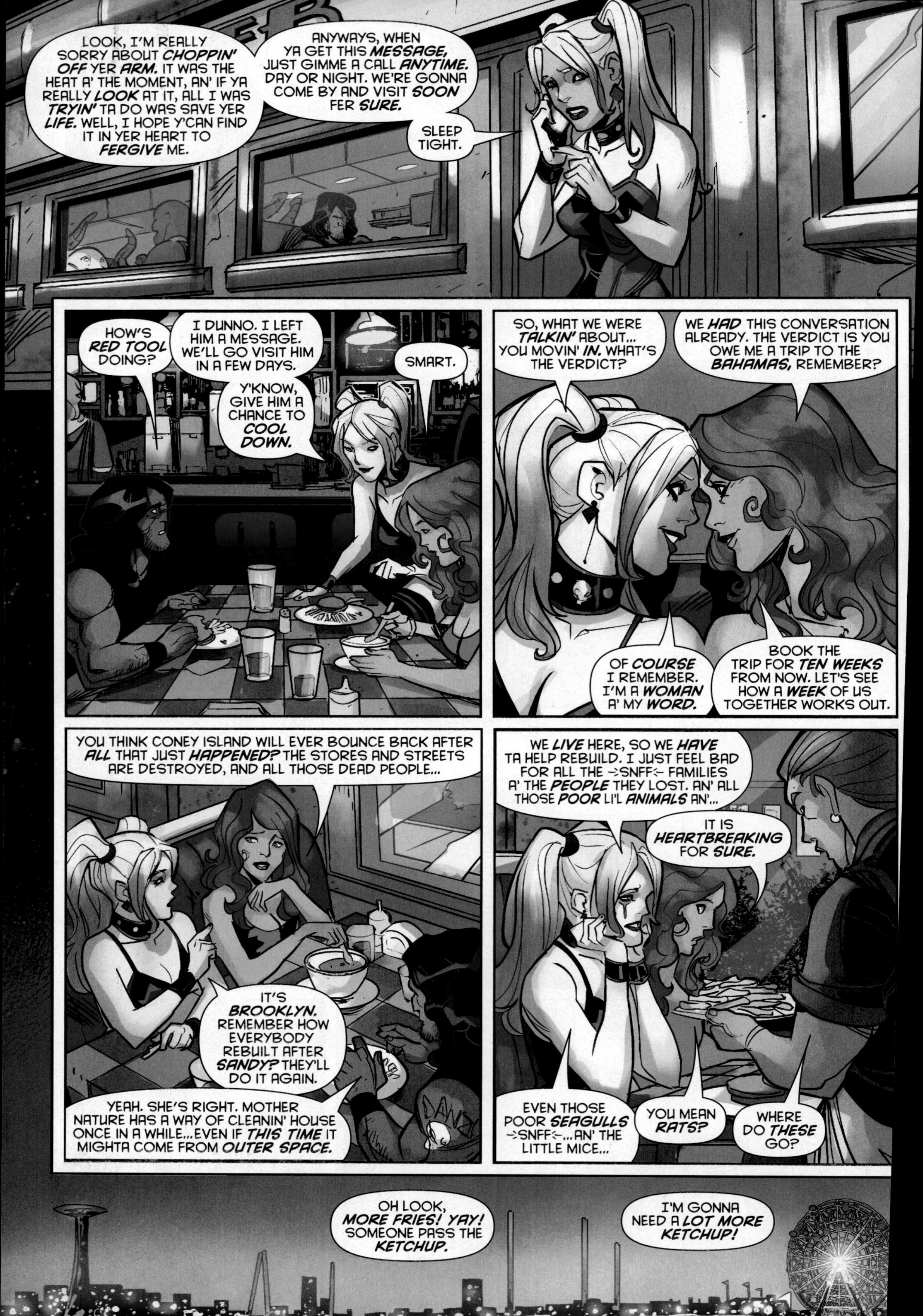
LOOK, I'M REALLY SORRY ABOUT CHOPPIN' OFF YER ARM. IT WAS THE HEAT A' THE MOMENT, AN' IF YA REALLY LOOK AT IT, ALL I WAS TRYIN' TA DO WAS SAVE YER LIFE. WELL, I HOPE Y'CAN FIND IT IN YER HEART TO FERGIVE ME.
ANYWAYS, WHEN YA GET THIS MESSAGE, JUST GIMME A CALL ANYTIME. DAY OR NIGHT. WE'RE GONNA COME BY AND VISIT SOON FER SURE.
SLEEP TIGHT.
HOW'S RED TOOL DOING?
I DUNNO. I LEFT HIM A MESSAGE. WE'LL GO VISIT HIM IN A FEW DAYS.
SMART.
Y'KNOW, GIVE HIM A CHANCE TO COOL DOWN.
SO, WHAT WE WERE TALKIN' ABOUT... YOU MOVIN' IN. WHAT'S THE VERDICT?
WE HAD THIS CONVERSATION ALREADY. THE VERDICT IS YOU OWE ME A TRIP TO THE BAHAMAS, REMEMBER?
OF COURSE I REMEMBER. I'M A WOMAN A' MY WORD.
BOOK THE TRIP FOR TEN WEEKS FROM NOW. LET'S SEE HOW A WEEK OF US TOGETHER WORKS OUT.
YOU THINK CONEY ISLAND WILL EVER BOUNCE BACK AFTER ALL THAT JUST HAPPENED? THE STORES AND STREETS ARE DESTROYED, AND ALL THOSE DEAD PEOPLE...
IT'S BROOKLYN. REMEMBER HOW EVERYBODY REBUILT AFTER SANDY? THEY'LL DO IT AGAIN.
YEAH. SHE'S RIGHT. MOTHER NATURE HAS A WAY OF CLEANIN' HOUSE ONCE IN A WHILE...EVEN IF THIS TIME IT MIGHTA COME FROM OUTER SPACE.
WE LIVE HERE, SO WE HAVE TA HELP REBUILD. I JUST FEEL BAD FOR ALL THE ⇒SNFF⇐ FAMILIES A' THE PEOPLE THEY LOST. AN' ALL THOSE POOR LI'L ANIMALS AN'...
IT IS HEARTBREAKING FOR SURE.
EVEN THOSE POOR SEAGULLS ⇒SNFF⇐...AN' THE LITTLE MICE...
YOU MEAN RATS?
WHERE DO THESE GO?
OH LOOK, MORE FRIES! YAY! SOMEONE PASS THE KETCHUP.
I'M GONNA NEED A LOT MORE KETCHUP!

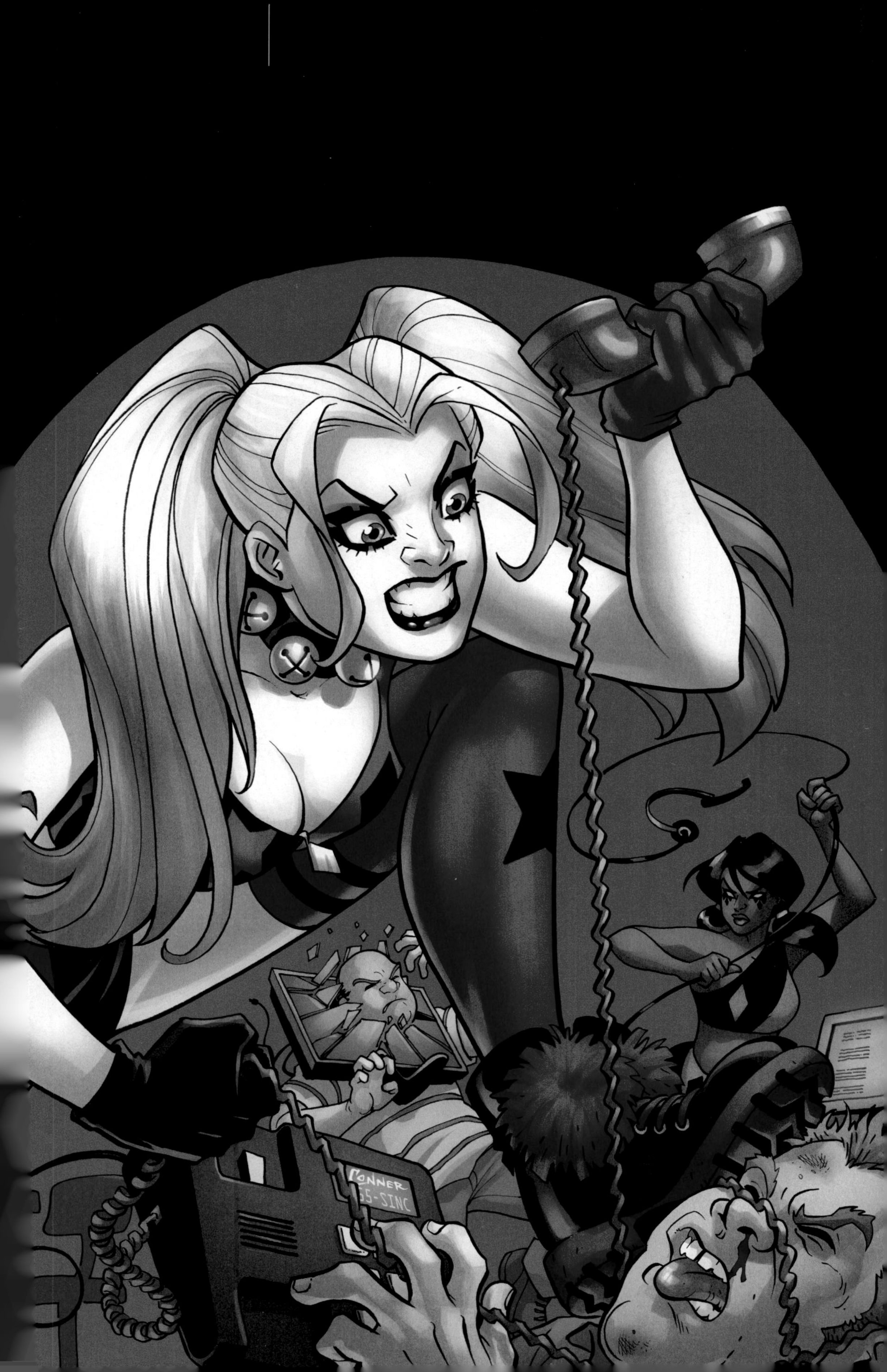
CONNER
55-SINC

108 MILLION WAYS TO DIE

JIMMY PALMIOTTI and AMANDA CONNER writers * JOSEPH MICHAEL LINSNER artist
ALEX SINCLAIR colorist * DAVE SHARPE letterer

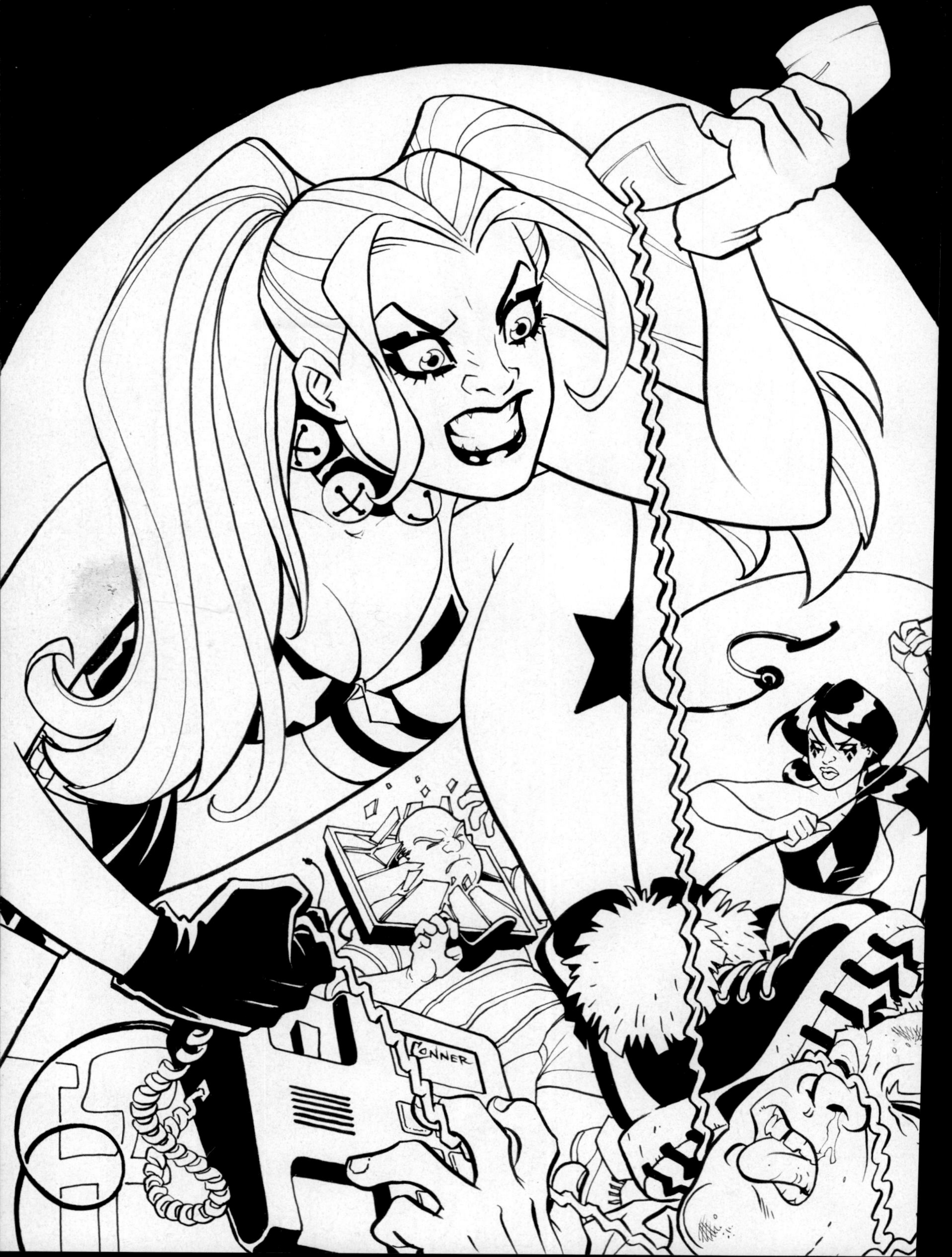

CONNER

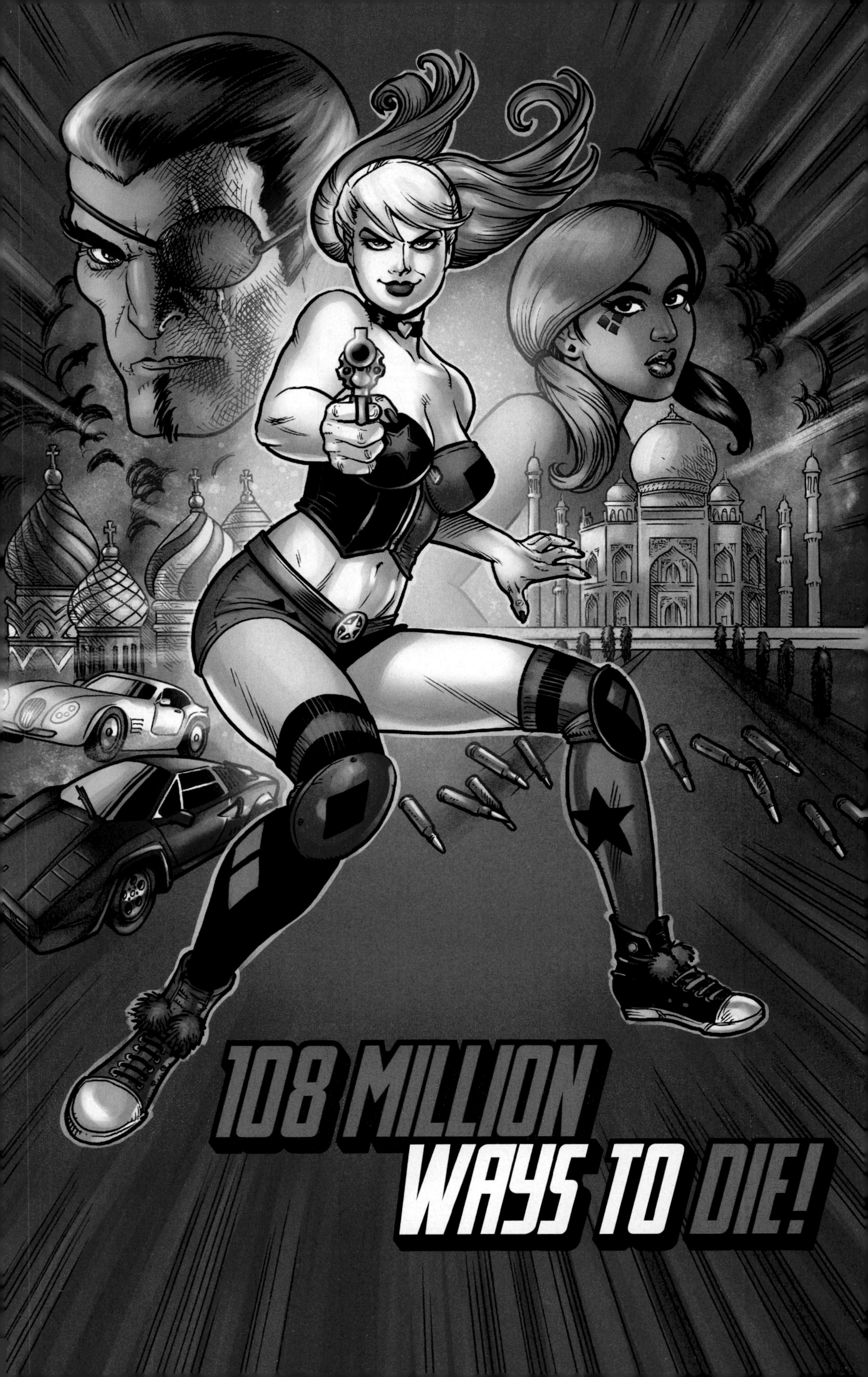
108 MILLION
WAYS TO DIE!

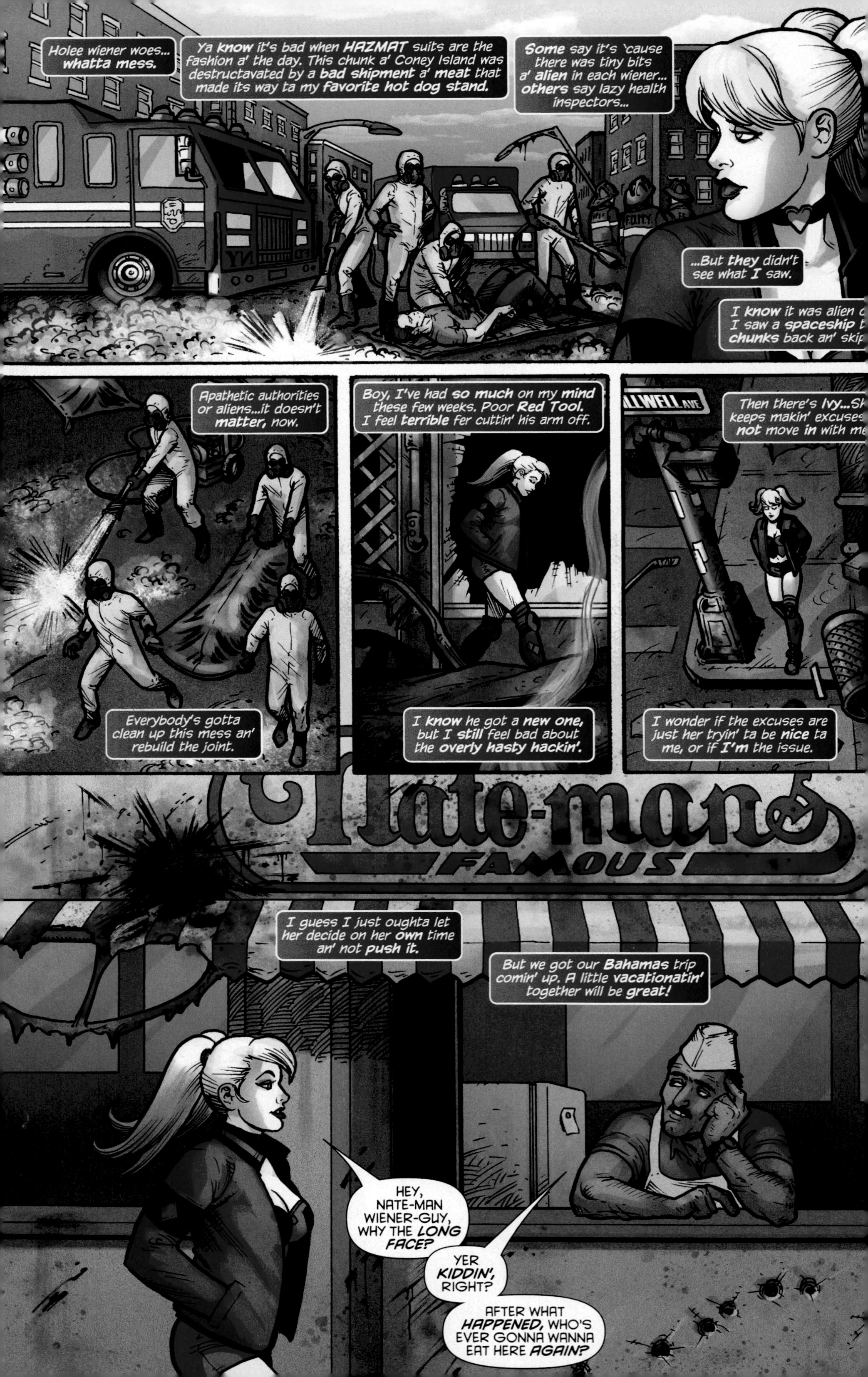
Holee wiener woes... whatta mess.
Ya know it's bad when HAZMAT suits are the fashion a' the day. This chunk a' Coney Island was destructavated by a bad shipment a' meat that made its way ta my favorite hot dog stand.
Some say it's 'cause there was tiny bits a' alien in each wiener... others say lazy health inspectors...
...But they didn't see what I saw.
I know it was alien c
I saw a spaceship t
chunks back an' skip
Apathetic authorities or aliens...it doesn't matter, now.
Everybody's gotta clean up this mess an' rebuild the joint.
Boy, I've had so much on my mind these few weeks. Poor Red Tool. I feel terrible fer cuttin' his arm off.
I know he got a new one, but I still feel bad about the overly hasty hackin'.
Then there's Ivy...Sh
keeps makin' excuses
not move in with me
I wonder if the excuses are just her tryin' ta be nice ta me, or if I'm the issue.
Nate-mans
FAMOUS
I guess I just oughta let her decide on her own time an' not push it.
But we got our Bahamas trip comin' up. A little vacationatin' together will be great!
HEY, NATE-MAN WIENER-GUY, WHY THE LONG FACE?
YER KIDDIN', RIGHT?
AFTER WHAT HAPPENED, WHO'S EVER GONNA WANNA EAT HERE AGAIN?

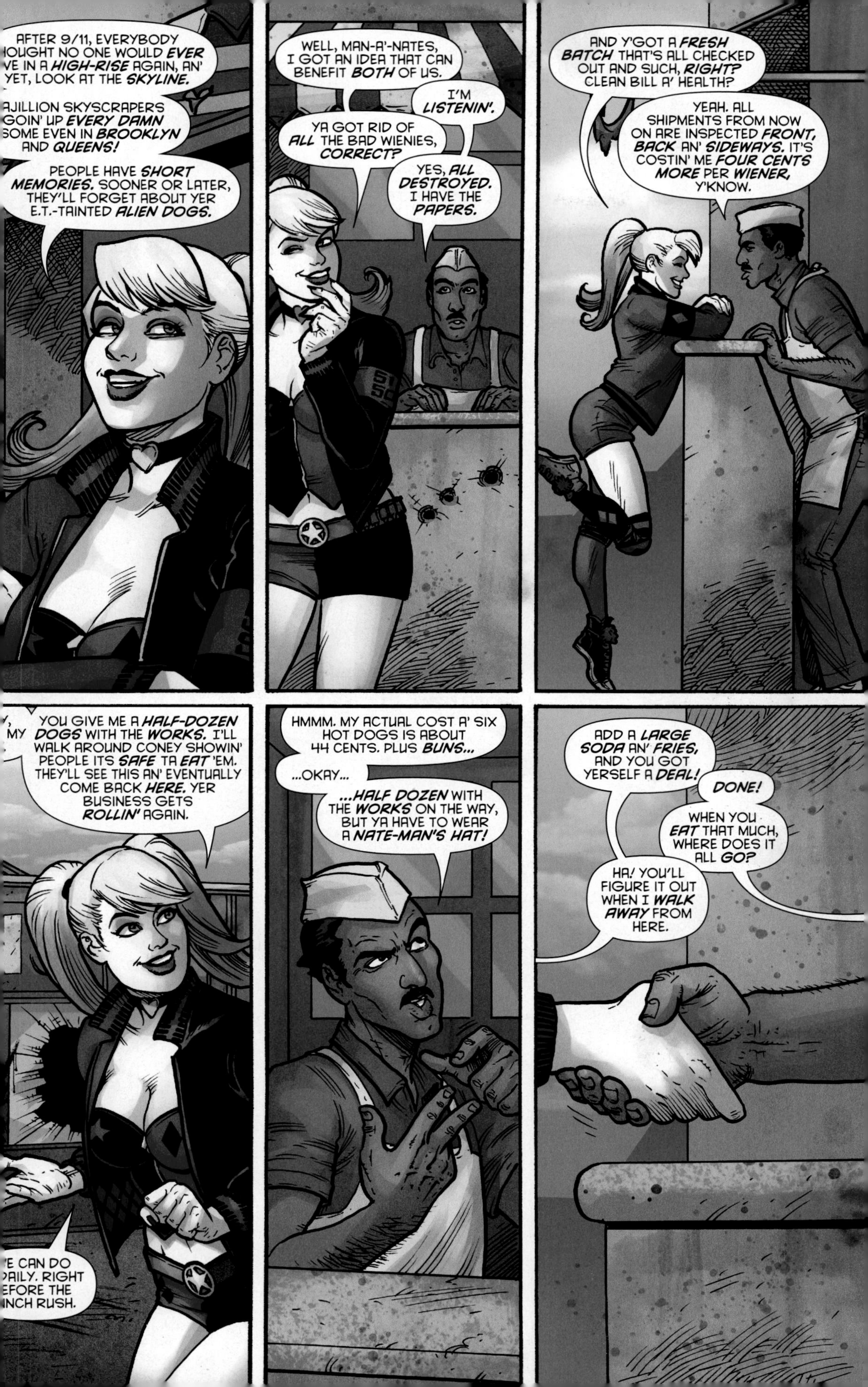

AFTER 9/11, EVERYBODY
HOUGHT NO ONE WOULD EVER
VE IN A HIGH-RISE AGAIN, AN'
YET, LOOK AT THE SKYLINE.
AJILLION SKYSCRAPERS
GOIN' UP EVERY DAMN
SOME EVEN IN BROOKLYN
AND QUEENS!
PEOPLE HAVE SHORT MEMORIES. SOONER OR LATER, THEY'LL FORGET ABOUT YER E.T.-TAINTED ALIEN DOGS.
WELL, MAN-A'-NATES, I GOT AN IDEA THAT CAN BENEFIT BOTH OF US.
I'M LISTENIN'.
YA GOT RID OF ALL THE BAD WIENIES, CORRECT?
YES, ALL DESTROYED. I HAVE THE PAPERS.
AND Y'GOT A FRESH BATCH THAT'S ALL CHECKED OUT AND SUCH, RIGHT? CLEAN BILL A' HEALTH?
YEAH. ALL SHIPMENTS FROM NOW ON ARE INSPECTED FRONT, BACK AN' SIDEWAYS. IT'S COSTIN' ME FOUR CENTS MORE PER WIENER, Y'KNOW.
MY
YOU GIVE ME A HALF-DOZEN DOGS WITH THE WORKS. I'LL WALK AROUND CONEY SHOWIN' PEOPLE ITS SAFE TA EAT 'EM. THEY'LL SEE THIS AN' EVENTUALLY COME BACK HERE. YER BUSINESS GETS ROLLIN' AGAIN.
E CAN DO
AILY. RIGHT
EFORE THE
NCH RUSH.
HMMM. MY ACTUAL COST A' SIX HOT DOGS IS ABOUT 44 CENTS. PLUS BUNS...
...OKAY...
...HALF DOZEN WITH THE WORKS ON THE WAY, BUT YA HAVE TO WEAR A NATE-MAN'S HAT!
ADD A LARGE SODA AN' FRIES, AND YOU GOT YERSELF A DEAL!
DONE!
WHEN YOU EAT THAT MUCH, WHERE DOES IT ALL GO?
HA! YOU'LL FIGURE IT OUT WHEN I WALK AWAY FROM HERE.

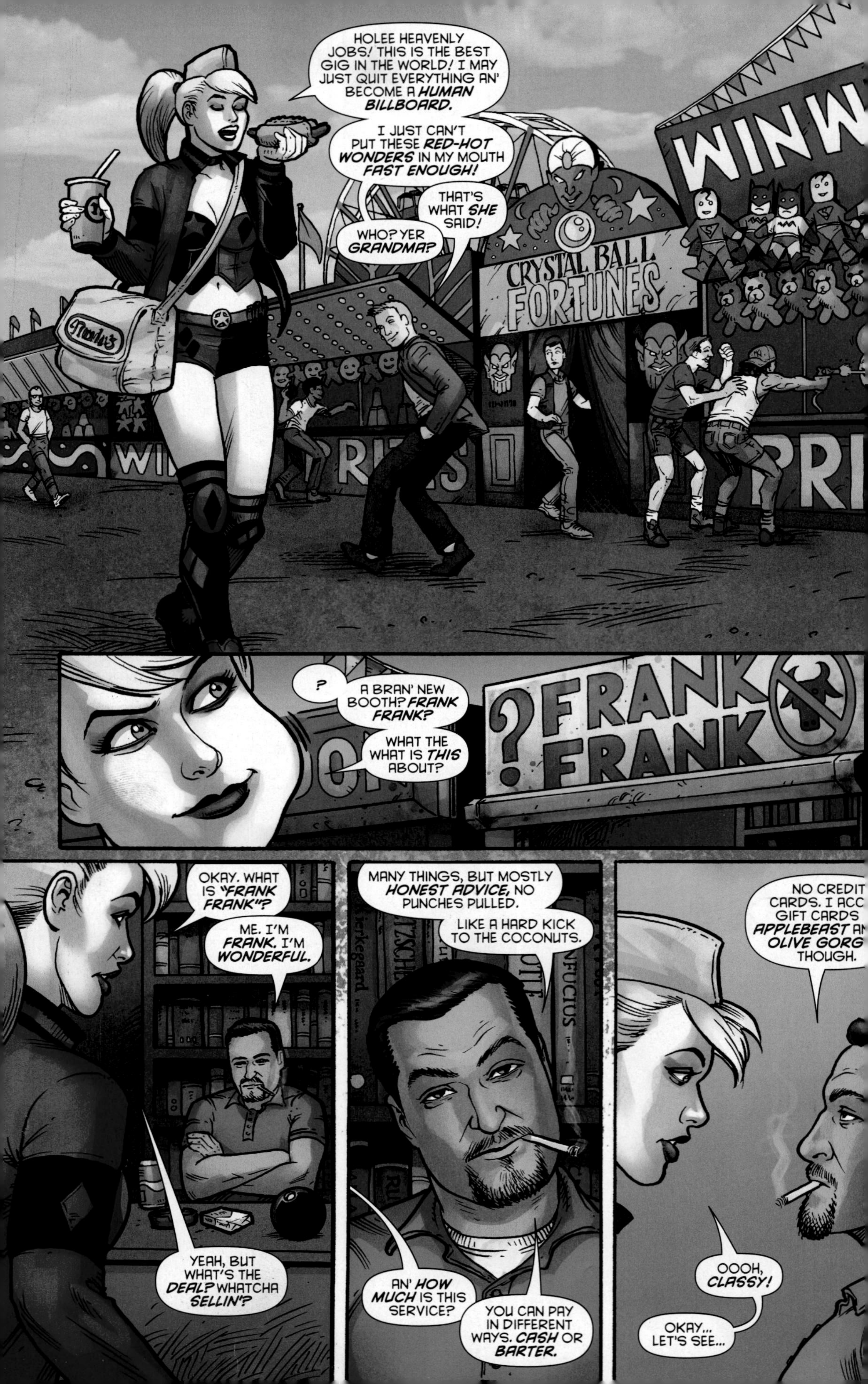
HOLEE HEAVENLY JOBS! THIS IS THE BEST GIG IN THE WORLD! I MAY JUST QUIT EVERYTHING AN' BECOME A HUMAN BILLBOARD.
I JUST CAN'T PUT THESE RED-HOT WONDERS IN MY MOUTH FAST ENOUGH!
THAT'S WHAT SHE SAID!
WHO? YER GRANDMA?
CRYSTAL BALL FORTUNES
WINW
?
A BRAN' NEW BOOTH? FRANK FRANK?
WHAT THE WHAT IS THIS ABOUT?
? FRANK FRANK
OKAY. WHAT IS "FRANK FRANK"?
ME. I'M FRANK. I'M WONDERFUL.
YEAH, BUT WHAT'S THE DEAL? WHATCHA SELLIN'?
MANY THINGS, BUT MOSTLY HONEST ADVICE, NO PUNCHES PULLED.
LIKE A HARD KICK TO THE COCONUTS.
AN' HOW MUCH IS THIS SERVICE?
YOU CAN PAY IN DIFFERENT WAYS. CASH OR BARTER.
NO CREDIT CARDS. I ACC GIFT CARDS APPLEBEAST AN OLIVE GORG THOUGH.
OOOH, CLASSY!
OKAY... LET'S SEE...

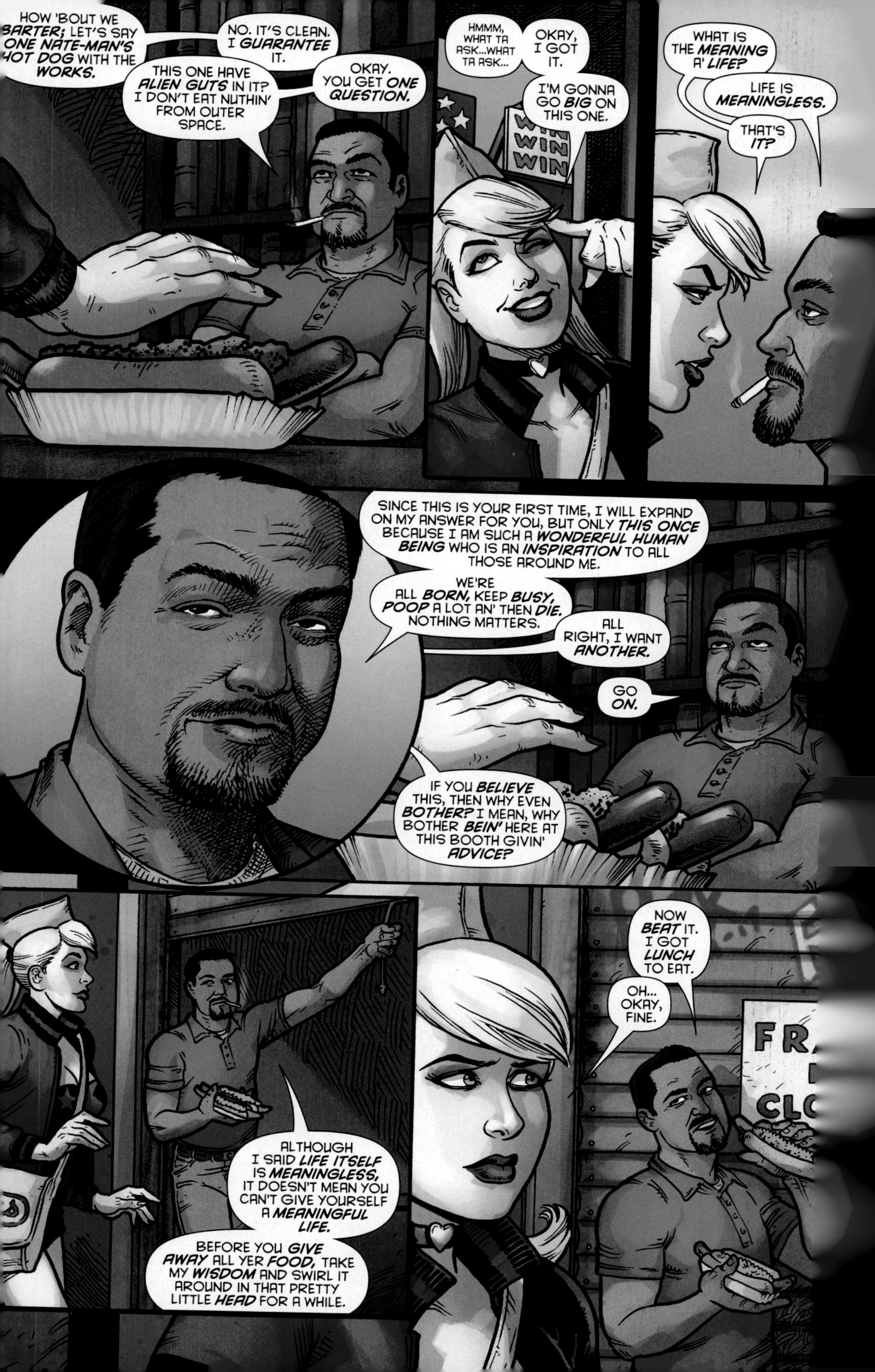
HOW 'BOUT WE BARTER; LET'S SAY ONE NATE-MAN'S HOT DOG WITH THE WORKS.
THIS ONE HAVE ALIEN GUTS IN IT? I DON'T EAT NUTHIN' FROM OUTER SPACE.
NO. IT'S CLEAN. I GUARANTEE IT.
OKAY. YOU GET ONE QUESTION.
HMMM, WHAT TA ASK...WHAT TA ASK...
OKAY, I GOT IT.
I'M GONNA GO BIG ON THIS ONE.
WIN WIN WIN
WHAT IS THE MEANING A' LIFE?
LIFE IS MEANINGLESS.
THAT'S IT?
SINCE THIS IS YOUR FIRST TIME, I WILL EXPAND ON MY ANSWER FOR YOU, BUT ONLY THIS ONCE BECAUSE I AM SUCH A WONDERFUL HUMAN BEING WHO IS AN INSPIRATION TO ALL THOSE AROUND ME.
WE'RE ALL BORN, KEEP BUSY, POOP A LOT AN' THEN DIE. NOTHING MATTERS.
ALL RIGHT, I WANT ANOTHER.
GO ON.
IF YOU BELIEVE THIS, THEN WHY EVEN BOTHER? I MEAN, WHY BOTHER BEIN' HERE AT THIS BOOTH GIVIN' ADVICE?
ALTHOUGH I SAID LIFE ITSELF IS MEANINGLESS, IT DOESN'T MEAN YOU CAN'T GIVE YOURSELF A MEANINGFUL LIFE.
BEFORE YOU GIVE AWAY ALL YER FOOD, TAKE MY WISDOM AND SWIRL IT AROUND IN THAT PRETTY LITTLE HEAD FOR A WHILE.
NOW BEAT IT. I GOT LUNCH TO EAT.
OH... OKAY, FINE.

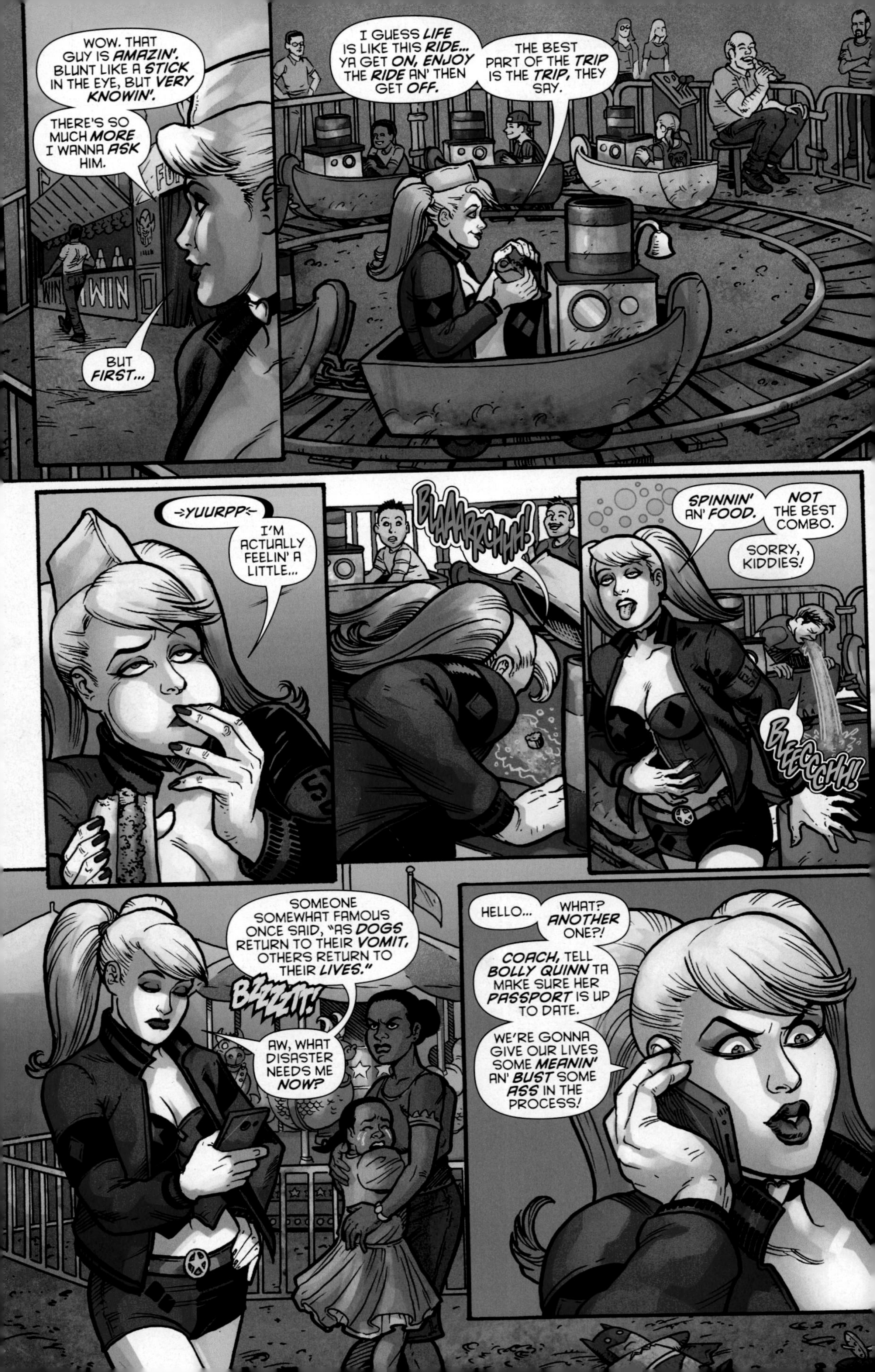

WOW. THAT GUY IS AMAZIN'. BLUNT LIKE A STICK IN THE EYE, BUT VERY KNOWIN'.
THERE'S SO MUCH MORE I WANNA ASK HIM.
BUT FIRST...
I GUESS LIFE IS LIKE THIS RIDE... YA GET ON, ENJOY THE RIDE AN' THEN GET OFF.
THE BEST PART OF THE TRIP IS THE TRIP, THEY SAY.
YUURPP
I'M ACTUALLY FEELIN' A LITTLE...
BLAAARRCHHH!
SPINNIN' AN' FOOD.
NOT THE BEST COMBO.
SORRY, KIDDIES!
BLEECCHH!
SOMEONE SOMEWHAT FAMOUS ONCE SAID, "AS DOGS RETURN TO THEIR VOMIT, OTHERS RETURN TO THEIR LIVES."
BZZZTT!
AW, WHAT DISASTER NEEDS ME NOW?
HELLO...
WHAT? ANOTHER ONE?!
COACH, TELL BOLLY QUINN TA MAKE SURE HER PASSPORT IS UP TO DATE.
WE'RE GONNA GIVE OUR LIVES SOME MEANIN' AN' BUST SOME ASS IN THE PROCESS!

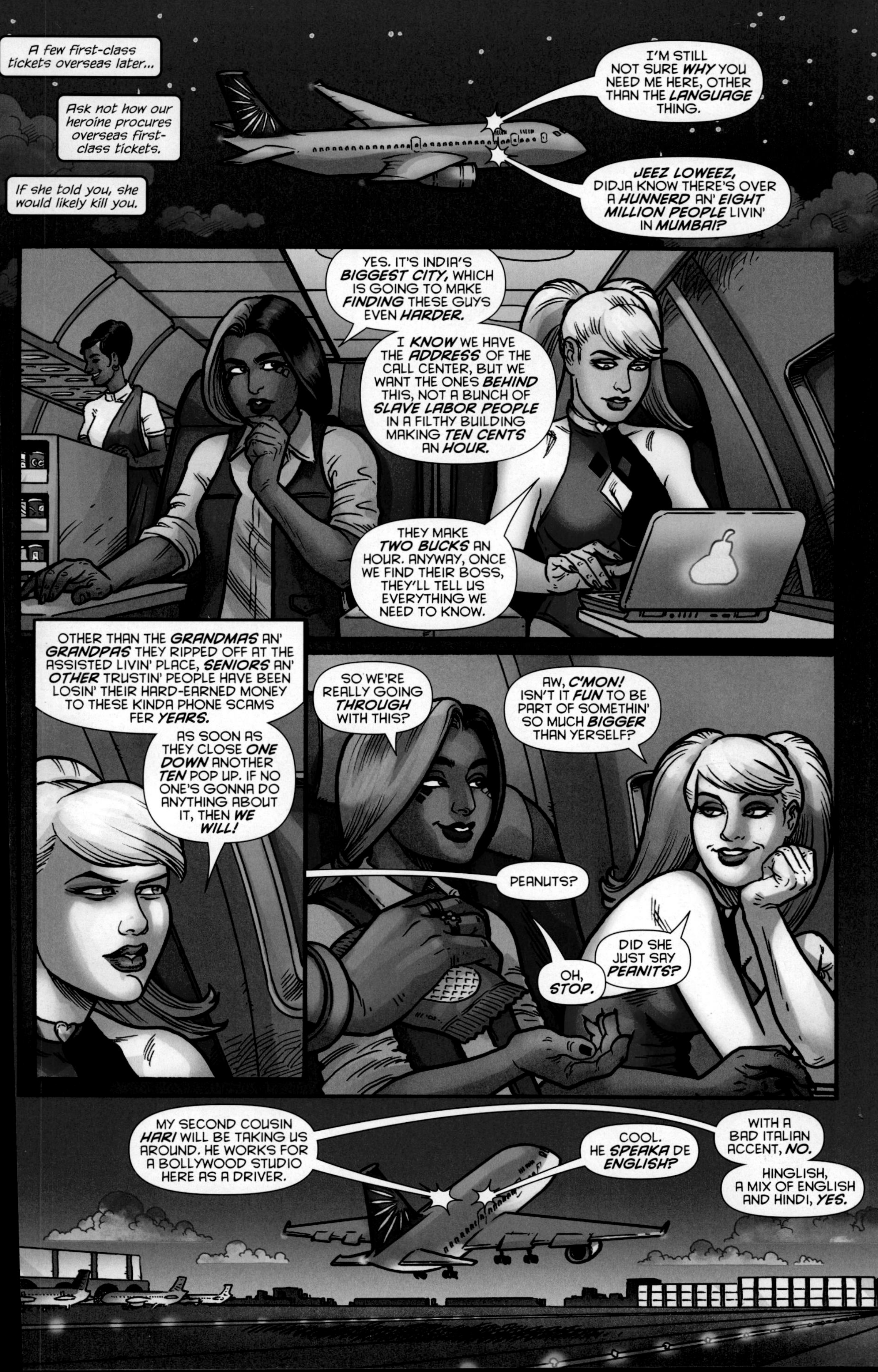
A few first-class tickets overseas later...
Ask not how our heroine procures overseas first-class tickets.
If she told you, she would likely kill you.
I'M STILL NOT SURE WHY YOU NEED ME HERE, OTHER THAN THE LANGUAGE THING.
JEEZ LOWEEZ, DIDJA KNOW THERE'S OVER A HUNNERD AN' EIGHT MILLION PEOPLE LIVIN' IN MUMBAI?
YES. IT'S INDIA'S BIGGEST CITY, WHICH IS GOING TO MAKE FINDING THESE GUYS EVEN HARDER.
I KNOW WE HAVE THE ADDRESS OF THE CALL CENTER, BUT WE WANT THE ONES BEHIND THIS, NOT A BUNCH OF SLAVE LABOR PEOPLE IN A FILTHY BUILDING MAKING TEN CENTS AN HOUR.
THEY MAKE TWO BUCKS AN HOUR. ANYWAY, ONCE WE FIND THEIR BOSS, THEY'LL TELL US EVERYTHING WE NEED TO KNOW.
OTHER THAN THE GRANDMAS AN' GRANDPAS THEY RIPPED OFF AT THE ASSISTED LIVIN' PLACE, SENIORS AN' OTHER TRUSTIN' PEOPLE HAVE BEEN LOSIN' THEIR HARD-EARNED MONEY TO THESE KINDA PHONE SCAMS FER YEARS.
AS SOON AS THEY CLOSE ONE DOWN ANOTHER TEN POP UP. IF NO ONE'S GONNA DO ANYTHING ABOUT IT, THEN WE WILL!
SO WE'RE REALLY GOING THROUGH WITH THIS?
AW, C'MON! ISN'T IT FUN TO BE PART OF SOMETHIN' SO MUCH BIGGER THAN YERSELF?
PEANUTS?
DID SHE JUST SAY PEANITS?
OH, STOP.
MY SECOND COUSIN HARI WILL BE TAKING US AROUND. HE WORKS FOR A BOLLYWOOD STUDIO HERE AS A DRIVER.
COOL. HE SPEAKA DE ENGLISH?
WITH A BAD ITALIAN ACCENT, NO.
HINGLISH, A MIX OF ENGLISH AND HINDI, YES.

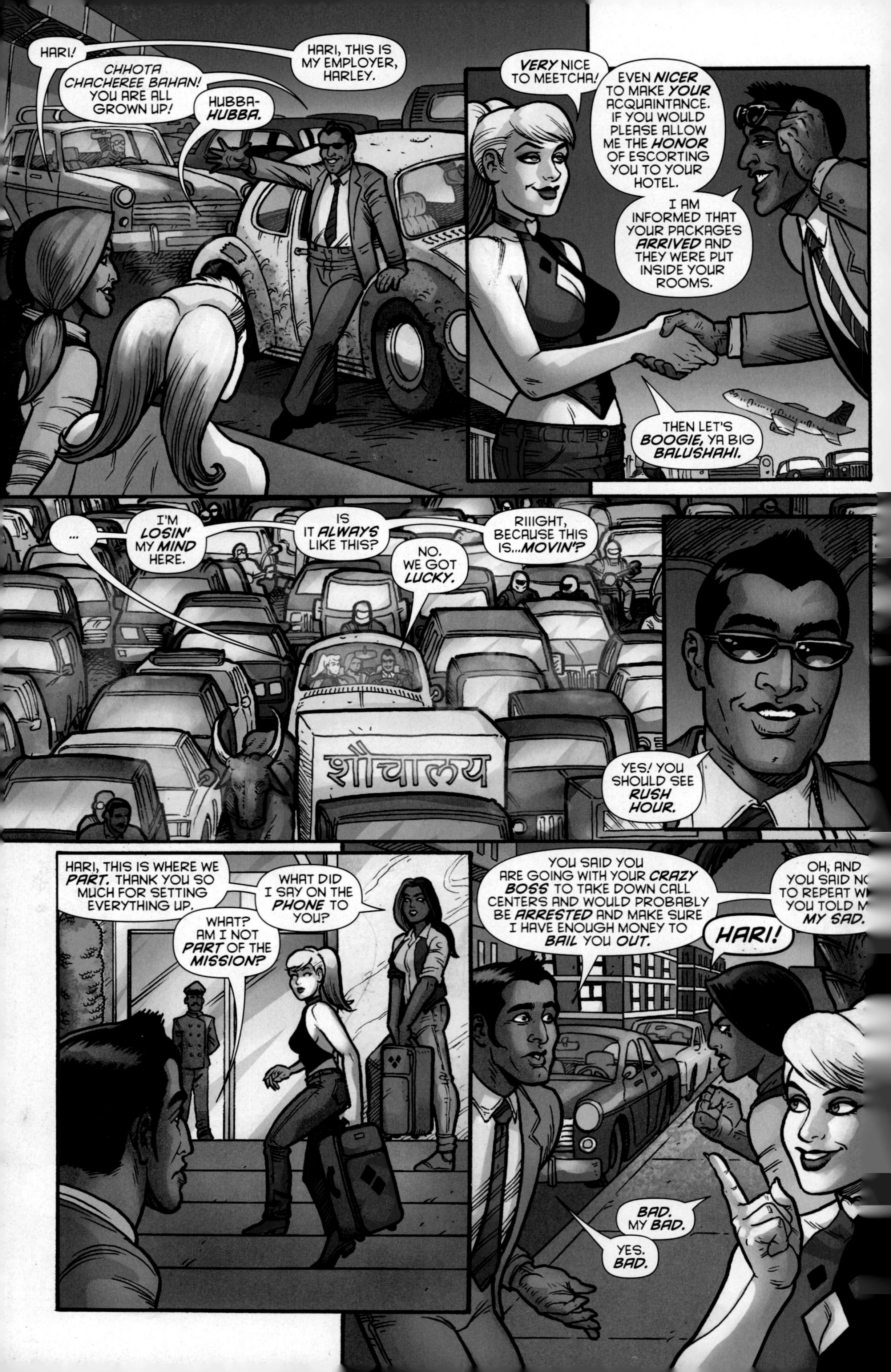
HARI!
CHHOTA CHACHEREE BAHAN! YOU ARE ALL GROWN UP!
HARI, THIS IS MY EMPLOYER, HARLEY.
HUBBA-HUBBA.
VERY NICE TO MEETCHA!
EVEN NICER TO MAKE YOUR ACQUAINTANCE. IF YOU WOULD PLEASE ALLOW ME THE HONOR OF ESCORTING YOU TO YOUR HOTEL.
I AM INFORMED THAT YOUR PACKAGES ARRIVED AND THEY WERE PUT INSIDE YOUR ROOMS.
THEN LET'S BOOGIE, YA BIG BALUSHAHI.
...
I'M LOSIN' MY MIND HERE.
IS IT ALWAYS LIKE THIS?
NO. WE GOT LUCKY.
RIIIGHT, BECAUSE THIS IS...MOVIN'?
शौचालय
YES! YOU SHOULD SEE RUSH HOUR.
HARI, THIS IS WHERE WE PART. THANK YOU SO MUCH FOR SETTING EVERYTHING UP.
WHAT? AM I NOT PART OF THE MISSION?
WHAT DID I SAY ON THE PHONE TO YOU?
YOU SAID YOU ARE GOING WITH YOUR CRAZY BOSS TO TAKE DOWN CALL CENTERS AND WOULD PROBABLY BE ARRESTED AND MAKE SURE I HAVE ENOUGH MONEY TO BAIL YOU OUT.
OH, AND YOU SAID N TO REPEAT W YOU TOLD M MY SAD.
HARI!
BAD. MY BAD.
YES. BAD.

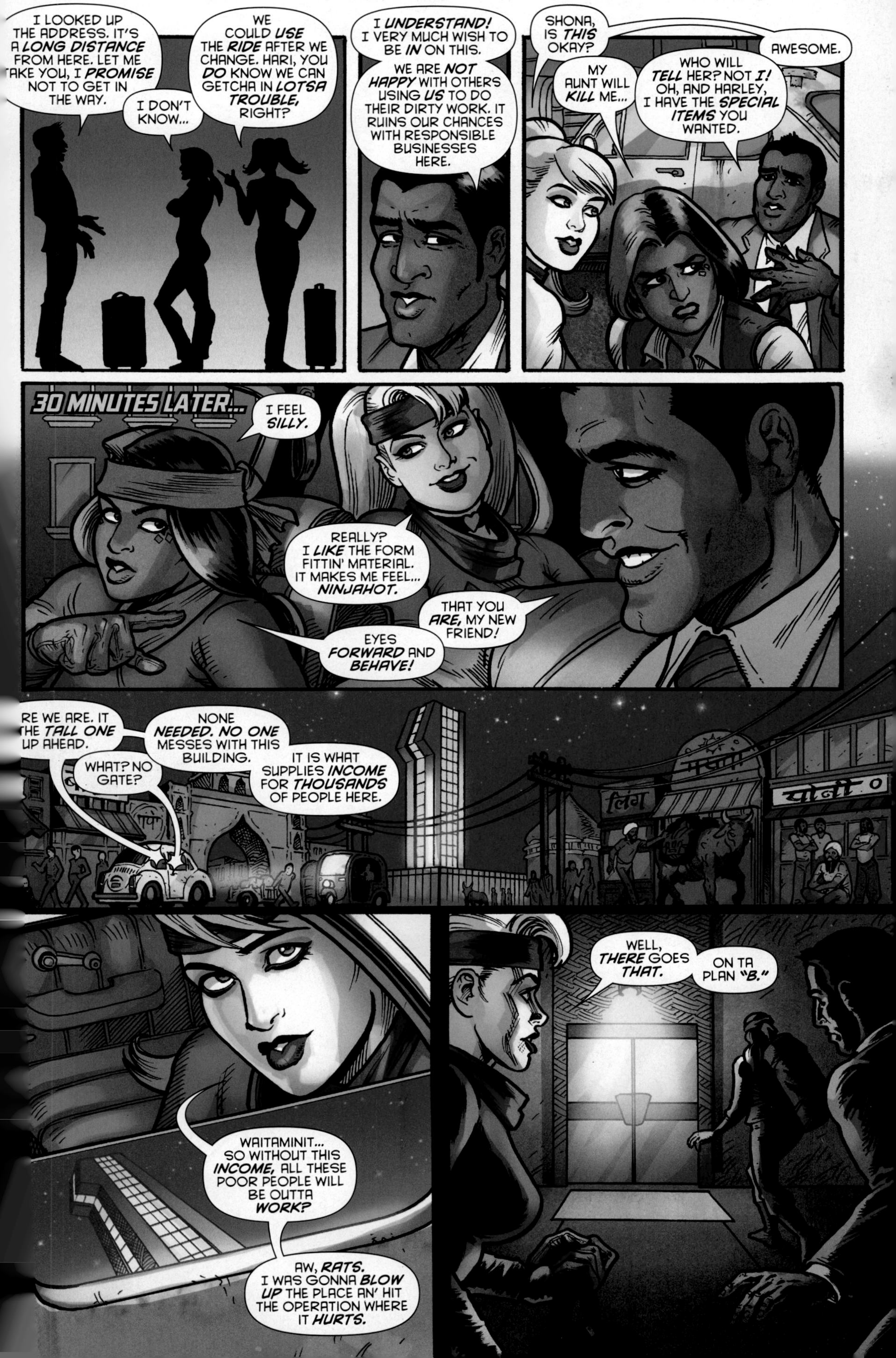

I LOOKED UP THE ADDRESS. IT'S A LONG DISTANCE FROM HERE. LET ME TAKE YOU, I PROMISE NOT TO GET IN THE WAY.
I DON'T KNOW...
WE COULD USE THE RIDE AFTER WE CHANGE. HARI, YOU DO KNOW WE CAN GETCHA IN LOTSA TROUBLE, RIGHT?
I UNDERSTAND! I VERY MUCH WISH TO BE IN ON THIS.
WE ARE NOT HAPPY WITH OTHERS USING US TO DO THEIR DIRTY WORK. IT RUINS OUR CHANCES WITH RESPONSIBLE BUSINESSES HERE.
SHONA, IS THIS OKAY?
MY AUNT WILL KILL ME...
AWESOME.
WHO WILL TELL HER? NOT I! OH, AND HARLEY, I HAVE THE SPECIAL ITEMS YOU WANTED.
30 MINUTES LATER...
I FEEL SILLY.
REALLY? I LIKE THE FORM FITTIN' MATERIAL. IT MAKES ME FEEL... NINJAHOT.
THAT YOU ARE, MY NEW FRIEND!
EYES FORWARD AND BEHAVE!
RE WE ARE. IT THE TALL ONE UP AHEAD.
WHAT? NO GATE?
NONE NEEDED. NO ONE MESSES WITH THIS BUILDING.
IT IS WHAT SUPPLIES INCOME FOR THOUSANDS OF PEOPLE HERE.
WAITAMINIT... SO WITHOUT THIS INCOME, ALL THESE POOR PEOPLE WILL BE OUTTA WORK?
AW, RATS. I WAS GONNA BLOW UP THE PLACE AN' HIT THE OPERATION WHERE IT HURTS.
WELL, THERE GOES THAT.
ON TA PLAN "B."

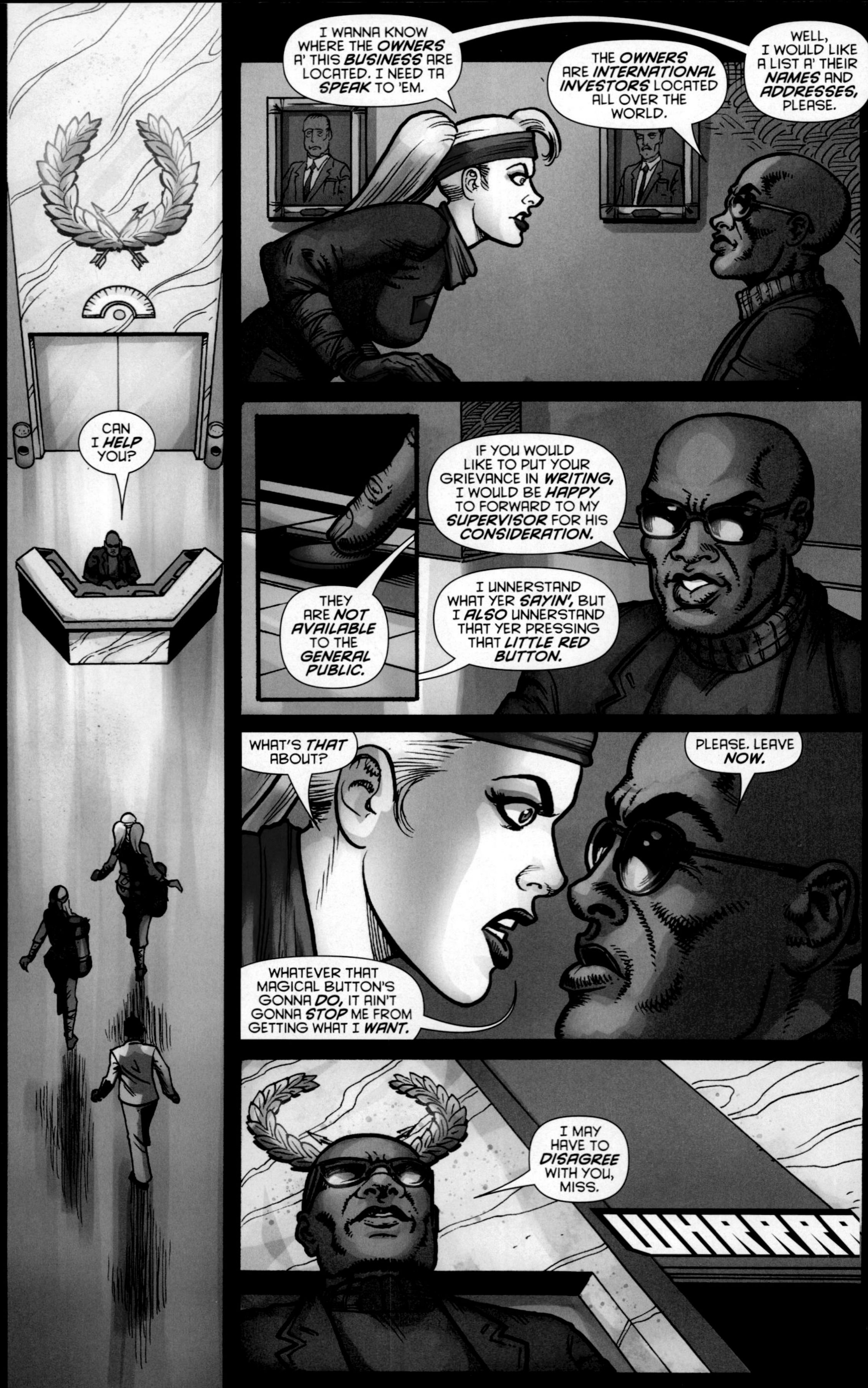
CAN I HELP YOU?
I WANNA KNOW WHERE THE OWNERS A' THIS BUSINESS ARE LOCATED. I NEED TA SPEAK TO 'EM.
THE OWNERS ARE INTERNATIONAL INVESTORS LOCATED ALL OVER THE WORLD.
WELL, I WOULD LIKE A LIST A' THEIR NAMES AND ADDRESSES, PLEASE.
THEY ARE NOT AVAILABLE TO THE GENERAL PUBLIC.
IF YOU WOULD LIKE TO PUT YOUR GRIEVANCE IN WRITING, I WOULD BE HAPPY TO FORWARD TO MY SUPERVISOR FOR HIS CONSIDERATION.
I UNNERSTAND WHAT YER SAYIN', BUT I ALSO UNNERSTAND THAT YER PRESSING THAT LITTLE RED BUTTON.
WHAT'S THAT ABOUT?
PLEASE. LEAVE NOW.
WHATEVER THAT MAGICAL BUTTON'S GONNA DO, IT AIN'T GONNA STOP ME FROM GETTING WHAT I WANT.
I MAY HAVE TO DISAGREE WITH YOU, MISS.
WHRRRR

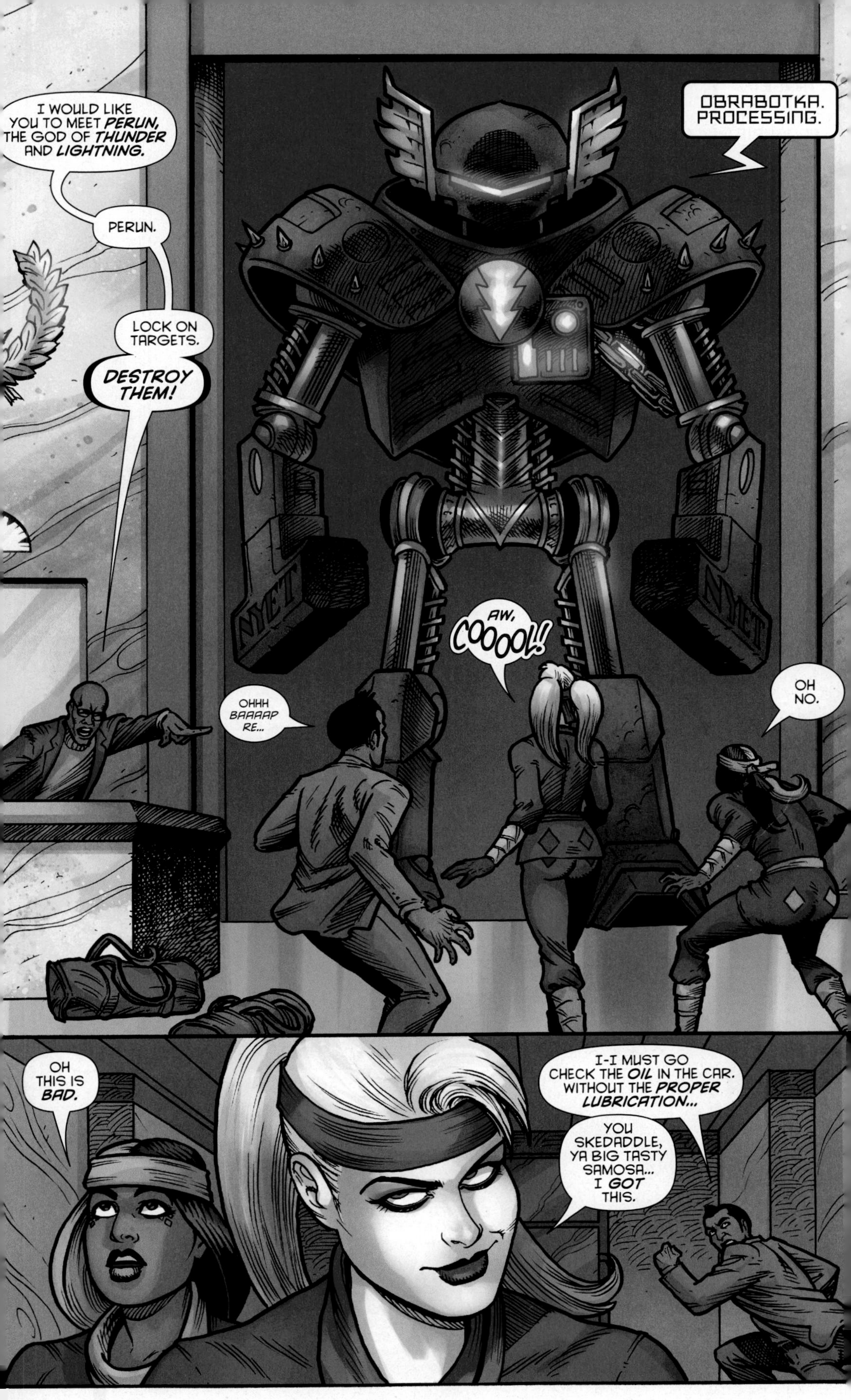
I WOULD LIKE YOU TO MEET PERUN, THE GOD OF THUNDER AND LIGHTNING.
PERUN.
LOCK ON TARGETS.
DESTROY THEM!
OBRABOTKA. PROCESSING.
NYET
NYET
AW, COOOOL!!
OHHH BAAAAP RE...
OH NO.
OH THIS IS BAD.
I-I MUST GO CHECK THE OIL IN THE CAR. WITHOUT THE PROPER LUBRICATION...
YOU SKEDADDLE, YA BIG TASTY SAMOSA... I GOT THIS.

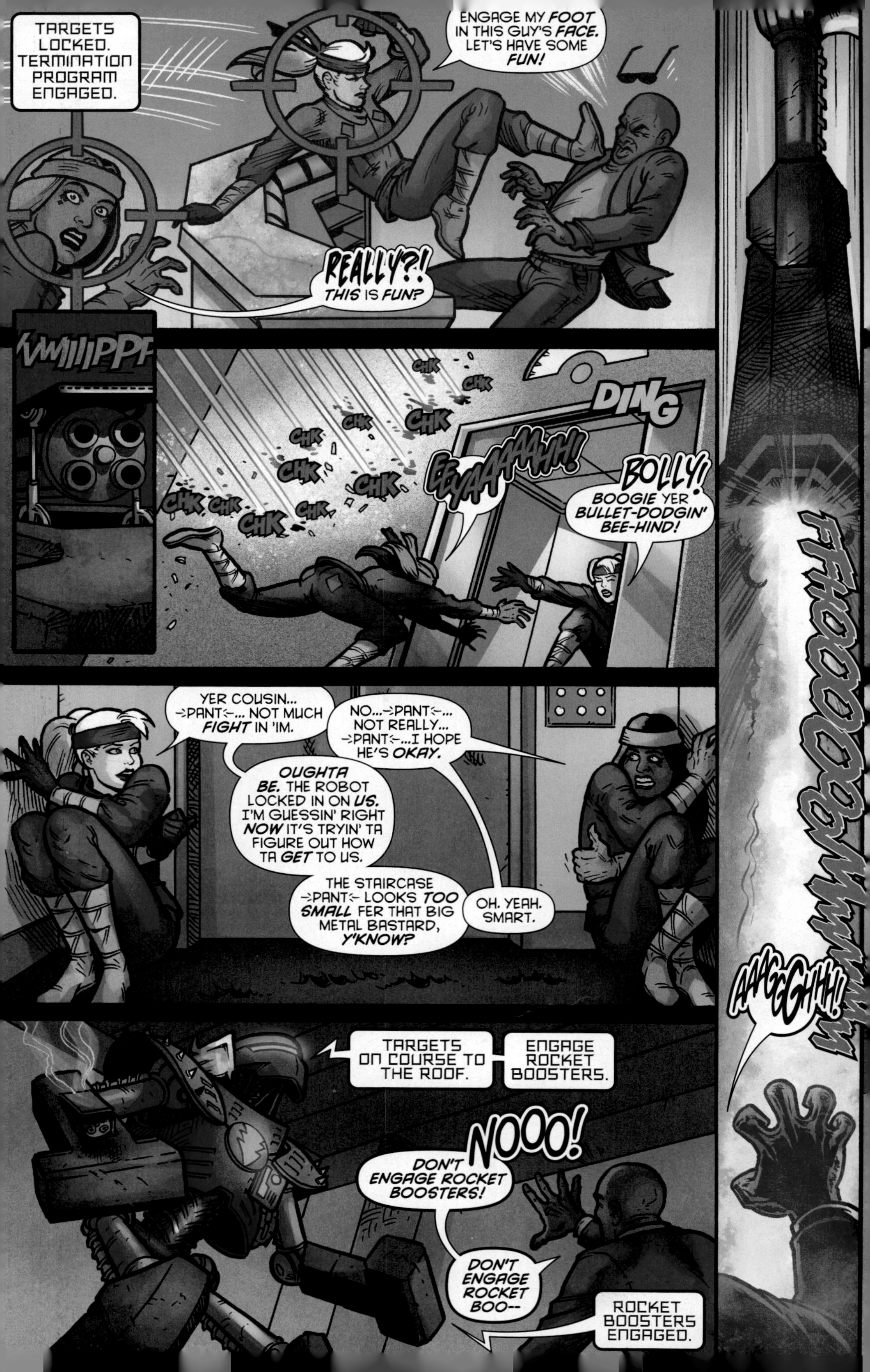
TARGETS LOCKED. TERMINATION PROGRAM ENGAGED.
ENGAGE MY FOOT IN THIS GUY'S FACE. LET'S HAVE SOME FUN!
REALLY?! THIS IS FUN?
KWIIIIPPP
CHK CHK CHK CHK CHK CHK CHK CHK CHK CHK
DING
EEYAAAAAAH!
BOLLY! BOOGIE YER BULLET-DODGIN' BEE-HIND!
YER COUSIN... ->PANT<-... NOT MUCH FIGHT IN 'IM.
NO... ->PANT<-... NOT REALLY... ->PANT<-...I HOPE HE'S OKAY.
OUGHTA BE. THE ROBOT LOCKED IN ON US. I'M GUESSIN' RIGHT NOW IT'S TRYIN' TA FIGURE OUT HOW TA GET TO US.
THE STAIRCASE ->PANT<- LOOKS TOO SMALL FER THAT BIG METAL BASTARD, Y'KNOW?
OH. YEAH. SMART.
TARGETS ON COURSE TO THE ROOF.
ENGAGE ROCKET BOOSTERS.
NOOO!
DON'T ENGAGE ROCKET BOOSTERS!
DON'T ENGAGE ROCKET BOO--
ROCKET BOOSTERS ENGAGED.
FFHOOOOOOMMMMM
AAAGGGHHH!

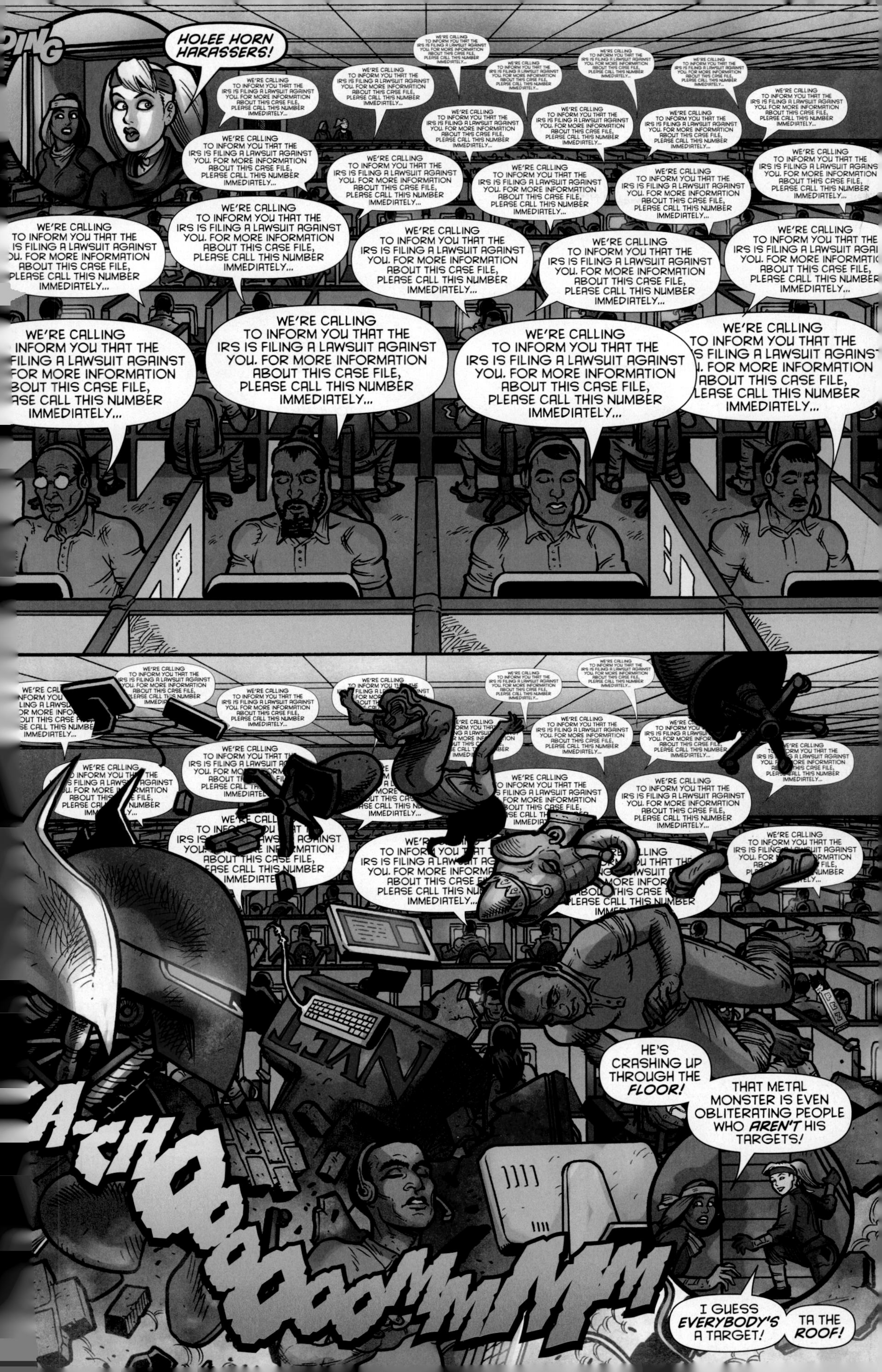

HOLEE HORN HARASSERS!
WE'RE CALLING TO INFORM YOU THAT THE IRS IS FILING A LAWSUIT AGAINST YOU. FOR MORE INFORMATION ABOUT THIS CASE FILE, PLEASE CALL THIS NUMBER IMMEDIATELY...
WE'RE CALLING TO INFORM YOU THAT THE IRS IS FILING A LAWSUIT AGAINST YOU. FOR MORE INFORMATION ABOUT THIS CASE FILE, PLEASE CALL THIS NUMBER IMMEDIATELY...
WE'RE CALLING TO INFORM YOU THAT THE IRS IS FILING A LAWSUIT AGAINST YOU. FOR MORE INFORMATION ABOUT THIS CASE FILE, PLEASE CALL THIS NUMBER IMMEDIATELY...
WE'RE CALLING TO INFORM YOU THAT THE IRS IS FILING A LAWSUIT AGAINST YOU. FOR MORE INFORMATION ABOUT THIS CASE FILE, PLEASE CALL THIS NUMBER IMMEDIATELY...
HE'S CRASHING UP THROUGH THE *FLOOR!*
THAT METAL MONSTER IS EVEN OBLITERATING PEOPLE WHO *AREN'T* HIS TARGETS!
I GUESS *EVERYBODY'S* A TARGET!
TA THE *ROOF!*

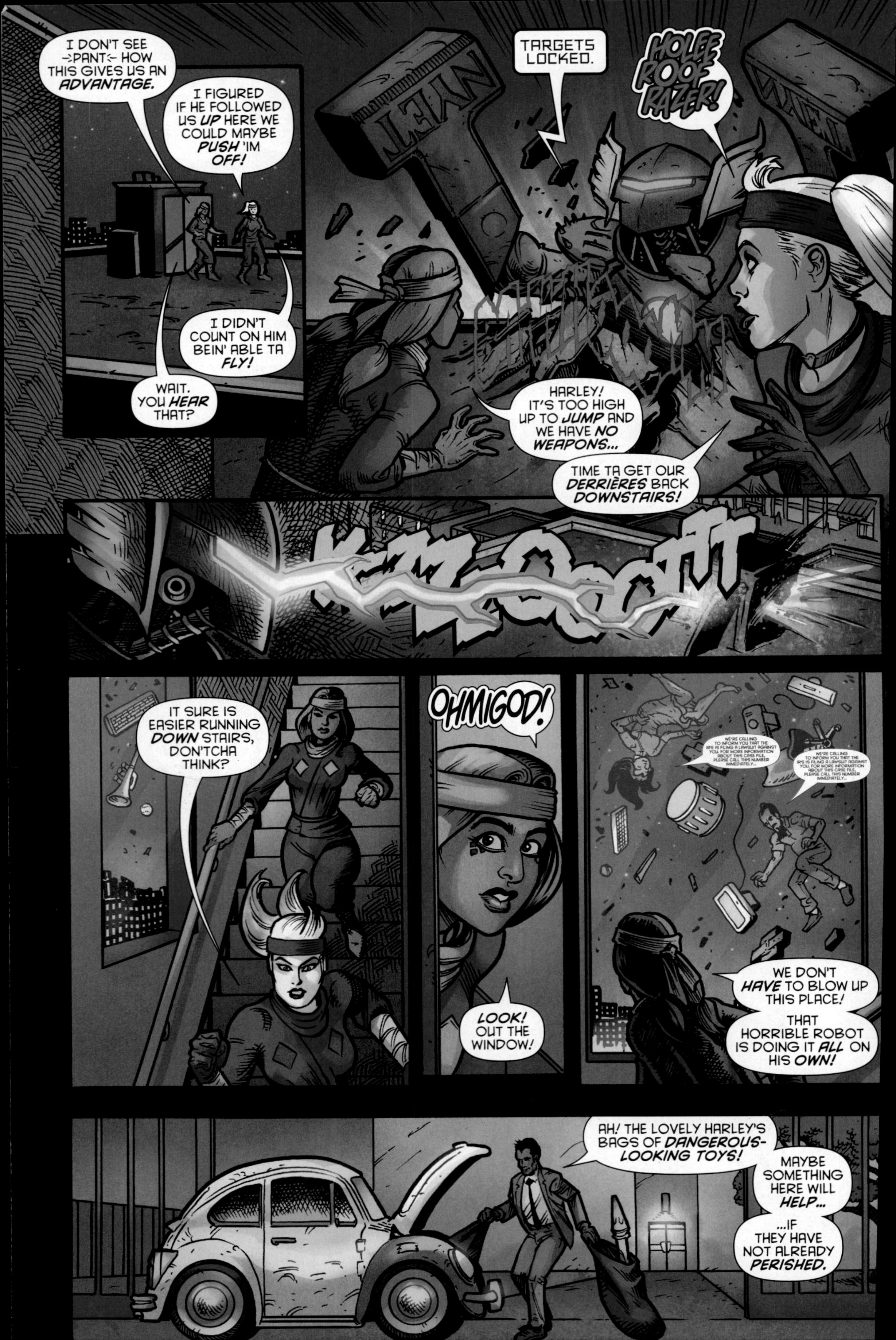
I DON'T SEE
⇒PANT⇐ HOW THIS GIVES US AN ADVANTAGE.
I FIGURED IF HE FOLLOWED US UP HERE WE COULD MAYBE PUSH 'IM OFF!
I DIDN'T COUNT ON HIM BEIN' ABLE TA FLY!
WAIT. YOU HEAR THAT?
TARGETS LOCKED.
HOLEE ROOF RAZER!
HARLEY! IT'S TOO HIGH UP TO JUMP AND WE HAVE NO WEAPONS...
TIME TA GET OUR DERRIÈRES BACK DOWNSTAIRS!
KZZ-OOOTT
IT SURE IS EASIER RUNNING DOWN STAIRS, DON'TCHA THINK?
OHMIGOD!
LOOK! OUT THE WINDOW!
WE'RE CALLING TO INFORM YOU THAT THE IRS IS FILING A LAWSUIT AGAINST YOU. FOR MORE INFORMATION ABOUT THIS CASE FILE, PLEASE CALL THIS NUMBER IMMEDIATELY...
WE'RE CALLING TO INFORM YOU THAT THE IRS IS FILING A LAWSUIT AGAINST YOU. FOR MORE INFORMATION ABOUT THIS CASE FILE, PLEASE CALL THIS NUMBER IMMEDIATELY...
WE DON'T HAVE TO BLOW UP THIS PLACE!
THAT HORRIBLE ROBOT IS DOING IT ALL ON HIS OWN!
AH! THE LOVELY HARLEY'S BAGS OF DANGEROUS-LOOKING TOYS!
MAYBE SOMETHING HERE WILL HELP...
...IF THEY HAVE NOT ALREADY PERISHED.

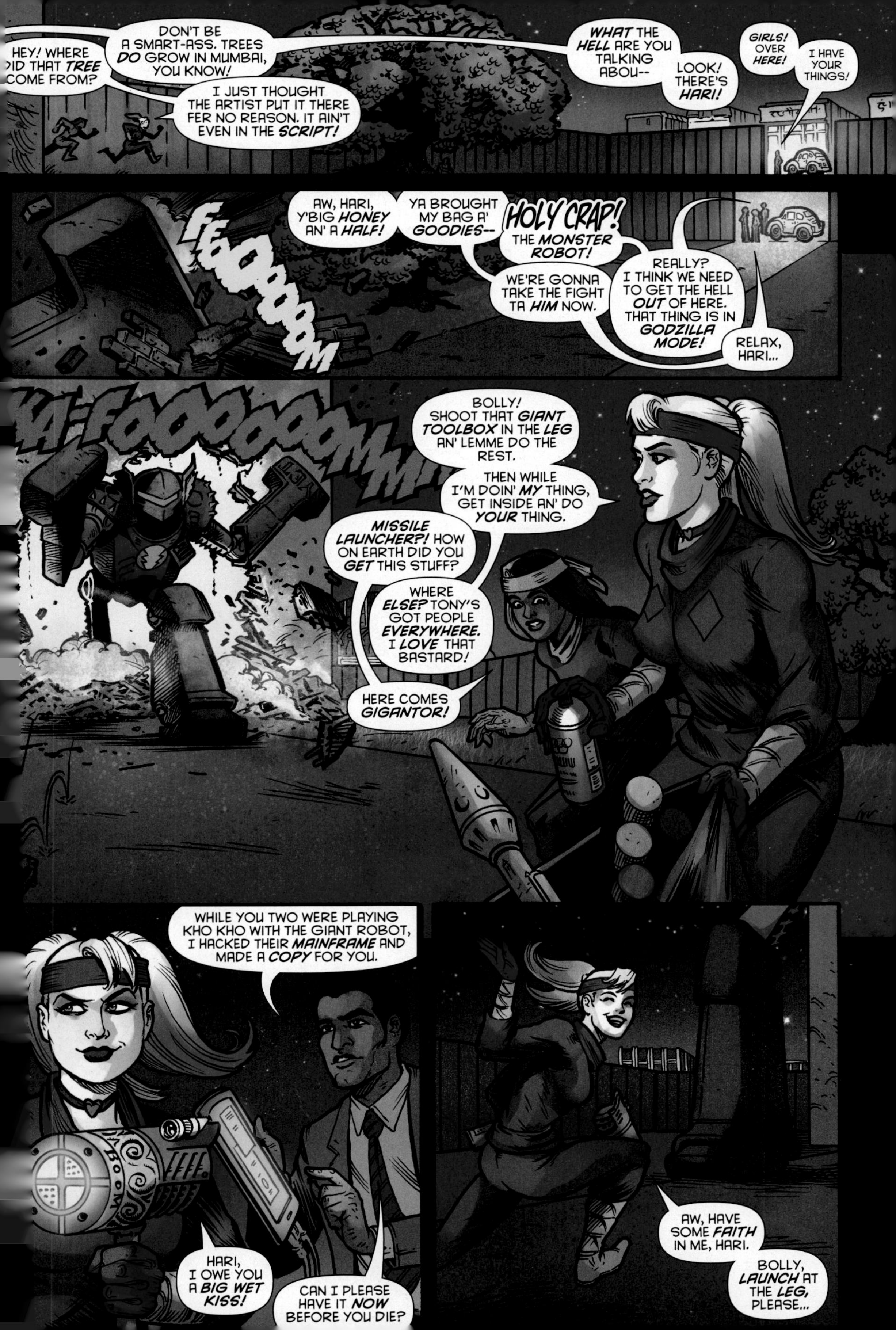
HEY! WHERE DID THAT TREE COME FROM?
DON'T BE A SMART-ASS. TREES DO GROW IN MUMBAI, YOU KNOW!
I JUST THOUGHT THE ARTIST PUT IT THERE FER NO REASON. IT AIN'T EVEN IN THE SCRIPT!
WHAT THE HELL ARE YOU TALKING ABOU--
LOOK! THERE'S HARI!
GIRLS! OVER HERE!
I HAVE YOUR THINGS!
FOOOOOOM
AW, HARI, Y'BIG HONEY AN' A HALF!
YA BROUGHT MY BAG A' GOODIES--
HOLY CRAP! THE MONSTER ROBOT!
WE'RE GONNA TAKE THE FIGHT TA HIM NOW.
REALLY? I THINK WE NEED TO GET THE HELL OUT OF HERE. THAT THING IS IN GODZILLA MODE!
RELAX, HARI...
KA-FOOOOOOMMM!
BOLLY! SHOOT THAT GIANT TOOLBOX IN THE LEG AN' LEMME DO THE REST.
THEN WHILE I'M DOIN' MY THING, GET INSIDE AN' DO YOUR THING.
MISSILE LAUNCHER?! HOW ON EARTH DID YOU GET THIS STUFF?
WHERE ELSE? TONY'S GOT PEOPLE EVERYWHERE. I LOVE THAT BASTARD!
HERE COMES GIGANTOR!
WHILE YOU TWO WERE PLAYING KHO KHO WITH THE GIANT ROBOT, I HACKED THEIR MAINFRAME AND MADE A COPY FOR YOU.
HARI, I OWE YOU A BIG WET KISS!
CAN I PLEASE HAVE IT NOW BEFORE YOU DIE?
AW, HAVE SOME FAITH IN ME, HARI.
BOLLY, LAUNCH AT THE LEG, PLEASE...

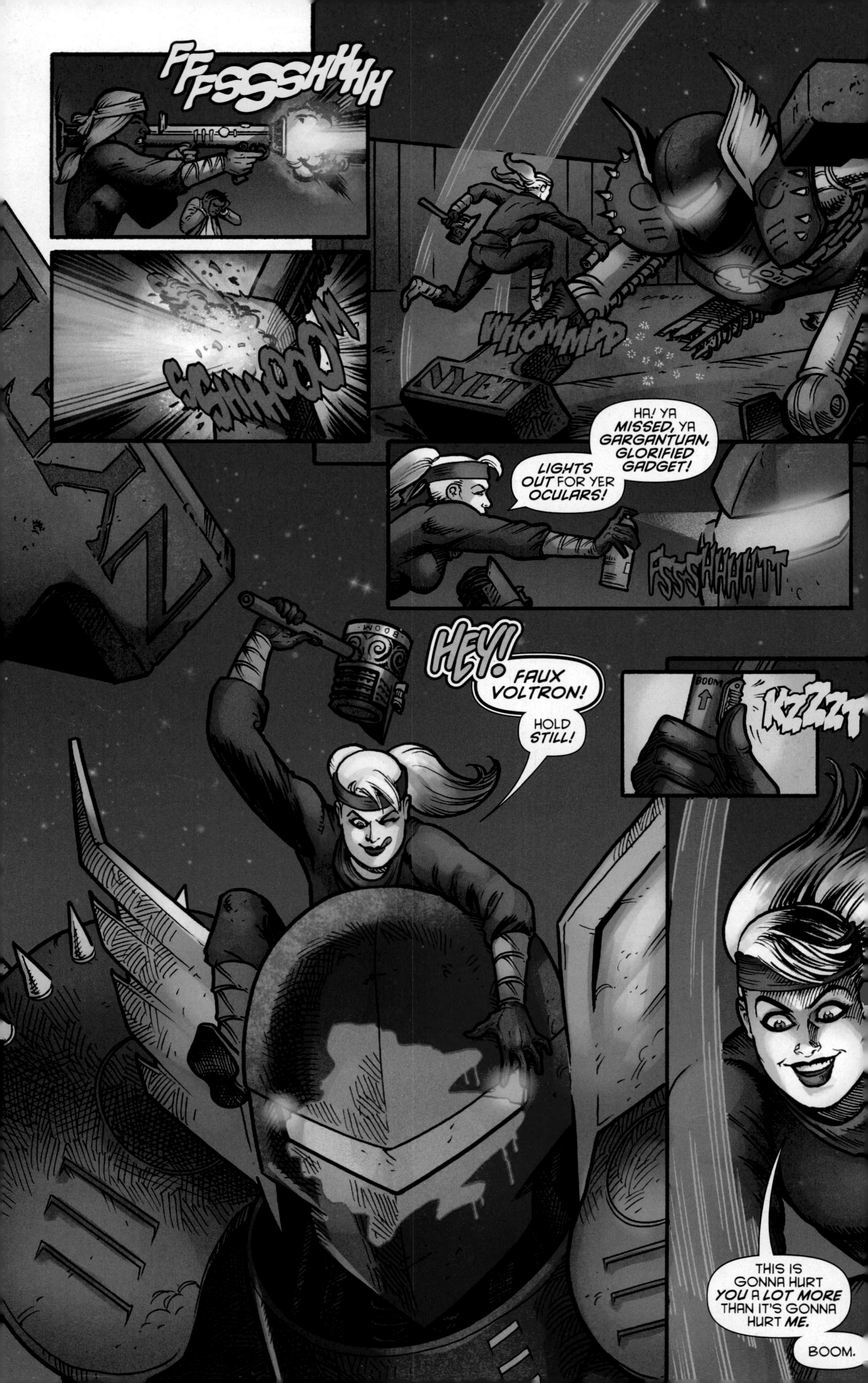
FFFSSSHHHHH
SSCHHOOOOM
WHOMMPP
NYET
HA! YA MISSED, YA GARGANTUAN, GLORIFIED GADGET!
LIGHTS OUT FOR YER OCULARS!
FSSSHHHHTT
HEY! FAUX VOLTRON!
HOLD STILL!
BOOM
KZZZT
THIS IS GONNA HURT YOU A LOT MORE THAN IT'S GONNA HURT ME.
BOOM.

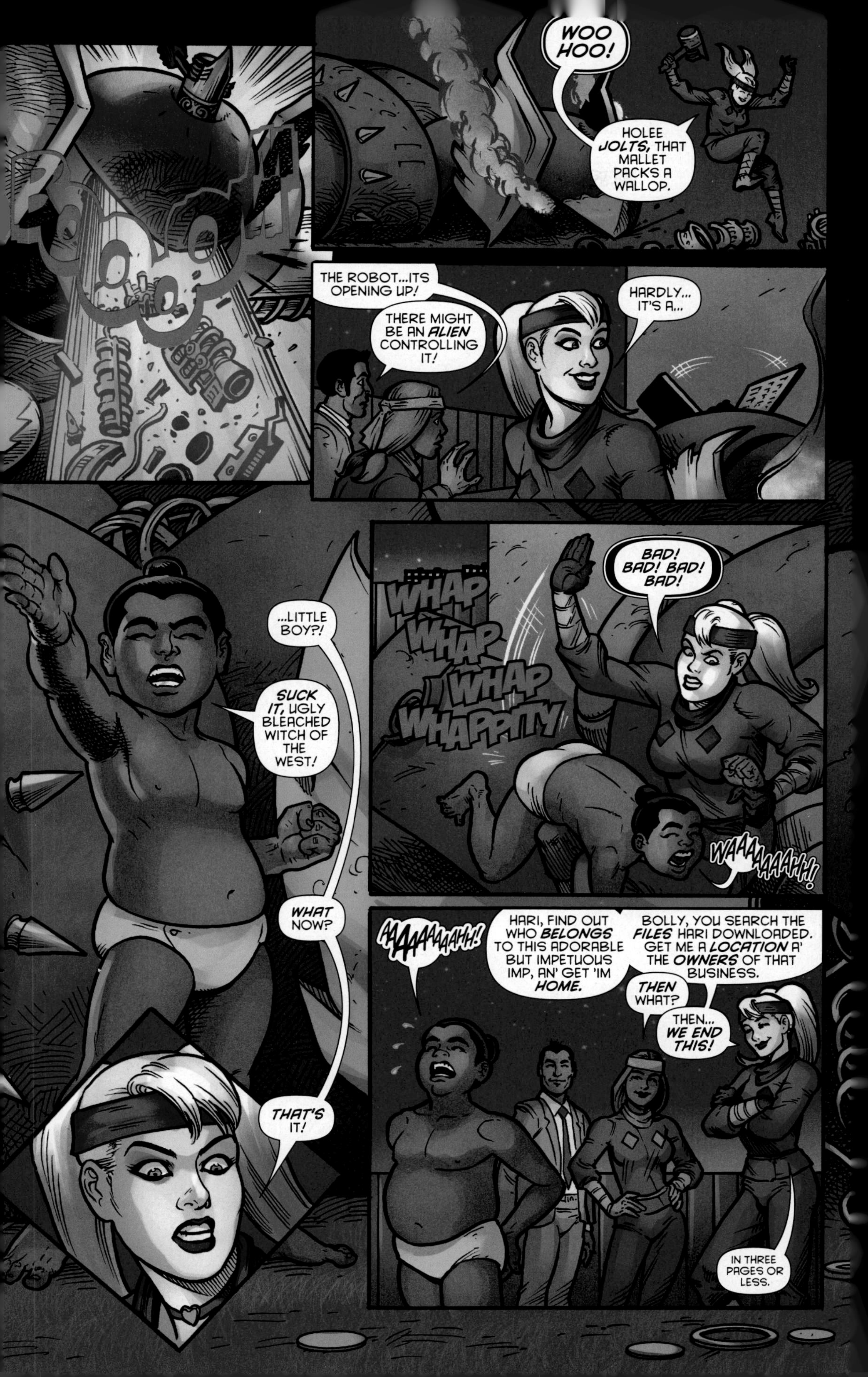
WOO HOO!
HOLEE JOLTS, THAT MALLET PACKS A WALLOP.
THE ROBOT...ITS OPENING UP!
THERE MIGHT BE AN ALIEN CONTROLLING IT!
HARDLY... IT'S A...
...LITTLE BOY?!
SUCK IT, UGLY BLEACHED WITCH OF THE WEST!
WHAT NOW?
THAT'S IT!
BAD! BAD! BAD! BAD!
WHAP WHAP WHAP WHAPPITY
WAAAAAAAAHH!
AAAAAAAAAHH!
HARI, FIND OUT WHO BELONGS TO THIS ADORABLE BUT IMPETUOUS IMP, AN' GET 'IM HOME.
BOLLY, YOU SEARCH THE FILES HARI DOWNLOADED. GET ME A LOCATION A' THE OWNERS OF THAT BUSINESS.
THEN WHAT?
THEN... WE END THIS!
IN THREE PAGES OR LESS.

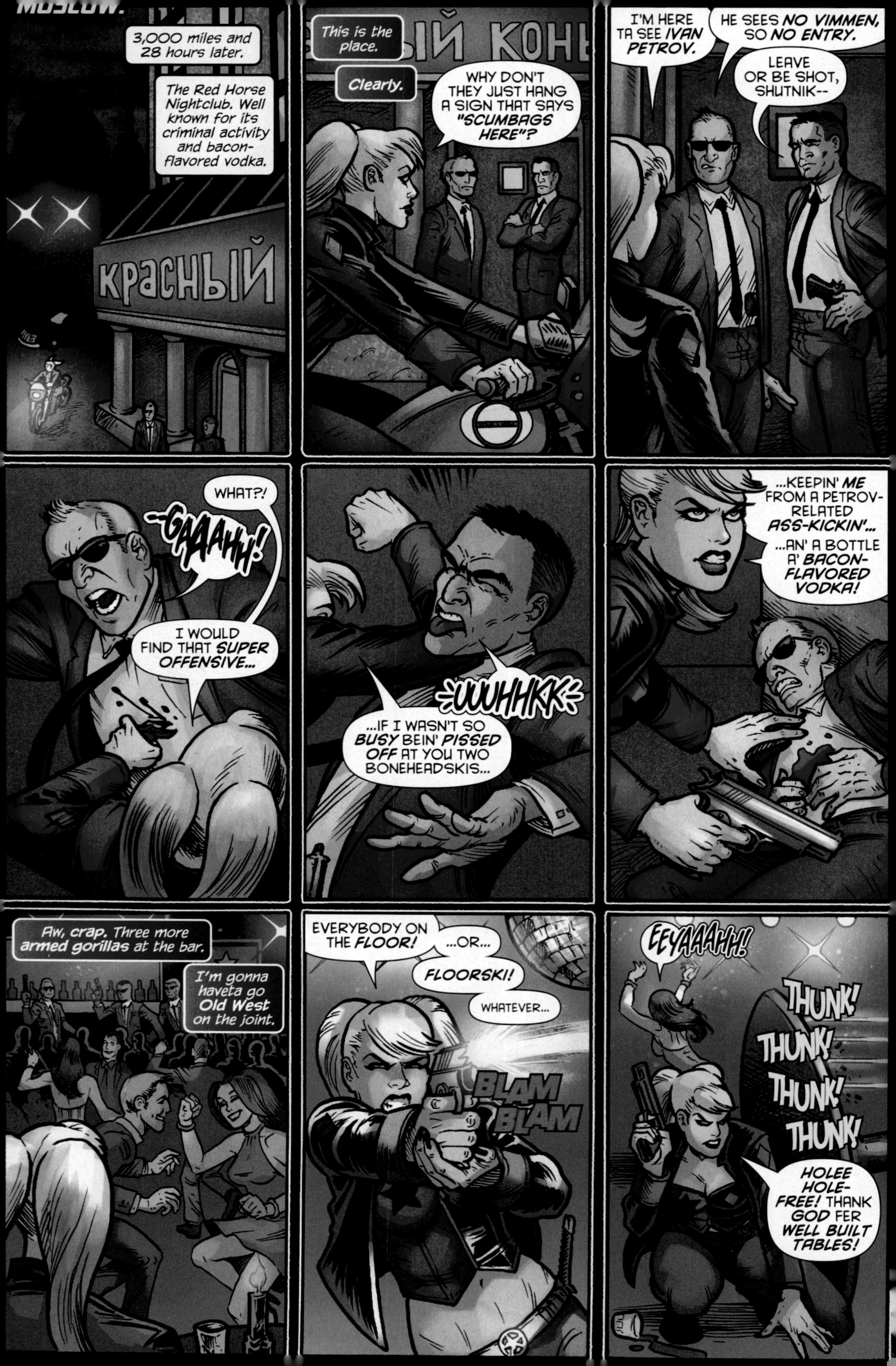
MOSCOW.
3,000 miles and 28 hours later.
The Red Horse Nightclub. Well known for its criminal activity and bacon-flavored vodka.
КРАСНЫЙ
This is the place.
Clearly.
WHY DON'T THEY JUST HANG A SIGN THAT SAYS "SCUMBAGS HERE"?
ЫЙ КОН
I'M HERE TA SEE IVAN PETROV.
HE SEES NO VIMMEN, SO NO ENTRY.
LEAVE OR BE SHOT, SHUTNIK--
WHAT?!
GAAAHH!
I WOULD FIND THAT SUPER OFFENSIVE...
UUUHHKK
...IF I WASN'T SO BUSY BEIN' PISSED OFF AT YOU TWO BONEHEADSKIS...
...KEEPIN' ME FROM A PETROV-RELATED ASS-KICKIN'...
...AN' A BOTTLE A' BACON-FLAVORED VODKA!
Aw, crap. Three more armed gorillas at the bar.
I'm gonna haveta go Old West on the joint.
EVERYBODY ON THE FLOOR!
...OR...
FLOORSKI!
WHATEVER...
BLAM BLAM
EEYAAAHH!
THUNK! THUNK! THUNK! THUNK!
HOLEE HOLE-FREE! THANK GOD FER WELL BUILT TABLES!

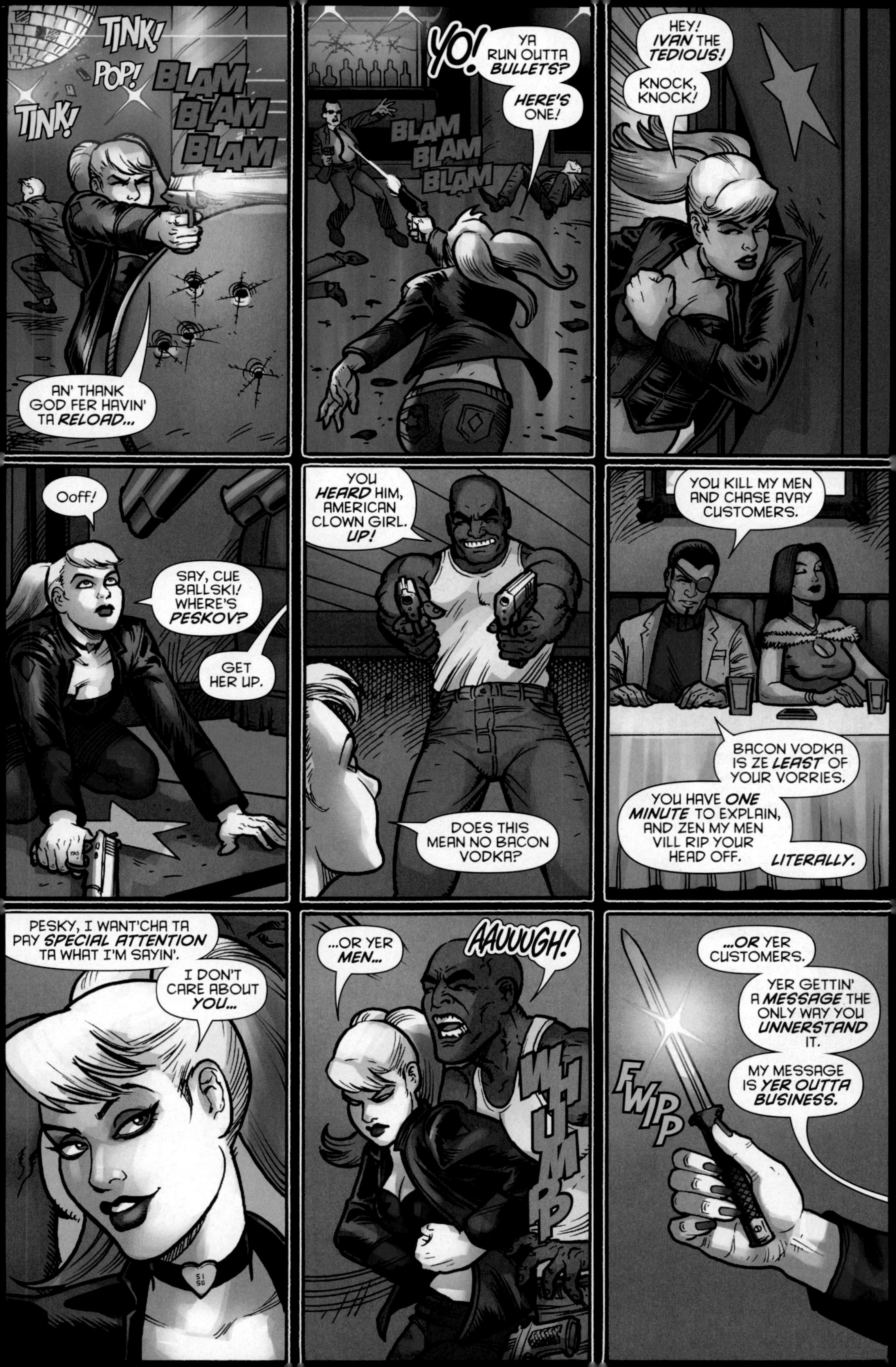
TINK!
POP!
BLAM BLAM BLAM
TINK!
AN' THANK GOD FER HAVIN' TA RELOAD...
YO!
YA RUN OUTTA BULLETS?
HERE'S ONE!
BLAM BLAM BLAM
HEY! IVAN THE TEDIOUS!
KNOCK, KNOCK!
Ooff!
SAY, CUE BALLSKI! WHERE'S PESKOV?
GET HER UP.
YOU HEARD HIM, AMERICAN CLOWN GIRL. UP!
DOES THIS MEAN NO BACON VODKA?
YOU KILL MY MEN AND CHASE AVAY CUSTOMERS.
BACON VODKA IS ZE LEAST OF YOUR VORRIES.
YOU HAVE ONE MINUTE TO EXPLAIN, AND ZEN MY MEN VILL RIP YOUR HEAD OFF. LITERALLY.
PESKY, I WANT'CHA TA PAY SPECIAL ATTENTION TA WHAT I'M SAYIN'.
I DON'T CARE ABOUT YOU...
...OR YER MEN...
AAUUUGH!
WHUMP
...OR YER CUSTOMERS.
YER GETTIN' A MESSAGE THE ONLY WAY YOU UNNERSTAND IT.
MY MESSAGE IS YER OUTTA BUSINESS.
FWIPP

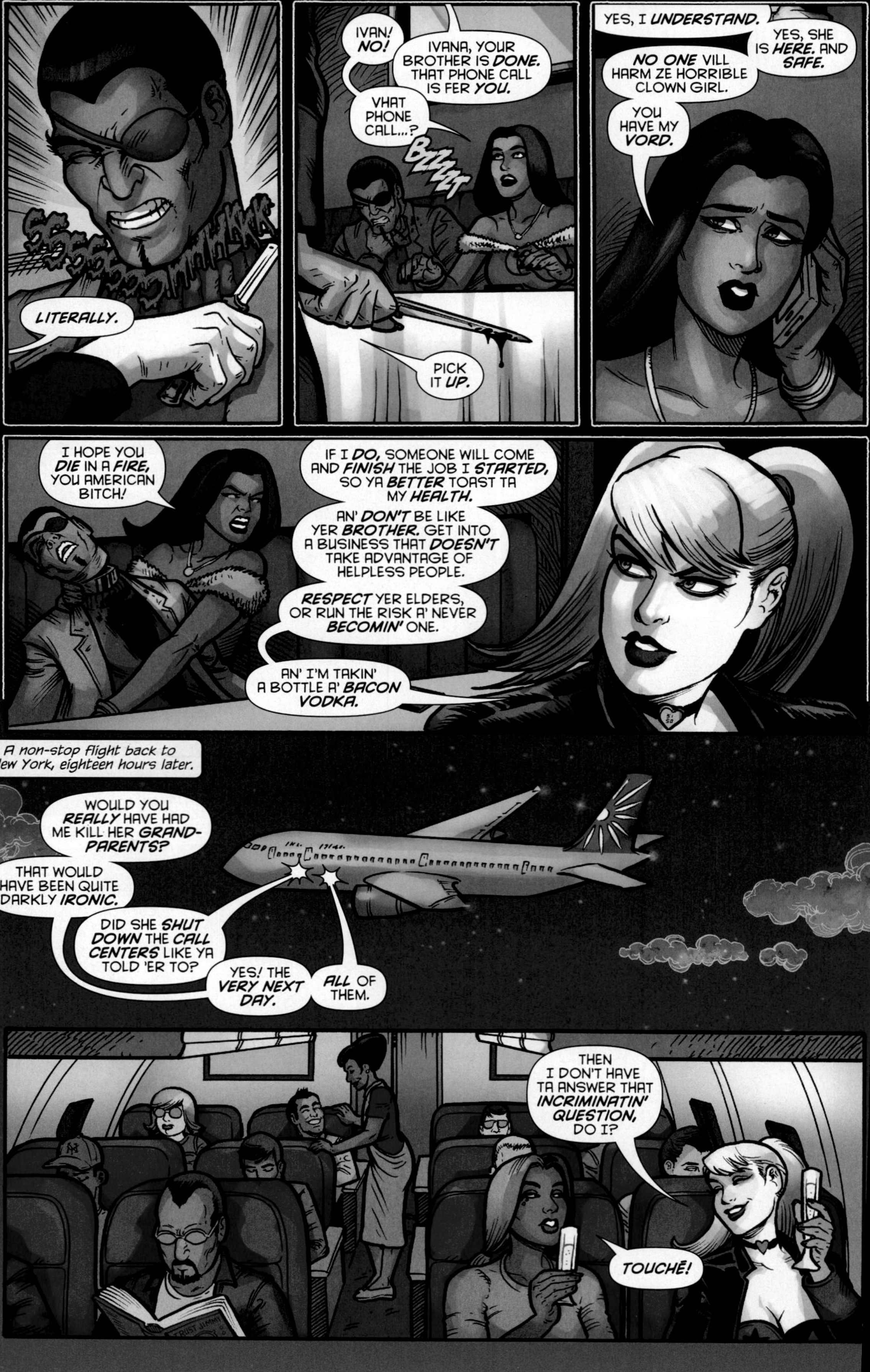
SSSSSSSHHHHKKK
LITERALLY.
IVAN! NO!
IVANA, YOUR BROTHER IS DONE. THAT PHONE CALL IS FER YOU.
VHAT PHONE CALL...?
BZZZZT
PICK IT UP.
YES, I UNDERSTAND.
YES, SHE IS HERE. AND SAFE.
NO ONE VILL HARM ZE HORRIBLE CLOWN GIRL.
YOU HAVE MY VORD.
I HOPE YOU DIE IN A FIRE, YOU AMERICAN BITCH!
IF I DO, SOMEONE WILL COME AND FINISH THE JOB I STARTED, SO YA BETTER TOAST TA MY HEALTH.
AN' DON'T BE LIKE YER BROTHER. GET INTO A BUSINESS THAT DOESN'T TAKE ADVANTAGE OF HELPLESS PEOPLE.
RESPECT YER ELDERS, OR RUN THE RISK A' NEVER BECOMIN' ONE.
AN' I'M TAKIN' A BOTTLE A' BACON VODKA.
A non-stop flight back to New York, eighteen hours later.
WOULD YOU REALLY HAVE HAD ME KILL HER GRAND-PARENTS?
THAT WOULD HAVE BEEN QUITE DARKLY IRONIC.
DID SHE SHUT DOWN THE CALL CENTERS LIKE YA TOLD 'ER TO?
YES! THE VERY NEXT DAY.
ALL OF THEM.
THEN I DON'T HAVE TA ANSWER THAT INCRIMINATIN' QUESTION, DO I?
TOUCHÉ!

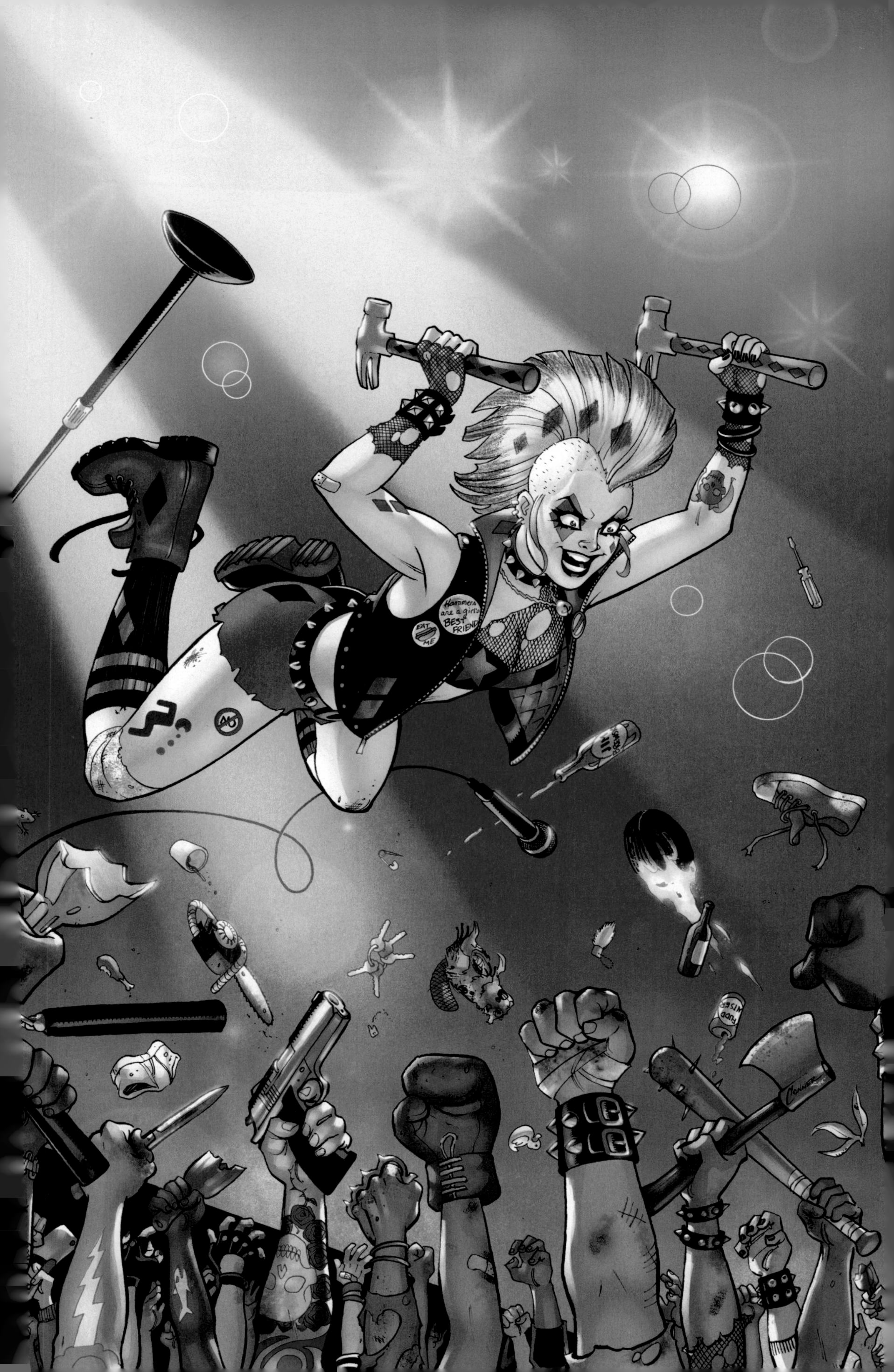
Hammers are a girl's BEST FRIEND
EAT ME
FUDD WISER
CONNER

UNDERCOVER PUNKER PART 1: EAT TO THIS BEAT

AMANDA CONNER and JIMMY PALMIOTTI writers ∗ JOHN TIMMS artist
ALEX SINCLAIR colorist ∗ DAVE SHARPE letterer

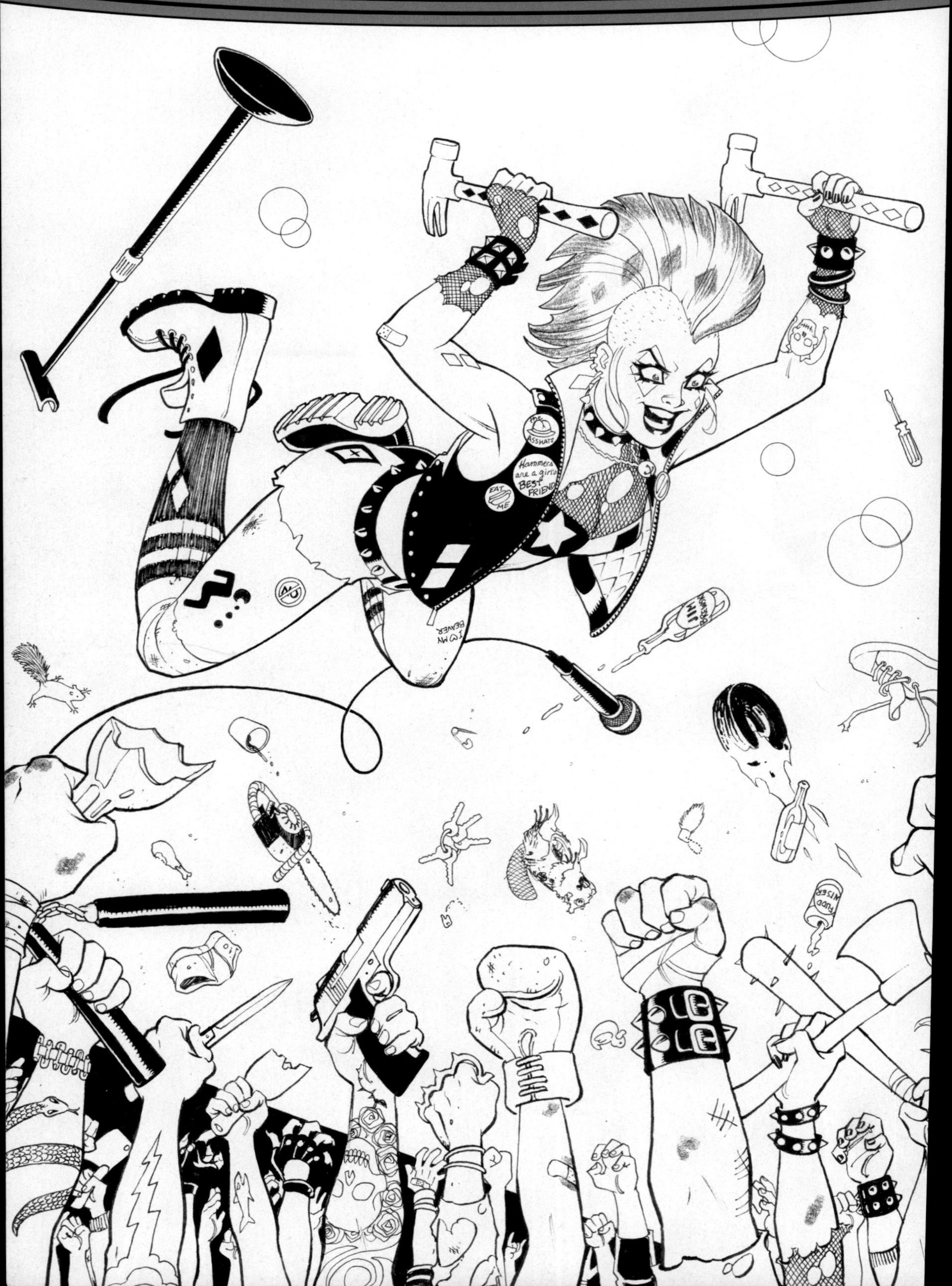

The ASSHATS
Hammers are a girl's BEST FRIEND
EAT ME

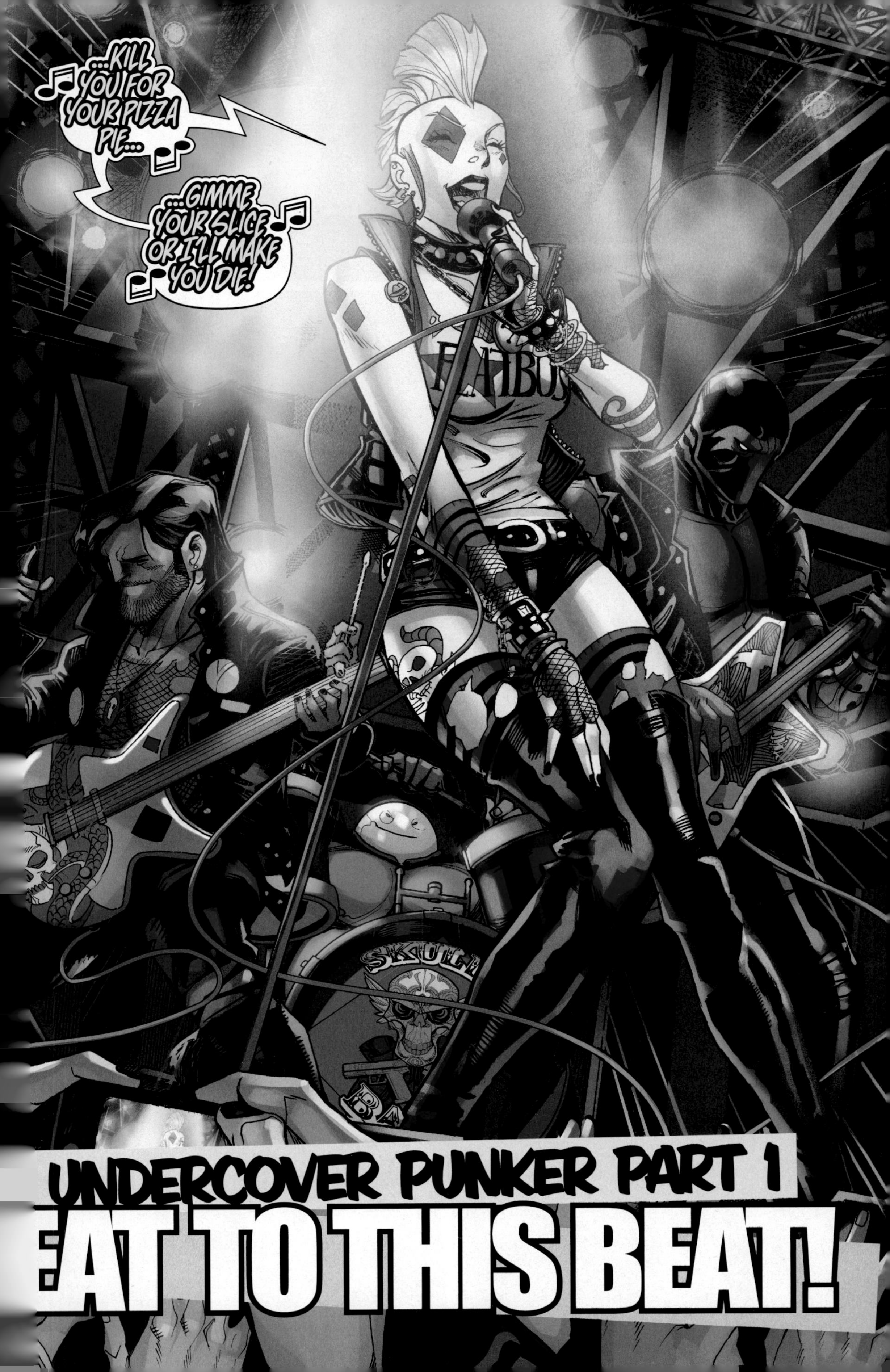
...KILL YOU FOR YOUR PIZZA PIE...
...GIMME YOUR SLICE OR I'LL MAKE YOU DIE!
UNDERCOVER PUNKER PART 1
EAT TO THIS BEAT!

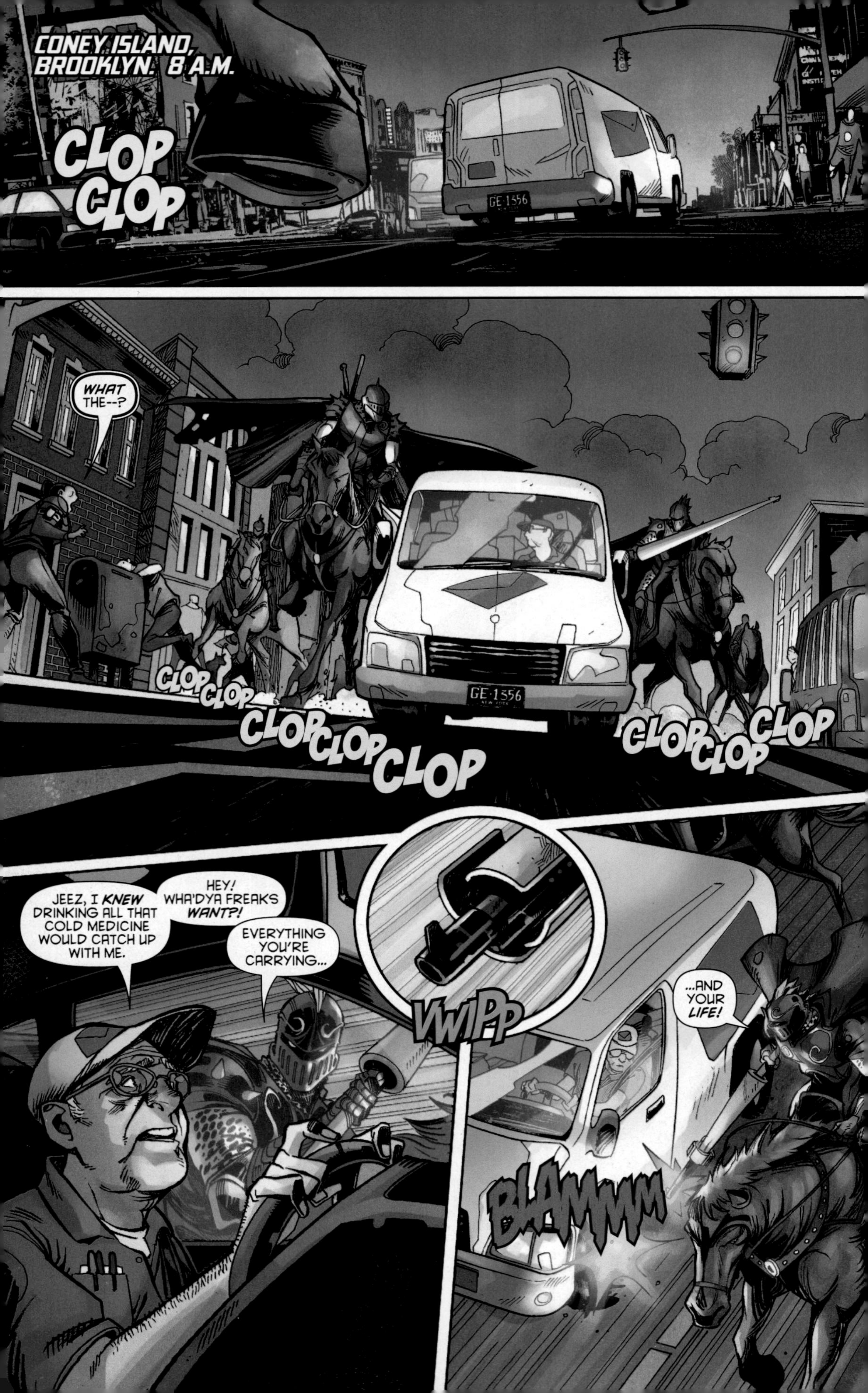
CONEY ISLAND, BROOKLYN. 8 A.M.
CLOP CLOP
WHAT THE--?
CLOP CLOP CLOP CLOP CLOP
CLOP CLOP CLOP
JEEZ, I KNEW DRINKING ALL THAT COLD MEDICINE WOULD CATCH UP WITH ME.
HEY! WHA'DYA FREAKS WANT?!
EVERYTHING YOU'RE CARRYING...
VWIPP
...AND YOUR LIFE!
BLAMMM

SMASH

SSKKRREEELLE

BOK

WHAT THE *HELL* WAS *THAT?*

HOPEFULLY THE *BOUNDLESS BEAVER DAM* OF *ETERNITY,* SO'S I CAN GO BACK TA *SLEEP.*

RRROOOHHH

Y'*HEAR* THAT, TONY?! WE'RE *UNDER ATTACK!*

RELAX, NUTBAGS. IT SOUNDED LIKE A *CAR CRASH.*

WELL THEN WHY ARE YA CARRYIN' A *SHOTGUN?*

SHOT*GUNS.* I BROUGHT ONE FOR *YOU.*

AWW, THAT'S SO *THOUGHTFUL.*

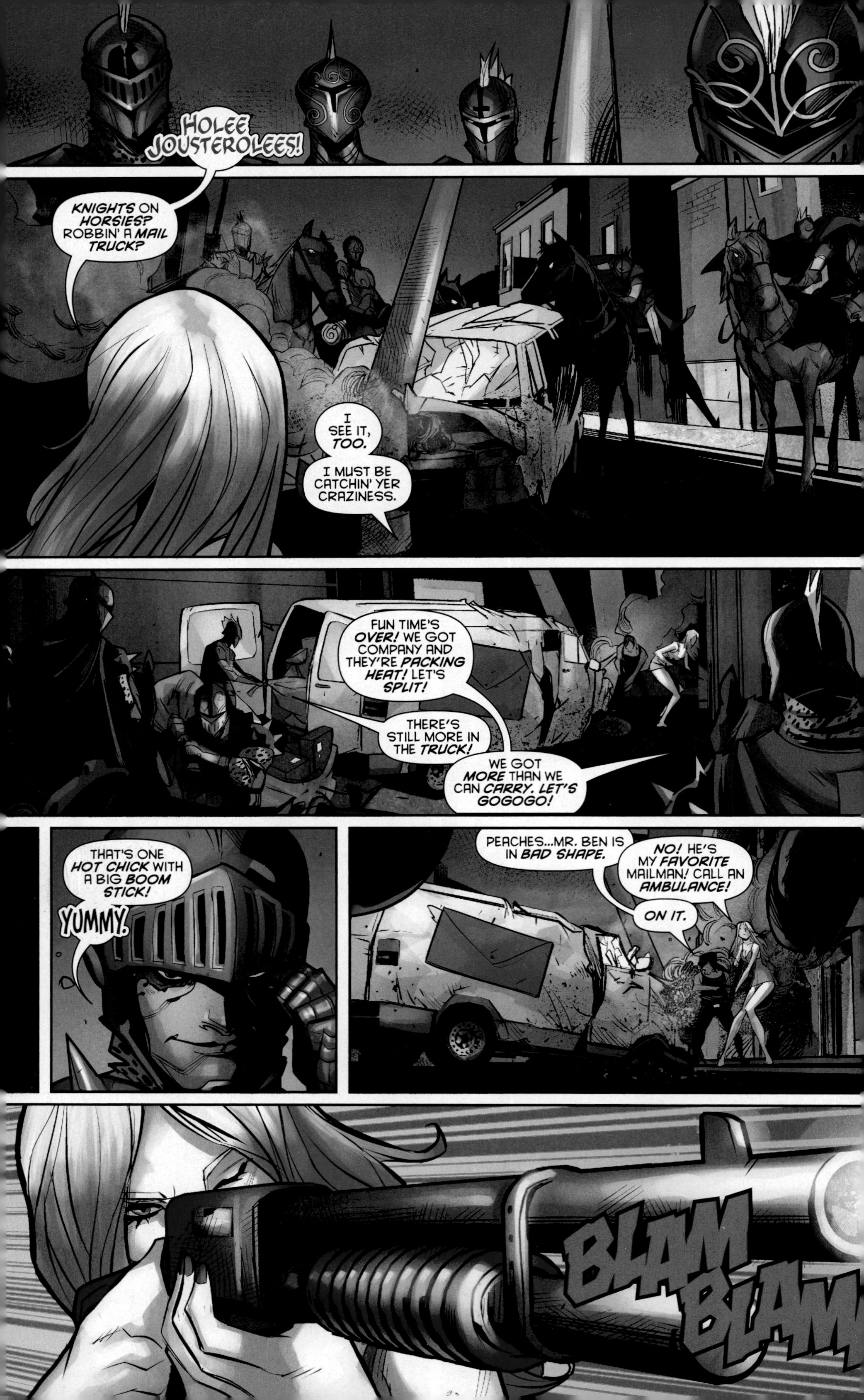
HOLEE JOUSTEROLEES!
KNIGHTS ON HORSIES? ROBBIN' A MAIL TRUCK?
I SEE IT, TOO.
I MUST BE CATCHIN' YER CRAZINESS.
FUN TIME'S OVER! WE GOT COMPANY AND THEY'RE PACKING HEAT! LET'S SPLIT!
THERE'S STILL MORE IN THE TRUCK!
WE GOT MORE THAN WE CAN CARRY. LET'S GOGOGO!
THAT'S ONE HOT CHICK WITH A BIG BOOM STICK!
YUMMY.
PEACHES...MR. BEN IS IN BAD SHAPE.
NO! HE'S MY FAVORITE MAILMAN! CALL AN AMBULANCE!
ON IT.
BLAM
BLAM

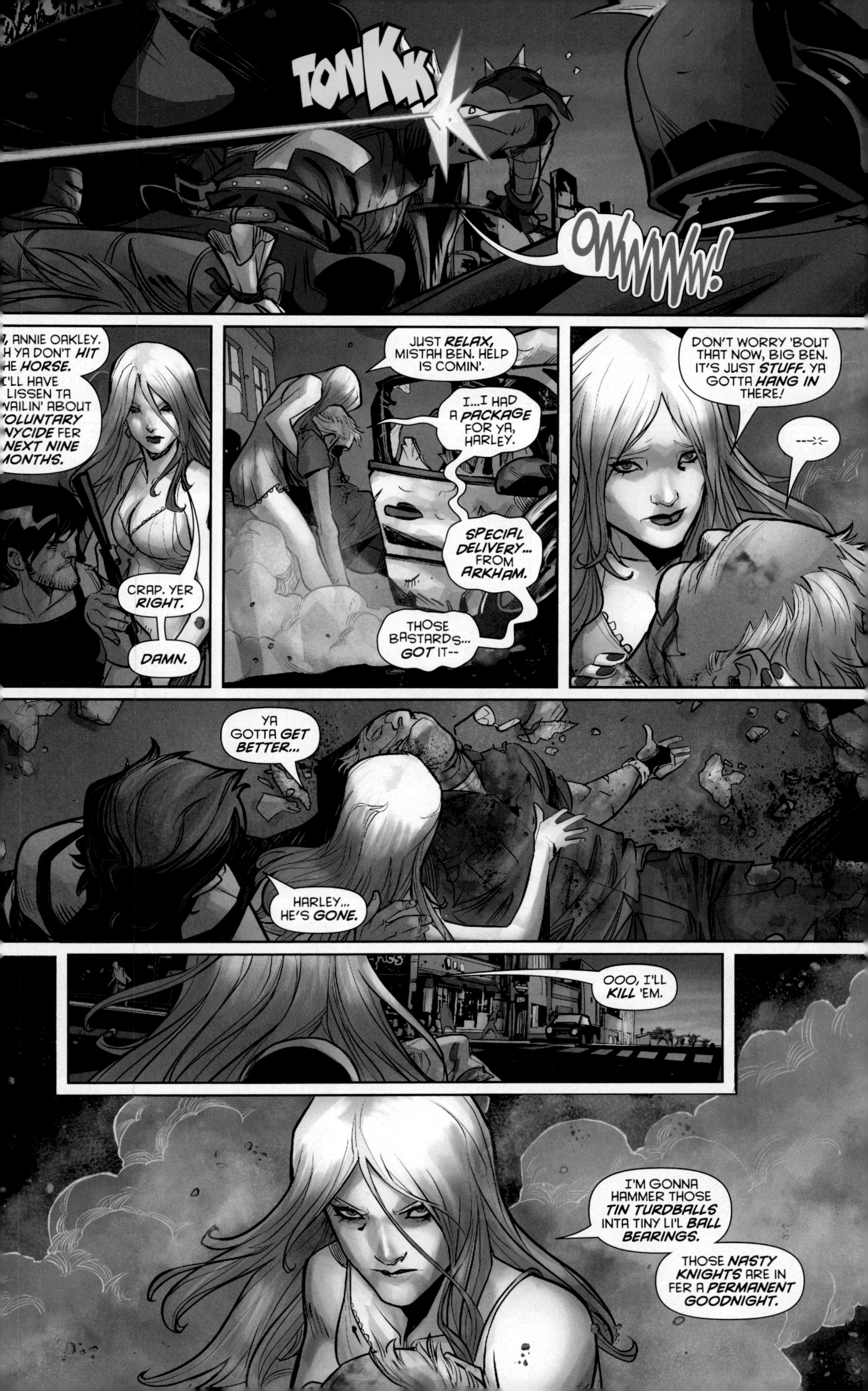
TONKK
OWWWW!
, ANNIE OAKLEY. H YA DON'T HIT HE HORSE. 'LL HAVE LISSEN TA WAILIN' ABOUT VOLUNTARY NYCIDE FER NEXT NINE MONTHS.
CRAP. YER RIGHT.
DAMN.
JUST RELAX, MISTAH BEN. HELP IS COMIN'.
I...I HAD A PACKAGE FOR YA, HARLEY.
SPECIAL DELIVERY... FROM ARKHAM.
THOSE BASTARDS... GOT IT--
DON'T WORRY 'BOUT THAT NOW, BIG BEN. IT'S JUST STUFF. YA GOTTA HANG IN THERE!
--:-
YA GOTTA GET BETTER...
HARLEY... HE'S GONE.
OOO, I'LL KILL 'EM.
I'M GONNA HAMMER THOSE TIN TURDBALLS INTA TINY LI'L BALL BEARINGS.
THOSE NASTY KNIGHTS ARE IN FER A PERMANENT GOODNIGHT.

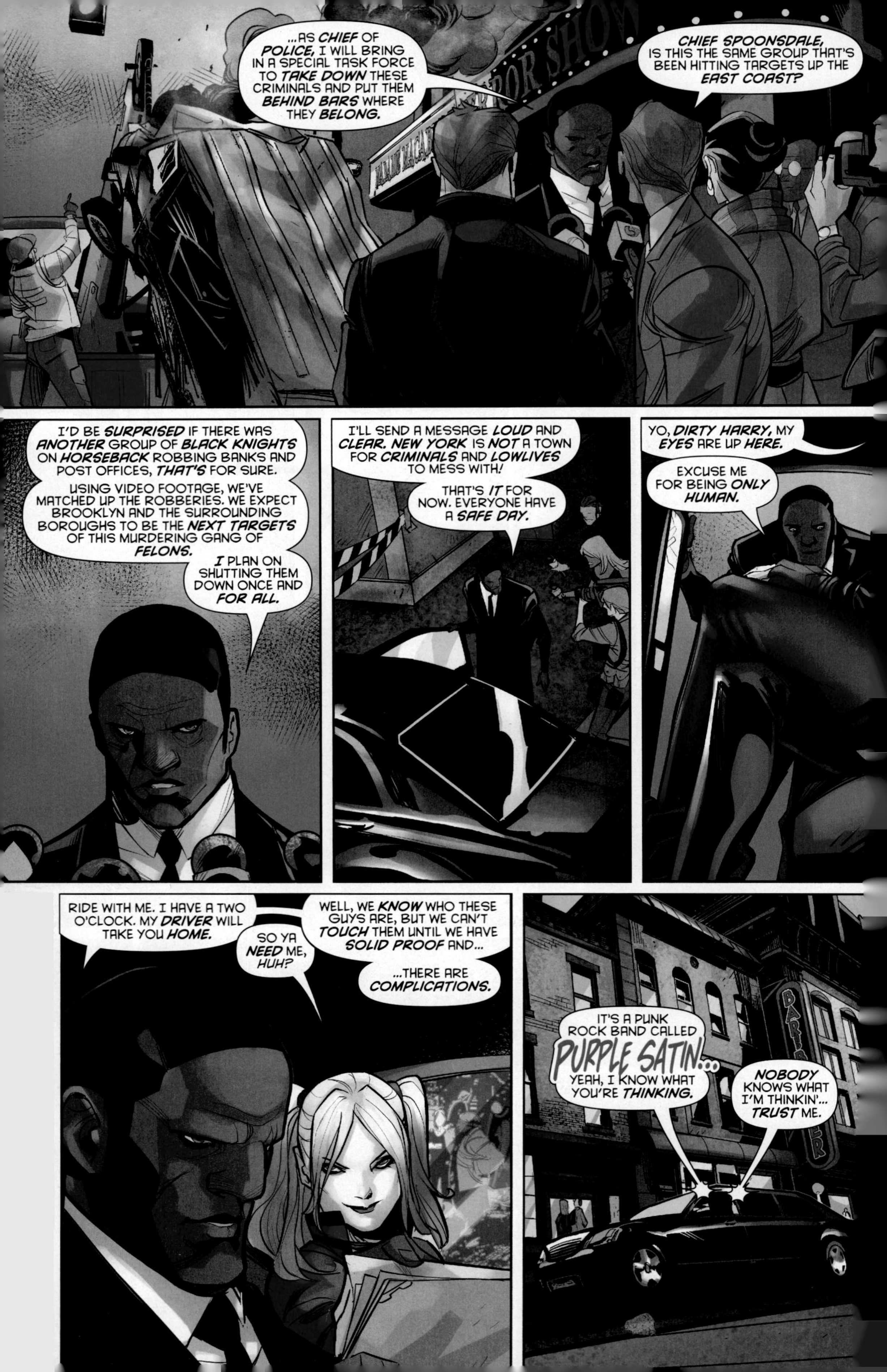
...AS CHIEF OF POLICE, I WILL BRING IN A SPECIAL TASK FORCE TO TAKE DOWN THESE CRIMINALS AND PUT THEM BEHIND BARS WHERE THEY BELONG.
CHIEF SPOONSDALE, IS THIS THE SAME GROUP THAT'S BEEN HITTING TARGETS UP THE EAST COAST?
I'D BE SURPRISED IF THERE WAS ANOTHER GROUP OF BLACK KNIGHTS ON HORSEBACK ROBBING BANKS AND POST OFFICES, THAT'S FOR SURE.
USING VIDEO FOOTAGE, WE'VE MATCHED UP THE ROBBERIES. WE EXPECT BROOKLYN AND THE SURROUNDING BOROUGHS TO BE THE NEXT TARGETS OF THIS MURDERING GANG OF FELONS.
I PLAN ON SHUTTING THEM DOWN ONCE AND FOR ALL.
I'LL SEND A MESSAGE LOUD AND CLEAR. NEW YORK IS NOT A TOWN FOR CRIMINALS AND LOWLIVES TO MESS WITH!
THAT'S IT FOR NOW. EVERYONE HAVE A SAFE DAY.
YO, DIRTY HARRY, MY EYES ARE UP HERE.
EXCUSE ME FOR BEING ONLY HUMAN.
RIDE WITH ME. I HAVE A TWO O'CLOCK. MY DRIVER WILL TAKE YOU HOME.
SO YA NEED ME, HUH?
WELL, WE KNOW WHO THESE GUYS ARE, BUT WE CAN'T TOUCH THEM UNTIL WE HAVE SOLID PROOF AND...
...THERE ARE COMPLICATIONS.
IT'S A PUNK ROCK BAND CALLED PURPLE SATIN...
YEAH, I KNOW WHAT YOU'RE THINKING.
NOBODY KNOWS WHAT I'M THINKIN'... TRUST ME.

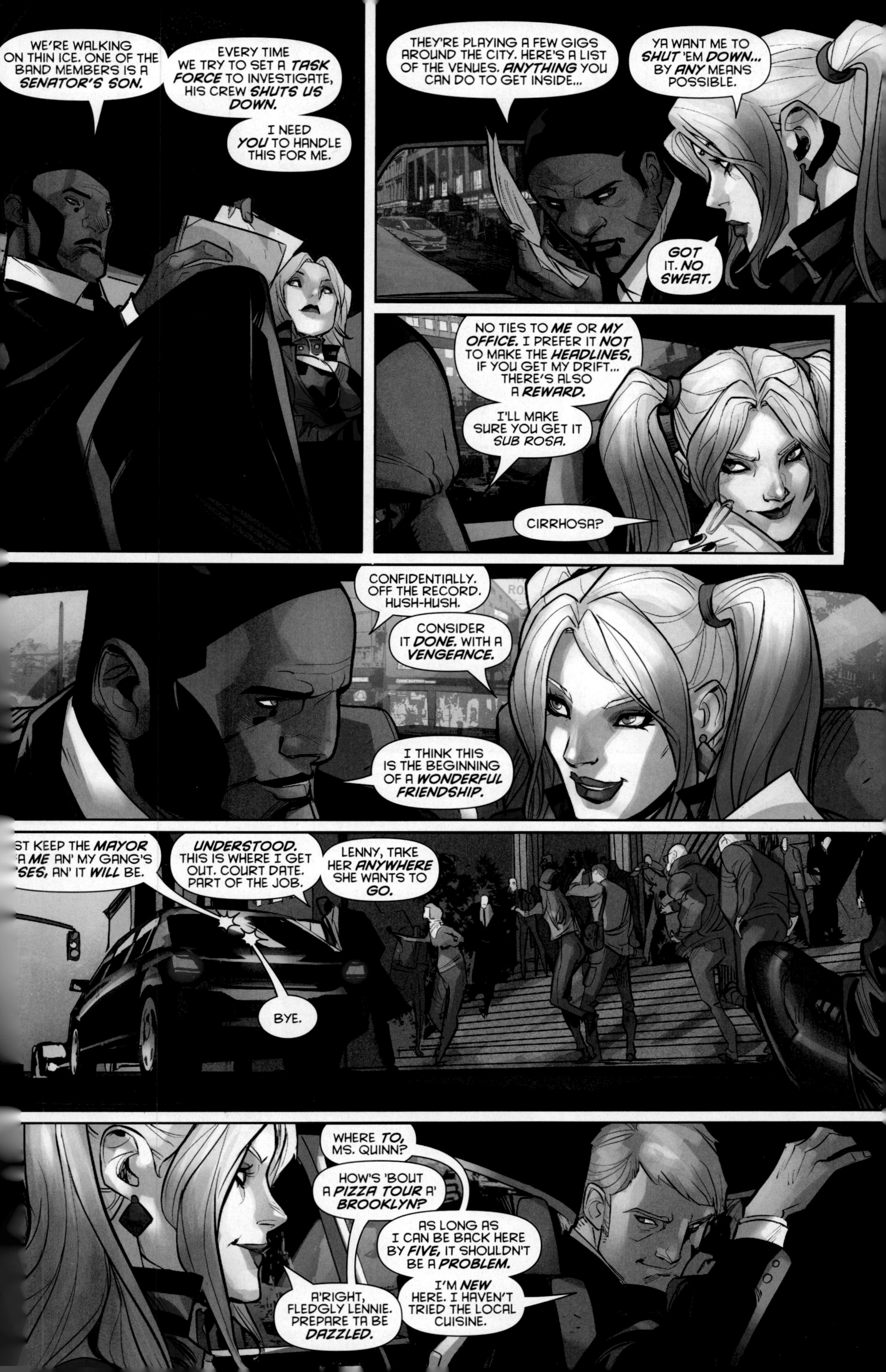
WE'RE WALKING ON THIN ICE. ONE OF THE BAND MEMBERS IS A SENATOR'S SON.
EVERY TIME WE TRY TO SET A TASK FORCE TO INVESTIGATE, HIS CREW SHUTS US DOWN.
I NEED YOU TO HANDLE THIS FOR ME.
THEY'RE PLAYING A FEW GIGS AROUND THE CITY. HERE'S A LIST OF THE VENUES. ANYTHING YOU CAN DO TO GET INSIDE...
YA WANT ME TO SHUT 'EM DOWN... BY ANY MEANS POSSIBLE.
GOT IT. NO SWEAT.
NO TIES TO ME OR MY OFFICE. I PREFER IT NOT TO MAKE THE HEADLINES, IF YOU GET MY DRIFT... THERE'S ALSO A REWARD.
I'LL MAKE SURE YOU GET IT SUB ROSA.
CIRRHOSA?
CONFIDENTIALLY. OFF THE RECORD. HUSH-HUSH.
CONSIDER IT DONE. WITH A VENGEANCE.
I THINK THIS IS THE BEGINNING OF A WONDERFUL FRIENDSHIP.
ST KEEP THE MAYOR
A ME AN' MY GANG'S
SES, AN' IT WILL BE.
UNDERSTOOD. THIS IS WHERE I GET OUT. COURT DATE. PART OF THE JOB.
LENNY, TAKE HER ANYWHERE SHE WANTS TO GO.
BYE.
WHERE TO, MS. QUINN?
HOW'S 'BOUT A PIZZA TOUR A' BROOKLYN?
AS LONG AS I CAN BE BACK HERE BY FIVE, IT SHOULDN'T BE A PROBLEM.
I'M NEW HERE. I HAVEN'T TRIED THE LOCAL CUISINE.
A'RIGHT, FLEDGLY LENNIE. PREPARE TA BE DAZZLED.

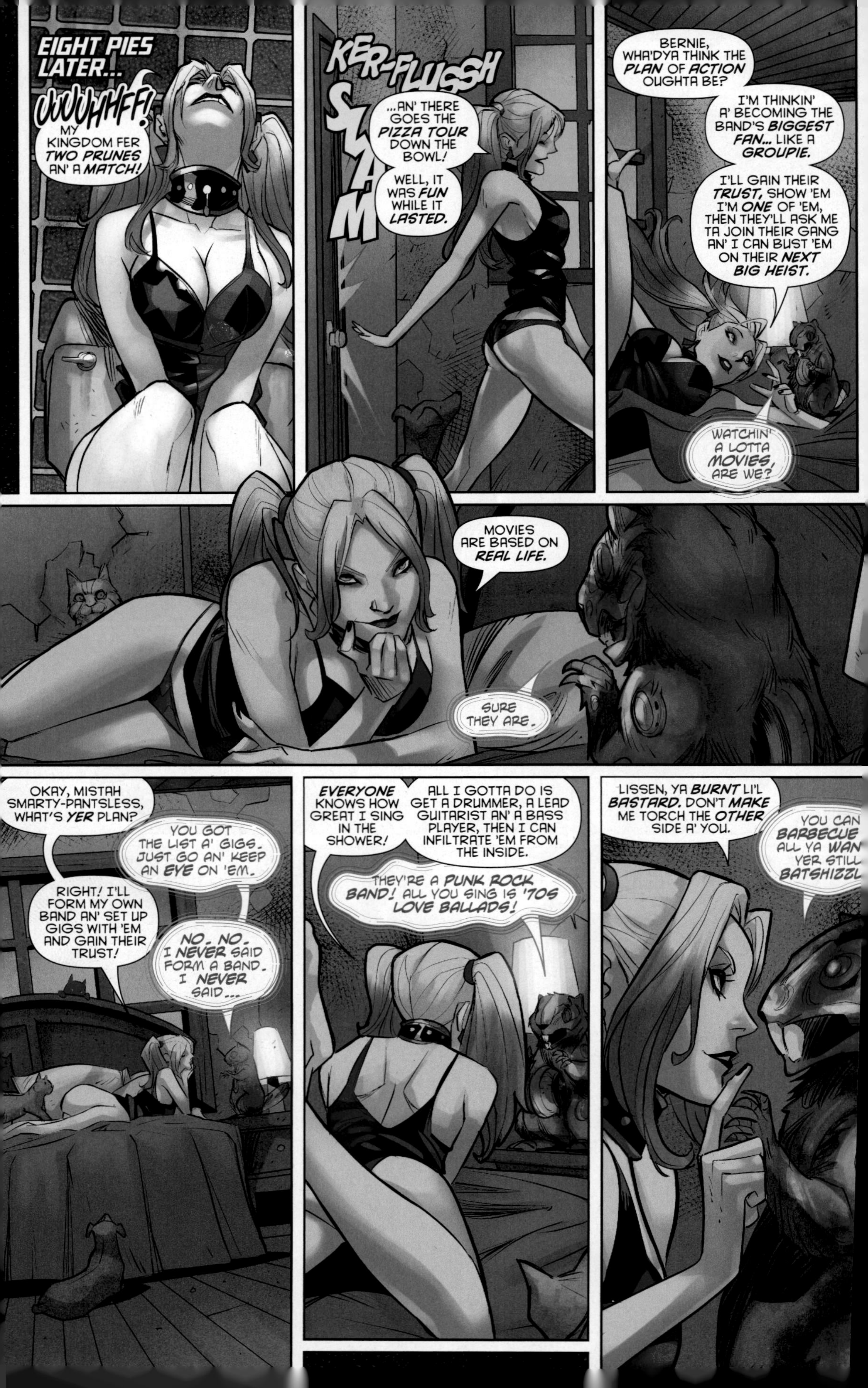
EIGHT PIES LATER...
OOOUHHFF!
MY KINGDOM FER TWO PRUNES AN' A MATCH!
KER-FLUSSH
SLAM
...AN' THERE GOES THE PIZZA TOUR DOWN THE BOWL!
WELL, IT WAS FUN WHILE IT LASTED.
BERNIE, WHA'DYA THINK THE PLAN OF ACTION OUGHTA BE?
I'M THINKIN' A' BECOMING THE BAND'S BIGGEST FAN... LIKE A GROUPIE.
I'LL GAIN THEIR TRUST, SHOW 'EM I'M ONE OF 'EM, THEN THEY'LL ASK ME TA JOIN THEIR GANG AN' I CAN BUST 'EM ON THEIR NEXT BIG HEIST.
WATCHIN' A LOTTA MOVIES, ARE WE?
MOVIES ARE BASED ON REAL LIFE.
SURE THEY ARE.
OKAY, MISTAH SMARTY-PANTSLESS, WHAT'S YER PLAN?
YOU GOT THE LIST A' GIGS. JUST GO AN' KEEP AN EYE ON 'EM.
RIGHT! I'LL FORM MY OWN BAND AN' SET UP GIGS WITH 'EM AND GAIN THEIR TRUST!
NO. NO. I NEVER SAID FORM A BAND. I NEVER SAID...
EVERYONE KNOWS HOW GREAT I SING IN THE SHOWER!
ALL I GOTTA DO IS GET A DRUMMER, A LEAD GUITARIST AN' A BASS PLAYER, THEN I CAN INFILTRATE 'EM FROM THE INSIDE.
THEY'RE A PUNK ROCK BAND! ALL YOU SING IS '70S LOVE BALLADS!
LISSEN, YA BURNT LI'L BASTARD. DON'T MAKE ME TORCH THE OTHER SIDE A' YOU.
YOU CAN BARBECUE ALL YA WAN YER STILL BATSHIZZL

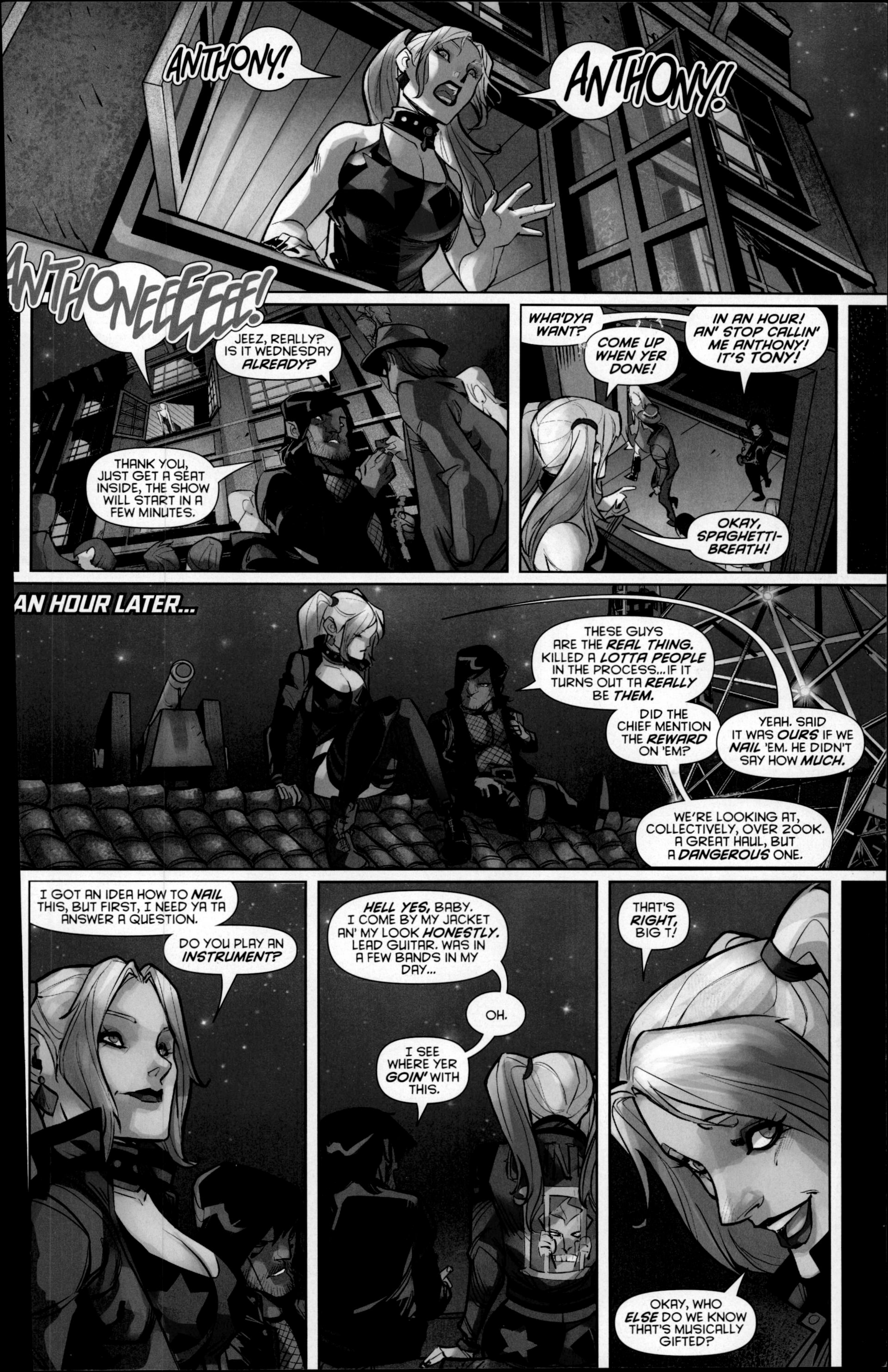
ANTHONY!
ANTHONY!
ANTHONEEEEEEE!
JEEZ, REALLY? IS IT WEDNESDAY ALREADY?
THANK YOU, JUST GET A SEAT INSIDE, THE SHOW WILL START IN A FEW MINUTES.
WHA'DYA WANT?
COME UP WHEN YER DONE!
IN AN HOUR! AN' STOP CALLIN' ME ANTHONY! IT'S TONY!
OKAY, SPAGHETTI-BREATH!
AN HOUR LATER...
THESE GUYS ARE THE REAL THING. KILLED A LOTTA PEOPLE IN THE PROCESS...IF IT TURNS OUT TA REALLY BE THEM.
DID THE CHIEF MENTION THE REWARD ON 'EM?
YEAH. SAID IT WAS OURS IF WE NAIL 'EM. HE DIDN'T SAY HOW MUCH.
WE'RE LOOKING AT, COLLECTIVELY, OVER 200K. A GREAT HAUL, BUT A DANGEROUS ONE.
I GOT AN IDEA HOW TO NAIL THIS, BUT FIRST, I NEED YA TA ANSWER A QUESTION.
DO YOU PLAY AN INSTRUMENT?
HELL YES, BABY. I COME BY MY JACKET AN' MY LOOK HONESTLY. LEAD GUITAR. WAS IN A FEW BANDS IN MY DAY...
OH.
I SEE WHERE YER GOIN' WITH THIS.
THAT'S RIGHT, BIG T!
OKAY, WHO ELSE DO WE KNOW THAT'S MUSICALLY GIFTED?

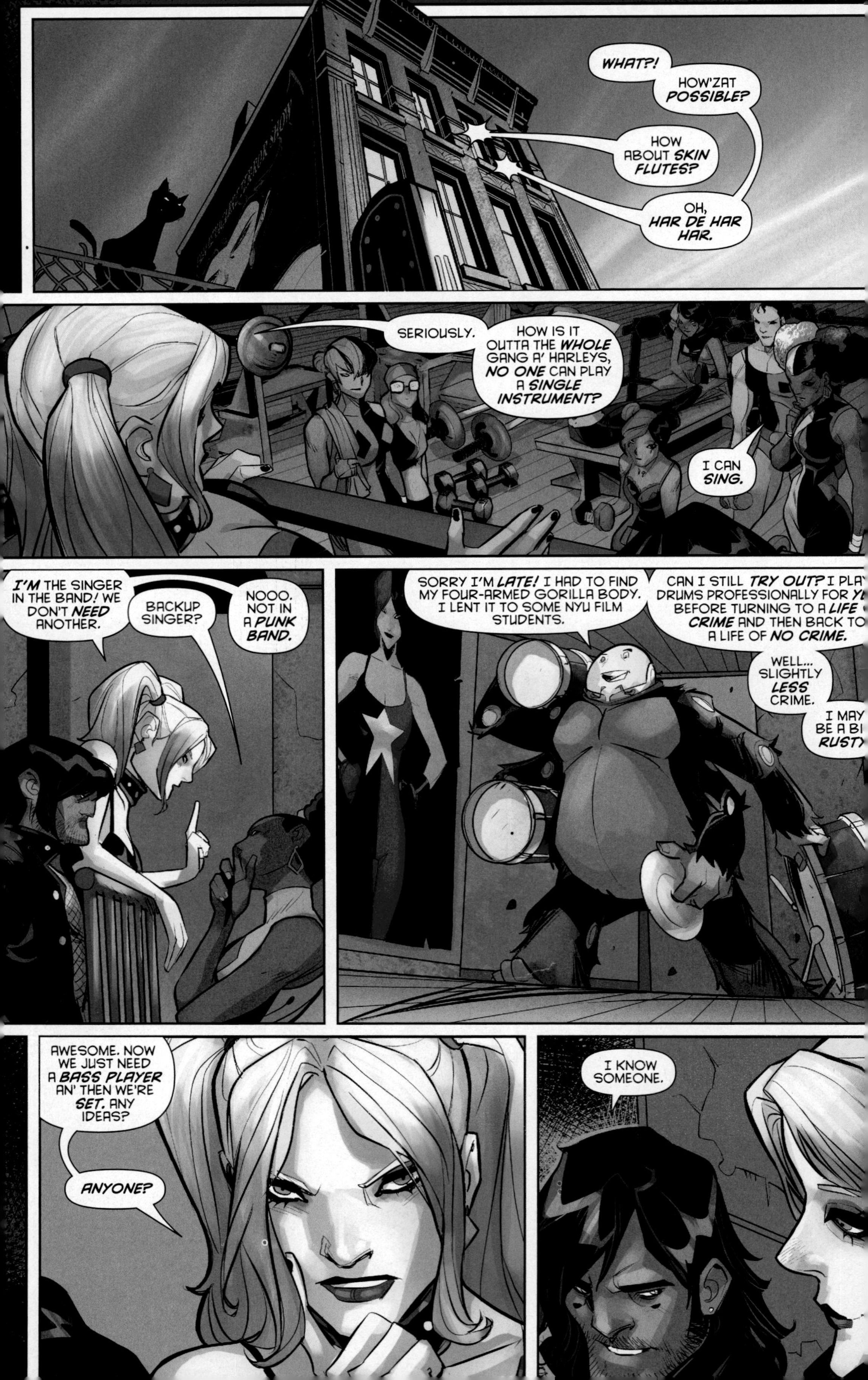

WHAT?!
HOW'ZAT POSSIBLE?
HOW ABOUT SKIN FLUTES?
OH, HAR DE HAR HAR.
SERIOUSLY.
HOW IS IT OUTTA THE WHOLE GANG A' HARLEYS, NO ONE CAN PLAY A SINGLE INSTRUMENT?
I CAN SING.
I'M THE SINGER IN THE BAND! WE DON'T NEED ANOTHER.
BACKUP SINGER?
NOOO. NOT IN A PUNK BAND.
SORRY I'M LATE! I HAD TO FIND MY FOUR-ARMED GORILLA BODY. I LENT IT TO SOME NYU FILM STUDENTS.
CAN I STILL TRY OUT? I PLA
DRUMS PROFESSIONALLY FOR Y
BEFORE TURNING TO A LIFE
CRIME AND THEN BACK TO
A LIFE OF NO CRIME.
WELL... SLIGHTLY LESS CRIME.
I MAY BE A BI RUSTY
AWESOME. NOW WE JUST NEED A BASS PLAYER AN' THEN WE'RE SET. ANY IDEAS?
ANYONE?
I KNOW SOMEONE.

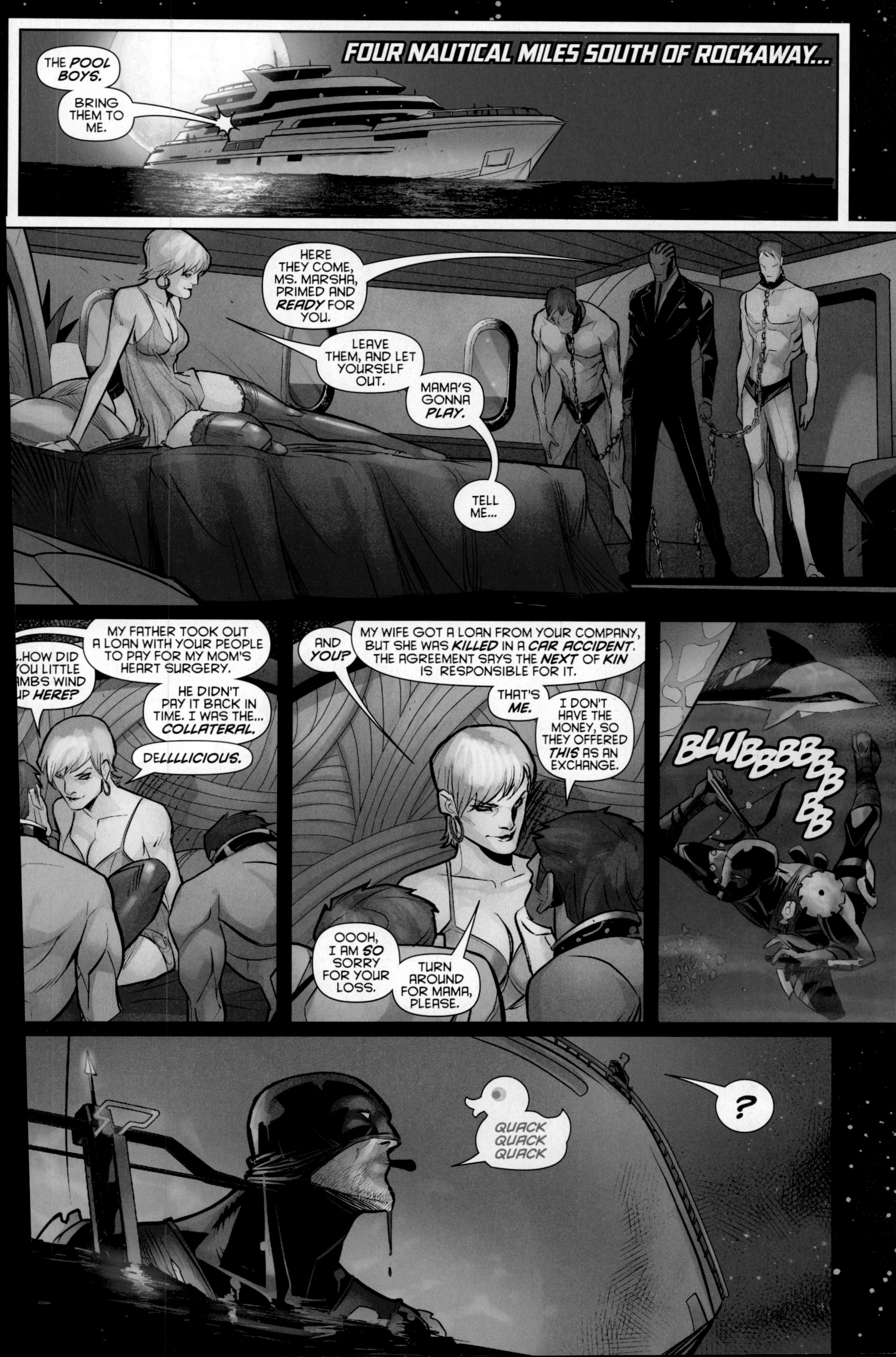
FOUR NAUTICAL MILES SOUTH OF ROCKAWAY...
THE POOL BOYS.
BRING THEM TO ME.
HERE THEY COME, MS. MARSHA, PRIMED AND READY FOR YOU.
LEAVE THEM, AND LET YOURSELF OUT.
MAMA'S GONNA PLAY.
TELL ME...
...HOW DID YOU LITTLE LAMBS WIND UP HERE?
MY FATHER TOOK OUT A LOAN WITH YOUR PEOPLE TO PAY FOR MY MOM'S HEART SURGERY.
HE DIDN'T PAY IT BACK IN TIME. I WAS THE... COLLATERAL.
DELLLLICIOUS.
AND YOU?
MY WIFE GOT A LOAN FROM YOUR COMPANY, BUT SHE WAS KILLED IN A CAR ACCIDENT. THE AGREEMENT SAYS THE NEXT OF KIN IS RESPONSIBLE FOR IT.
THAT'S ME.
I DON'T HAVE THE MONEY, SO THEY OFFERED THIS AS AN EXCHANGE.
OOOH, I AM SO SORRY FOR YOUR LOSS.
TURN AROUND FOR MAMA, PLEASE.
BLUBBBBBBBBB
QUACK QUACK QUACK
?

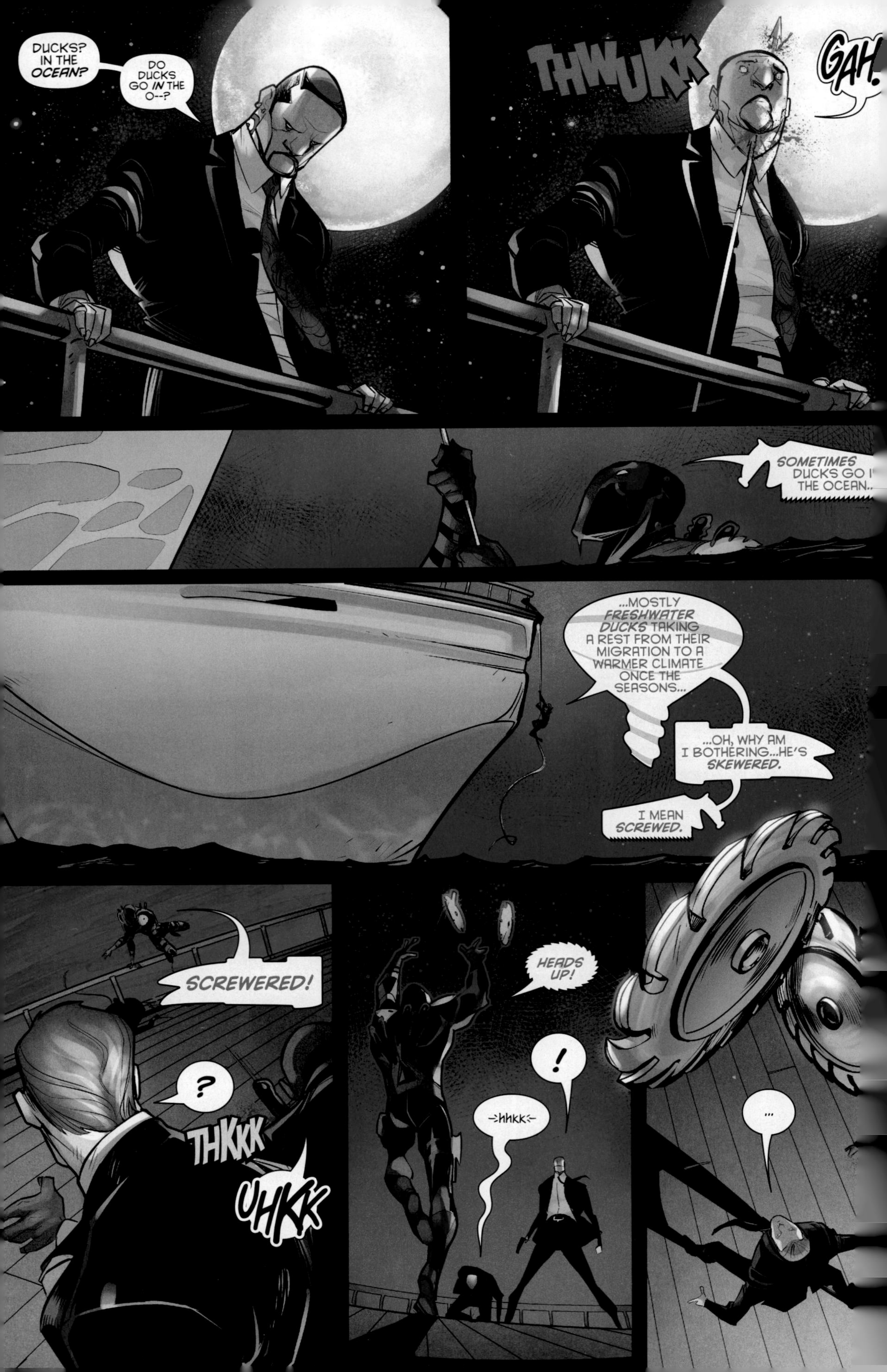
DUCKS? IN THE OCEAN?
DO DUCKS GO IN THE O--?
THWUKK
GAH!
SOMETIMES DUCKS GO IN THE OCEAN...
...MOSTLY FRESHWATER DUCKS TAKING A REST FROM THEIR MIGRATION TO A WARMER CLIMATE ONCE THE SEASONS...
...OH, WHY AM I BOTHERING...HE'S SKEWERED.
I MEAN SCREWED.
SCREWERED!
?
THKKK
UHKK
HEADS UP!
!
-hhkk-
...

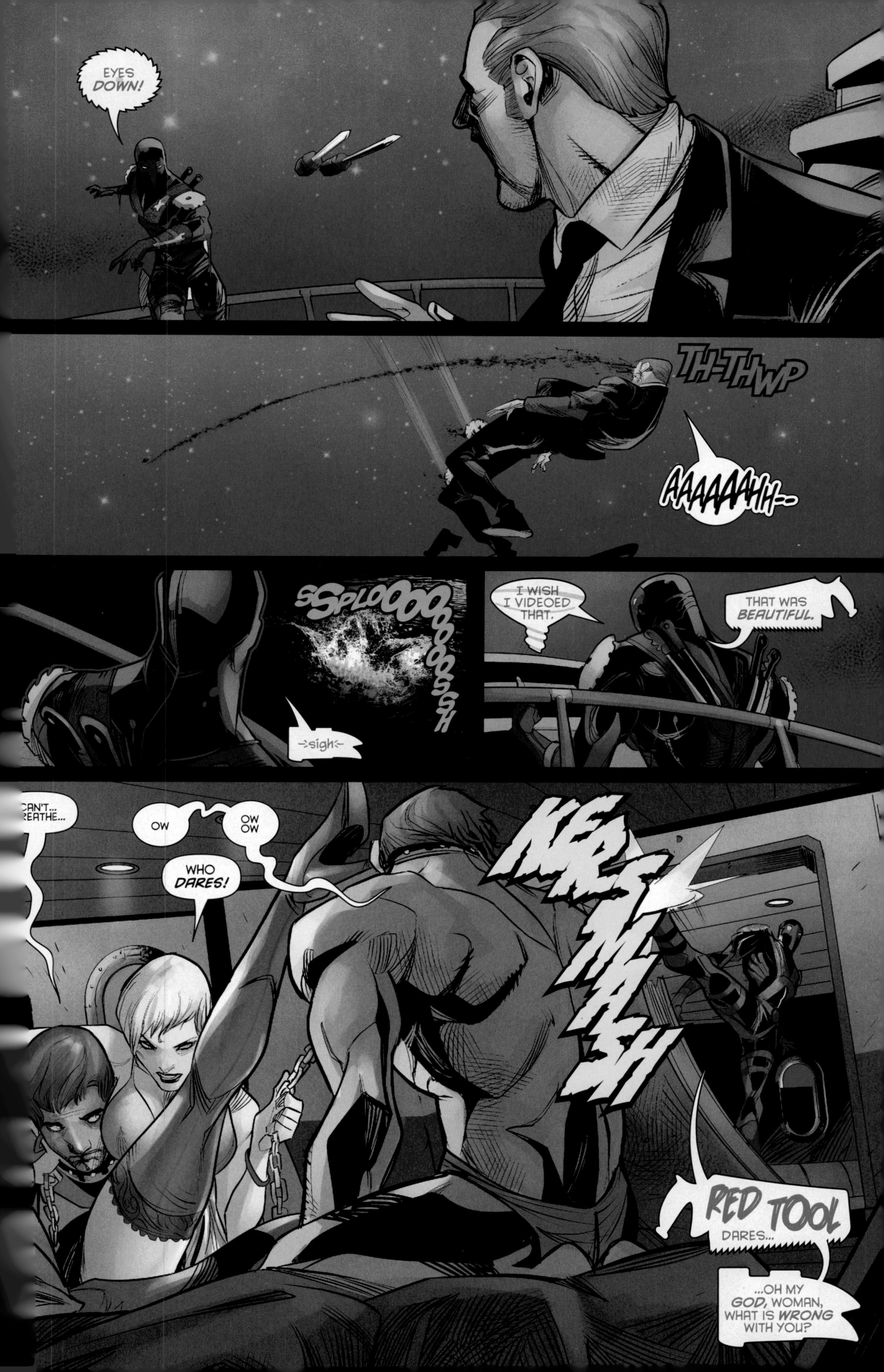

EYES DOWN!
TH-THWP
AAAAAAHH--
SSPLOOOOOOOOOOSSH
--sigh--
I WISH I VIDEOED THAT.
THAT WAS BEAUTIFUL.
CAN'T... BREATHE...
OW
OW OW
WHO DARES!
KERSMASH
RED TOOL DARES...
...OH MY GOD, WOMAN, WHAT IS WRONG WITH YOU?

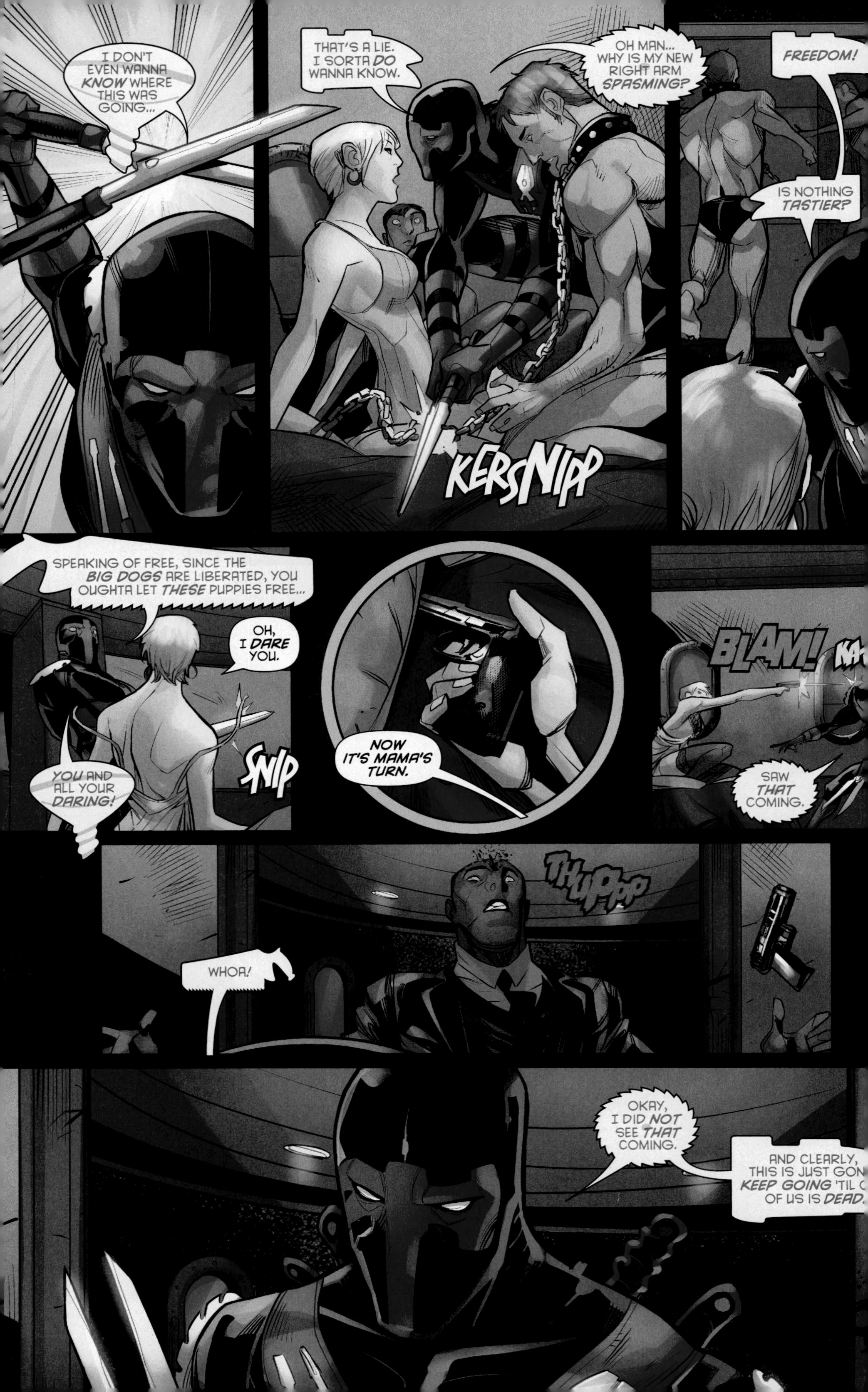
I DON'T EVEN WANNA KNOW WHERE THIS WAS GOING...
THAT'S A LIE. I SORTA DO WANNA KNOW.
OH MAN... WHY IS MY NEW RIGHT ARM SPASMING?
KERSNIPP
FREEDOM!
IS NOTHING TASTIER?
SPEAKING OF FREE, SINCE THE BIG DOGS ARE LIBERATED, YOU OUGHTA LET THESE PUPPIES FREE...
OH, I DARE YOU.
SNIP
YOU AND ALL YOUR DARING!
NOW IT'S MAMA'S TURN.
BLAM!
SAW THAT COMING.
THUPPP
WHOA!
OKAY, I DID NOT SEE THAT COMING.
AND CLEARLY, THIS IS JUST GON KEEP GOING 'TIL OF US IS DEAD.

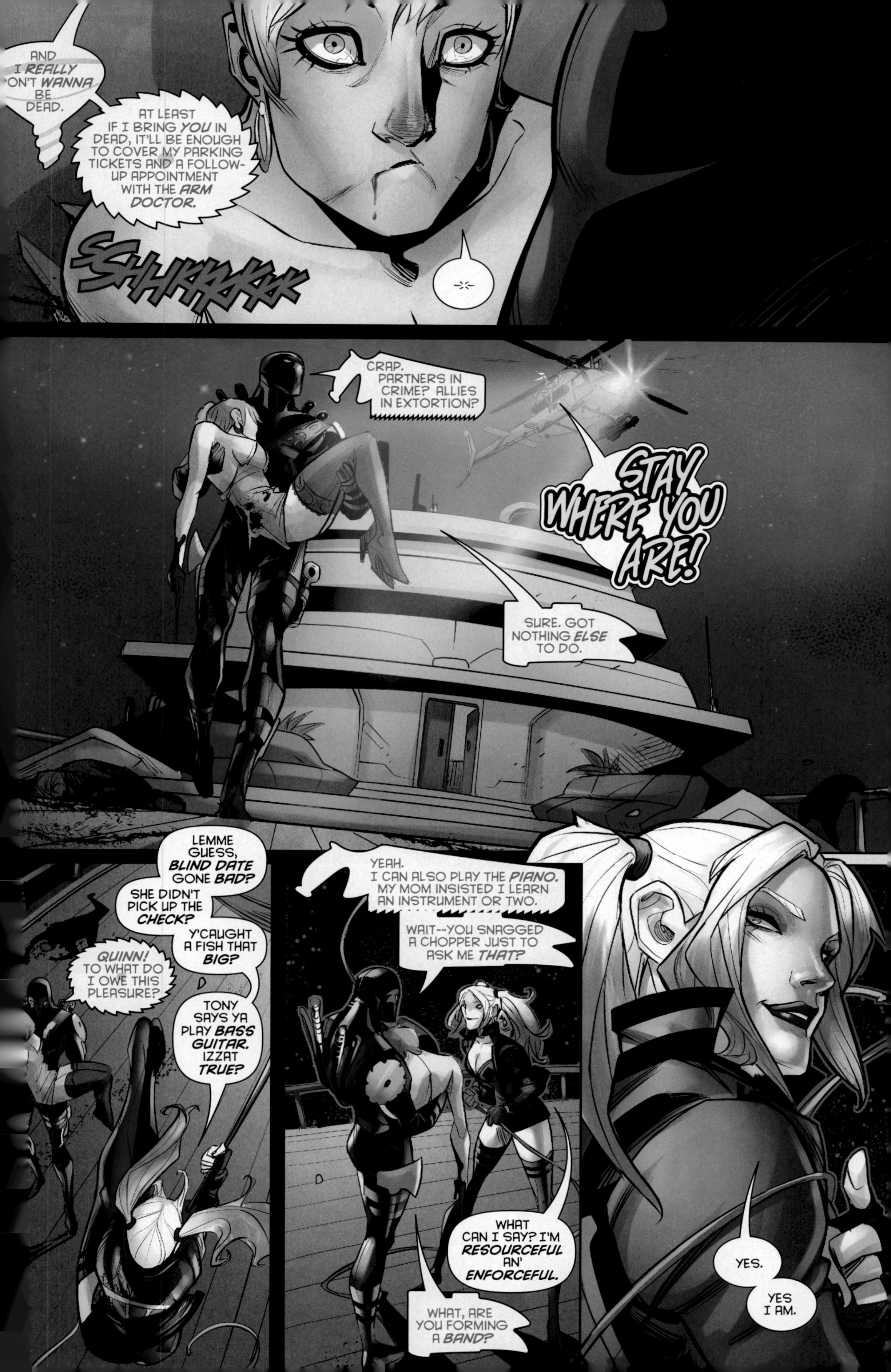

AND I REALLY DON'T WANNA BE DEAD.
AT LEAST IF I BRING YOU IN DEAD, IT'LL BE ENOUGH TO COVER MY PARKING TICKETS AND A FOLLOW-UP APPOINTMENT WITH THE ARM DOCTOR.
SSHHKKKKK
CRAP. PARTNERS IN CRIME? ALLIES IN EXTORTION?
STAY WHERE YOU ARE!
SURE. GOT NOTHING ELSE TO DO.
QUINN! TO WHAT DO I OWE THIS PLEASURE?
LEMME GUESS, BLIND DATE GONE BAD?
SHE DIDN'T PICK UP THE CHECK?
Y'CAUGHT A FISH THAT BIG?
TONY SAYS YA PLAY BASS GUITAR. IZZAT TRUE?
YEAH. I CAN ALSO PLAY THE PIANO. MY MOM INSISTED I LEARN AN INSTRUMENT OR TWO.
WAIT--YOU SNAGGED A CHOPPER JUST TO ASK ME THAT?
WHAT CAN I SAY? I'M RESOURCEFUL AN' ENFORCEFUL.
WHAT, ARE YOU FORMING A BAND?
YES.
YES I AM.

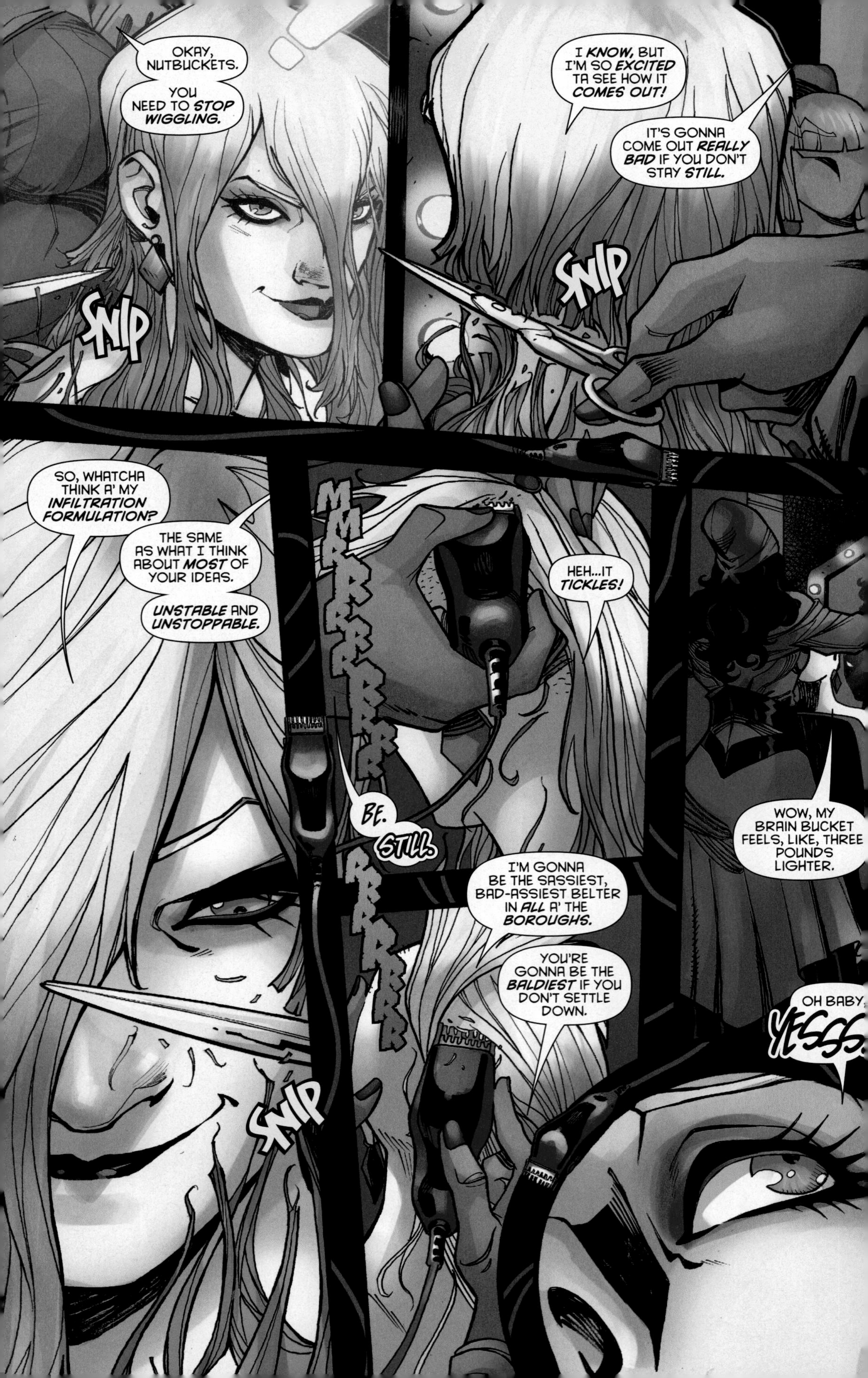
OKAY, NUTBUCKETS.
YOU NEED TO STOP WIGGLING.
SNIP
I KNOW, BUT I'M SO EXCITED TA SEE HOW IT COMES OUT!
IT'S GONNA COME OUT REALLY BAD IF YOU DON'T STAY STILL.
SNIP
SO, WHATCHA THINK A' MY INFILTRATION FORMULATION?
THE SAME AS WHAT I THINK ABOUT MOST OF YOUR IDEAS.
UNSTABLE AND UNSTOPPABLE.
MMRRRRRRRRRRR
HEH...IT TICKLES!
BE.
STILL.
I'M GONNA BE THE SASSIEST, BAD-ASSIEST BELTER IN ALL A' THE BOROUGHS.
YOU'RE GONNA BE THE BALDIEST IF YOU DON'T SETTLE DOWN.
SNIP
WOW, MY BRAIN BUCKET FEELS, LIKE, THREE POUNDS LIGHTER.
OH BABY,
YESSS.

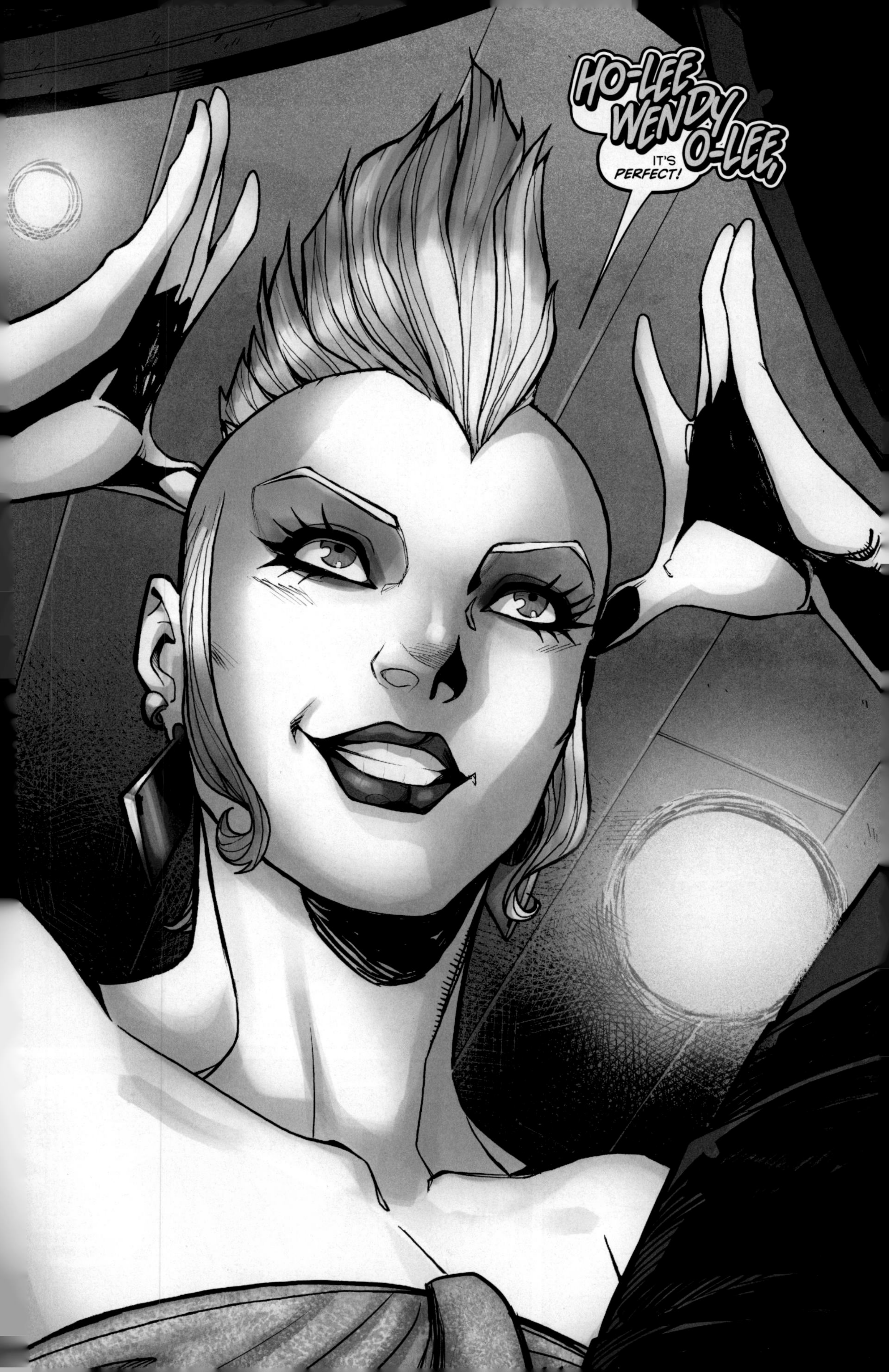
HO-LEE WENDY O-LEE, IT'S PERFECT!

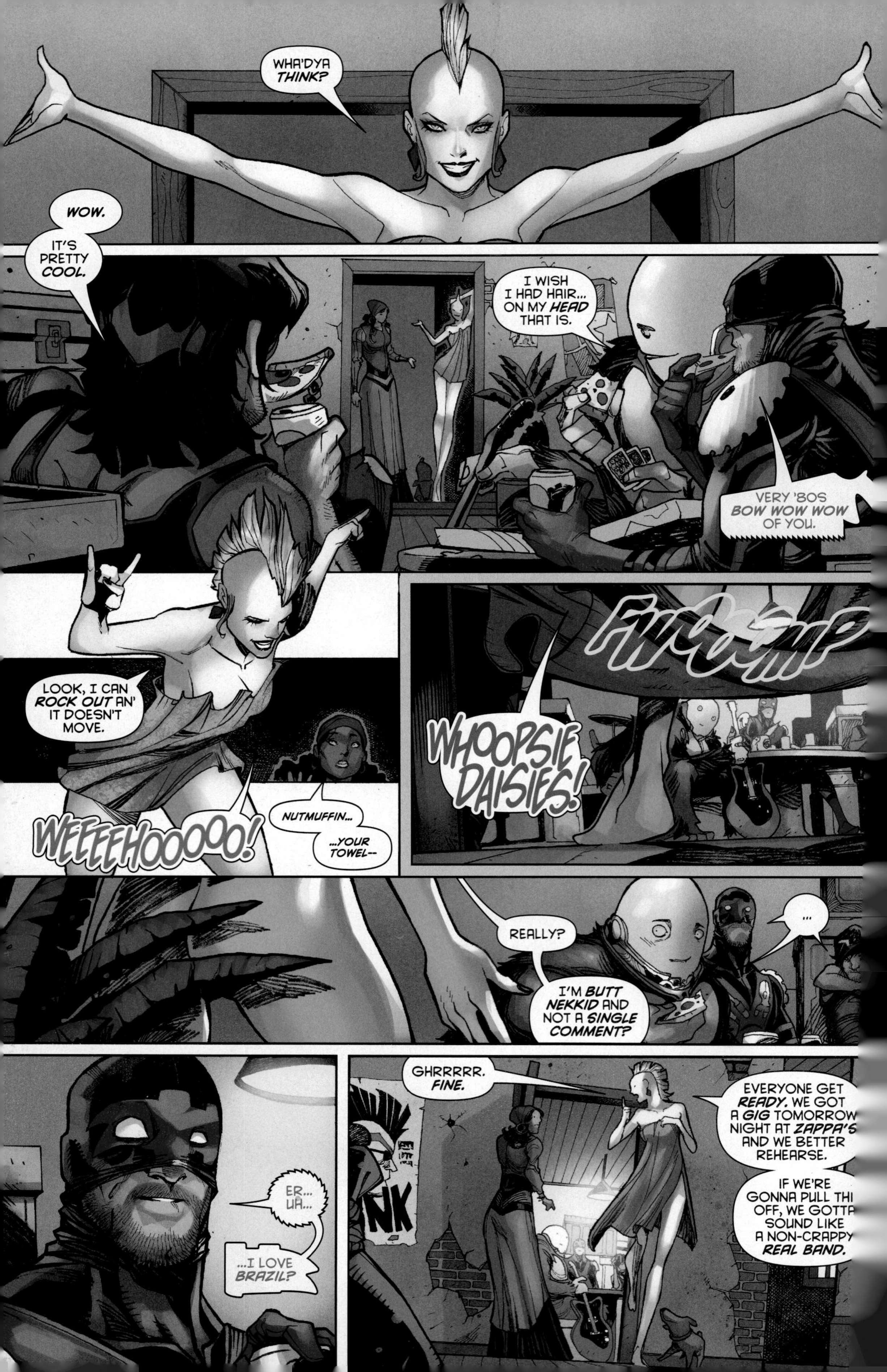
WHA'DYA THINK?
WOW.
IT'S PRETTY COOL.
I WISH I HAD HAIR... ON MY HEAD THAT IS.
VERY '80S BOW WOW WOW OF YOU.
LOOK, I CAN ROCK OUT AN' IT DOESN'T MOVE.
WEEEEHOOOOO!
NUTMUFFIN...
...YOUR TOWEL--
FWOOMP
WHOOPSIE DAISIES!
REALLY?
I'M BUTT NEKKID AND NOT A SINGLE COMMENT?
...
ER... UH...
...I LOVE BRAZIL?
GHRRRRR. FINE.
EVERYONE GET READY. WE GOT A GIG TOMORROW NIGHT AT ZAPPA'S AND WE BETTER REHEARSE.
IF WE'RE GONNA PULL THI OFF, WE GOTTA SOUND LIKE A NON-CRAPPY REAL BAND.

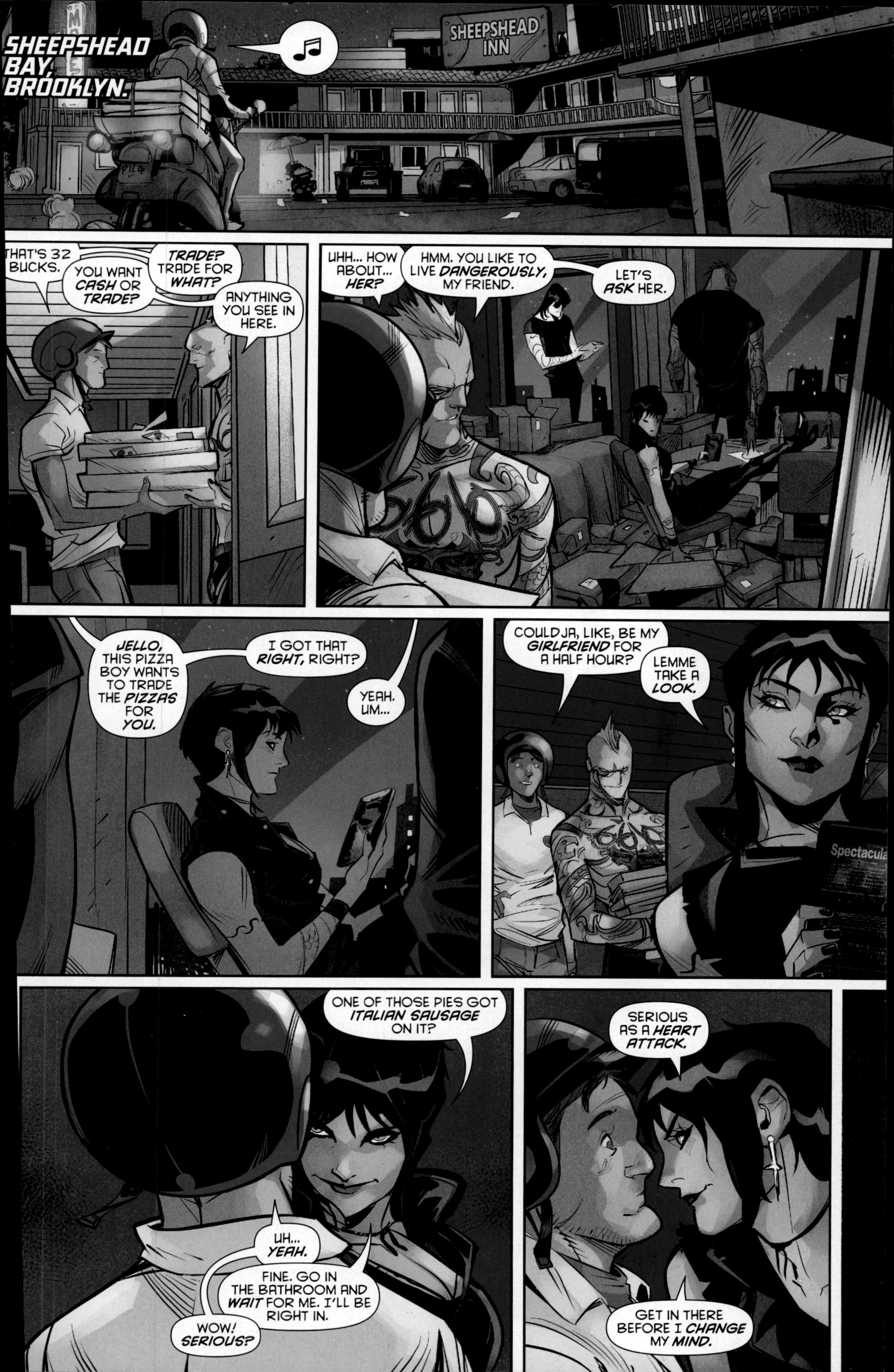
SHEEPSHEAD BAY, BROOKLYN.
SHEEPSHEAD INN
♫
THAT'S 32 BUCKS.
YOU WANT CASH OR TRADE?
TRADE? TRADE FOR WHAT?
ANYTHING YOU SEE IN HERE.
UHH... HOW ABOUT... HER?
HMM. YOU LIKE TO LIVE DANGEROUSLY, MY FRIEND.
LET'S ASK HER.
JELLO, THIS PIZZA BOY WANTS TO TRADE THE PIZZAS FOR YOU.
I GOT THAT RIGHT, RIGHT?
YEAH. UM...
COULDJA, LIKE, BE MY GIRLFRIEND FOR A HALF HOUR?
LEMME TAKE A LOOK.
ONE OF THOSE PIES GOT ITALIAN SAUSAGE ON IT?
UH... YEAH.
FINE. GO IN THE BATHROOM AND WAIT FOR ME. I'LL BE RIGHT IN.
WOW! SERIOUS?
SERIOUS AS A HEART ATTACK.
GET IN THERE BEFORE I CHANGE MY MIND.

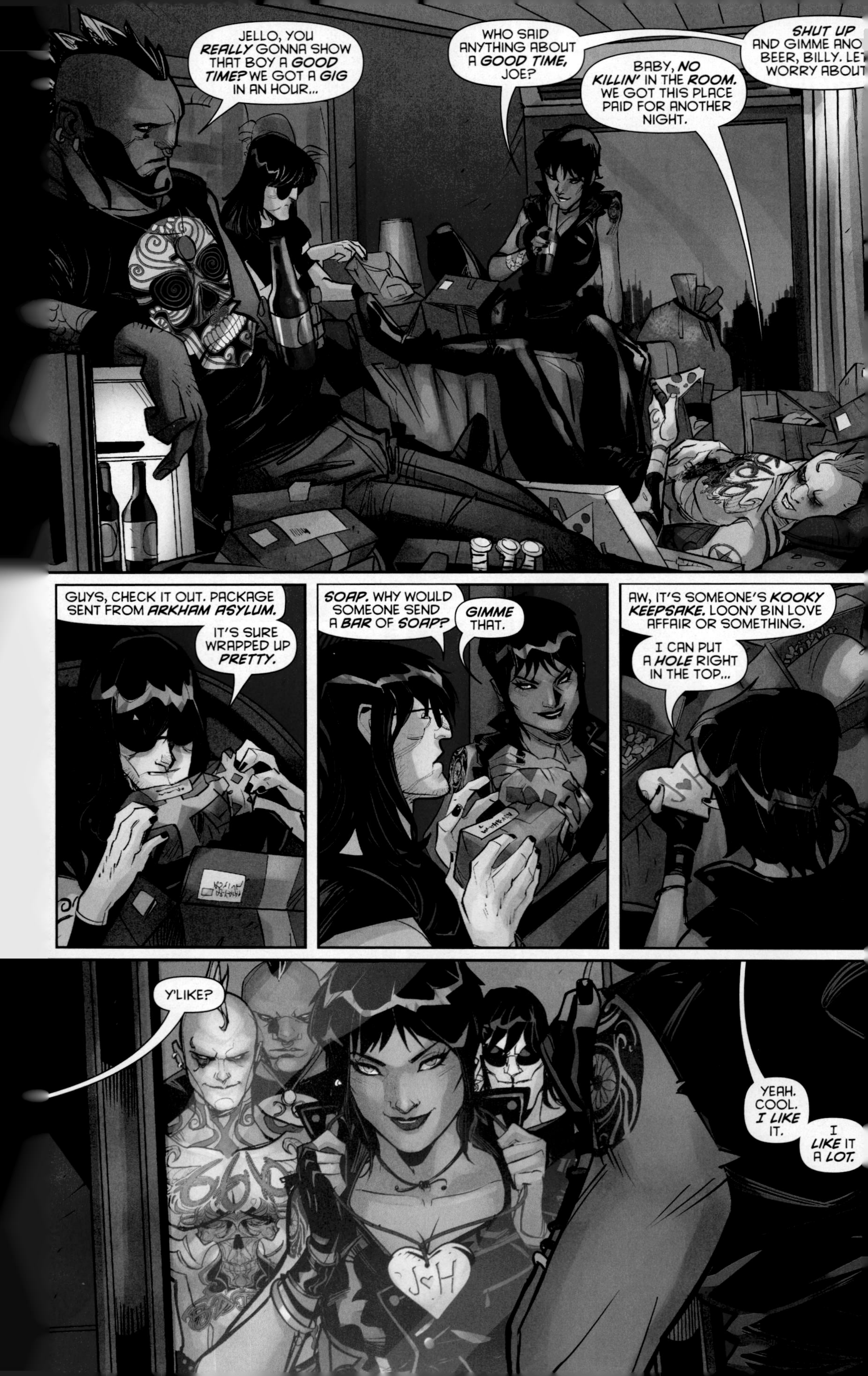

JELLO, YOU REALLY GONNA SHOW THAT BOY A GOOD TIME? WE GOT A GIG IN AN HOUR...
WHO SAID ANYTHING ABOUT A GOOD TIME, JOE?
SHUT UP AND GIMME ANO BEER, BILLY. LET WORRY ABOUT
BABY, NO KILLIN' IN THE ROOM. WE GOT THIS PLACE PAID FOR ANOTHER NIGHT.
GUYS, CHECK IT OUT. PACKAGE SENT FROM ARKHAM ASYLUM.
IT'S SURE WRAPPED UP PRETTY.
SOAP. WHY WOULD SOMEONE SEND A BAR OF SOAP?
GIMME THAT.
AW, IT'S SOMEONE'S KOOKY KEEPSAKE. LOONY BIN LOVE AFFAIR OR SOMETHING.
I CAN PUT A HOLE RIGHT IN THE TOP...
Y'LIKE?
YEAH. COOL. I LIKE IT.
I LIKE IT A LOT.

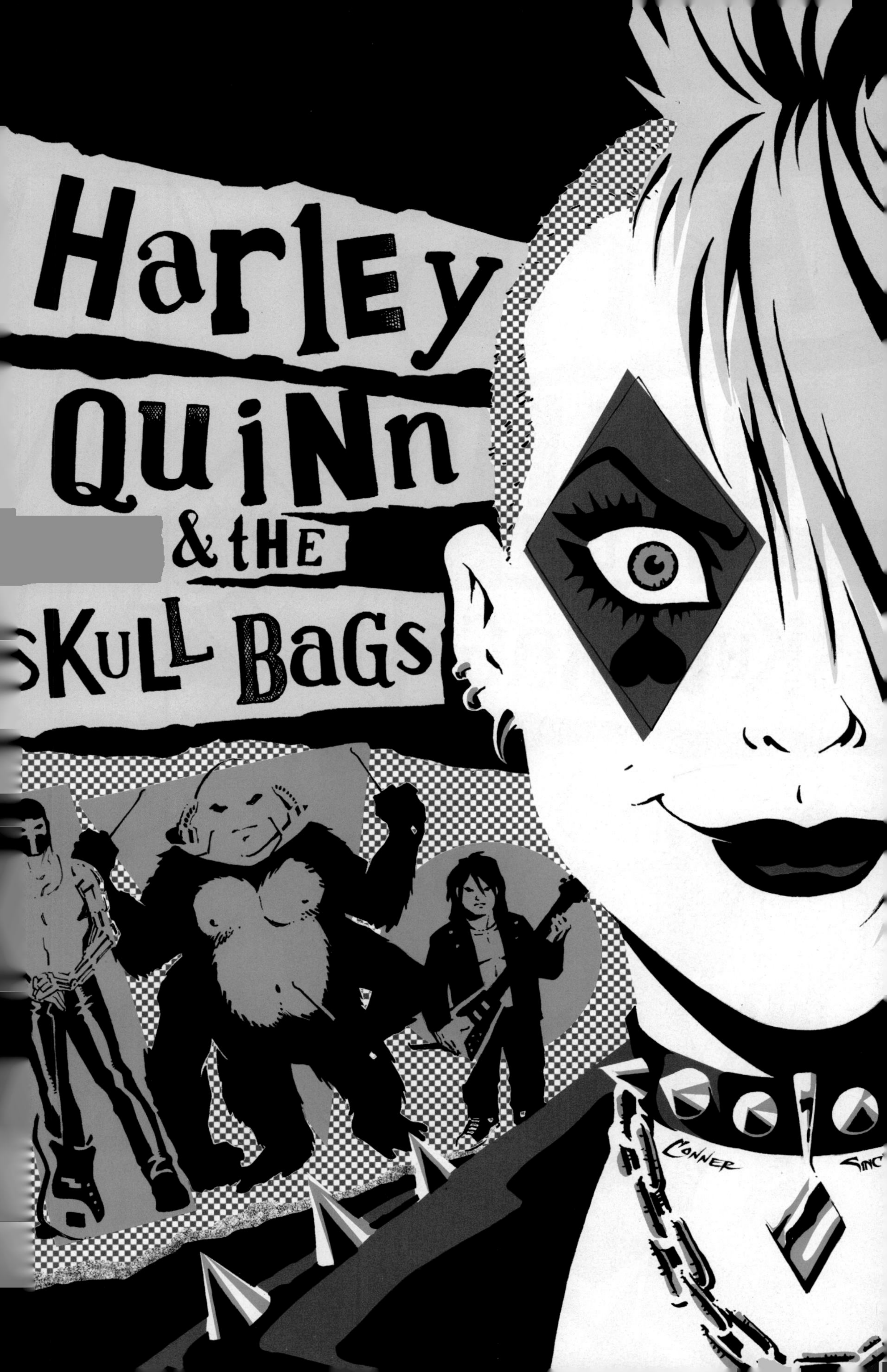
Harley Quinn
& the
Skull Bags
CONNER
SINC

UNDERCOVER PUNKER PART 2: THE SKULL BAGS' BIG SNAG

JIMMY PALMIOTTI and AMANDA CONNER writers * JOHN TIMMS artist
JILL THOMPSON flashback artist and colorist * ALEX SINCLAIR colorist * DAVE SHARPE letterer

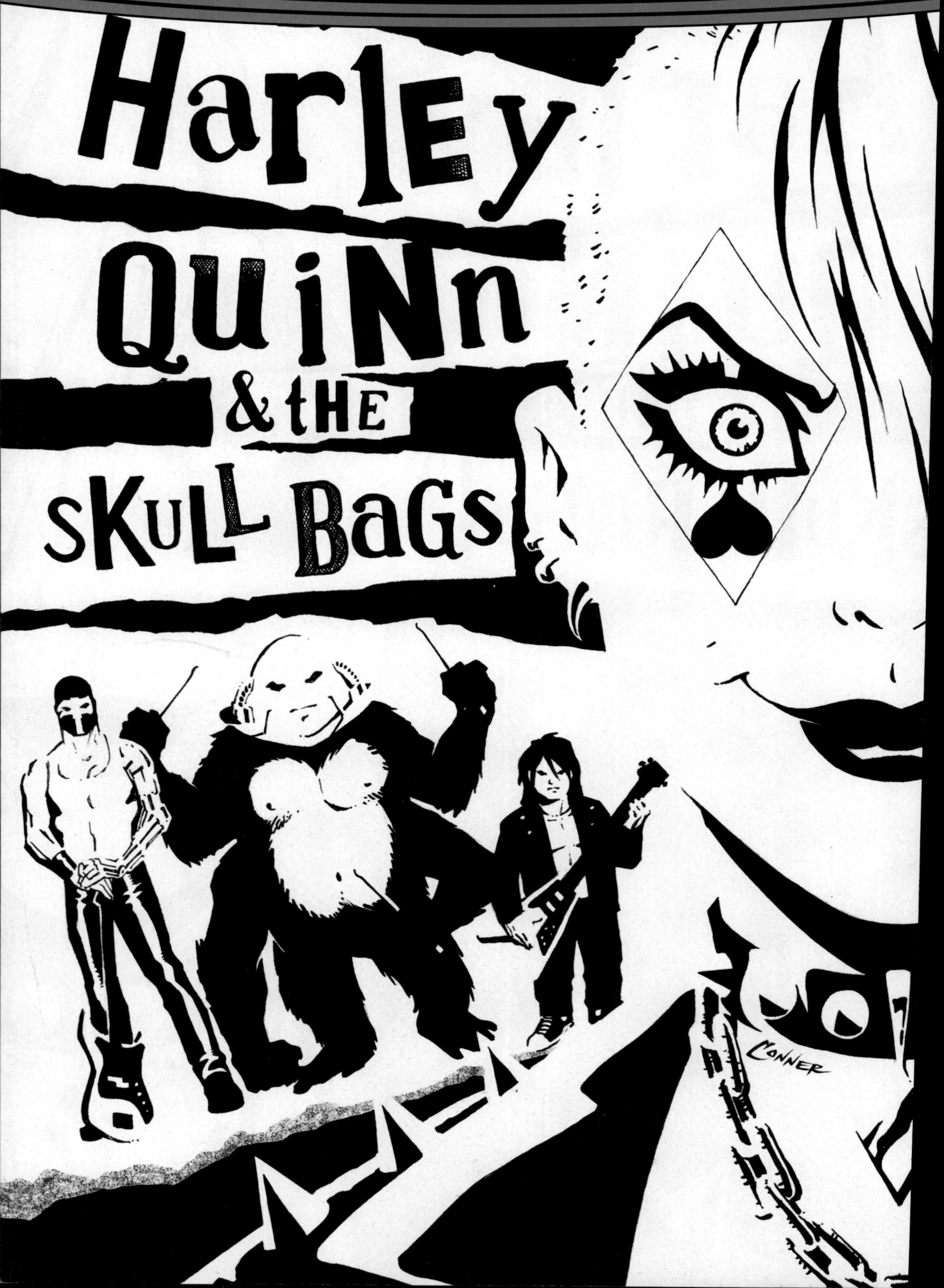

Harley Quinn & the Skull Bags
CONNER

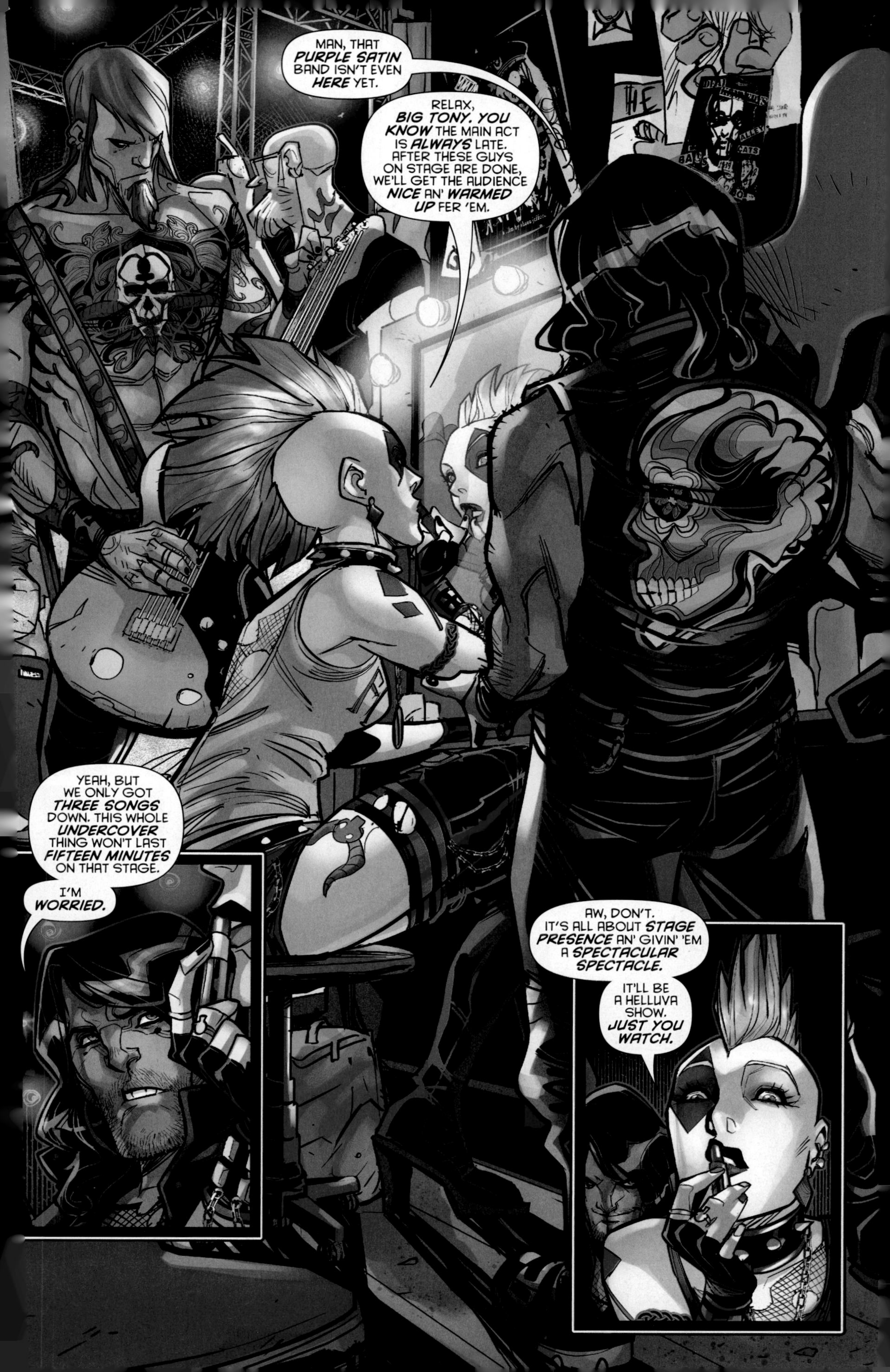
MAN, THAT PURPLE SATIN BAND ISN'T EVEN HERE YET.
RELAX, BIG TONY. YOU KNOW THE MAIN ACT IS ALWAYS LATE. AFTER THESE GUYS ON STAGE ARE DONE, WE'LL GET THE AUDIENCE NICE AN' WARMED UP FER 'EM.
YEAH, BUT WE ONLY GOT THREE SONGS DOWN. THIS WHOLE UNDERCOVER THING WON'T LAST FIFTEEN MINUTES ON THAT STAGE.
I'M WORRIED.
AW, DON'T. IT'S ALL ABOUT STAGE PRESENCE AN' GIVIN' 'EM A SPECTACULAR SPECTACLE.
IT'LL BE A HELLUVA SHOW. JUST YOU WATCH.

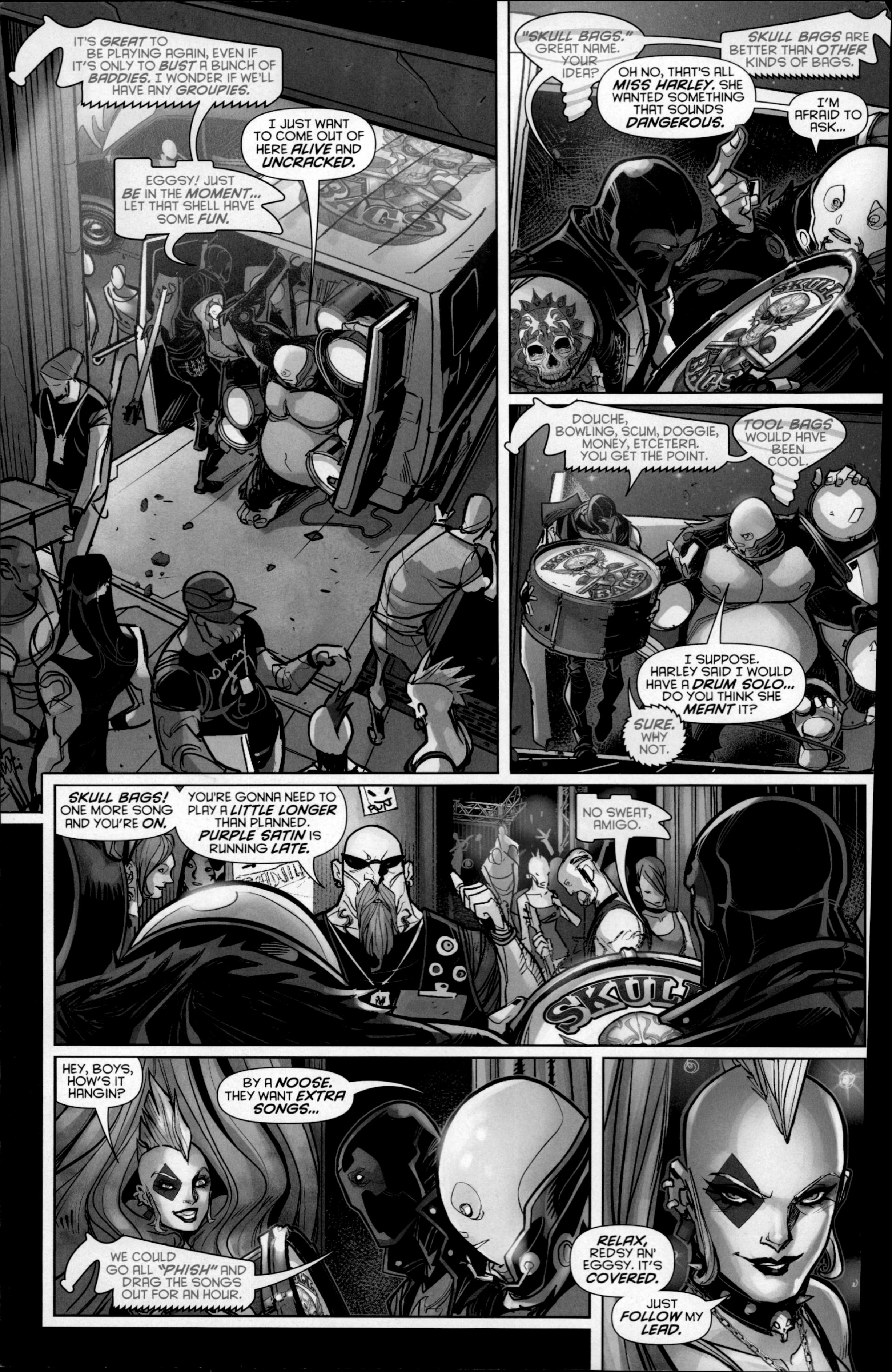

IT'S GREAT TO BE PLAYING AGAIN, EVEN IF IT'S ONLY TO BUST A BUNCH OF BADDIES. I WONDER IF WE'LL HAVE ANY GROUPIES.
I JUST WANT TO COME OUT OF HERE ALIVE AND UNCRACKED.
EGGSY! JUST BE IN THE MOMENT... LET THAT SHELL HAVE SOME FUN.
"SKULL BAGS." GREAT NAME. YOUR IDEA?
OH NO, THAT'S ALL MISS HARLEY. SHE WANTED SOMETHING THAT SOUNDS DANGEROUS.
SKULL BAGS ARE BETTER THAN OTHER KINDS OF BAGS.
I'M AFRAID TO ASK...
DOUCHE, BOWLING, SCUM, DOGGIE, MONEY, ETCETERA. YOU GET THE POINT.
TOOL BAGS WOULD HAVE BEEN COOL.
I SUPPOSE. HARLEY SAID I WOULD HAVE A DRUM SOLO... DO YOU THINK SHE MEANT IT?
SURE. WHY NOT.
SKULL BAGS! ONE MORE SONG AND YOU'RE ON.
YOU'RE GONNA NEED TO PLAY A LITTLE LONGER THAN PLANNED. PURPLE SATIN IS RUNNING LATE.
NO SWEAT, AMIGO.
HEY, BOYS, HOW'S IT HANGIN?
BY A NOOSE. THEY WANT EXTRA SONGS...
WE COULD GO ALL "PHISH" AND DRAG THE SONGS OUT FOR AN HOUR.
RELAX, REDSY AN' EGGSY. IT'S COVERED.
JUST FOLLOW MY LEAD.

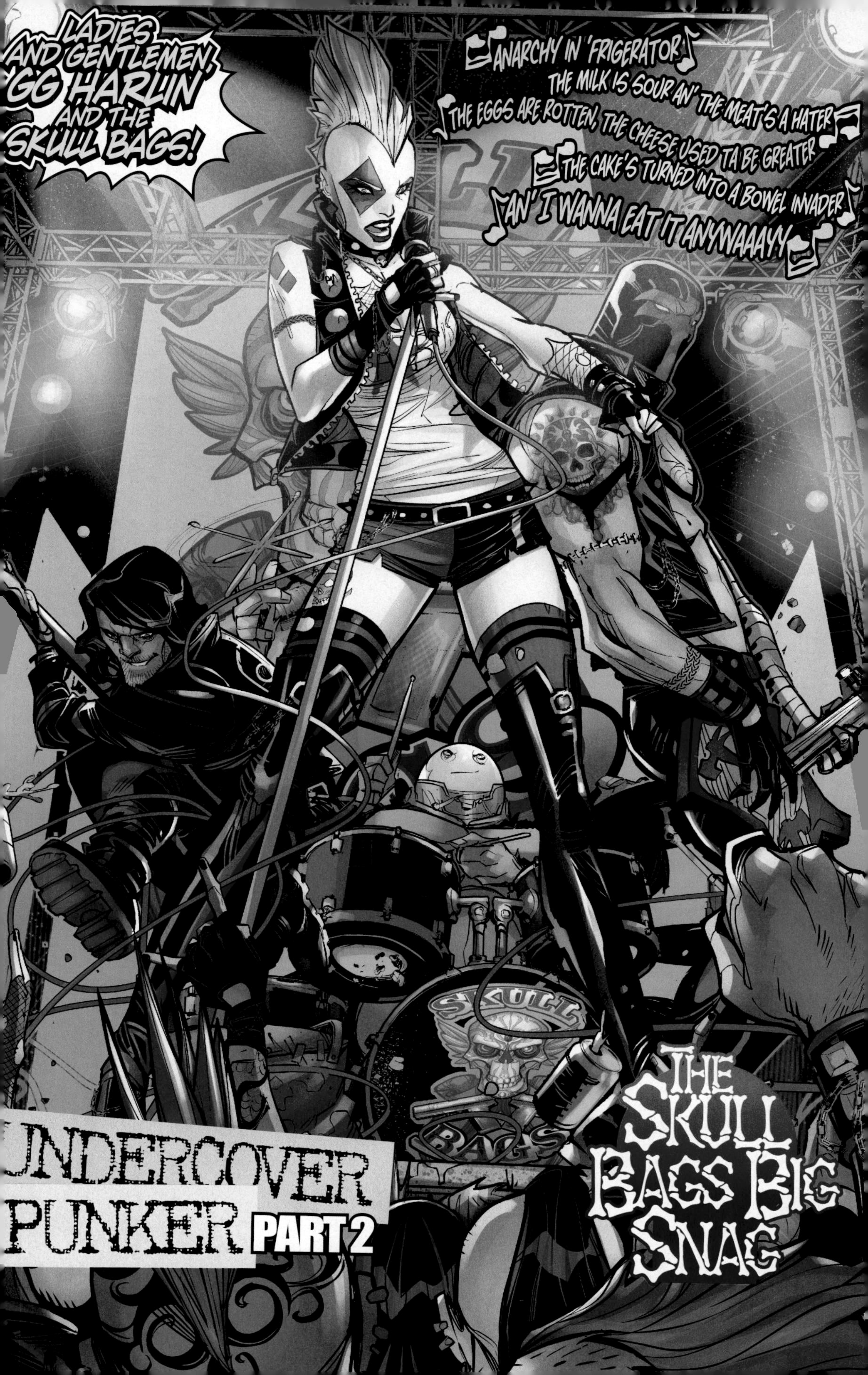
LADIES AND GENTLEMEN, GG HARLIN AND THE SKULL BAGS!
ANARCHY IN 'FRIGERATOR
THE MILK IS SOUR AN' THE MEAT'S A HATER
THE EGGS ARE ROTTEN, THE CHEESE USED TA BE GREATER
THE CAKE'S TURNED INTO A BOWEL INVADER
AN' I WANNA EAT IT ANYWAAAYY
UNDERCOVER PUNKER PART 2
THE SKULL BAGS BIG SNAG

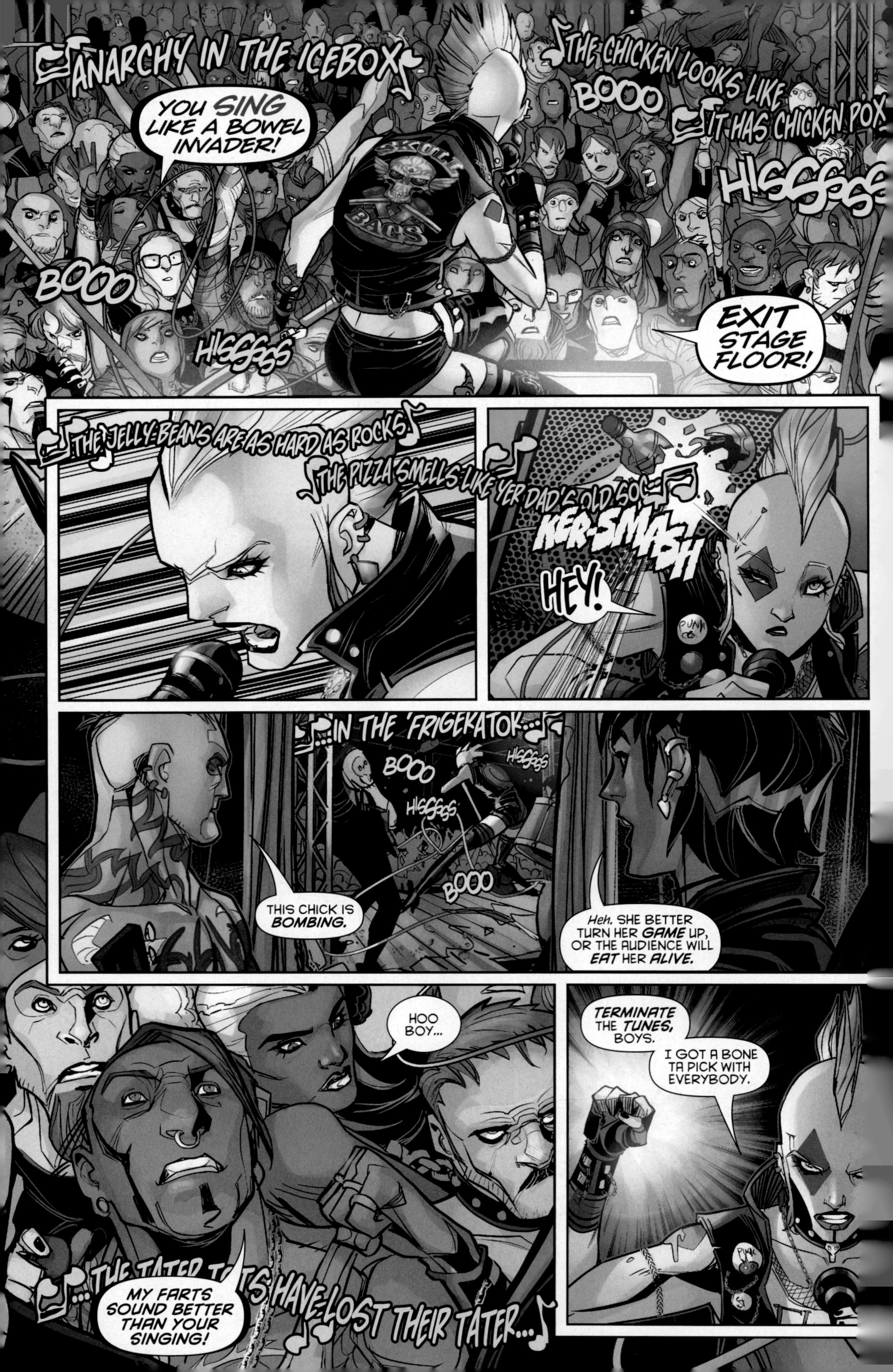
ANARCHY IN THE ICEBOX
YOU SING LIKE A BOWEL INVADER!
THE CHICKEN LOOKS LIKE
BOOO
IT HAS CHICKEN POX
HISSSSS
BOOO
HISSSSS
EXIT STAGE FLOOR!
THE JELLY-BEANS ARE AS HARD AS ROCKS
THE PIZZA SMELLS LIKE YER DAD'S OLD SOC
KER-SMASH
HEY!
PUNK
IN THE 'FRIGERATOR
BOOO
HISSSSS
HISSSSS
BOOO
THIS CHICK IS BOMBING.
Heh. SHE BETTER TURN HER GAME UP, OR THE AUDIENCE WILL EAT HER ALIVE.
HOO BOY...
...THE TATER TOTS HAVE LOST THEIR TATER...
MY FARTS SOUND BETTER THAN YOUR SINGING!
TERMINATE THE TUNES, BOYS.
I GOT A BONE TA PICK WITH EVERYBODY.

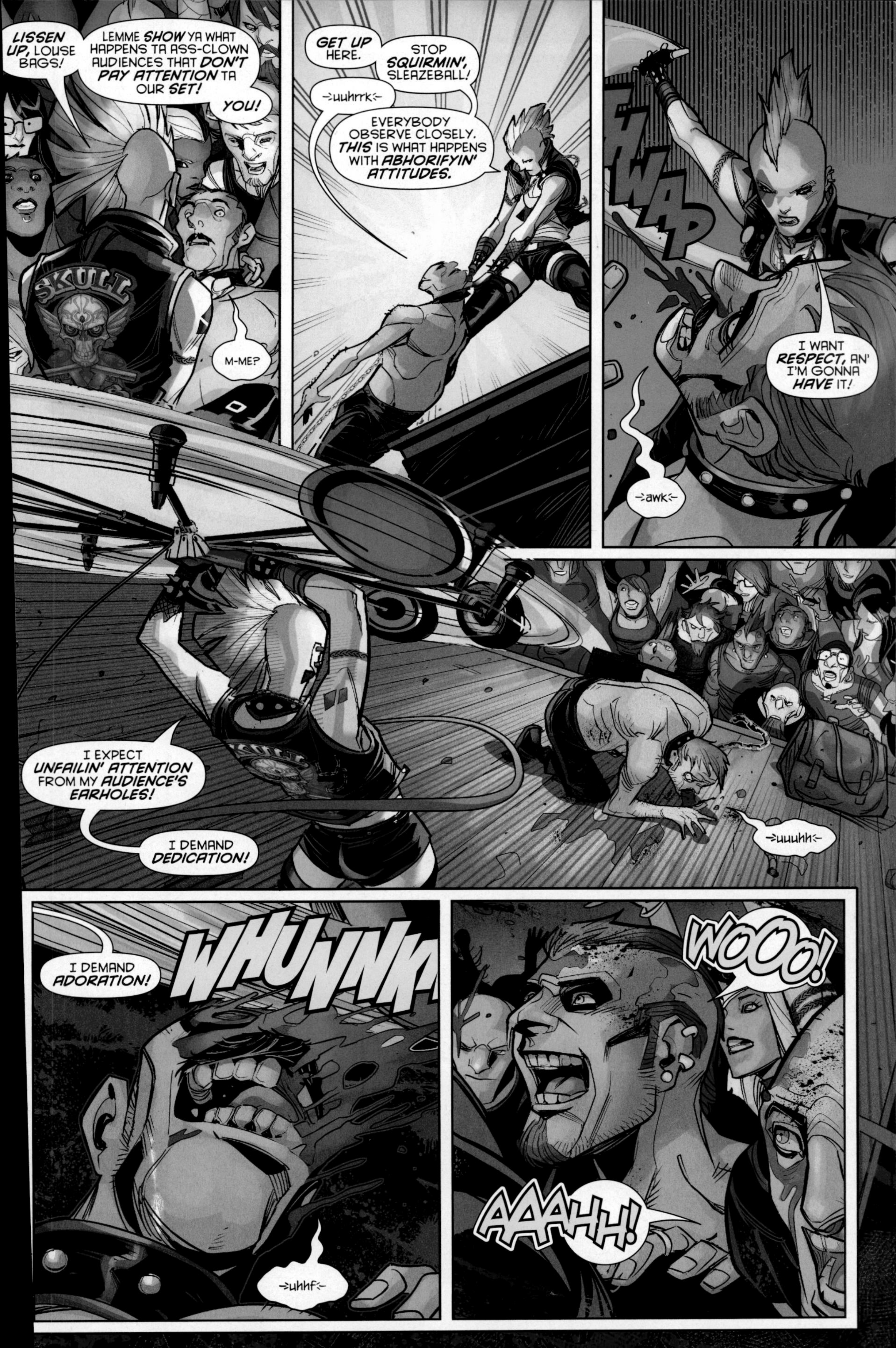
LISSEN UP, LOUSE BAGS!
LEMME SHOW YA WHAT HAPPENS TA ASS-CLOWN AUDIENCES THAT DON'T PAY ATTENTION TA OUR SET!
YOU!
M-ME?
GET UP HERE.
STOP SQUIRMIN', SLEAZEBALL!
uuhrrk
EVERYBODY OBSERVE CLOSELY. THIS IS WHAT HAPPENS WITH ABHORIFYIN' ATTITUDES.
WAP
I WANT RESPECT, AN' I'M GONNA HAVE IT!
awk
I EXPECT UNFAILIN' ATTENTION FROM MY AUDIENCE'S EARHOLES!
I DEMAND DEDICATION!
uuuhh
I DEMAND ADORATION!
WHUNNK
uhhf
WOOO!
AAAHH!

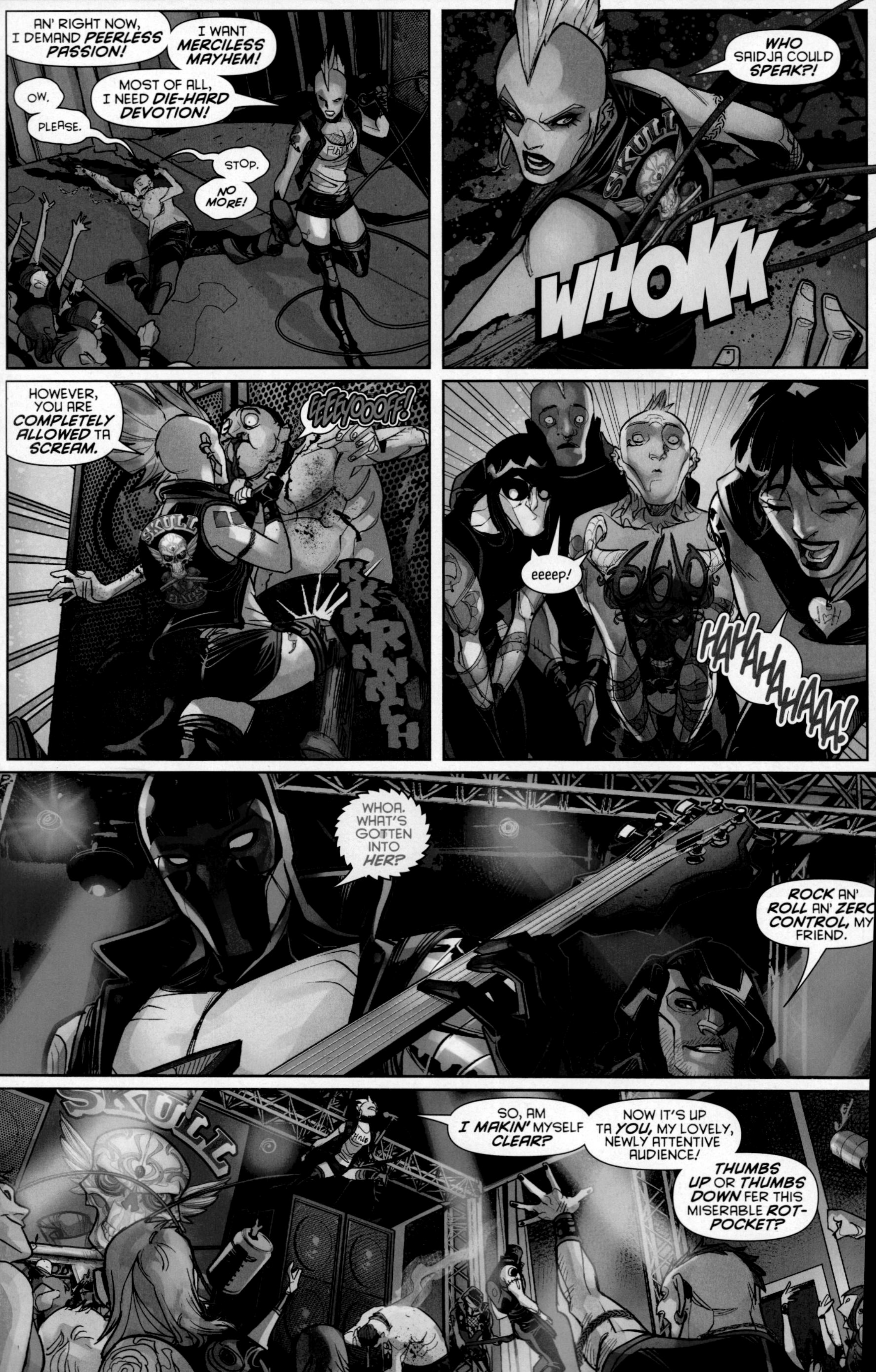

AN' RIGHT NOW, I DEMAND PEERLESS PASSION!
I WANT MERCILESS MAYHEM!
MOST OF ALL, I NEED DIE-HARD DEVOTION!
OW.
PLEASE.
STOP.
NO MORE!
WHO SAIDJA COULD SPEAK?!
WHOKK
HOWEVER, YOU ARE COMPLETELY ALLOWED TA SCREAM.
EEEEYOOOFF!
KKRRNNCH
eeeep!
HAHAHAHAHAAA!
WHOA. WHAT'S GOTTEN INTO HER?
ROCK AN' ROLL AN' ZERO CONTROL, MY FRIEND.
SO, AM I MAKIN' MYSELF CLEAR?
NOW IT'S UP TA YOU, MY LOVELY, NEWLY ATTENTIVE AUDIENCE!
THUMBS UP OR THUMBS DOWN FER THIS MISERABLE ROT-POCKET?

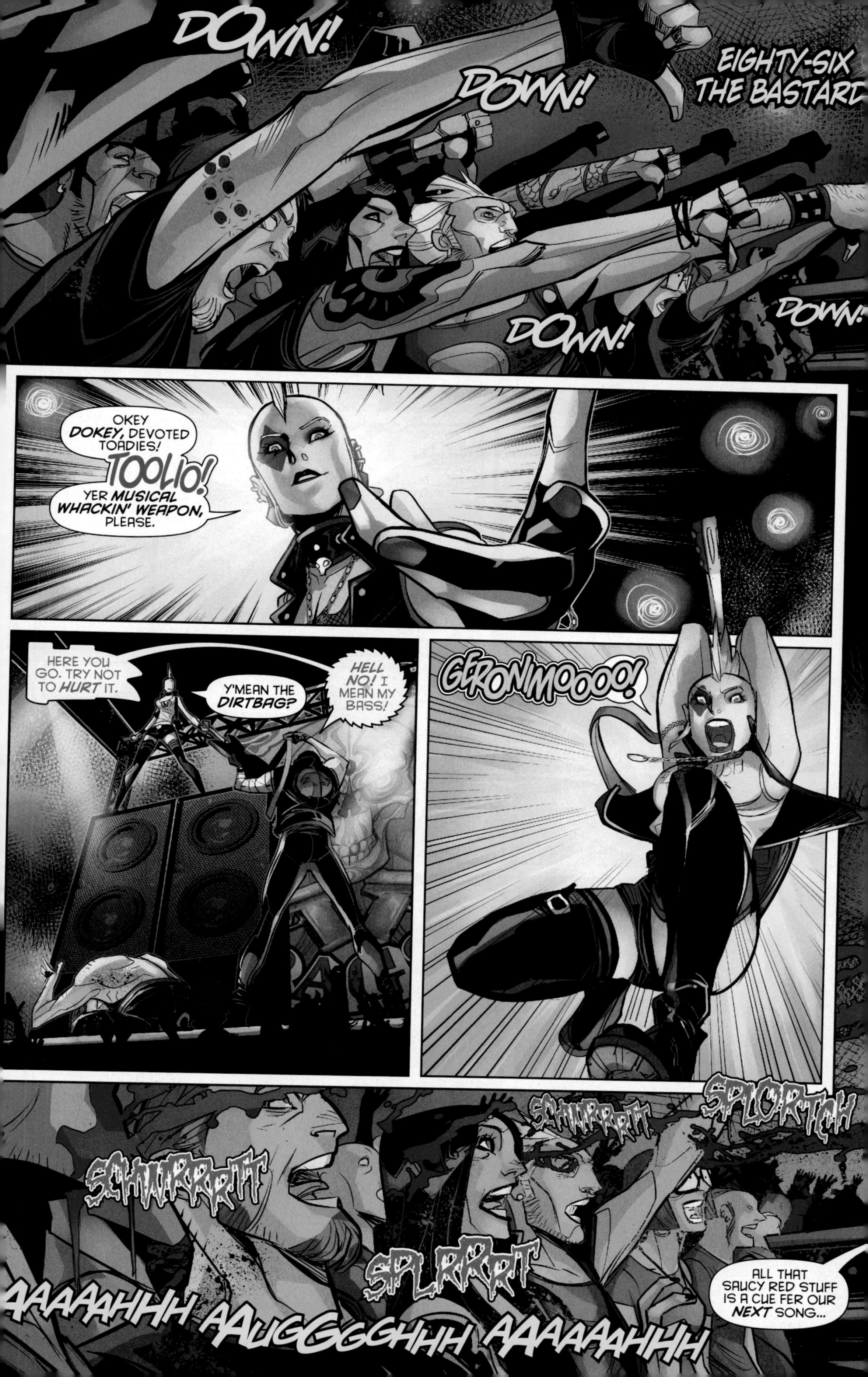
DOWN!
DOWN!
EIGHTY-SIX THE BASTARD
DOWN!
DOWN!
OKEY DOKEY, DEVOTED TOADIES! TOOLIO! YER MUSICAL WHACKIN' WEAPON, PLEASE.
HERE YOU GO. TRY NOT TO HURT IT.
Y'MEAN THE DIRTBAG?
HELL NO! I MEAN MY BASS!
GERONIMOOOO!
SCHHIRRRTT
SPLORTCH
SCHHIRRRTT
SPLRRRT
AAAAAHHH AAUGGGGHHH AAAAAAHHH
ALL THAT SAUCY RED STUFF IS A CUE FER OUR NEXT SONG...

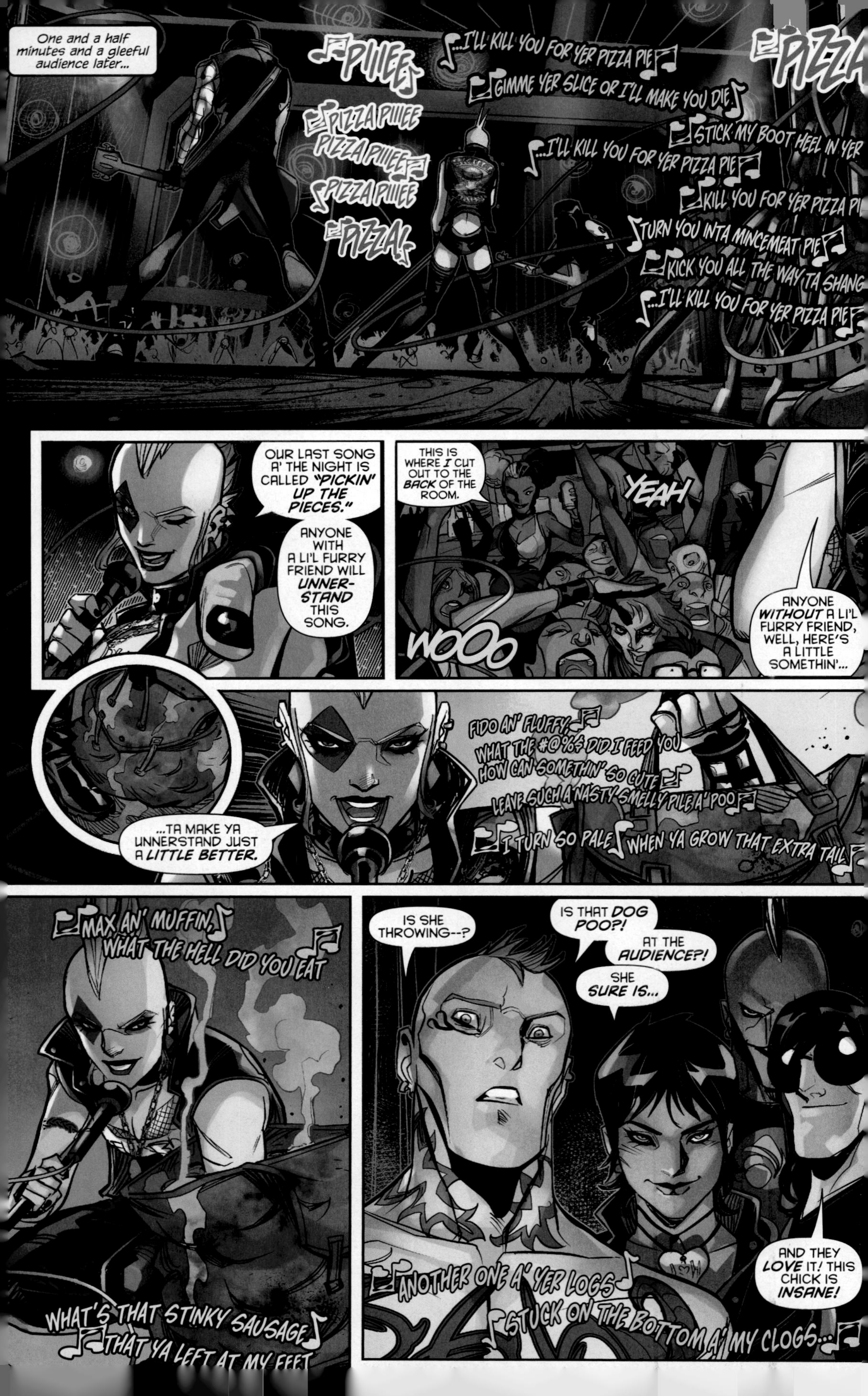
One and a half minutes and a gleeful audience later...
PIIIEE
PIZZA PIIIEE
PIZZA PIIIEE
PIZZA PIIIEE
PIZZA!
...I'LL KILL YOU FOR YER PIZZA PIE
GIMME YER SLICE OR I'LL MAKE YOU DIE
STICK MY BOOT HEEL IN YER
...I'LL KILL YOU FOR YER PIZZA PIE
KILL YOU FOR YER PIZZA PI
TURN YOU INTA MINCEMEAT PIE
KICK YOU ALL THE WAY TA SHANG
...I'LL KILL YOU FOR YER PIZZA PIE
PIZZA
OUR LAST SONG A' THE NIGHT IS CALLED "PICKIN' UP THE PIECES."
ANYONE WITH A LI'L FURRY FRIEND WILL UNNER-STAND THIS SONG.
THIS IS WHERE I CUT OUT TO THE BACK OF THE ROOM.
YEAH
WOOO
ANYONE WITHOUT A LI'L FURRY FRIEND, WELL, HERE'S A LITTLE SOMETHIN'...
...TA MAKE YA UNNERSTAND JUST A LITTLE BETTER.
FIDO AN' FLUFFY
WHAT THE #@%$ DID I FEED YOU
HOW CAN SOMETHIN' SO CUTE
LEAVE SUCH A NASTY SMELLY PILE A' POO
I TURN SO PALE
WHEN YA GROW THAT EXTRA TAIL
MAX AN' MUFFIN,
WHAT THE HELL DID YOU EAT
WHAT'S THAT STINKY SAUSAGE
THAT YA LEFT AT MY FEET
IS SHE THROWING--?
IS THAT DOG POO?!
AT THE AUDIENCE?!
SHE SURE IS...
AND THEY LOVE IT! THIS CHICK IS INSANE!
ANOTHER ONE A' YER LOGS
STUCK ON THE BOTTOM A' MY CLOGS...

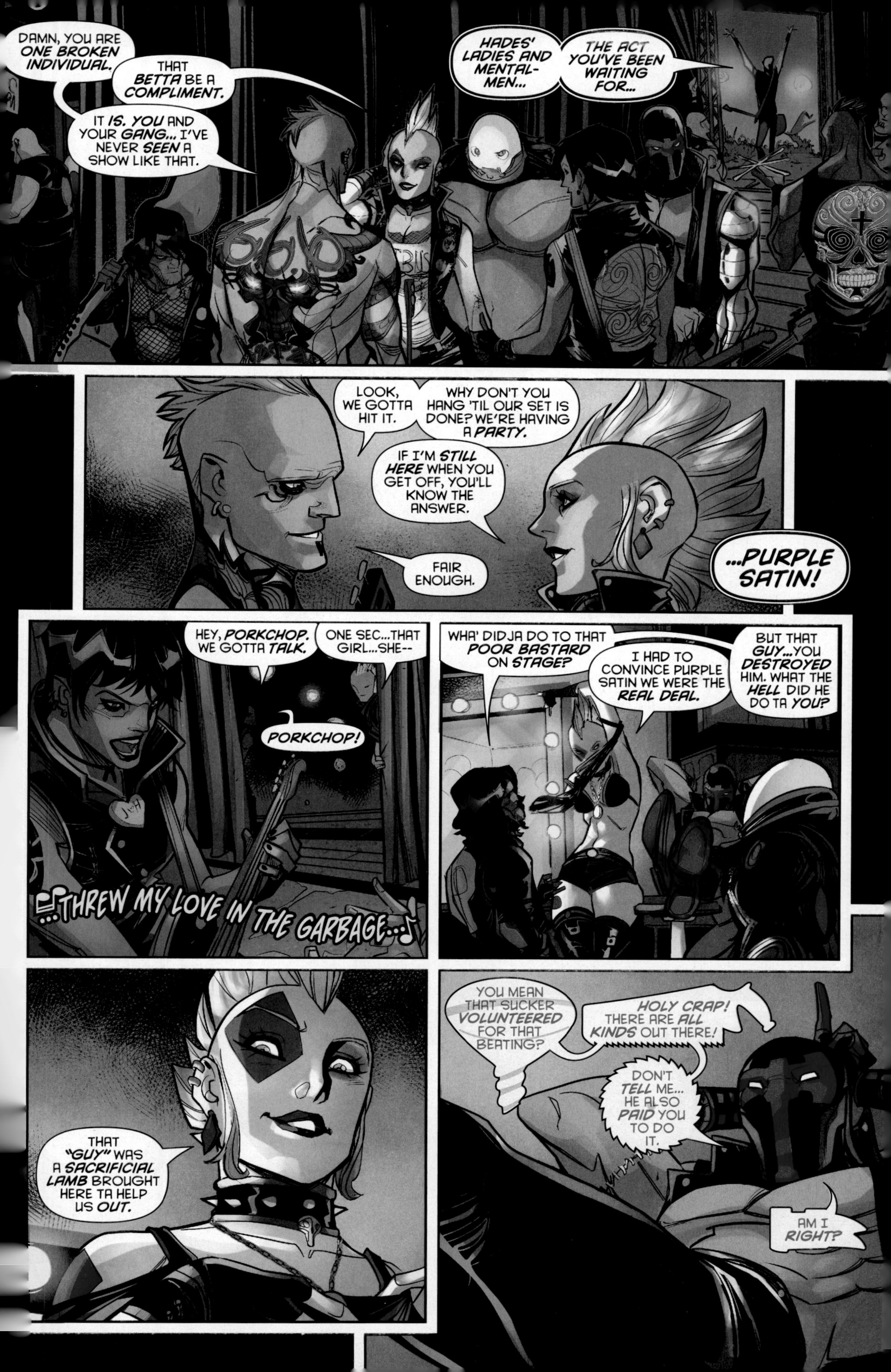
DAMN, YOU ARE ONE BROKEN INDIVIDUAL.
THAT BETTA BE A COMPLIMENT.
IT IS. YOU AND YOUR GANG... I'VE NEVER SEEN A SHOW LIKE THAT.
HADES' LADIES AND MENTAL-MEN...
THE ACT YOU'VE BEEN WAITING FOR...
LOOK, WE GOTTA HIT IT.
WHY DON'T YOU HANG 'TIL OUR SET IS DONE? WE'RE HAVING A PARTY.
IF I'M STILL HERE WHEN YOU GET OFF, YOU'LL KNOW THE ANSWER.
FAIR ENOUGH.
...PURPLE SATIN!
HEY, PORKCHOP. WE GOTTA TALK.
ONE SEC...THAT GIRL...SHE--
PORKCHOP!
...THREW MY LOVE IN THE GARBAGE...
WHA' DIDJA DO TO THAT POOR BASTARD ON STAGE?
I HAD TO CONVINCE PURPLE SATIN WE WERE THE REAL DEAL.
BUT THAT GUY...YOU DESTROYED HIM. WHAT THE HELL DID HE DO TA YOU?
THAT "GUY" WAS A SACRIFICIAL LAMB BROUGHT HERE TA HELP US OUT.
YOU MEAN THAT SUCKER VOLUNTEERED FOR THAT BEATING?
HOLY CRAP! THERE ARE ALL KINDS OUT THERE!
DON'T TELL ME... HE ALSO PAID YOU TO DO IT.
AM I RIGHT?

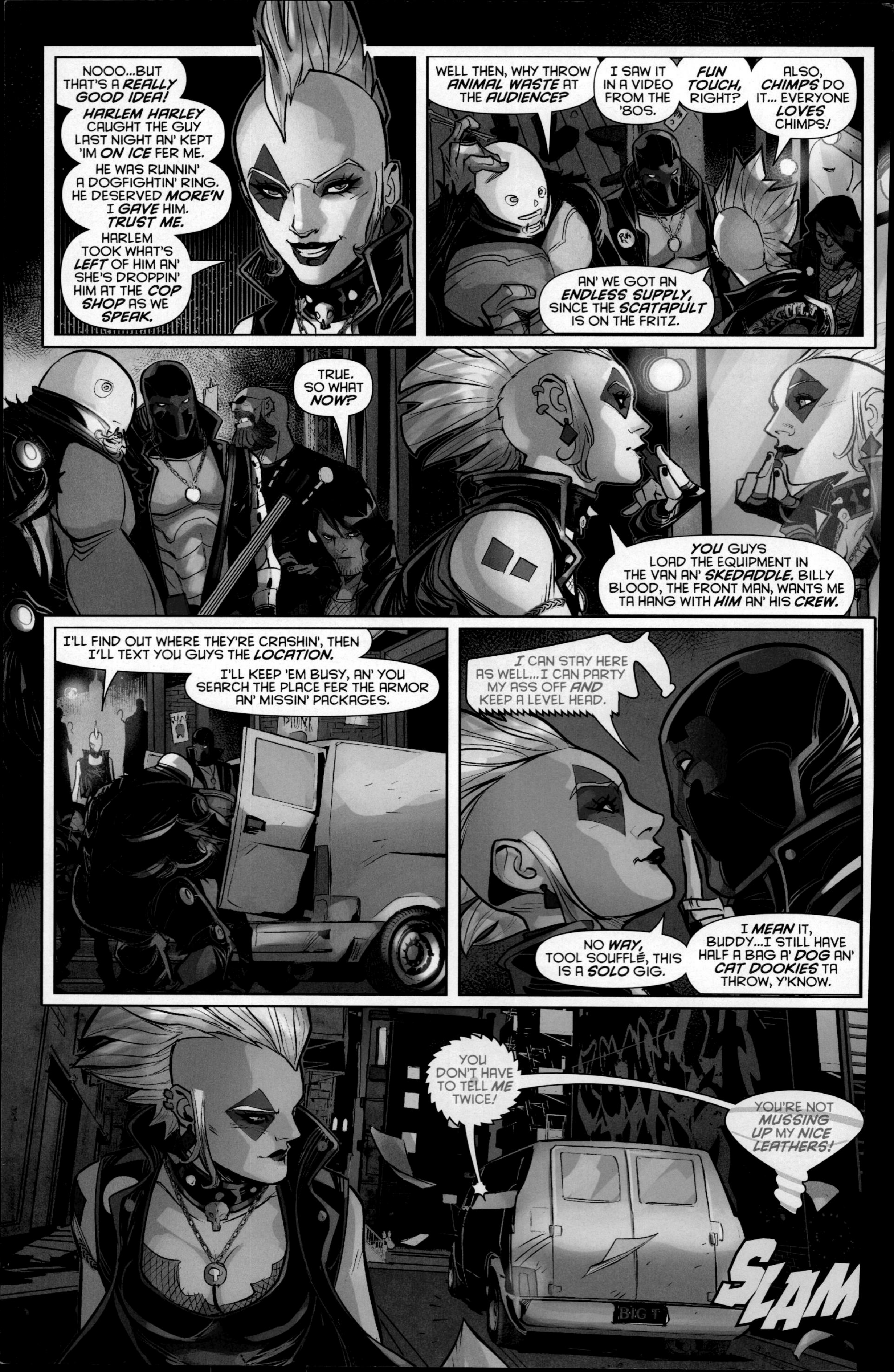
NOOO...BUT THAT'S A REALLY GOOD IDEA!
HARLEM HARLEY CAUGHT THE GUY LAST NIGHT AN' KEPT 'IM ON ICE FER ME.
HE WAS RUNNIN' A DOGFIGHTIN' RING. HE DESERVED MORE'N I GAVE HIM. TRUST ME.
HARLEM TOOK WHAT'S LEFT OF HIM AN' SHE'S DROPPIN' HIM AT THE COP SHOP AS WE SPEAK.
WELL THEN, WHY THROW ANIMAL WASTE AT THE AUDIENCE?
I SAW IT IN A VIDEO FROM THE '80S.
FUN TOUCH, RIGHT?
ALSO, CHIMPS DO IT... EVERYONE LOVES CHIMPS!
AN' WE GOT AN ENDLESS SUPPLY, SINCE THE SCATAPULT IS ON THE FRITZ.
TRUE. SO WHAT NOW?
YOU GUYS LOAD THE EQUIPMENT IN THE VAN AN' SKEDADDLE. BILLY BLOOD, THE FRONT MAN, WANTS ME TA HANG WITH HIM AN' HIS CREW.
I'LL FIND OUT WHERE THEY'RE CRASHIN', THEN I'LL TEXT YOU GUYS THE LOCATION.
I'LL KEEP 'EM BUSY, AN' YOU SEARCH THE PLACE FER THE ARMOR AN' MISSIN' PACKAGES.
I CAN STAY HERE AS WELL...I CAN PARTY MY ASS OFF AND KEEP A LEVEL HEAD.
NO WAY, TOOL SOUFFLÉ, THIS IS A SOLO GIG.
I MEAN IT, BUDDY...I STILL HAVE HALF A BAG A' DOG AN' CAT DOOKIES TA THROW, Y'KNOW.
YOU DON'T HAVE TO TELL ME TWICE!
YOU'RE NOT MUSSING UP MY NICE LEATHERS!
BIG T
SLAM

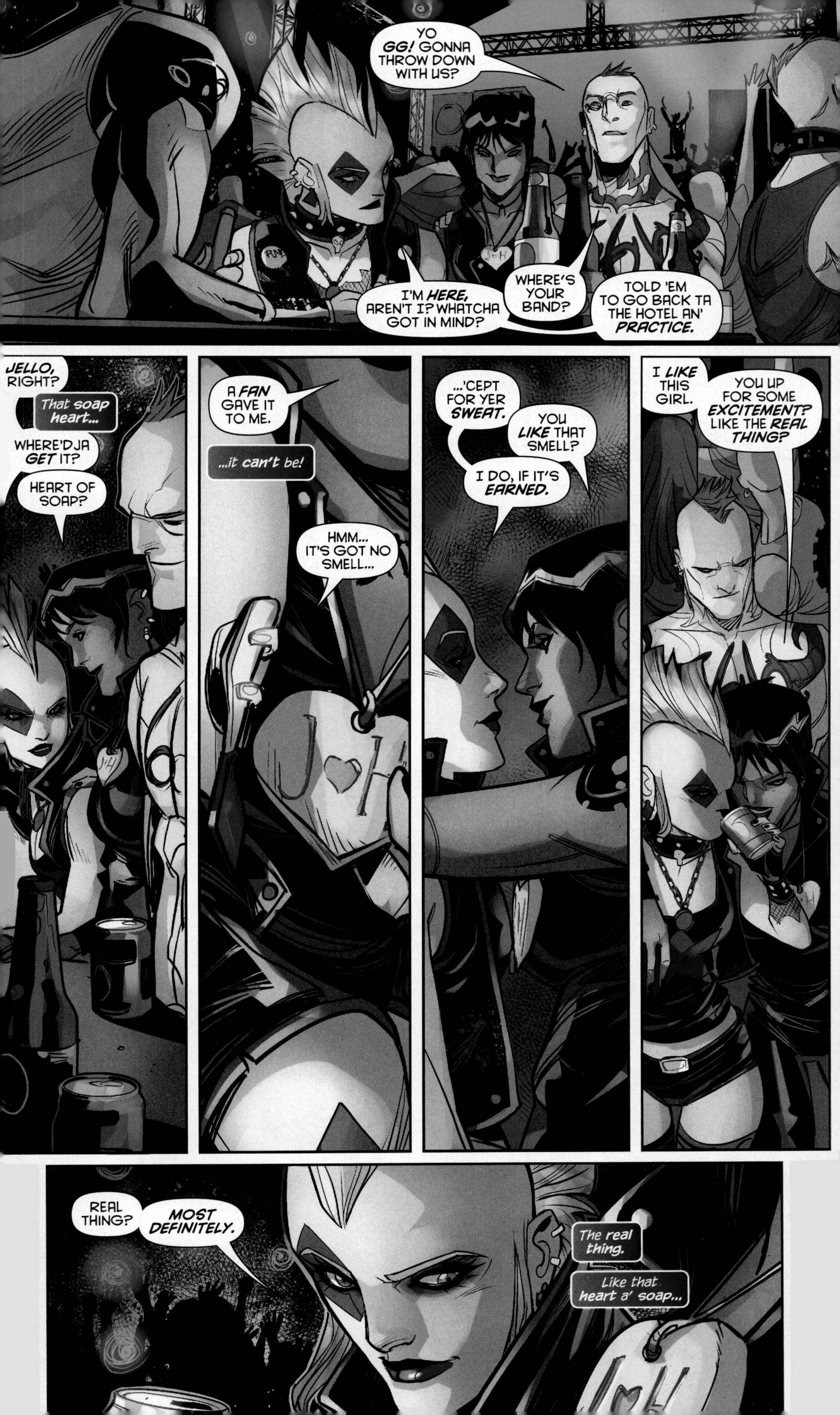
YO GG! GONNA THROW DOWN WITH US?
I'M HERE, AREN'T I? WHATCHA GOT IN MIND?
WHERE'S YOUR BAND?
TOLD 'EM TO GO BACK TA THE HOTEL AN' PRACTICE.
JELLO, RIGHT?
That soap heart...
WHERE'DJA GET IT?
HEART OF SOAP?
A FAN GAVE IT TO ME.
...it can't be!
HMM... IT'S GOT NO SMELL...
...'CEPT FOR YER SWEAT.
YOU LIKE THAT SMELL?
I DO, IF IT'S EARNED.
I LIKE THIS GIRL.
YOU UP FOR SOME EXCITEMENT? LIKE THE REAL THING?
REAL THING?
MOST DEFINITELY.
The real thing.
Like that heart a' soap...

...I haven't seen it in *years.*

DR. QUINZEL, YOUR LAST APPOINTMENT OF THE DAY IS HERE.

PLEASE, SEND HIM *IN.*

DOCTOR... I SEE YOU SAVED THE *BEST* FOR LAST.

SHUT YOUR *MOUTH,* PRISONER.

INTERTWINE YOUR FINGERS AND RELAX YOUR ARMS.

WHATEVER YOU *SAY.*

OTHER HAND.

THAT ISN'T NECESSARY, SINCE YOU *WILL* BE STATIONED OUTSIDE MY DOOR, *RIGHT?*

THIS PRISONER IS TO BE RESTRAINED AT *ALL TIMES.* RULES.

FINE.

FRIENDLY FELLOW, DON'T YA THINK?

THE REPORT SAYS YOU HAD AN ALTERCATION WITH ANOTHER PRISONER.

YOU BIT HIS LEF EAR OFF AND SLAMM HEAD WITH A DOOR, C MULTIPLE FRACTURES CONCUSSION.

LET'S *TALK* ABC THAT. MAY I ASK WH WERE FEELING TO E ABOUT SUCH A OUTBURST?

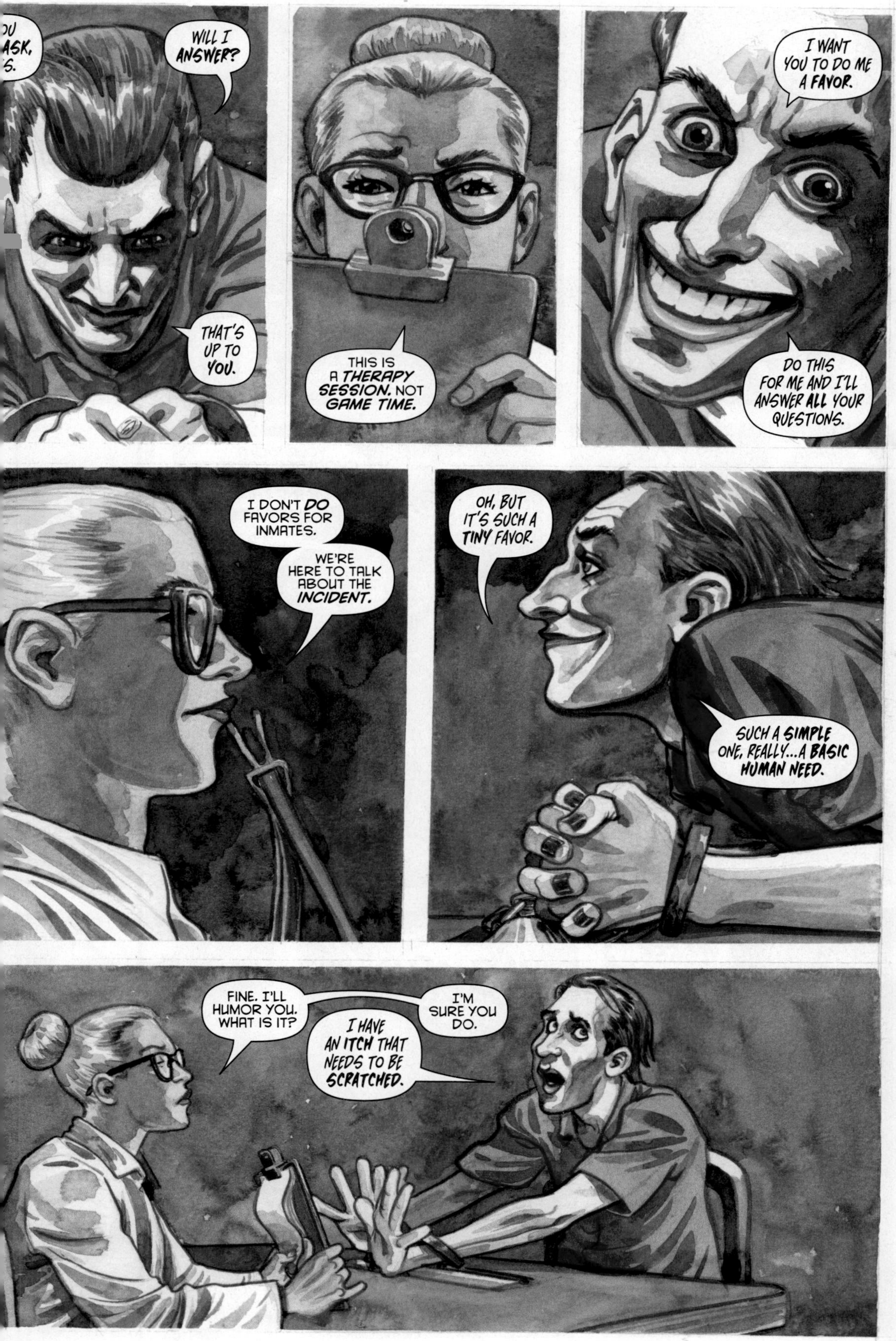
WILL I ANSWER?
THAT'S UP TO YOU.
THIS IS A THERAPY SESSION. NOT GAME TIME.
I WANT YOU TO DO ME A FAVOR.
DO THIS FOR ME AND I'LL ANSWER ALL YOUR QUESTIONS.
I DON'T DO FAVORS FOR INMATES.
WE'RE HERE TO TALK ABOUT THE INCIDENT.
OH, BUT IT'S SUCH A TINY FAVOR.
SUCH A SIMPLE ONE, REALLY...A BASIC HUMAN NEED.
FINE. I'LL HUMOR YOU. WHAT IS IT?
I'M SURE YOU DO.
I HAVE AN ITCH THAT NEEDS TO BE SCRATCHED.

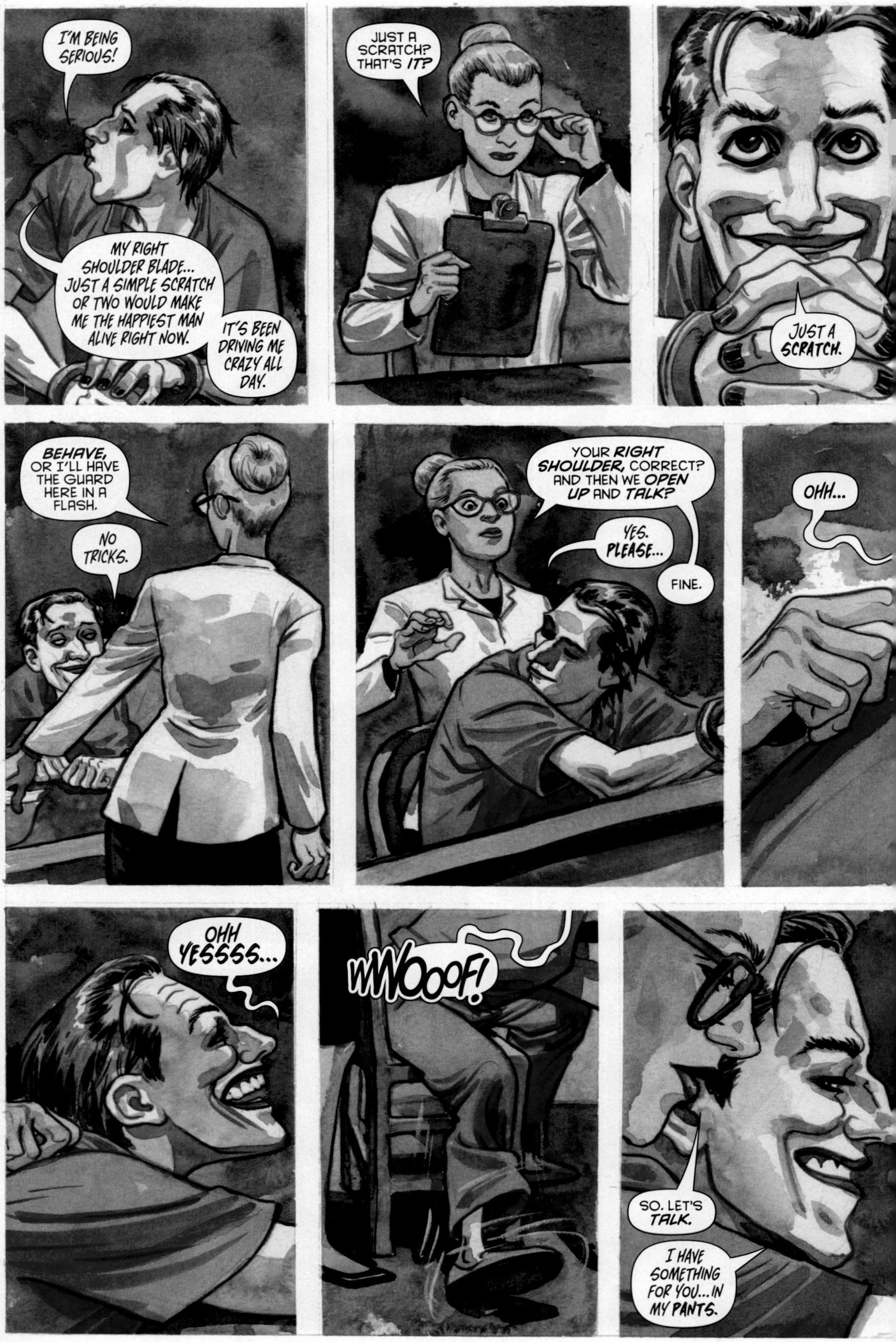
I'M BEING SERIOUS!
MY RIGHT SHOULDER BLADE... JUST A SIMPLE SCRATCH OR TWO WOULD MAKE ME THE HAPPIEST MAN ALIVE RIGHT NOW.
IT'S BEEN DRIVING ME CRAZY ALL DAY.
JUST A SCRATCH? THAT'S IT?
JUST A SCRATCH.
BEHAVE, OR I'LL HAVE THE GUARD HERE IN A FLASH.
NO TRICKS.
YOUR RIGHT SHOULDER, CORRECT? AND THEN WE OPEN UP AND TALK?
YES. PLEASE...
FINE.
OHH...
OHH YESSSS...
WWOOOF!
SO. LET'S TALK.
I HAVE SOMETHING FOR YOU... IN MY PANTS.

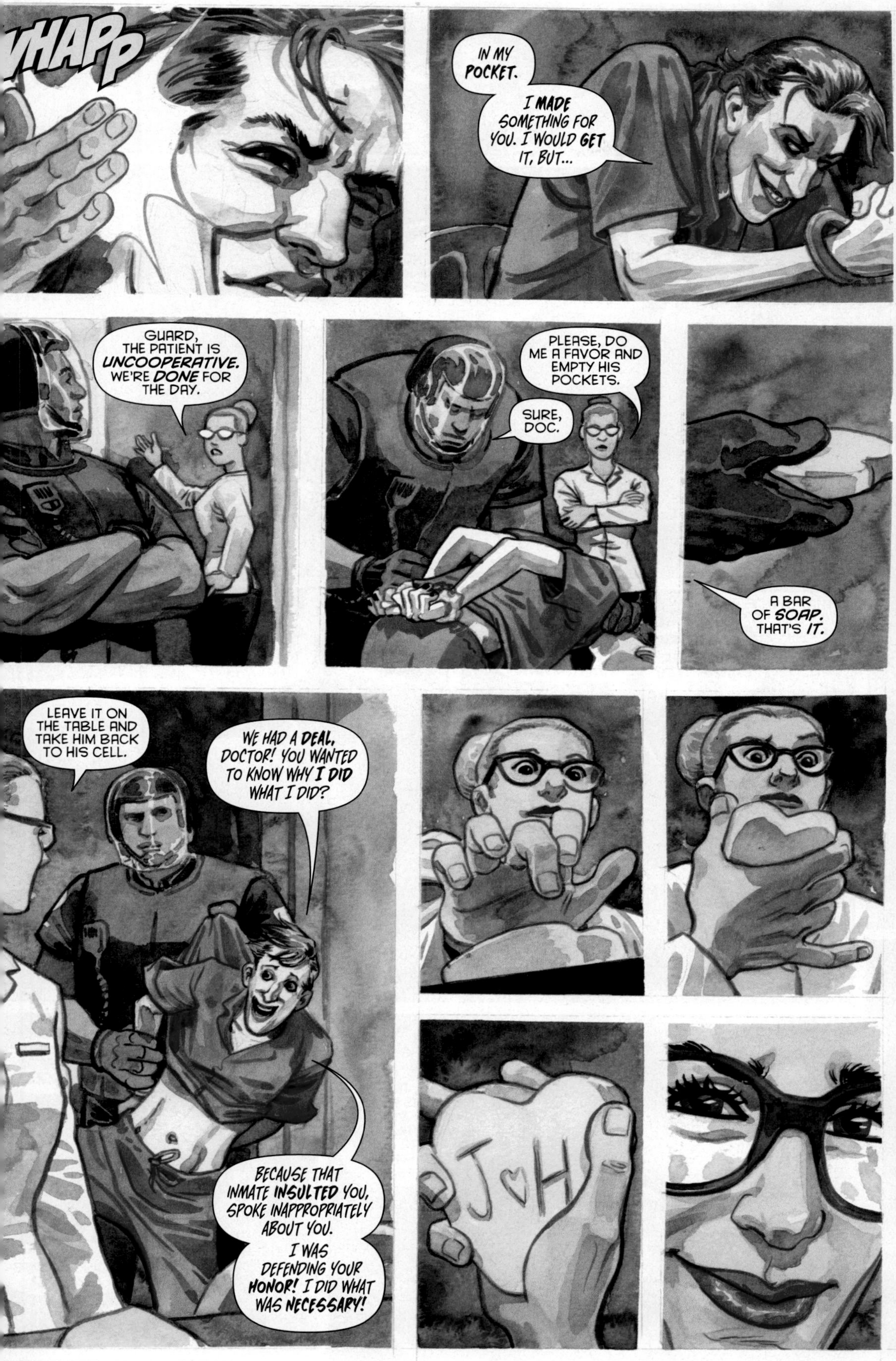
WHAPP
IN MY POCKET.
I MADE SOMETHING FOR YOU. I WOULD GET IT, BUT...
GUARD, THE PATIENT IS UNCOOPERATIVE. WE'RE DONE FOR THE DAY.
PLEASE, DO ME A FAVOR AND EMPTY HIS POCKETS.
SURE, DOC.
A BAR OF SOAP. THAT'S IT.
LEAVE IT ON THE TABLE AND TAKE HIM BACK TO HIS CELL.
WE HAD A DEAL, DOCTOR! YOU WANTED TO KNOW WHY I DID WHAT I DID?
BECAUSE THAT INMATE INSULTED YOU, SPOKE INAPPROPRIATELY ABOUT YOU.
I WAS DEFENDING YOUR HONOR! I DID WHAT WAS NECESSARY!
J♡H

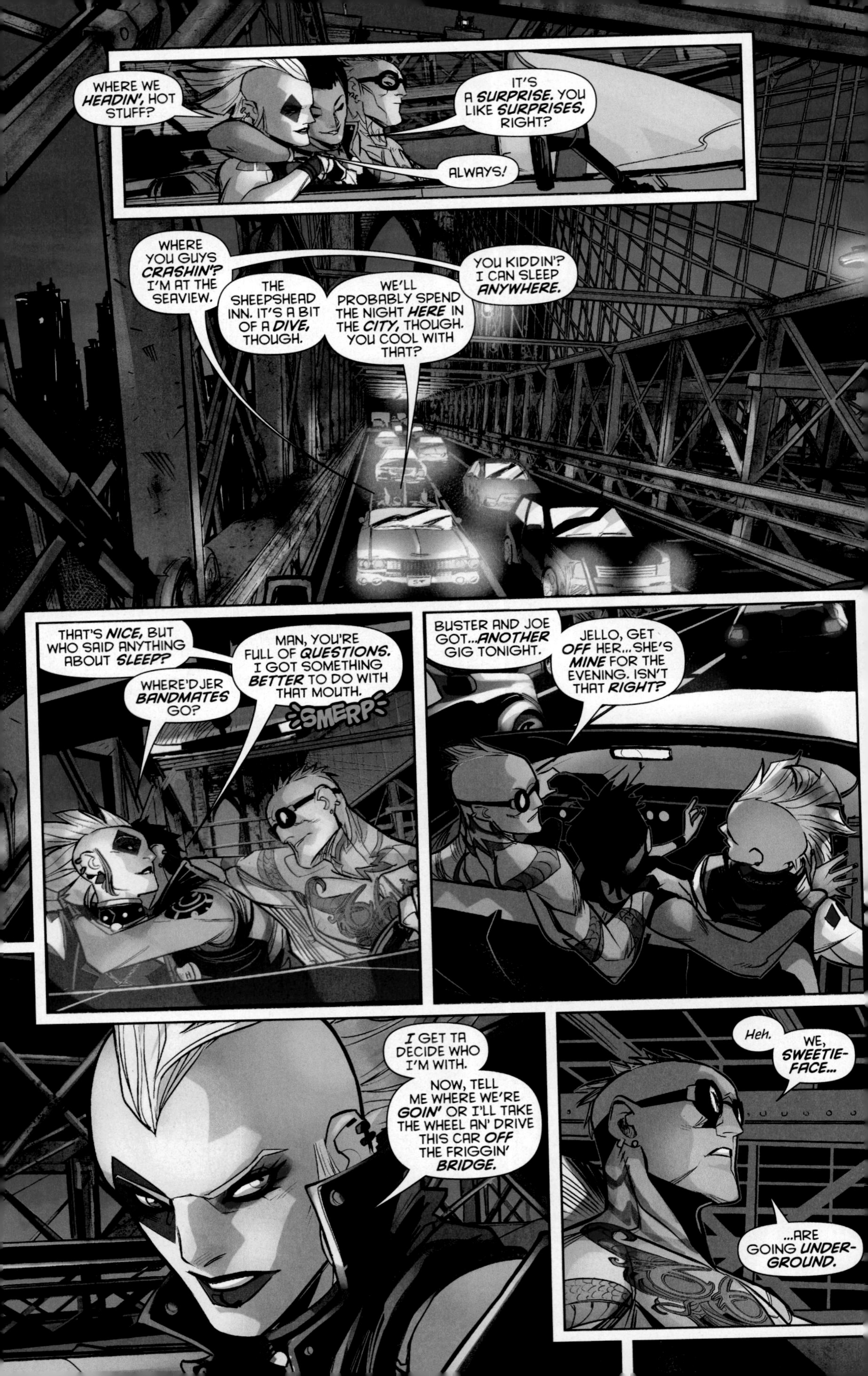

WHERE WE HEADIN', HOT STUFF?
IT'S A SURPRISE. YOU LIKE SURPRISES, RIGHT?
ALWAYS!
WHERE YOU GUYS CRASHIN'? I'M AT THE SEAVIEW.
THE SHEEPSHEAD INN. IT'S A BIT OF A DIVE, THOUGH.
WE'LL PROBABLY SPEND THE NIGHT HERE IN THE CITY, THOUGH. YOU COOL WITH THAT?
YOU KIDDIN'? I CAN SLEEP ANYWHERE.
THAT'S NICE, BUT WHO SAID ANYTHING ABOUT SLEEP?
WHERE'DJER BANDMATES GO?
MAN, YOU'RE FULL OF QUESTIONS. I GOT SOMETHING BETTER TO DO WITH THAT MOUTH.
SMERP
BUSTER AND JOE GOT...ANOTHER GIG TONIGHT.
JELLO, GET OFF HER...SHE'S MINE FOR THE EVENING. ISN'T THAT RIGHT?
I GET TA DECIDE WHO I'M WITH.
NOW, TELL ME WHERE WE'RE GOIN' OR I'LL TAKE THE WHEEL AN' DRIVE THIS CAR OFF THE FRIGGIN' BRIDGE.
Heh.
WE, SWEETIE-FACE...
...ARE GOING UNDER-GROUND.

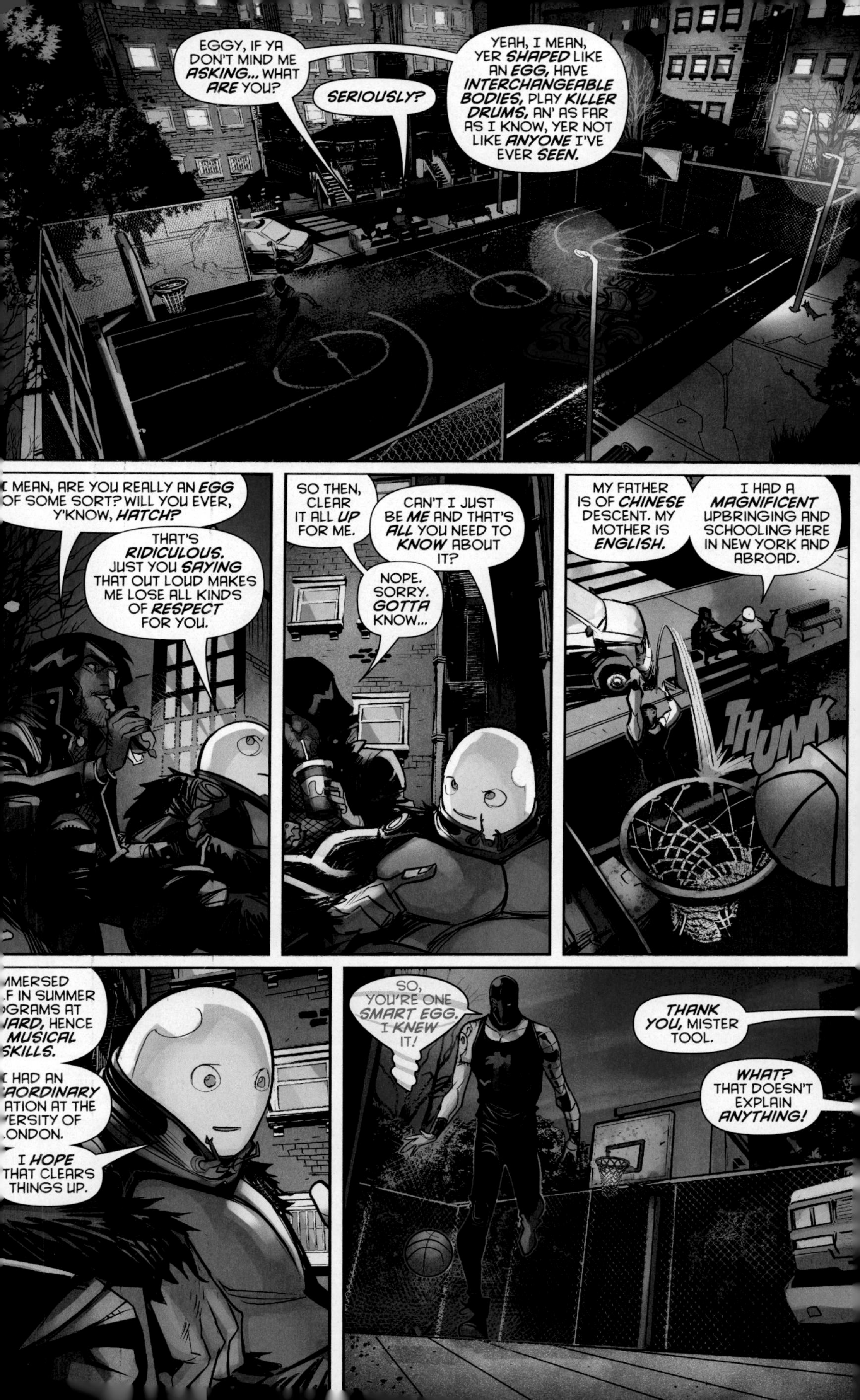
EGGY, IF YA DON'T MIND ME ASKING... WHAT ARE YOU?
SERIOUSLY?
YEAH, I MEAN, YER SHAPED LIKE AN EGG, HAVE INTERCHANGEABLE BODIES, PLAY KILLER DRUMS, AN' AS FAR AS I KNOW, YER NOT LIKE ANYONE I'VE EVER SEEN.
I MEAN, ARE YOU REALLY AN EGG OF SOME SORT? WILL YOU EVER, Y'KNOW, HATCH?
THAT'S RIDICULOUS. JUST YOU SAYING THAT OUT LOUD MAKES ME LOSE ALL KINDS OF RESPECT FOR YOU.
SO THEN, CLEAR IT ALL UP FOR ME.
CAN'T I JUST BE ME AND THAT'S ALL YOU NEED TO KNOW ABOUT IT?
NOPE. SORRY. GOTTA KNOW...
MY FATHER IS OF CHINESE DESCENT. MY MOTHER IS ENGLISH.
I HAD A MAGNIFICENT UPBRINGING AND SCHOOLING HERE IN NEW YORK AND ABROAD.
THUNK
MMERSED LF IN SUMMER OGRAMS AT IARD, HENCE MUSICAL SKILLS.
I HAD AN AORDINARY ATION AT THE VERSITY OF LONDON.
I HOPE THAT CLEARS THINGS UP.
SO, YOU'RE ONE SMART EGG. I KNEW IT!
THANK YOU, MISTER TOOL.
WHAT? THAT DOESN'T EXPLAIN ANYTHING!

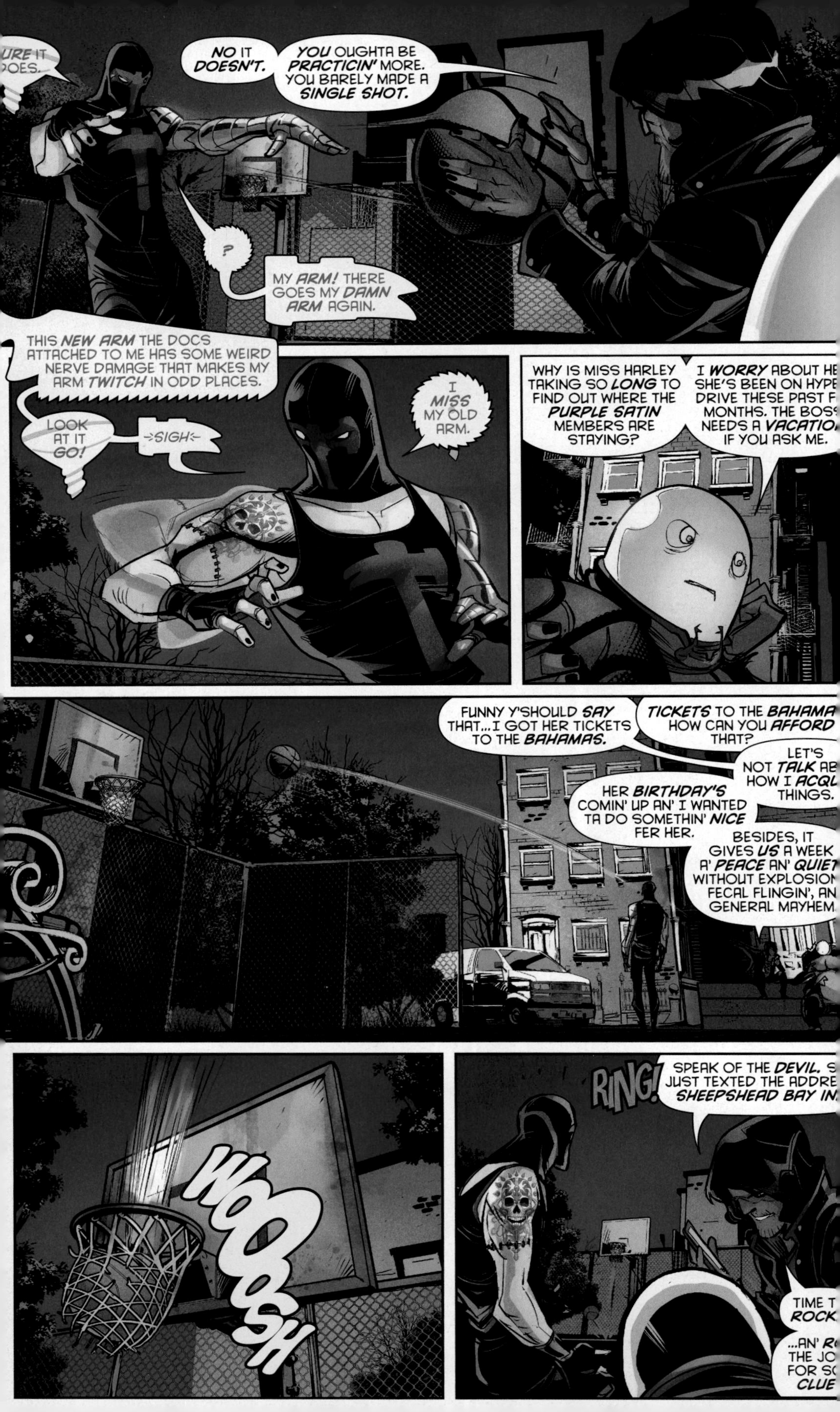
URE IT
DOES.
NO IT DOESN'T.
YOU OUGHTA BE PRACTICIN' MORE. YOU BARELY MADE A SINGLE SHOT.
?
MY ARM! THERE GOES MY DAMN ARM AGAIN.
THIS NEW ARM THE DOCS ATTACHED TO ME HAS SOME WEIRD NERVE DAMAGE THAT MAKES MY ARM TWITCH IN ODD PLACES.
LOOK AT IT GO!
SIGH
I MISS MY OLD ARM.
WHY IS MISS HARLEY TAKING SO LONG TO FIND OUT WHERE THE PURPLE SATIN MEMBERS ARE STAYING?
I WORRY ABOUT HE
SHE'S BEEN ON HYPE
DRIVE THESE PAST F
MONTHS. THE BOS
NEEDS A VACATIO
IF YOU ASK ME.
FUNNY Y'SHOULD SAY THAT...I GOT HER TICKETS TO THE BAHAMAS.
TICKETS TO THE BAHAMA
HOW CAN YOU AFFORD
THAT?
LET'S
NOT TALK AB
HOW I ACQU
THINGS.
HER BIRTHDAY'S COMIN' UP AN' I WANTED TA DO SOMETHIN' NICE FER HER.
BESIDES, IT
GIVES US A WEEK
A' PEACE AN' QUIET
WITHOUT EXPLOSION
FECAL FLINGIN', AN
GENERAL MAYHEM.
WOOOSH
RING!
SPEAK OF THE DEVIL. S
JUST TEXTED THE ADDRE
SHEEPSHEAD BAY IN
TIME T
ROCK
...AN' R
THE JO
FOR S
CLUE

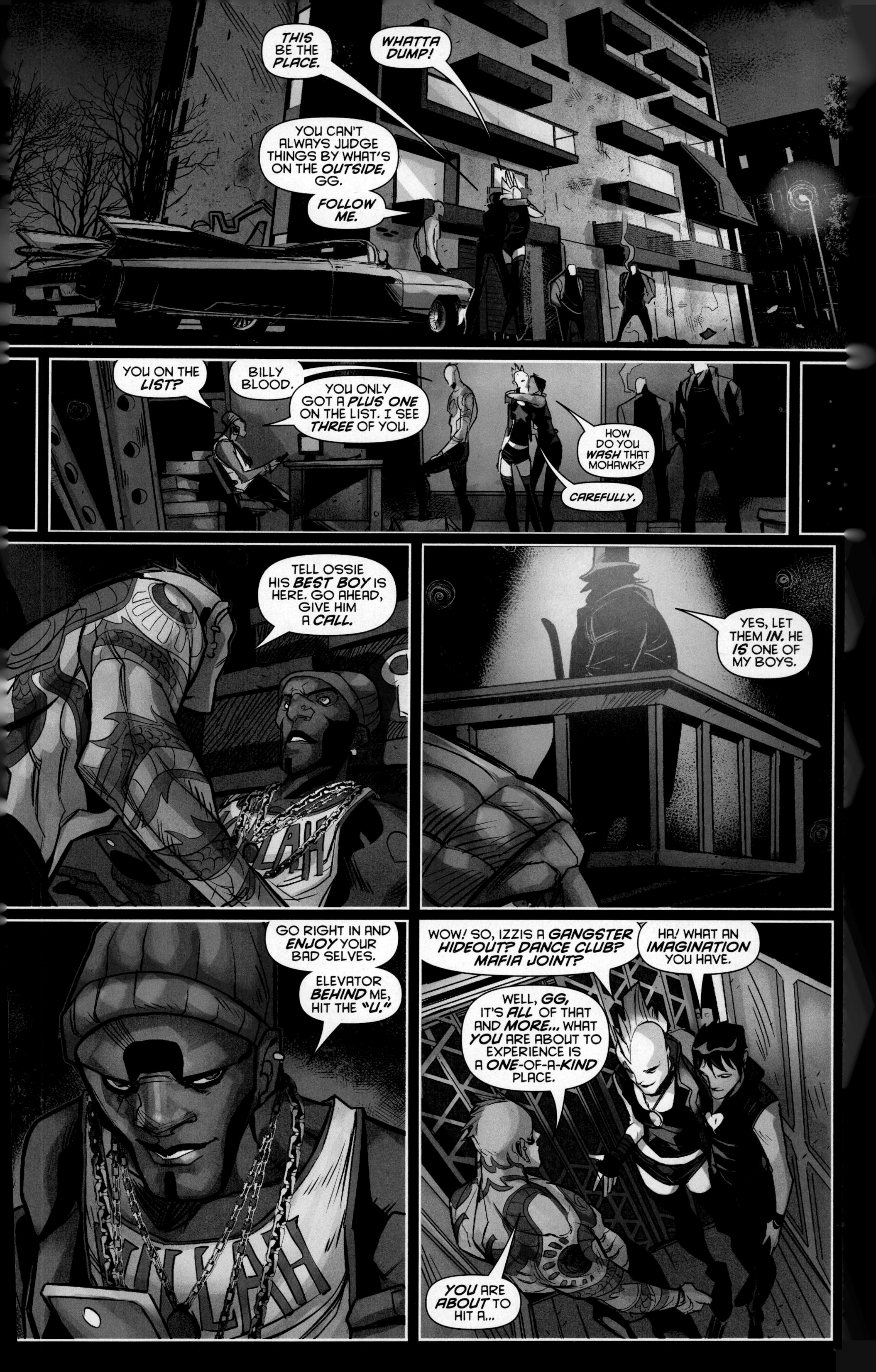
THIS BE THE PLACE.
WHATTA DUMP!
YOU CAN'T ALWAYS JUDGE THINGS BY WHAT'S ON THE OUTSIDE, GG.
FOLLOW ME.
YOU ON THE LIST?
BILLY BLOOD.
YOU ONLY GOT A PLUS ONE ON THE LIST. I SEE THREE OF YOU.
HOW DO YOU WASH THAT MOHAWK?
CAREFULLY.
TELL OSSIE HIS BEST BOY IS HERE. GO AHEAD, GIVE HIM A CALL.
YES, LET THEM IN. HE IS ONE OF MY BOYS.
GO RIGHT IN AND ENJOY YOUR BAD SELVES.
ELEVATOR BEHIND ME, HIT THE "U."
WOW! SO, IZZIS A GANGSTER HIDEOUT? DANCE CLUB? MAFIA JOINT?
HA! WHAT AN IMAGINATION YOU HAVE.
WELL, GG, IT'S ALL OF THAT AND MORE... WHAT YOU ARE ABOUT TO EXPERIENCE IS A ONE-OF-A-KIND PLACE.
YOU ARE ABOUT TO HIT A...

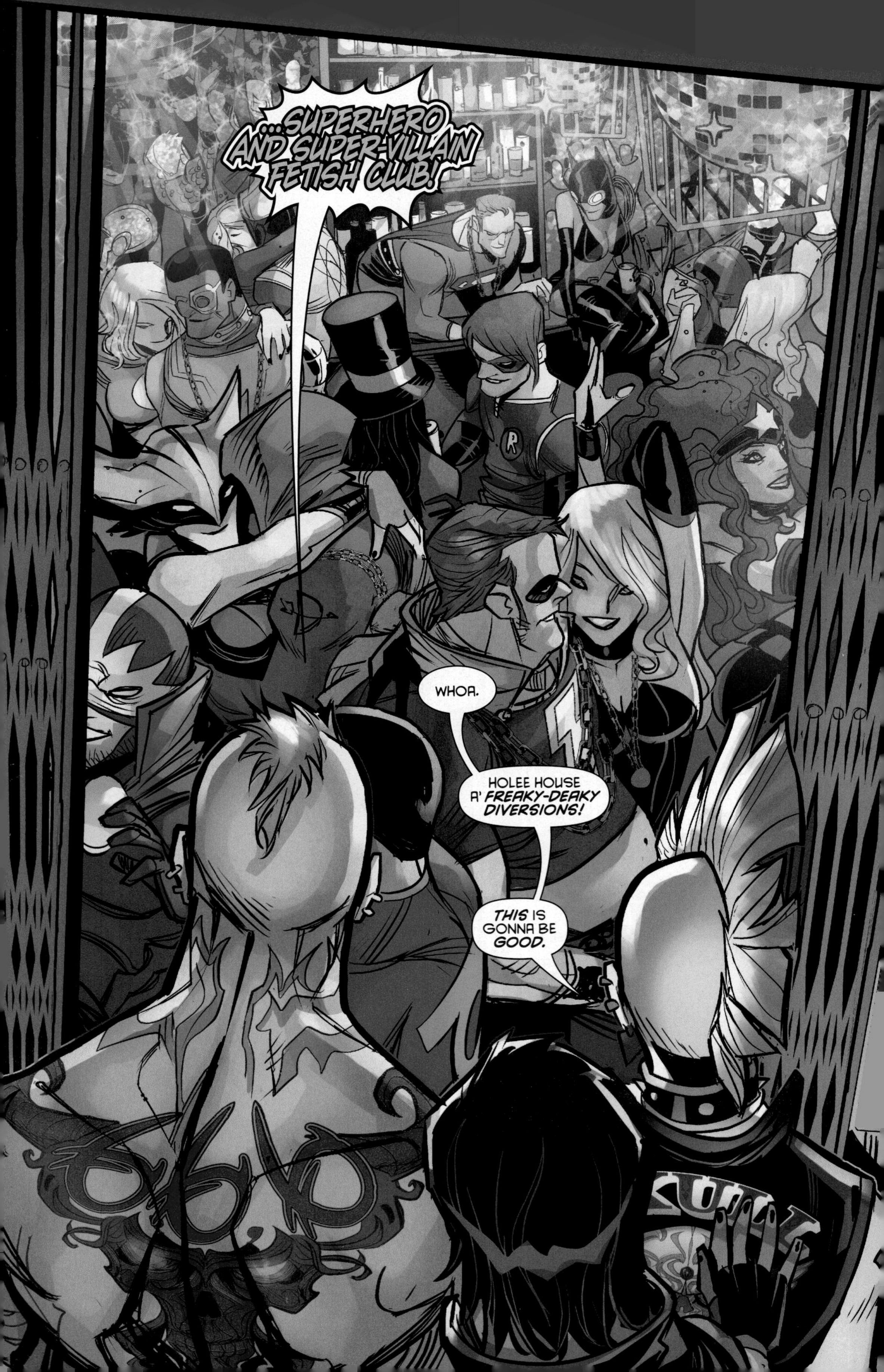
...SUPERHERO AND SUPER-VILLAIN FETISH CLUB!
WHOA.
HOLEE HOUSE A' FREAKY-DEAKY DIVERSIONS!
THIS IS GONNA BE GOOD.

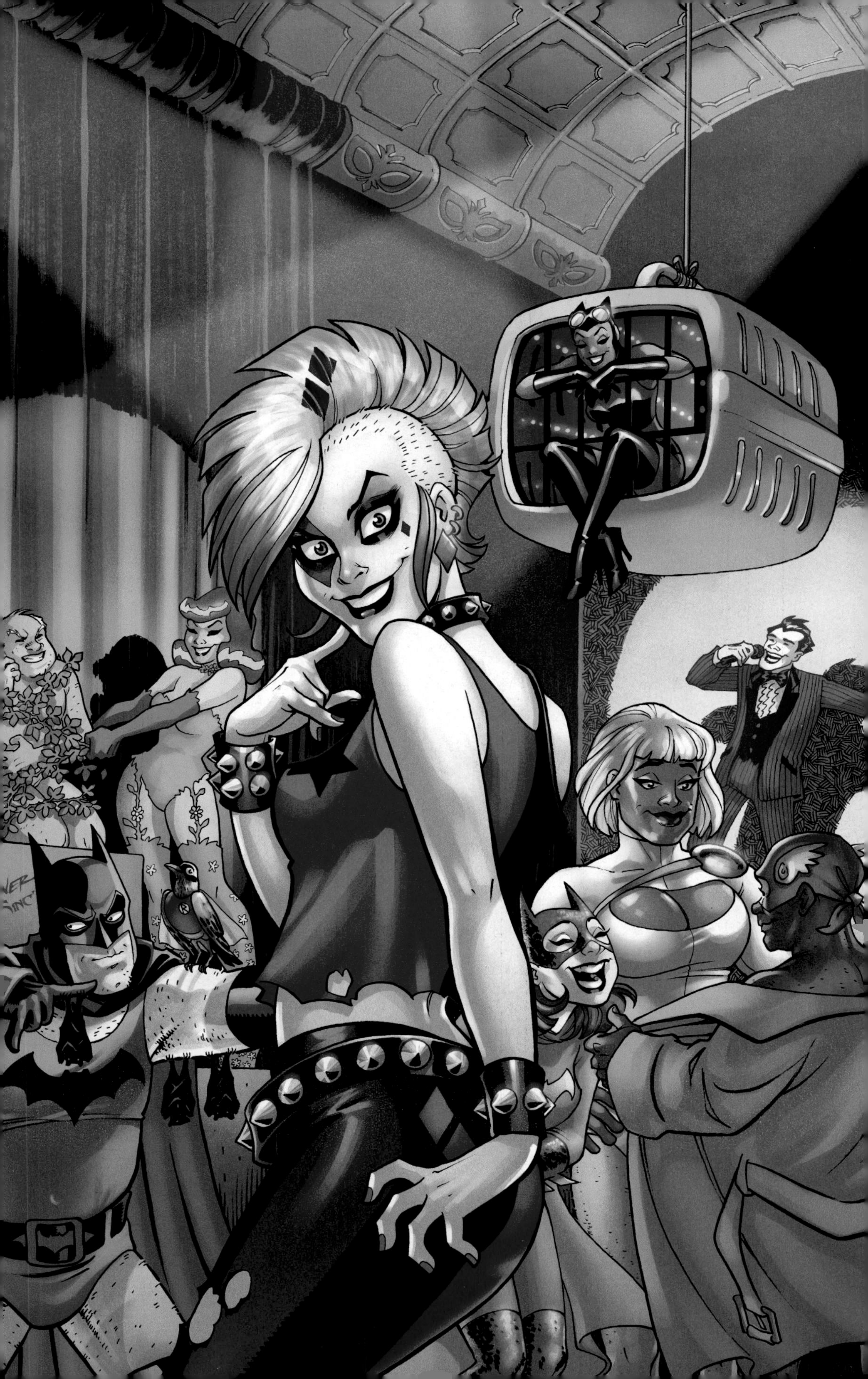

UNDERCOVER PUNKER PART 3: SATIN UNDERGROUND

AMANDA CONNER and JIMMY PALMIOTTI writers * JOHN TIMMS artist

ALEX SINCLAIR with HI-FI colorists * DAVE SHARPE letterer

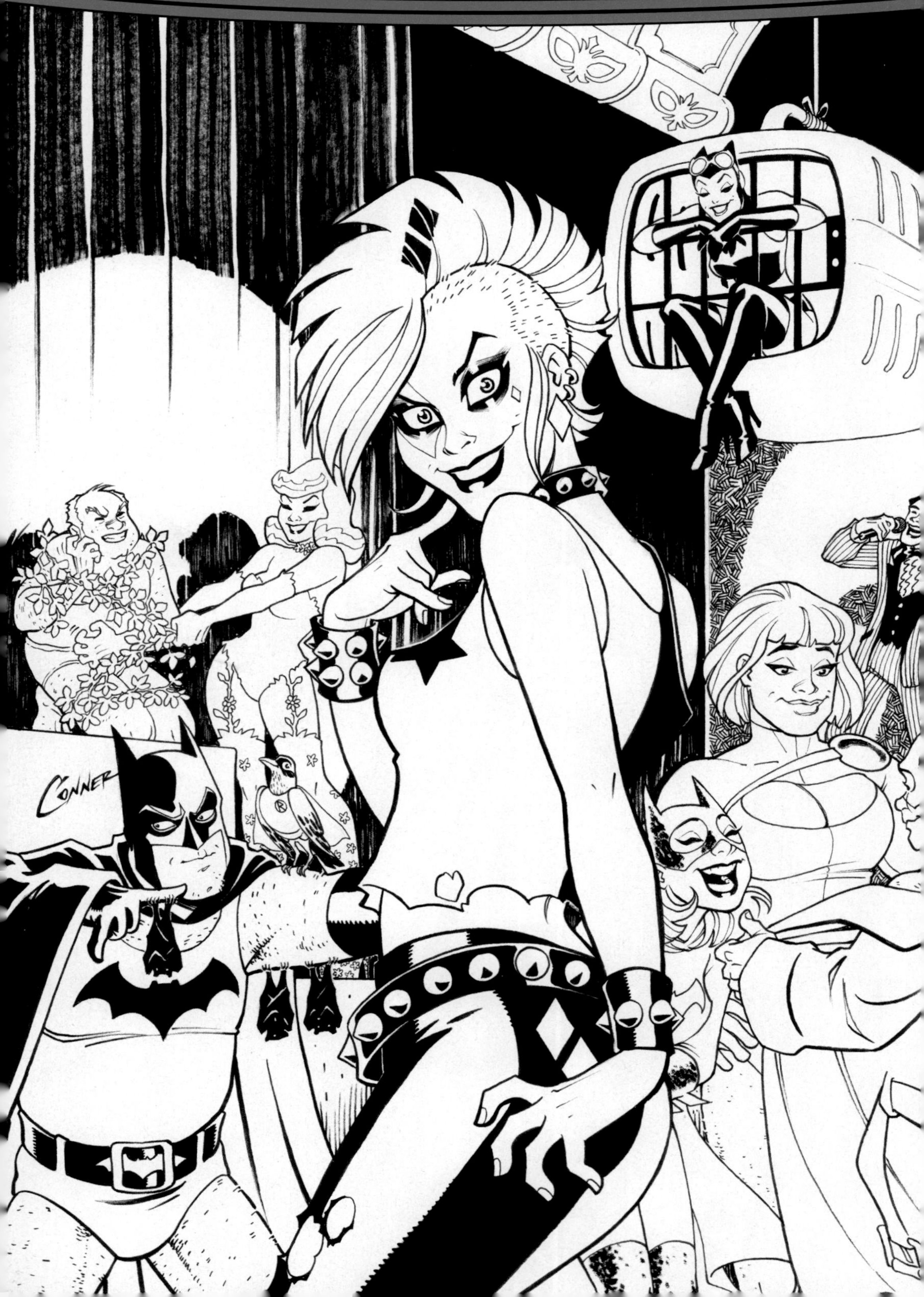
CONNER

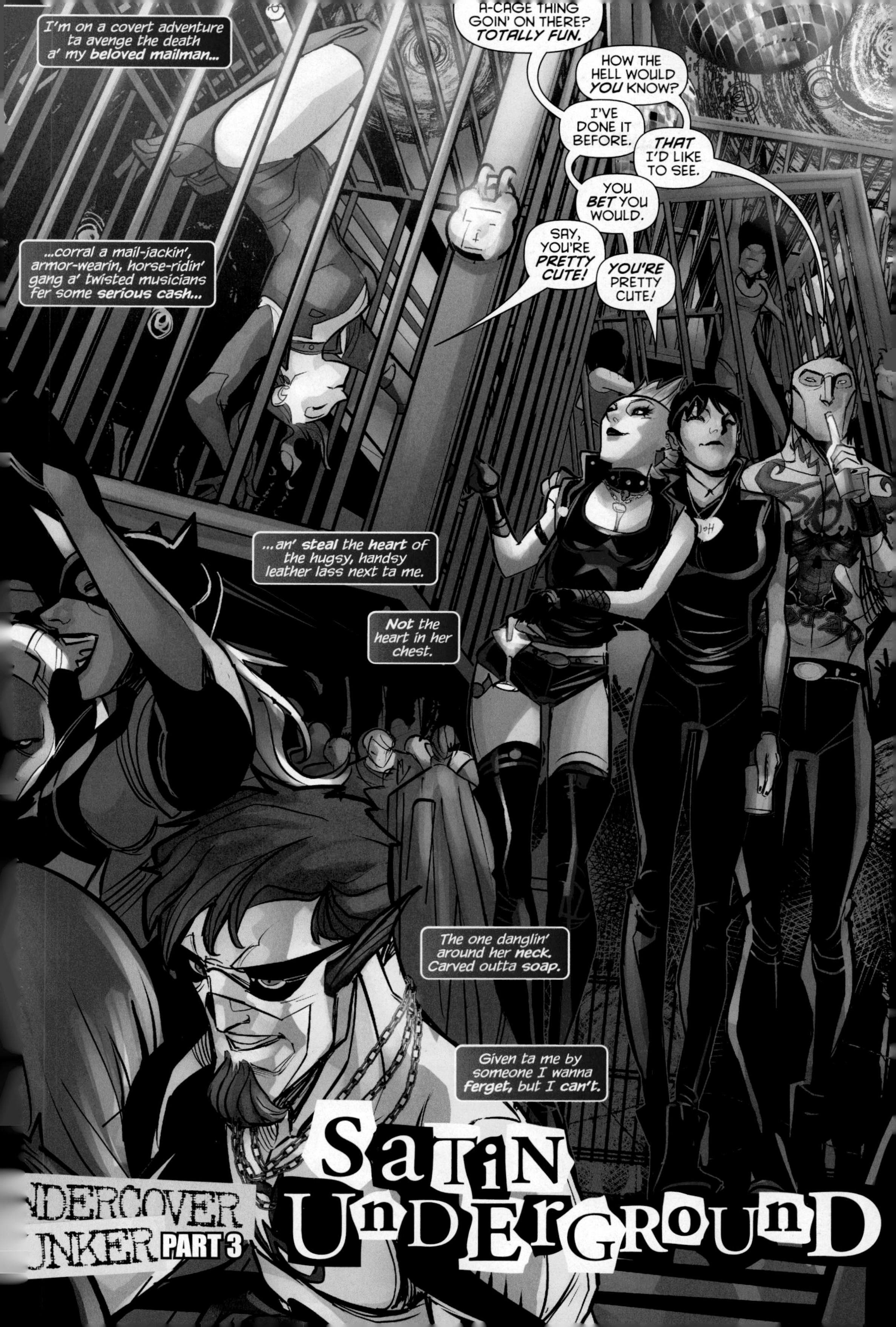

I'm on a covert adventure ta avenge the death a' my beloved mailman...
A-CAGE THING GOIN' ON THERE? TOTALLY FUN.
HOW THE HELL WOULD YOU KNOW?
I'VE DONE IT BEFORE.
THAT I'D LIKE TO SEE.
YOU BET YOU WOULD.
SAY, YOU'RE PRETTY CUTE!
YOU'RE PRETTY CUTE!
...corral a mail-jackin', armor-wearin, horse-ridin' gang a' twisted musicians fer some serious cash...
...an' steal the heart of the hugsy, handsy leather lass next ta me.
Not the heart in her chest.
The one danglin' around her neck. Carved outta soap.
Given ta me by someone I wanna ferget, but I can't.
SATIN UNDERGROUND
NDERCOVER
UNKER PART 3

THIS PLACE IS *A-FRIGGIN'-MAZIN'!* I'M GONNA COME HERE EVERY--

WOLEE-H2-FIN-SLAPPIN'-OLEE!

C'MON, YOU SACK OF NUTS! LET'S GO.

YO, LOSE THE ROPE. WE'RE GUESTS OF *OSWALD.*

CHECKING.

ALL CLEAR. ENTER.

PRETTY *WILD,* EH?

AND *HOW!* Y'NEVER SEE *REAL* BATMAN KICKIN' BACK LIKE THAT.

HOW DO YOU KNOW *THAT?*

I'M JUST *SAYIN'...*

...SO, IT'S ALL *DRESS-UP* AN' *PARTIES* IN THAT MAIN HALL? THERE ANY *OTHER* ROOMS IN THIS JOINT?

OH, THERE ARE *MANY* OTHER ROOMS. WANNA *EXPLORE?*

SURE, BUT LEMME HIT THE *CAN* FIRST. BE RIGHT BACK.

YOU SURE YOU DON'T WANT *COMPANY?*

JEEZ, *ENOUGH* ALREADY, JELLO.

GG, G DO YO *DUTY.* W BE HER

BILLY, THE BOSS WANTS A *WORD* WITH YOU.

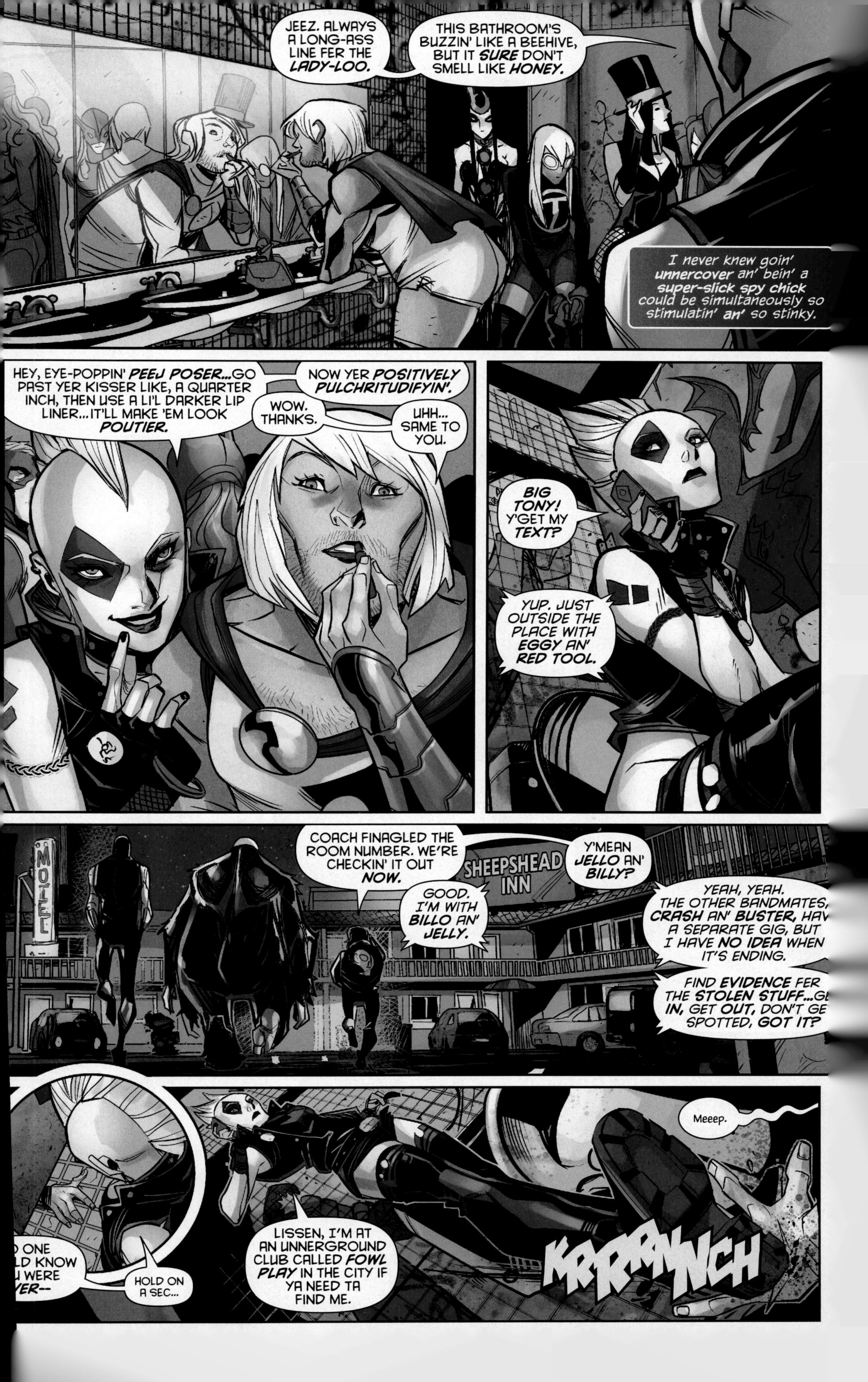

JEEZ. ALWAYS A LONG-ASS LINE FER THE LADY-LOO.
THIS BATHROOM'S BUZZIN' LIKE A BEEHIVE, BUT IT SURE DON'T SMELL LIKE HONEY.
I never knew goin' unnercover an' bein' a super-slick spy chick could be simultaneously so stimulatin' an' so stinky.
HEY, EYE-POPPIN' PEEJ POSER...GO PAST YER KISSER LIKE, A QUARTER INCH, THEN USE A LI'L DARKER LIP LINER...IT'LL MAKE 'EM LOOK POUTIER.
NOW YER POSITIVELY PULCHRITUDIFYIN'.
WOW. THANKS.
UHH... SAME TO YOU.
BIG TONY! Y'GET MY TEXT?
YUP. JUST OUTSIDE THE PLACE WITH EGGY AN' RED TOOL.
MOTEL
SHEEPSHEAD INN
COACH FINAGLED THE ROOM NUMBER. WE'RE CHECKIN' IT OUT NOW.
GOOD. I'M WITH BILLO AN' JELLY.
Y'MEAN JELLO AN' BILLY?
YEAH, YEAH. THE OTHER BANDMATES, CRASH AN' BUSTER, HAV A SEPARATE GIG, BUT I HAVE NO IDEA WHEN IT'S ENDING.
FIND EVIDENCE FER THE STOLEN STUFF...GE IN, GET OUT, DON'T GE SPOTTED, GOT IT?
D ONE LD KNOW U WERE VER--
HOLD ON A SEC...
LISSEN, I'M AT AN UNNERGROUND CLUB CALLED FOWL PLAY IN THE CITY IF YA NEED TA FIND ME.
Meeep.
KRRRNNCH

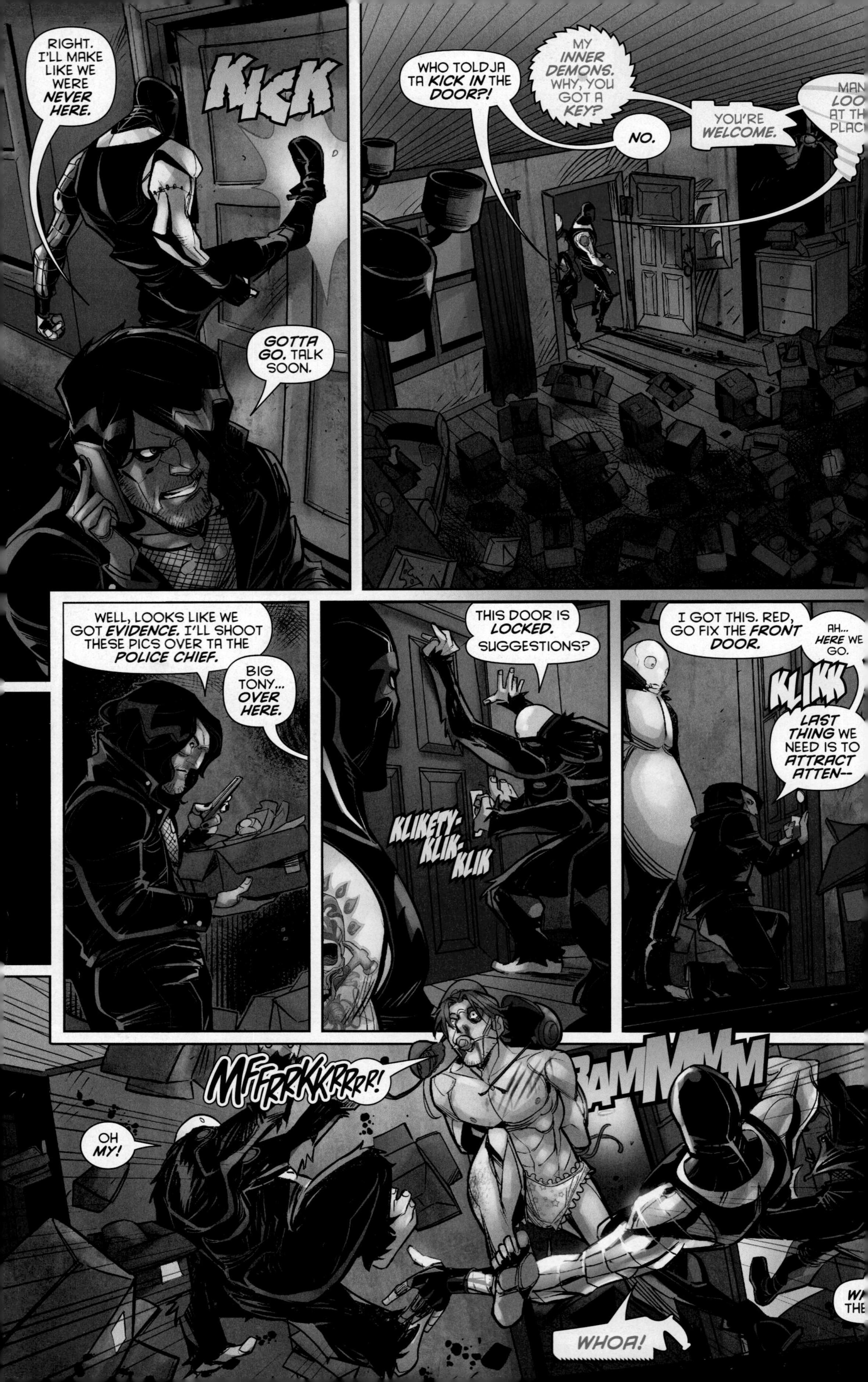
RIGHT. I'LL MAKE LIKE WE WERE NEVER HERE.
KICK
GOTTA GO. TALK SOON.
WHO TOLDJA TA KICK IN THE DOOR?!
MY INNER DEMONS. WHY, YOU GOT A KEY?
NO.
YOU'RE WELCOME.
WELL, LOOKS LIKE WE GOT EVIDENCE. I'LL SHOOT THESE PICS OVER TA THE POLICE CHIEF.
BIG TONY... OVER HERE.
THIS DOOR IS LOCKED. SUGGESTIONS?
KLIKETY-KLIK-KLIK
I GOT THIS. RED, GO FIX THE FRONT DOOR.
AH... HERE WE GO.
KLIKK
LAST THING WE NEED IS TO ATTRACT ATTEN--
MFFRRKKRRRR!
BAMMMMM
OH MY!
WHOA!

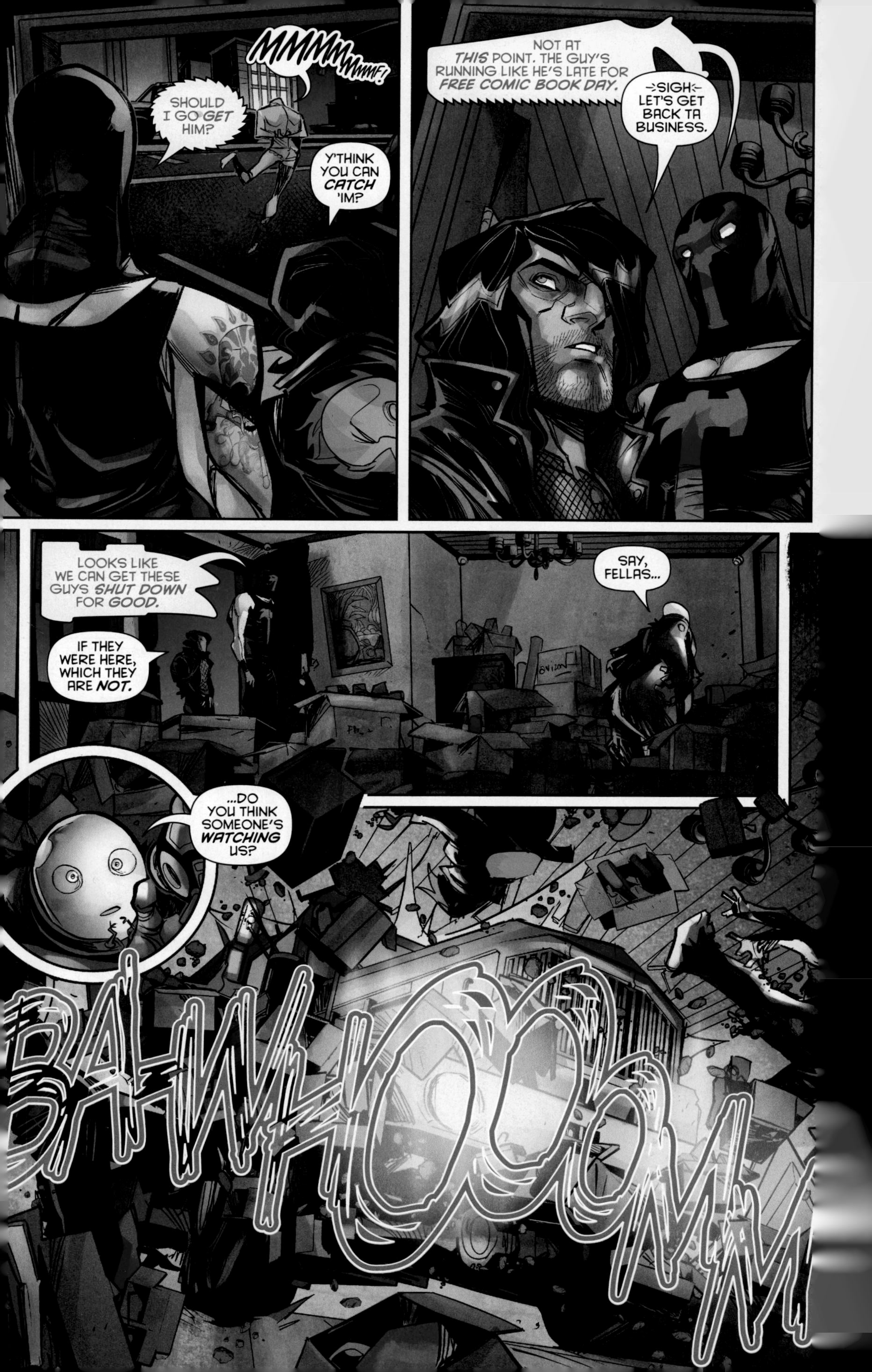
MMMMMMMMF!
SHOULD I GO GET HIM?
Y'THINK YOU CAN CATCH 'IM?
NOT AT THIS POINT. THE GUY'S RUNNING LIKE HE'S LATE FOR FREE COMIC BOOK DAY.
-SIGH- LET'S GET BACK TA BUSINESS.
LOOKS LIKE WE CAN GET THESE GUYS SHUT DOWN FOR GOOD.
IF THEY WERE HERE, WHICH THEY ARE NOT.
SAY, FELLAS...
...DO YOU THINK SOMEONE'S WATCHING US?
BAHWHOOOOMM

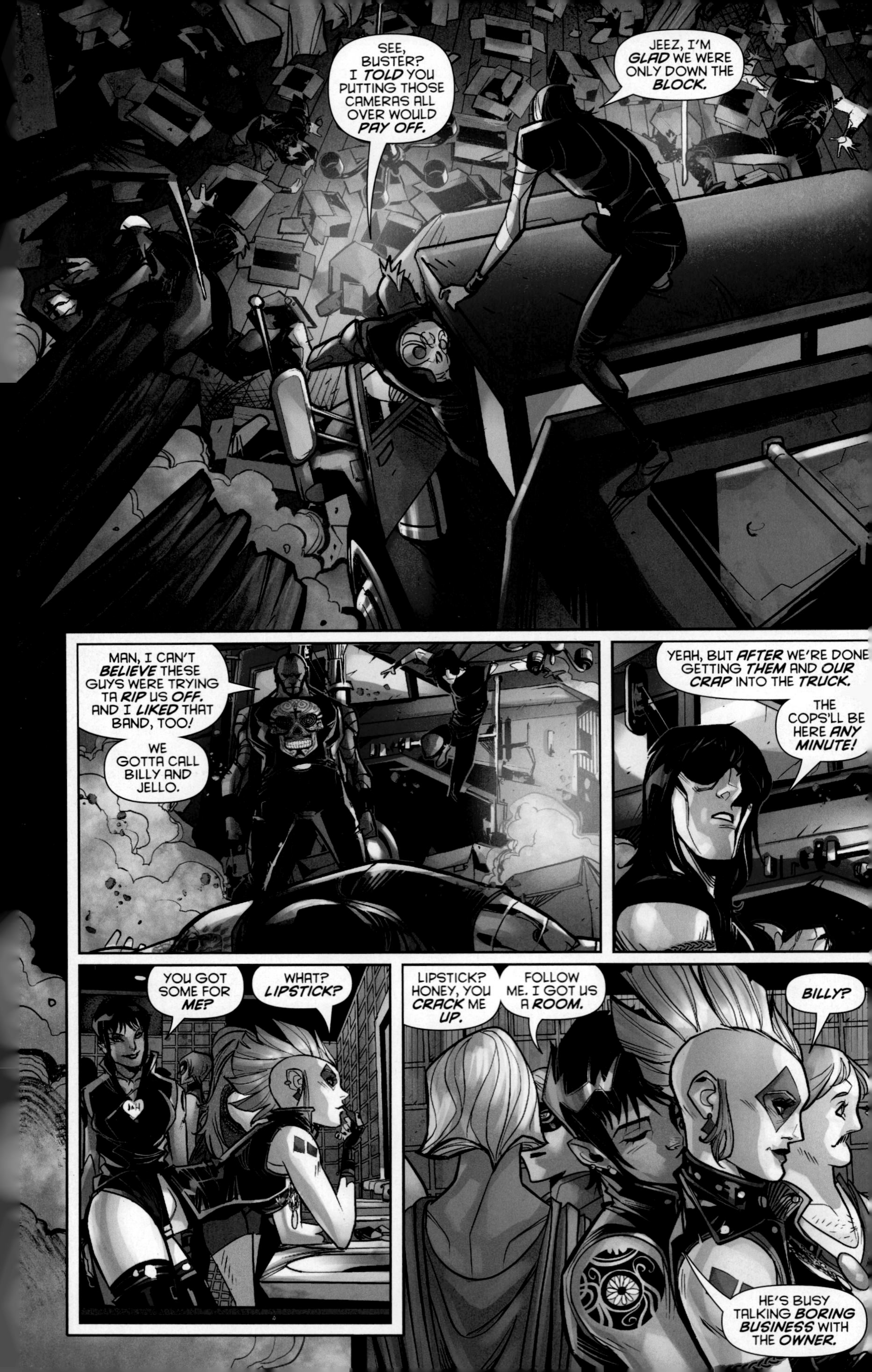

SEE, BUSTER? I TOLD YOU PUTTING THOSE CAMERAS ALL OVER WOULD PAY OFF.
JEEZ, I'M GLAD WE WERE ONLY DOWN THE BLOCK.
MAN, I CAN'T BELIEVE THESE GUYS WERE TRYING TA RIP US OFF. AND I LIKED THAT BAND, TOO!
WE GOTTA CALL BILLY AND JELLO.
YEAH, BUT AFTER WE'RE DONE GETTING THEM AND OUR CRAP INTO THE TRUCK.
THE COPS'LL BE HERE ANY MINUTE!
YOU GOT SOME FOR ME?
WHAT? LIPSTICK?
LIPSTICK? HONEY, YOU CRACK ME UP.
FOLLOW ME. I GOT US A ROOM.
BILLY?
HE'S BUSY TALKING BORING BUSINESS WITH THE OWNER.

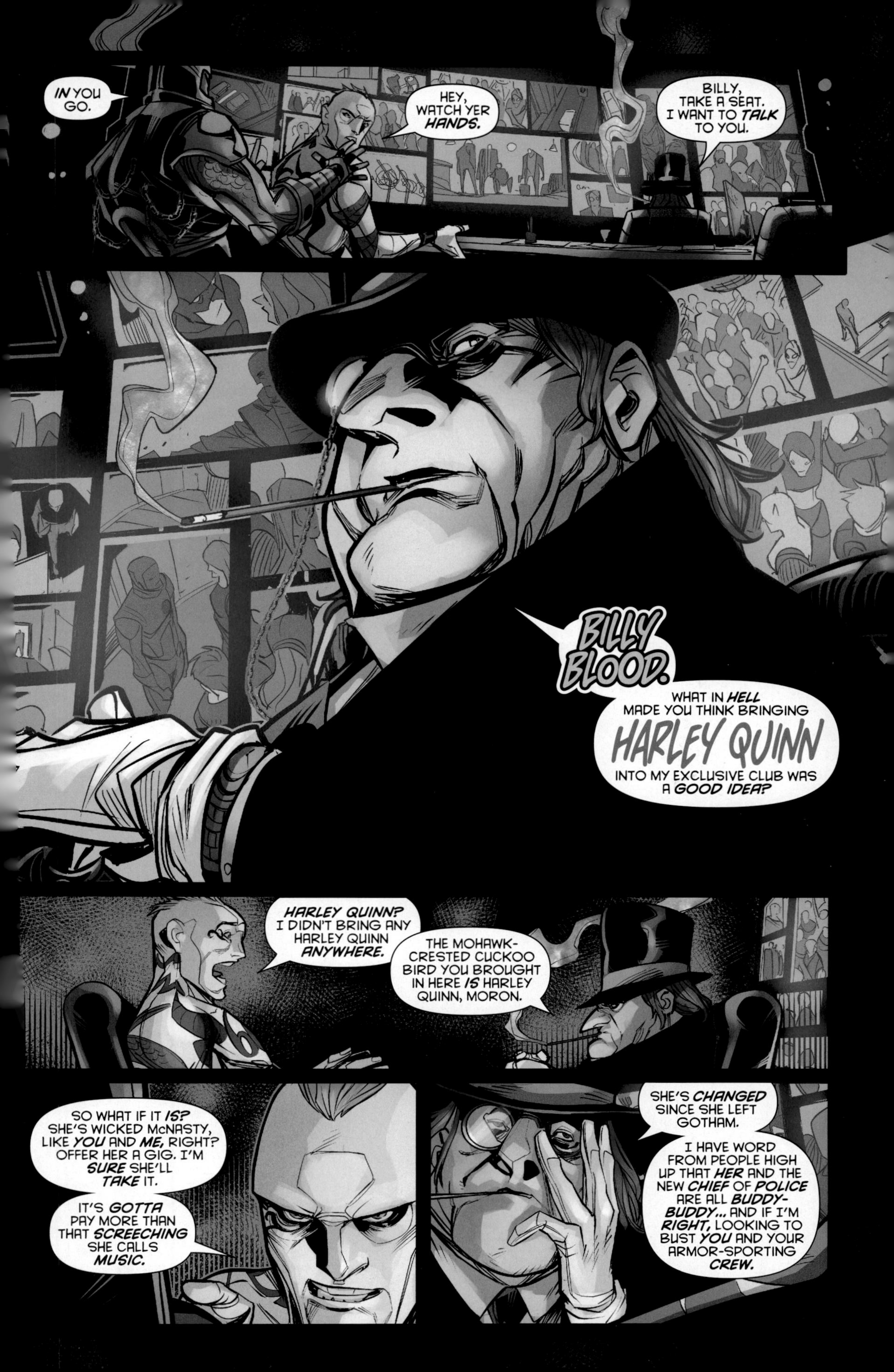

IN YOU GO.
HEY, WATCH YER HANDS.
BILLY, TAKE A SEAT. I WANT TO TALK TO YOU.
BILLY BLOOD.
WHAT IN HELL MADE YOU THINK BRINGING HARLEY QUINN INTO MY EXCLUSIVE CLUB WAS A GOOD IDEA?
HARLEY QUINN? I DIDN'T BRING ANY HARLEY QUINN ANYWHERE.
THE MOHAWK-CRESTED CUCKOO BIRD YOU BROUGHT IN HERE IS HARLEY QUINN, MORON.
SO WHAT IF IT IS? SHE'S WICKED McNASTY, LIKE YOU AND ME, RIGHT? OFFER HER A GIG. I'M SURE SHE'LL TAKE IT.
IT'S GOTTA PAY MORE THAN THAT SCREECHING SHE CALLS MUSIC.
SHE'S CHANGED SINCE SHE LEFT GOTHAM.
I HAVE WORD FROM PEOPLE HIGH UP THAT HER AND THE NEW CHIEF OF POLICE ARE ALL BUDDY-BUDDY... AND IF I'M RIGHT, LOOKING TO BUST YOU AND YOUR ARMOR-SPORTING CREW.

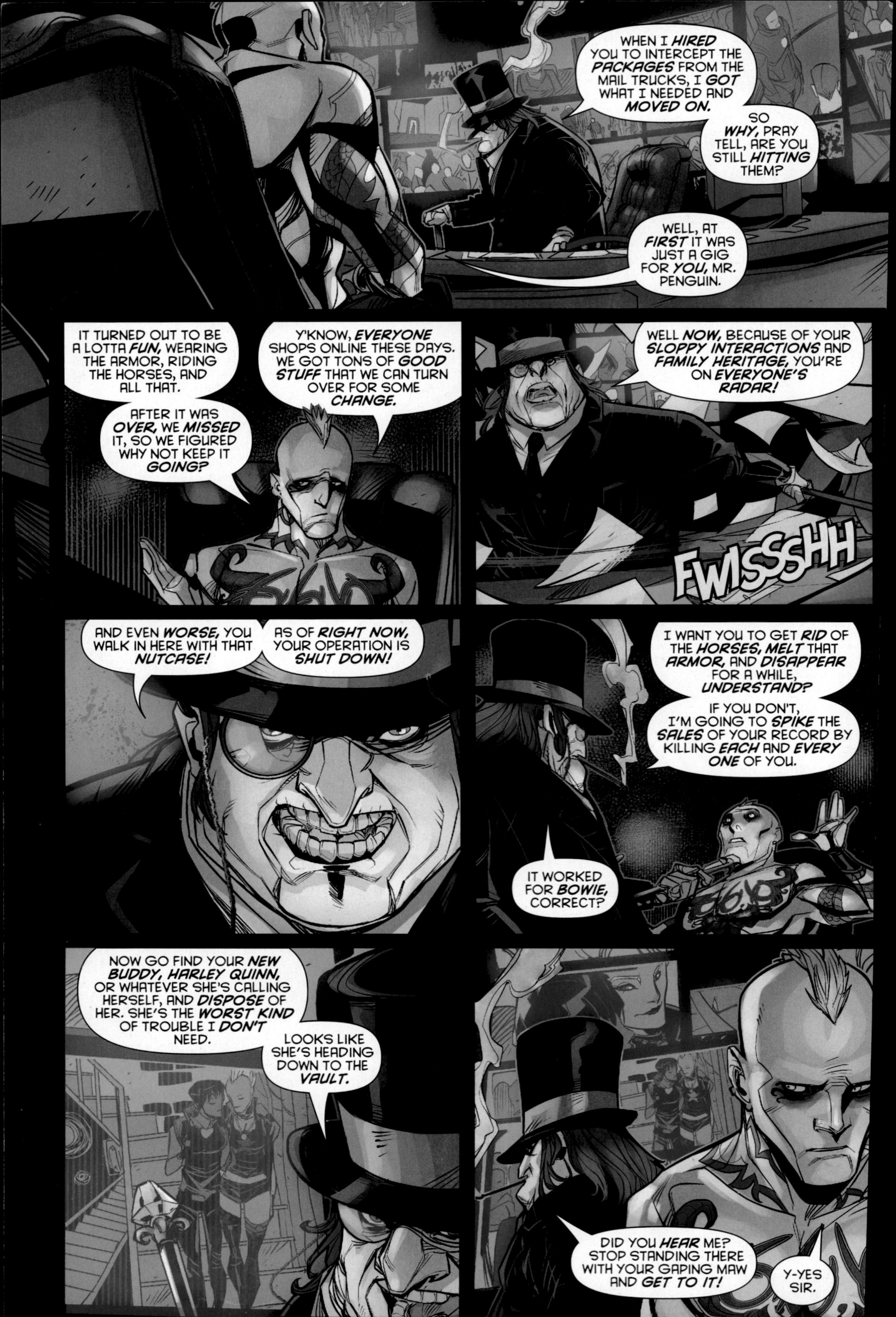

WHEN I *HIRED* YOU TO INTERCEPT THE *PACKAGES* FROM THE MAIL TRUCKS, I *GOT* WHAT I NEEDED AND *MOVED ON.*
SO *WHY,* PRAY TELL, ARE YOU STILL *HITTING* THEM?
WELL, AT *FIRST* IT WAS JUST A GIG FOR *YOU,* MR. PENGUIN.
IT TURNED OUT TO BE A LOTTA *FUN,* WEARING THE ARMOR, RIDING THE HORSES, AND ALL THAT.
AFTER IT WAS *OVER,* WE *MISSED* IT, SO WE FIGURED WHY NOT KEEP IT *GOING?*
Y'KNOW, *EVERYONE* SHOPS ONLINE THESE DAYS. WE GOT TONS OF *GOOD STUFF* THAT WE CAN TURN OVER FOR SOME *CHANGE.*
WELL *NOW,* BECAUSE OF YOUR *SLOPPY INTERACTIONS* AND *FAMILY HERITAGE,* YOU'RE ON *EVERYONE'S RADAR!*
FWISSSHH
AND EVEN *WORSE,* YOU WALK IN HERE WITH THAT *NUTCASE!*
AS OF *RIGHT NOW,* YOUR OPERATION IS *SHUT DOWN!*
I WANT YOU TO GET *RID* OF THE *HORSES, MELT* THAT *ARMOR,* AND *DISAPPEAR* FOR A WHILE, *UNDERSTAND?*
IF YOU DON'T, I'M GOING TO *SPIKE* THE *SALES* OF YOUR RECORD BY KILLING *EACH* AND *EVERY ONE* OF YOU.
IT WORKED FOR *BOWIE,* CORRECT?
NOW GO FIND YOUR *NEW BUDDY, HARLEY QUINN,* OR WHATEVER SHE'S CALLING HERSELF, AND *DISPOSE* OF HER. SHE'S THE *WORST KIND* OF TROUBLE I *DON'T* NEED.
LOOKS LIKE SHE'S HEADING DOWN TO THE *VAULT.*
DID YOU *HEAR* ME? STOP STANDING THERE WITH YOUR GAPING MAW AND *GET TO IT!*
Y-YES SIR.

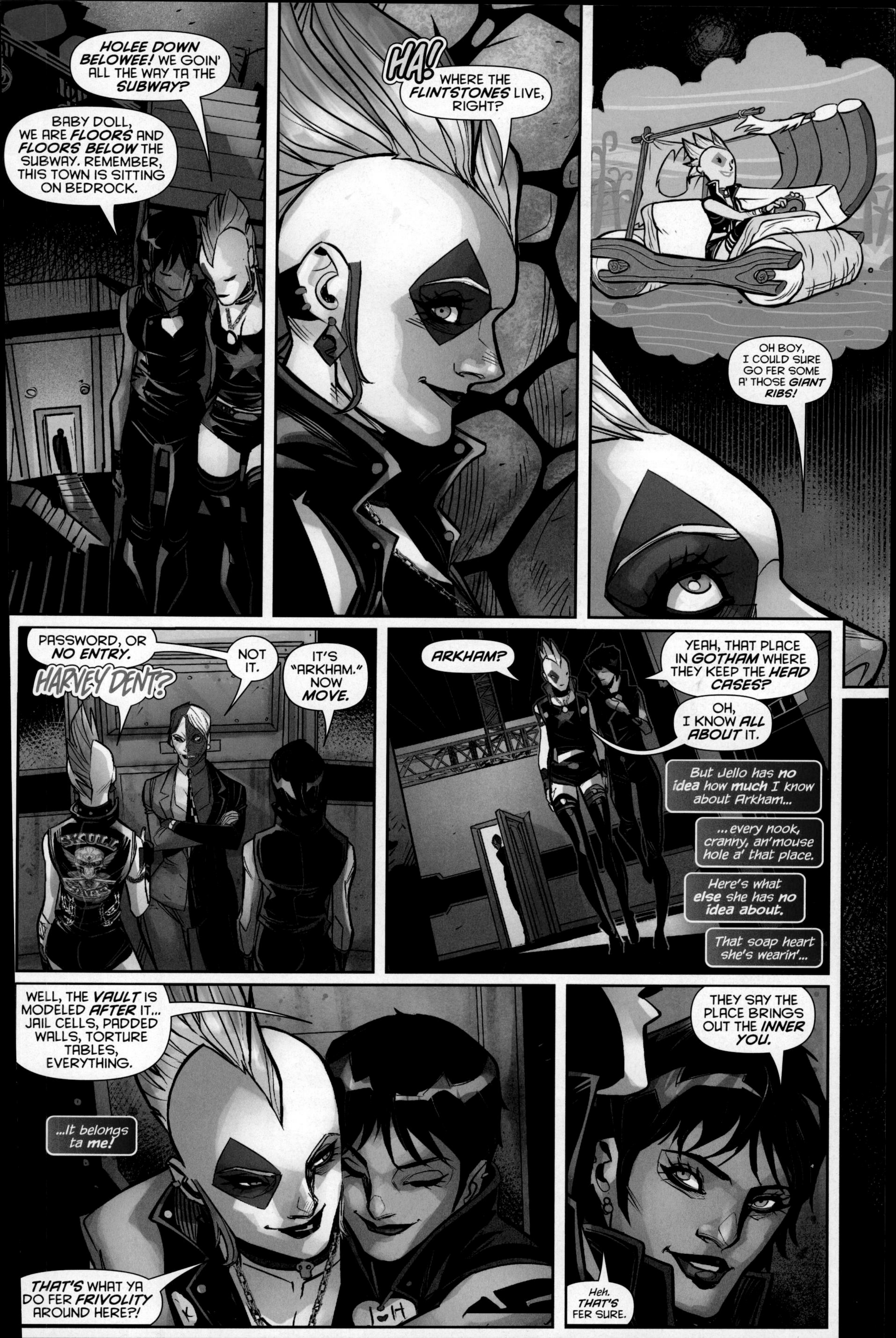
HOLEE DOWN BELOWEE! WE GOIN' ALL THE WAY TA THE SUBWAY?
BABY DOLL, WE ARE FLOORS AND FLOORS BELOW THE SUBWAY. REMEMBER, THIS TOWN IS SITTING ON BEDROCK.
HA!
WHERE THE FLINTSTONES LIVE, RIGHT?
OH BOY, I COULD SURE GO FER SOME A' THOSE GIANT RIBS!
PASSWORD, OR NO ENTRY.
HARVEY DENT?
NOT IT.
IT'S "ARKHAM." NOW MOVE.
ARKHAM?
YEAH, THAT PLACE IN GOTHAM WHERE THEY KEEP THE HEAD CASES?
OH, I KNOW ALL ABOUT IT.
But Jello has no idea how much I know about Arkham...
...every nook, cranny, an' mouse hole a' that place.
Here's what else she has no idea about.
That soap heart she's wearin'...
WELL, THE VAULT IS MODELED AFTER IT... JAIL CELLS, PADDED WALLS, TORTURE TABLES, EVERYTHING.
...It belongs ta me!
THAT'S WHAT YA DO FER FRIVOLITY AROUND HERE?!
THEY SAY THE PLACE BRINGS OUT THE INNER YOU.
Heh. THAT'S FER SURE.

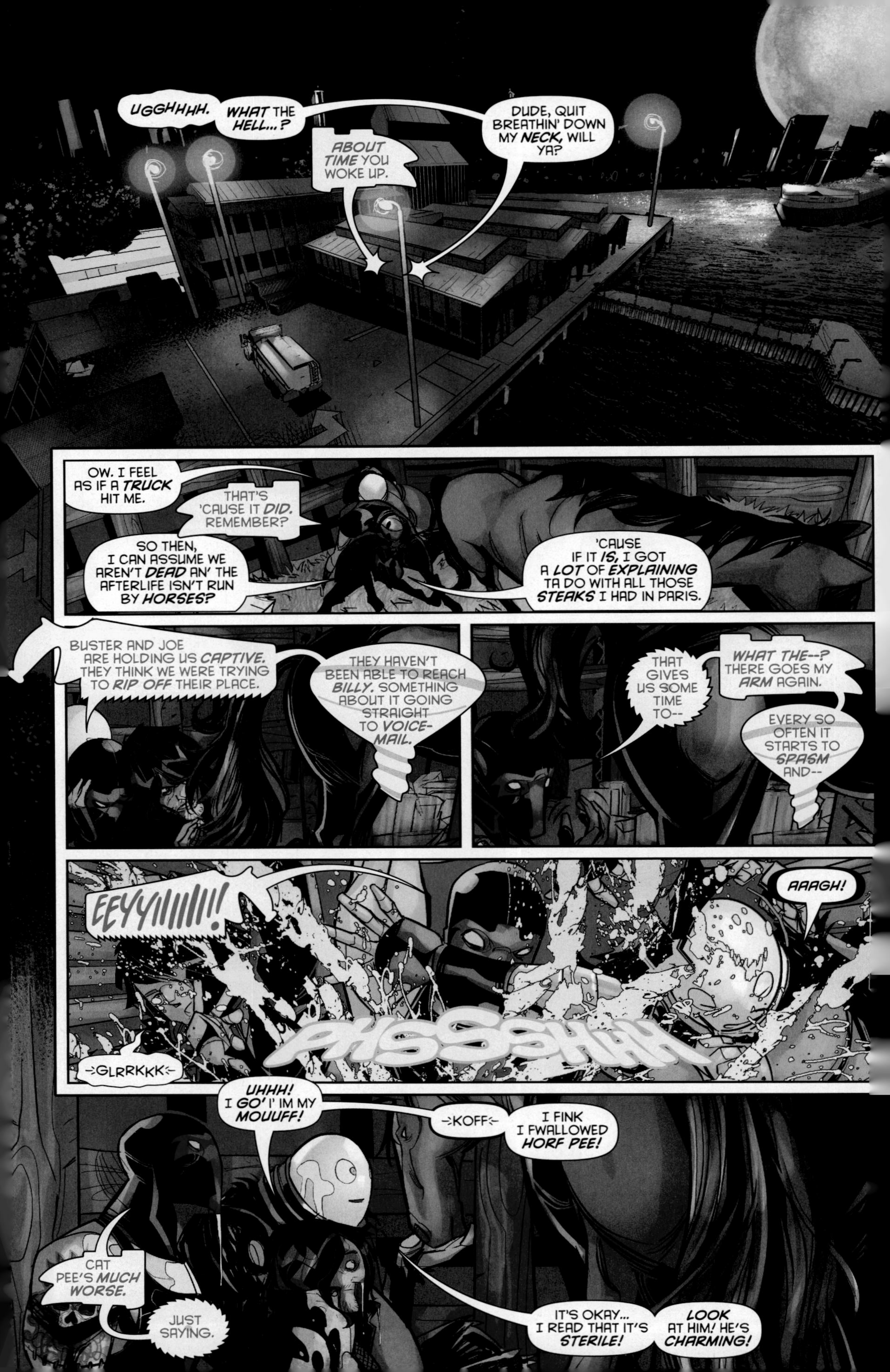
UGGHHHH.
WHAT THE HELL...?
ABOUT TIME YOU WOKE UP.
DUDE, QUIT BREATHIN' DOWN MY NECK, WILL YA?
OW. I FEEL AS IF A TRUCK HIT ME.
THAT'S 'CAUSE IT DID. REMEMBER?
SO THEN, I CAN ASSUME WE AREN'T DEAD AN' THE AFTERLIFE ISN'T RUN BY HORSES?
'CAUSE IF IT IS, I GOT A LOT OF EXPLAINING TA DO WITH ALL THOSE STEAKS I HAD IN PARIS.
BUSTER AND JOE ARE HOLDING US CAPTIVE. THEY THINK WE WERE TRYING TO RIP OFF THEIR PLACE.
THEY HAVEN'T BEEN ABLE TO REACH BILLY. SOMETHING ABOUT IT GOING STRAIGHT TO VOICE-MAIL.
THAT GIVES US SOME TIME TO--
WHAT THE--? THERE GOES MY ARM AGAIN.
EVERY SO OFTEN IT STARTS TO SPASM AND--
EEYYIIIIIIII!!
AAAGH!
PHSSSHHH
GLRRKKK
UHHH! I GO' I' IM MY MOUFF!
KOFF
I FINK I FWALLOWED HORF PEE!
CAT PEE'S MUCH WORSE.
JUST SAYING.
IT'S OKAY... I READ THAT IT'S STERILE!
LOOK AT HIM! HE'S CHARMING!

TRIXIE! *GOOD GIRL!*

I COULDN'T THINK OF A *BETTER WAY* TO *WAKE* YOU DISAPPOINTING DUDES *UP.*

SO WHAT'S THE *DEAL,* ROBBING OUR PLACE?

LIKE, COMPLETELY *NOT RESPECTFUL* OF FELLOW MUSICIANS.

WHAT THE HELL WERE YOU *LOOKING FOR,* ANYWAY? OUR *INSTRUMENTS?*

...OKAY, OKAY. YOU CAUGHT US *RED-HANDED.* WE *DESERVE* WHAT HAPPENED, BUT...

...BUSTER, WE *KNOW* YOU WRITE ALL THE *MUSIC* FOR THE BAND...AND JOE, THE *ARRANGEMENTS* YOU COME UP WITH...

...WAIT...YOU WERE *TRYING* TO *STEAL* OUR *GROOVES?*

DUDES...THAT'S *SCREWED UP. FLATTERING,* BUT SCREWED UP.

ALL YOU HAD TO DO WAS *APPROACH* US, MAN. WE WOULD'VE WRITTEN YOU GUYS A FEW TUNES.

REALLY...WE WOULDA BEEN *FLATTERED,* HONESTLY. GOD *KNOWS* YOU COULD USE THE *HELP.*

YEAH, YOU GUYS ARE *GOOD,* BUT YOUR *SONGS* ARE FOR...

...WELL, THINKING ABOUT IT, I DON'T *BLAME* YOU FOR TRYING TO GET OUR SONGBOOKS.

I WOULDA DONE THE *SAME.* DAMN.

WE *STILL* GOT A *PROBLEM* THOUGH; YOU SAW ALL THE *BOXES* AND *STUFF* WE RIPPED OFF.

WE DON'T *CARE,* DUDE. WE STOLE THE *CAR* TA GET OVER TA YER *HOTEL* EARLIER.

NO WAY!

YEAH! WE ALSO KNOCK OFF GROCERY STORES FOR SOME *FOOD* AND *CASH* ALMOST *EVERY* WEEK.

GET OUT! *SERIOUSLY?*

WE ALSO STEAL *CANES* FROM *BLIND PEOPLE!*

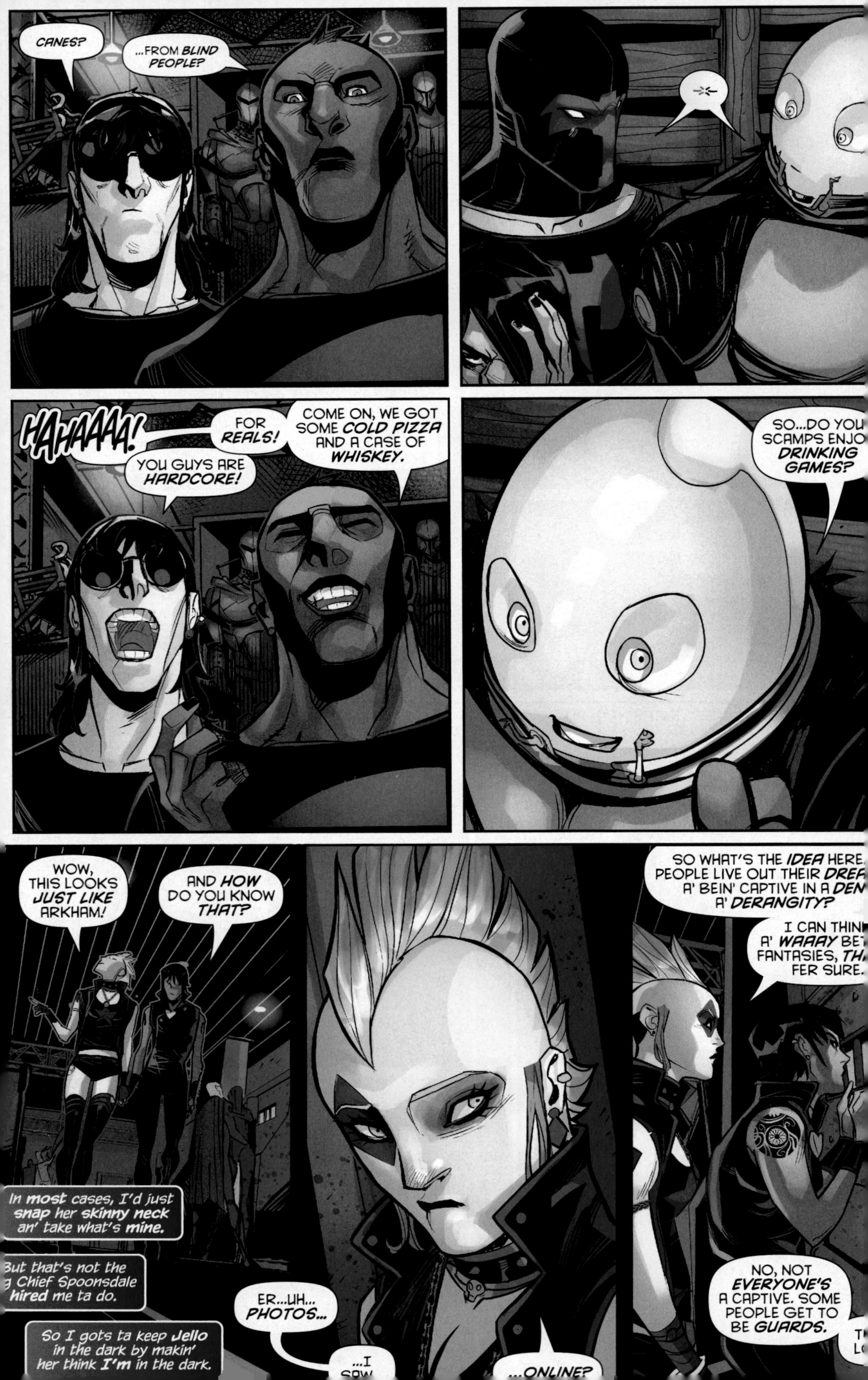
CANES?
...FROM BLIND PEOPLE?
HAHAAAA!
FOR REALS!
YOU GUYS ARE HARDCORE!
COME ON, WE GOT SOME COLD PIZZA AND A CASE OF WHISKEY.
SO...DO YOU SCAMPS ENJO DRINKING GAMES?
WOW, THIS LOOKS JUST LIKE ARKHAM!
AND HOW DO YOU KNOW THAT?
In most cases, I'd just snap her skinny neck an' take what's mine.
But that's not the g Chief Spoonsdale hired me ta do.
So I gots ta keep Jello in the dark by makin' her think I'm in the dark.
ER...UH... PHOTOS...
...I
...ONLINE?
SO WHAT'S THE IDEA HERE PEOPLE LIVE OUT THEIR DREA A' BEIN' CAPTIVE IN A DEN A' DERANGITY?
I CAN THIN A' WAAAY BE FANTASIES, TH FER SURE.
NO, NOT EVERYONE'S A CAPTIVE. SOME PEOPLE GET TO BE GUARDS.

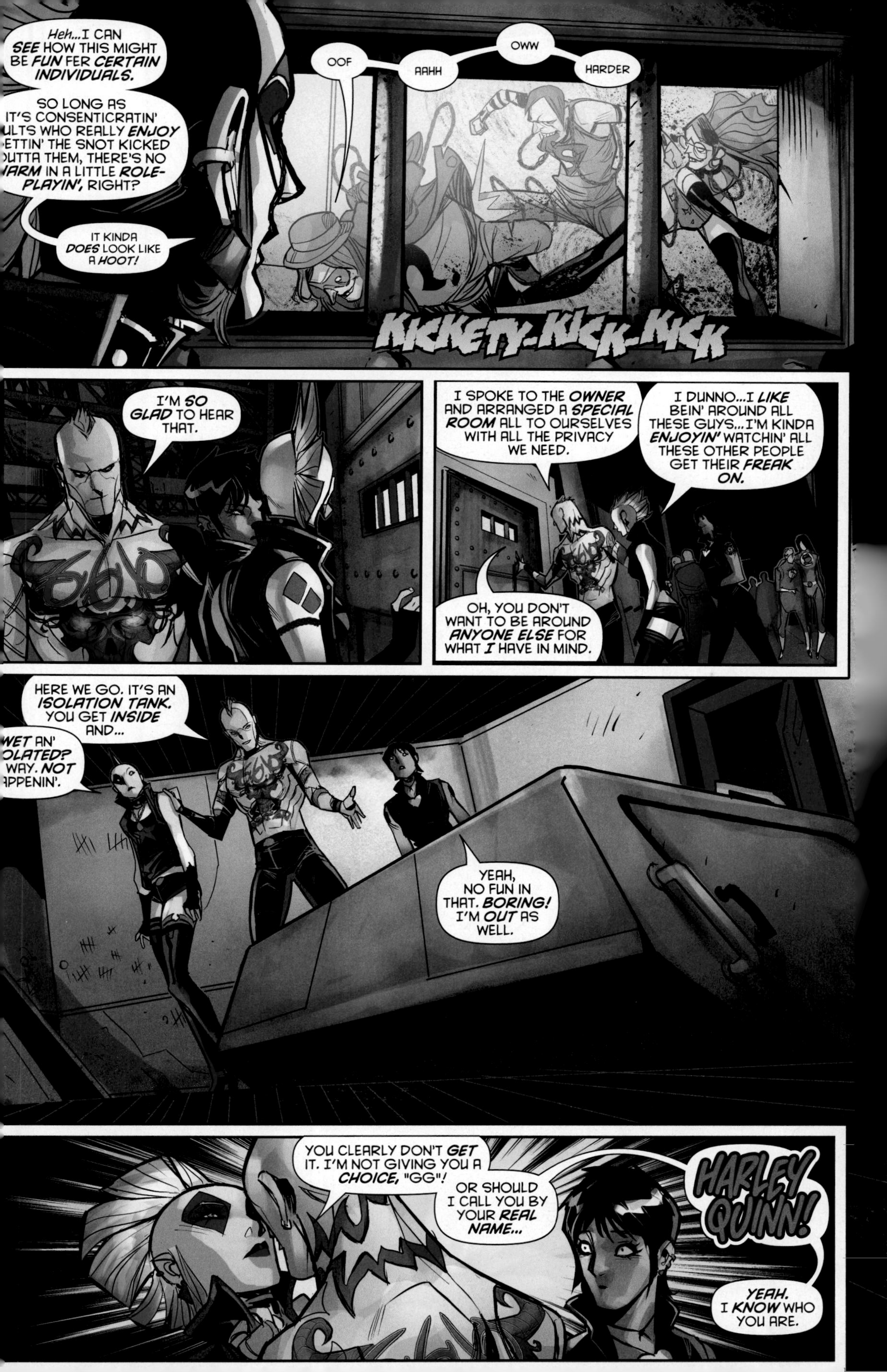

Heh...I CAN SEE HOW THIS MIGHT BE FUN FER CERTAIN INDIVIDUALS.
SO LONG AS IT'S CONSENTICRATIN' ULTS WHO REALLY ENJOY ETTIN' THE SNOT KICKED OUTTA THEM, THERE'S NO ARM IN A LITTLE ROLE-PLAYIN', RIGHT?
IT KINDA DOES LOOK LIKE A HOOT!
OOF
AAHH
OWW
HARDER
KICKETY-KICK-KICK
I'M SO GLAD TO HEAR THAT.
I SPOKE TO THE OWNER AND ARRANGED A SPECIAL ROOM ALL TO OURSELVES WITH ALL THE PRIVACY WE NEED.
I DUNNO...I LIKE BEIN' AROUND ALL THESE GUYS...I'M KINDA ENJOYIN' WATCHIN' ALL THESE OTHER PEOPLE GET THEIR FREAK ON.
OH, YOU DON'T WANT TO BE AROUND ANYONE ELSE FOR WHAT I HAVE IN MIND.
HERE WE GO. IT'S AN ISOLATION TANK. YOU GET INSIDE AND...
WET AN' OLATED? WAY. NOT APPENIN'.
YEAH, NO FUN IN THAT. BORING! I'M OUT AS WELL.
YOU CLEARLY DON'T GET IT. I'M NOT GIVING YOU A CHOICE, "GG"!
OR SHOULD I CALL YOU BY YOUR REAL NAME...
HARLEY QUINN!
YEAH. I KNOW WHO YOU ARE.

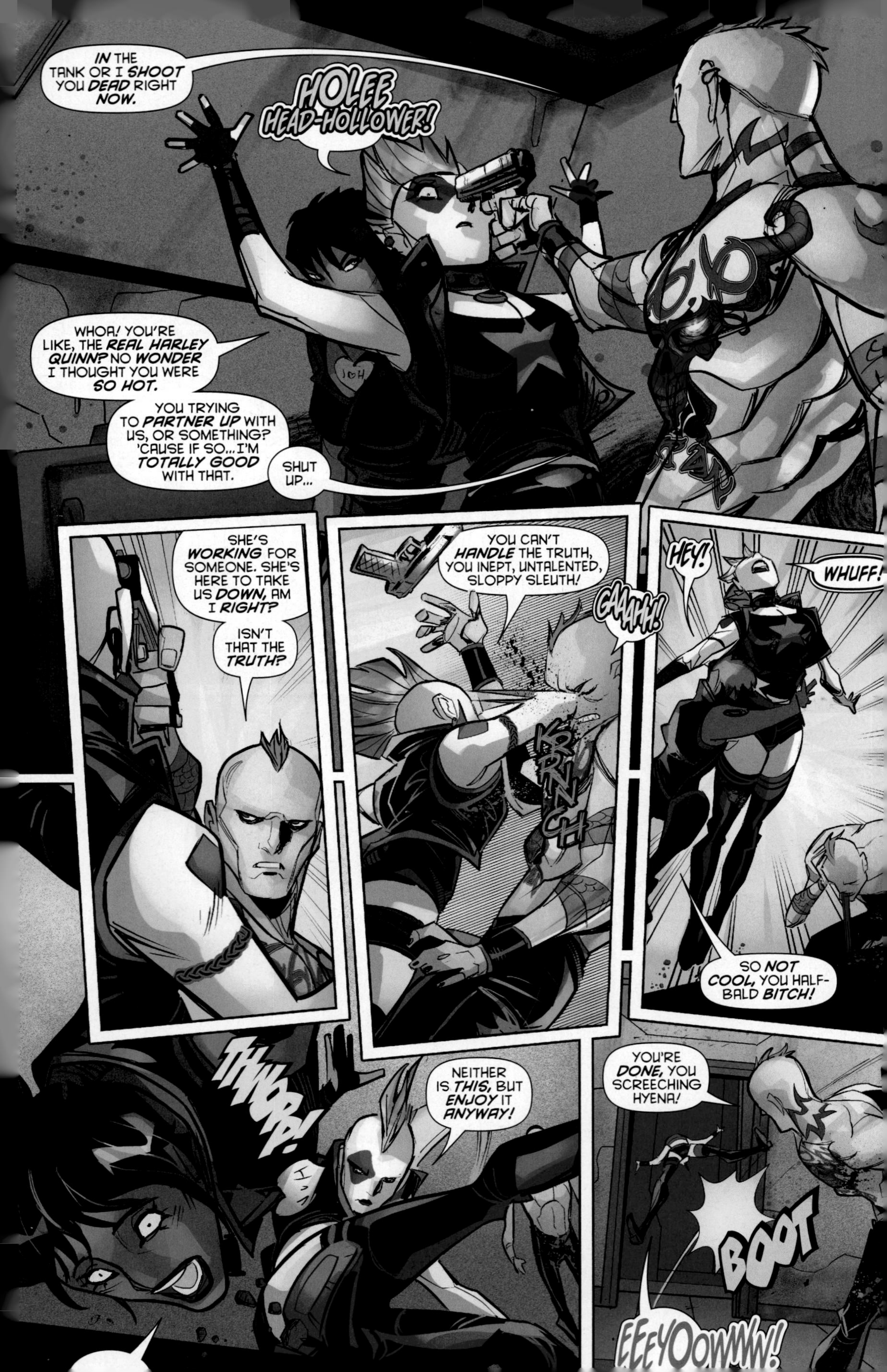
IN THE TANK OR I SHOOT YOU DEAD RIGHT NOW.
HOLEE HEAD-HOLLOWER!
WHOA! YOU'RE LIKE, THE REAL HARLEY QUINN? NO WONDER I THOUGHT YOU WERE SO HOT.
YOU TRYING TO PARTNER UP WITH US, OR SOMETHING? 'CAUSE IF SO...I'M TOTALLY GOOD WITH THAT.
SHUT UP...
SHE'S WORKING FOR SOMEONE. SHE'S HERE TO TAKE US DOWN, AM I RIGHT?
ISN'T THAT THE TRUTH?
YOU CAN'T HANDLE THE TRUTH, YOU INEPT, UNTALENTED, SLOPPY SLEUTH!
GAAAHH!
KRRNCH
HEY!
WHUFF!
SO NOT COOL, YOU HALF-BALD BITCH!
THWORP!
NEITHER IS THIS, BUT ENJOY IT ANYWAY!
YOU'RE DONE, YOU SCREECHING HYENA!
BOOT
EEEYOOWWW!

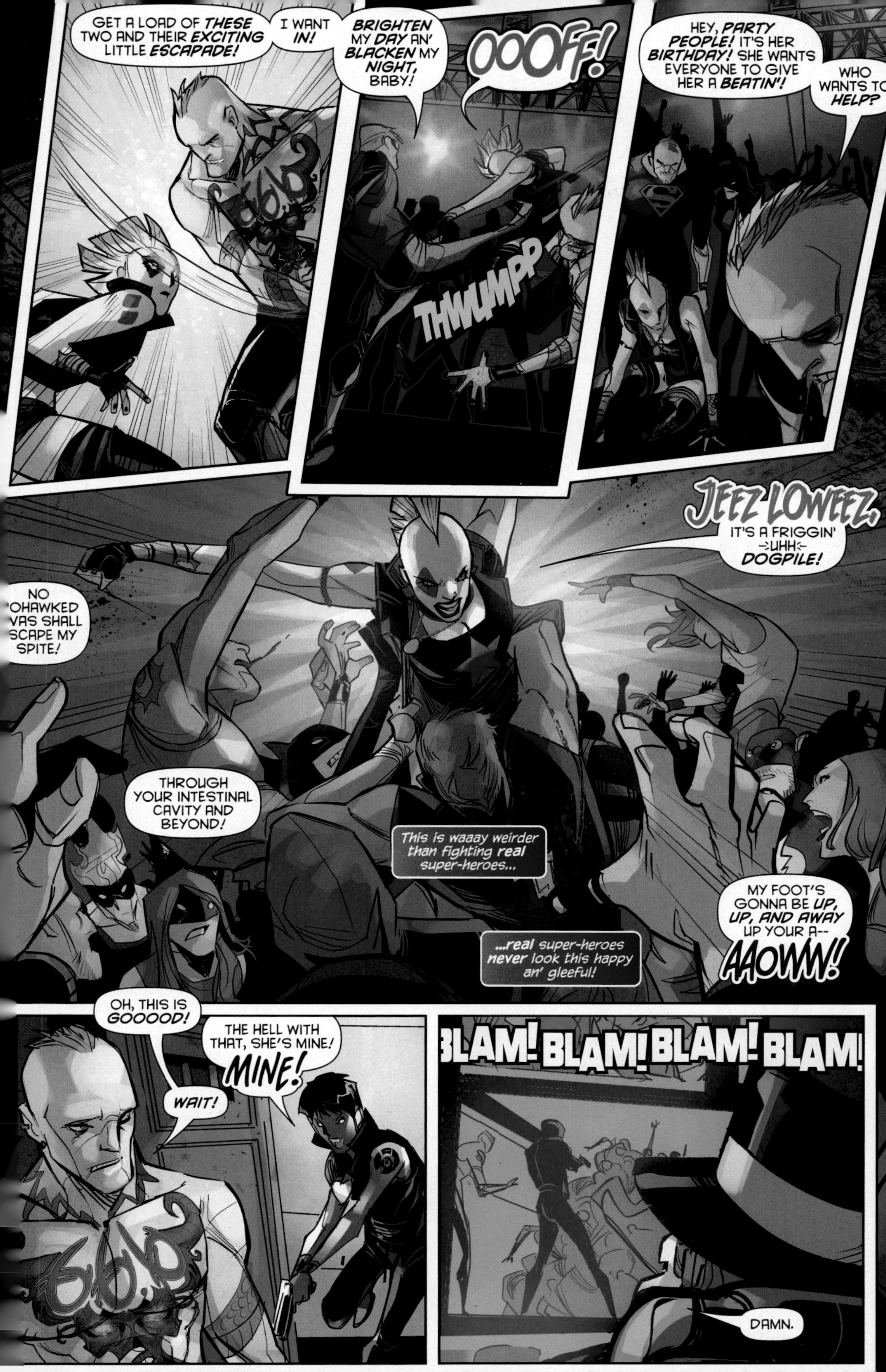

GET A LOAD OF THESE TWO AND THEIR EXCITING LITTLE ESCAPADE!
I WANT IN!
BRIGHTEN MY DAY AN' BLACKEN MY NIGHT, BABY!
OOOFF!
THWUMPP
HEY, PARTY PEOPLE! IT'S HER BIRTHDAY! SHE WANTS EVERYONE TO GIVE HER A BEATIN'!
WHO WANTS TO HELP?
JEEZ LOWEEZ,
IT'S A FRIGGIN' -UHH- DOGPILE!
NO OHAWKED VAS SHALL SCAPE MY SPITE!
THROUGH YOUR INTESTINAL CAVITY AND BEYOND!
This is waaay weirder than fighting real super-heroes...
...real super-heroes never look this happy an' gleeful!
MY FOOT'S GONNA BE UP, UP, AND AWAY UP YOUR A--
AAOWW!
OH, THIS IS GOOOOD!
THE HELL WITH THAT, SHE'S MINE!
MINE!
WAIT!
BLAM! BLAM! BLAM! BLAM!
DAMN.

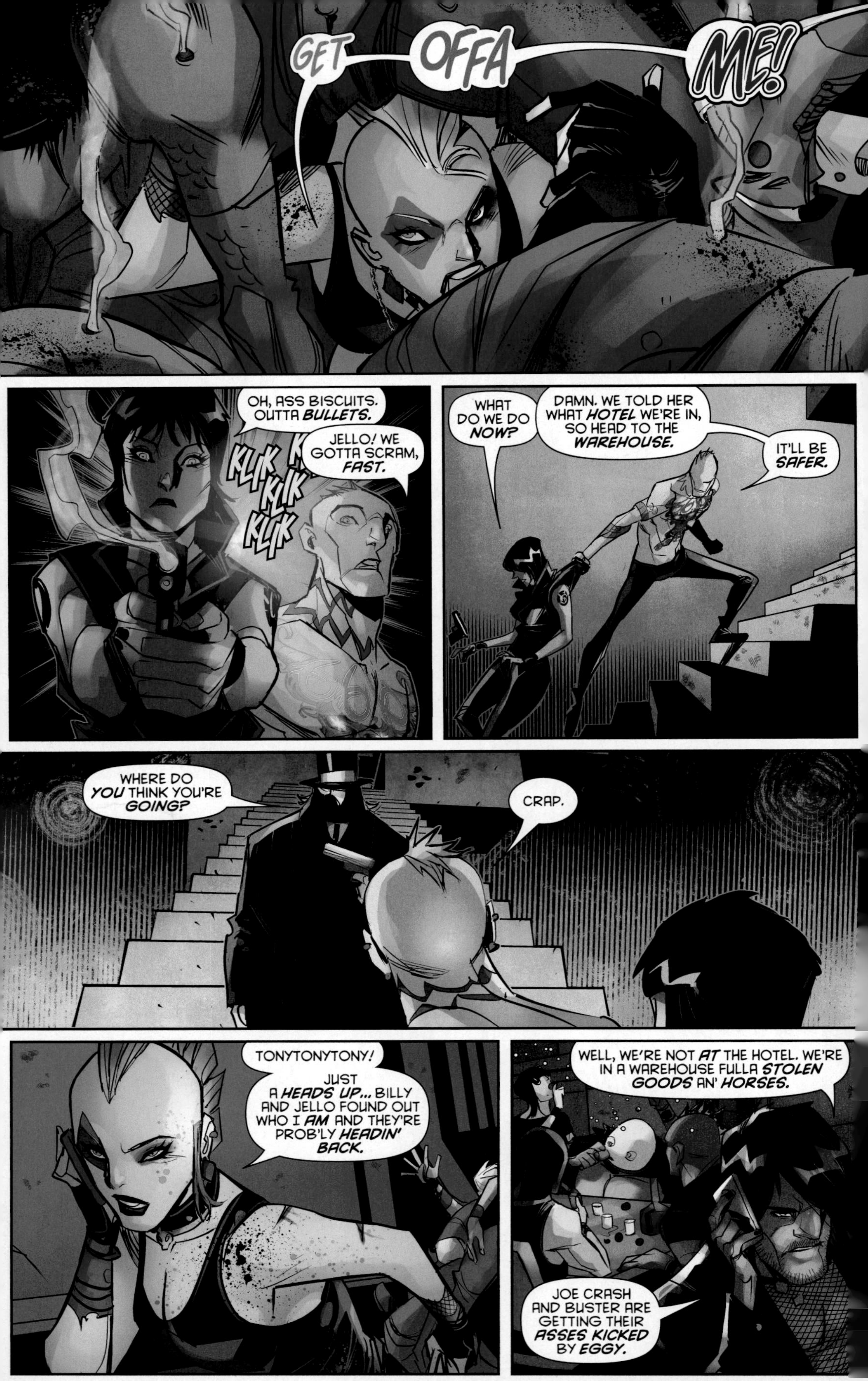
GET OFFA ME!
OH, ASS BISCUITS. OUTTA BULLETS.
KLIK KLIK KLIK KLIK
JELLO! WE GOTTA SCRAM, FAST.
WHAT DO WE DO NOW?
DAMN. WE TOLD HER WHAT HOTEL WE'RE IN, SO HEAD TO THE WAREHOUSE.
IT'LL BE SAFER.
WHERE DO YOU THINK YOU'RE GOING?
CRAP.
TONYTONYTONY!
JUST A HEADS UP... BILLY AND JELLO FOUND OUT WHO I AM AND THEY'RE PROB'LY HEADIN' BACK.
WELL, WE'RE NOT AT THE HOTEL. WE'RE IN A WAREHOUSE FULLA STOLEN GOODS AN' HORSES.
JOE CRASH AND BUSTER ARE GETTING THEIR ASSES KICKED BY EGGY.

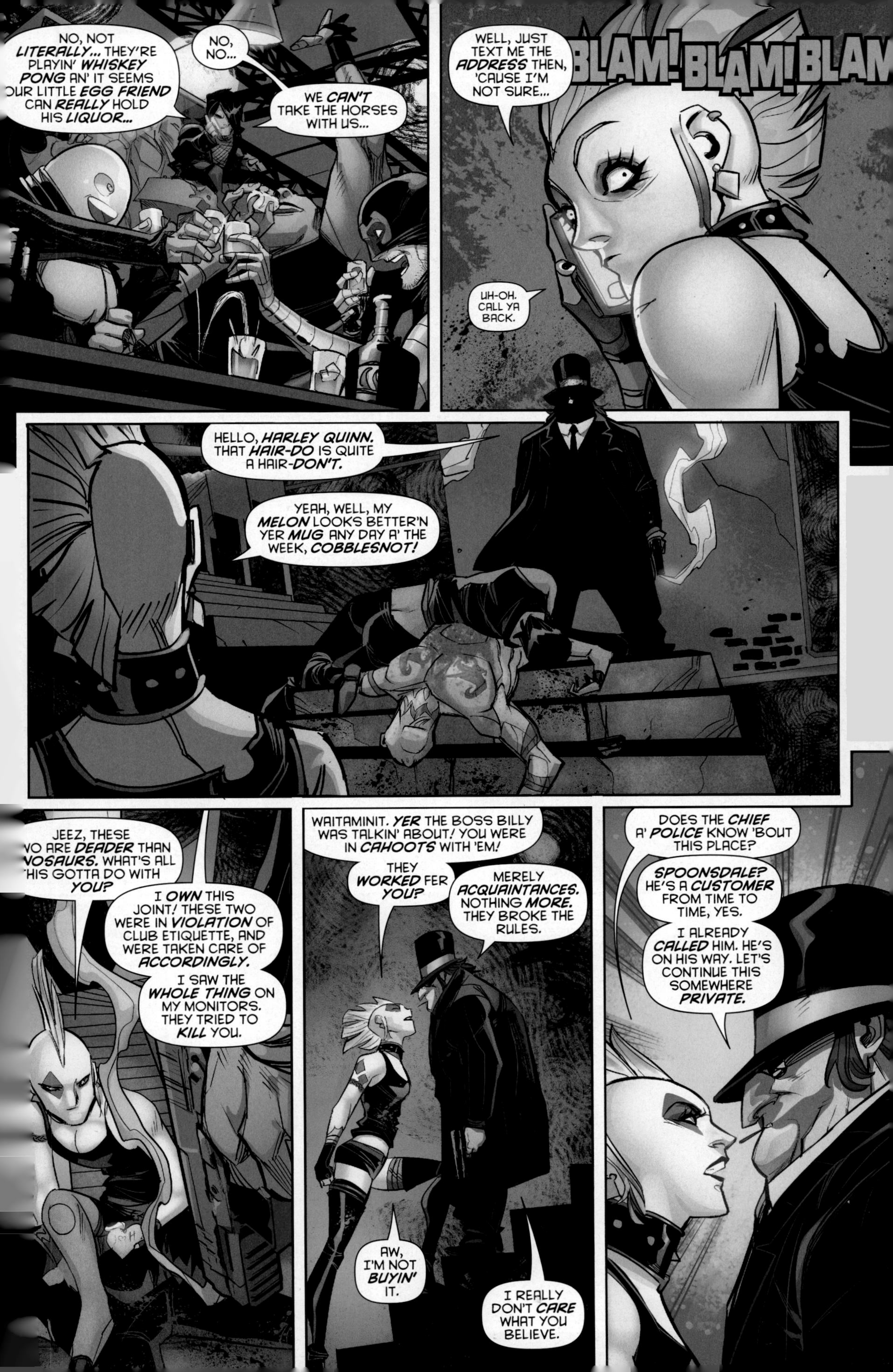

NO, NOT LITERALLY... THEY'RE PLAYIN' WHISKEY PONG AN' IT SEEMS OUR LITTLE EGG FRIEND CAN REALLY HOLD HIS LIQUOR...
NO, NO...
WE CAN'T TAKE THE HORSES WITH US...
WELL, JUST TEXT ME THE ADDRESS THEN, 'CAUSE I'M NOT SURE...
BLAM! BLAM! BLAM
UH-OH. CALL YA BACK.
HELLO, HARLEY QUINN. THAT HAIR-DO IS QUITE A HAIR-DON'T.
YEAH, WELL, MY MELON LOOKS BETTER'N YER MUG ANY DAY A' THE WEEK, COBBLESNOT!
JEEZ, THESE WO ARE DEADER THAN NOSAURS. WHAT'S ALL THIS GOTTA DO WITH YOU?
I OWN THIS JOINT! THESE TWO WERE IN VIOLATION OF CLUB ETIQUETTE, AND WERE TAKEN CARE OF ACCORDINGLY.
I SAW THE WHOLE THING ON MY MONITORS. THEY TRIED TO KILL YOU.
WAITAMINIT. YER THE BOSS BILLY WAS TALKIN' ABOUT! YOU WERE IN CAHOOTS WITH 'EM!
THEY WORKED FER YOU?
MERELY ACQUAINTANCES. NOTHING MORE. THEY BROKE THE RULES.
AW, I'M NOT BUYIN' IT.
I REALLY DON'T CARE WHAT YOU BELIEVE.
DOES THE CHIEF A' POLICE KNOW 'BOUT THIS PLACE?
SPOONSDALE? HE'S A CUSTOMER FROM TIME TO TIME, YES.
I ALREADY CALLED HIM. HE'S ON HIS WAY. LET'S CONTINUE THIS SOMEWHERE PRIVATE.

THIS ISN'T *YOUR CITY*, PENGUIN.

AND IT'S *YOURS*?

I WAS *BORN* HERE.

WELL, *THAT* CERTAINLY EXPLAINS THE *THICK BROOKLYN* ACCENT.

LISTEN, QUINN, I DON'T KNOW *WHAT* YOU WERE UP TO WITH THOSE TWO, BUT TAKE WHAT HAPPENED TO THEM AS A *WARNING* FOR YOU TO *MIND YOUR OWN BUSINESS*.

Oswald Cobblepot.

I shoulda *known* one a' the old *Arkham assclowns* would be *behind* all this. The masterful mock madhouse downstairs shoulda tipped me off.

I just *hope* that in spite a' Billy an' Jello bein' *newly deceased*, I can still collect my *payment* from the *chief*.

At least I salvage my soapy heart.

I KNOW ALL ABOUT YOUR *NEW HOME*, YOUR *NEW FRIENDS*, AND YOUR *GANG* OF *HARLEYS*. UP UNTIL NOW, *NONE* OF WHAT YOU DID FELL ON MY *RADAR*...

...UNTIL YOU WALKED INTO *MY PLACE*. ARE WE GOING TO HAVE A *PROBLEM*?

ARE YOU *DONE*, YA BEAKY BAG A' BUTT-NUGGETS?

WHAT *YOU* NEED TO UNNERSTAND IS THREATENING ME, *HERE*, IN *MY HOMETOWN*...

...Y'EVER TRY *PUNCHIN'* TORNADOES?

I'M NOT AN *IDIOT*, DUCK-MUG. YOU COULDA JAMMED THOSE TWO UP WITHOUT *KILLIN'* 'EM, BUT YA *DIDN'T*.

LISTEN TO YOURSEL[F]

YOU SOUND LIKE A CERT[AIN] *CAPED CRUSADER*

YOU TAKE THAT BACK.

I THINK YOU'RE ANGRY BECAUSE YOU DIDN'T GET TO *OFF* THEM *YOURSELF*.

YEAH, WELL... THEY DID 86 MY FAVORITE *MAILMAN*.

EVEN IF I *HAD* ANYTHING TO DO WITH WHATEVER YOU *THINK* I HAD SOMETHING TO DO WITH, WHAT'S IT TO *YOU*?

AGAIN, *POPPED POSTMAN*.

LOOK AT THAT... SPOONSDALE AND HIS MEN HAVE ARRIVED TO *CLEAN UP* YOUR *MESS*.

DO YOURSELF A *FAVOR*. TAKE YOUR PRETTY PUSS OUT OF MY CLUB BEFORE I HAVE IT *THROWN* OUT.

LISSEN, *FOWL-FACE*, THE REST A' THE BAND IS LOCKED DOWN WITH MY GUYS...

...IF I FIND OUT YA HAD **ANYTHING** TA DO WITH THIS...

SNATCH

...I'M GONNA **GRAB** YOU BY YER **SCRUFFY SKULL**...

KRISSHHH

...THEN I'M-A-GONNA **WRING** YER **WRINKLY, NOXIOUS NECK**...

KRASSHHH

...AND THEN I'LL **PLUCK** YOU **FRONT, BACK, A SIDEWAYS**...

...THEN **SKIN** THE **SKIN** RIGH OFFA YER **SLEAZ** SELF...

...AN' **COOK** YER **OVERLY-MARBLED ASS** TA **WAAAY** PAST **GOLDEN BROWN**...

...THEN I'M GONNA **EAT'CHA ALIVE!**

SMASSHH

FEEL **BETTER**?

YES. YES. MUCH BETTER.

I HEAR BILLY AND JELLO DIDN'T **MAKE** IT.

WE'RE GONNA HAVE ONE **VERY UPSET** SENATOR.

I DIDN'T **DO** IT.

LOOK, THIS ISN'T **DONE**. DRIVE ME.

I NEED TO BE **HERE**, ON THE SCENE TO--

I GOT **ANOTHER** SCEN YA NEED TA BE AT.

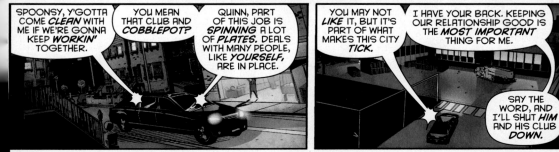

SPOONSY, Y'GOTTA COME **CLEAN** WITH ME IF WE'RE GONNA KEEP **WORKIN'** TOGETHER.

YOU MEAN THAT CLUB AND **COBBLEPOT**?

QUINN, PART OF THIS JOB IS **SPINNING** A LOT OF **PLATES**. DEALS WITH MANY PEOPLE, LIKE **YOURSELF**, ARE IN PLACE.

YOU MAY NOT **LIKE** IT, BUT IT'S PART OF WHAT MAKES THIS CITY **TICK**.

I HAVE YOUR BACK. KEEPING OUR RELATIONSHIP GOOD IS THE **MOST IMPORTANT** THING FOR ME.

SAY THE WORD, AND I'LL SHUT **HIM** AND HIS CLUB **DOWN**.

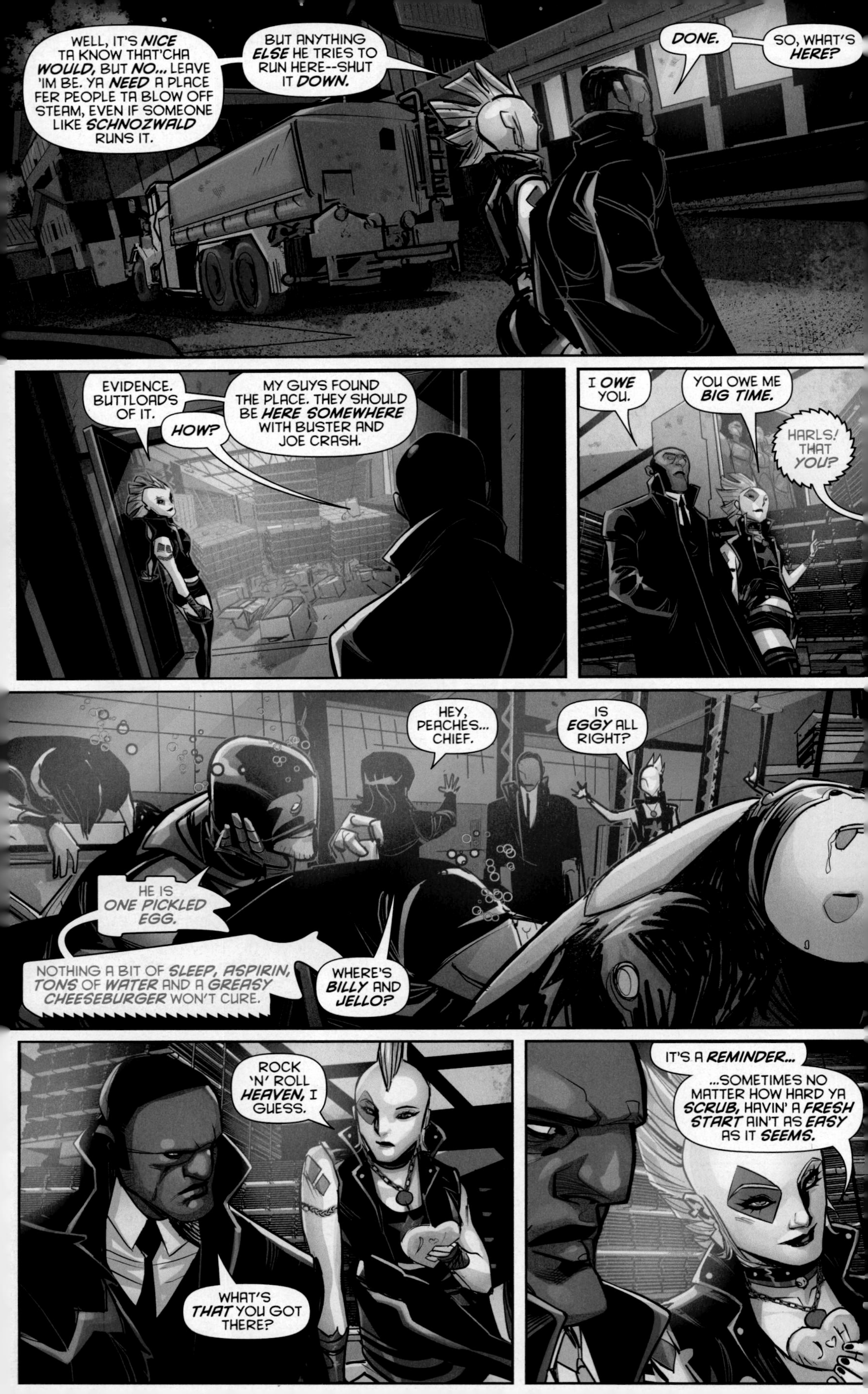
WELL, IT'S NICE TA KNOW THAT'CHA WOULD, BUT NO... LEAVE 'IM BE. YA NEED A PLACE FER PEOPLE TA BLOW OFF STEAM, EVEN IF SOMEONE LIKE SCHNOZWALD RUNS IT.
BUT ANYTHING ELSE HE TRIES TO RUN HERE--SHUT IT DOWN.
DONE.
SO, WHAT'S HERE?
EVIDENCE. BUTTLOADS OF IT.
HOW?
MY GUYS FOUND THE PLACE. THEY SHOULD BE HERE SOMEWHERE WITH BUSTER AND JOE CRASH.
I OWE YOU.
YOU OWE ME BIG TIME.
HARLS! THAT YOU?
HEY, PEACHES... CHIEF.
IS EGGY ALL RIGHT?
HE IS ONE PICKLED EGG.
NOTHING A BIT OF SLEEP, ASPIRIN, TONS OF WATER AND A GREASY CHEESEBURGER WON'T CURE.
WHERE'S BILLY AND JELLO?
ROCK 'N' ROLL HEAVEN, I GUESS.
WHAT'S THAT YOU GOT THERE?
IT'S A REMINDER...
...SOMETIMES NO MATTER HOW HARD YA SCRUB, HAVIN' A FRESH START AIN'T AS EASY AS IT SEEMS.

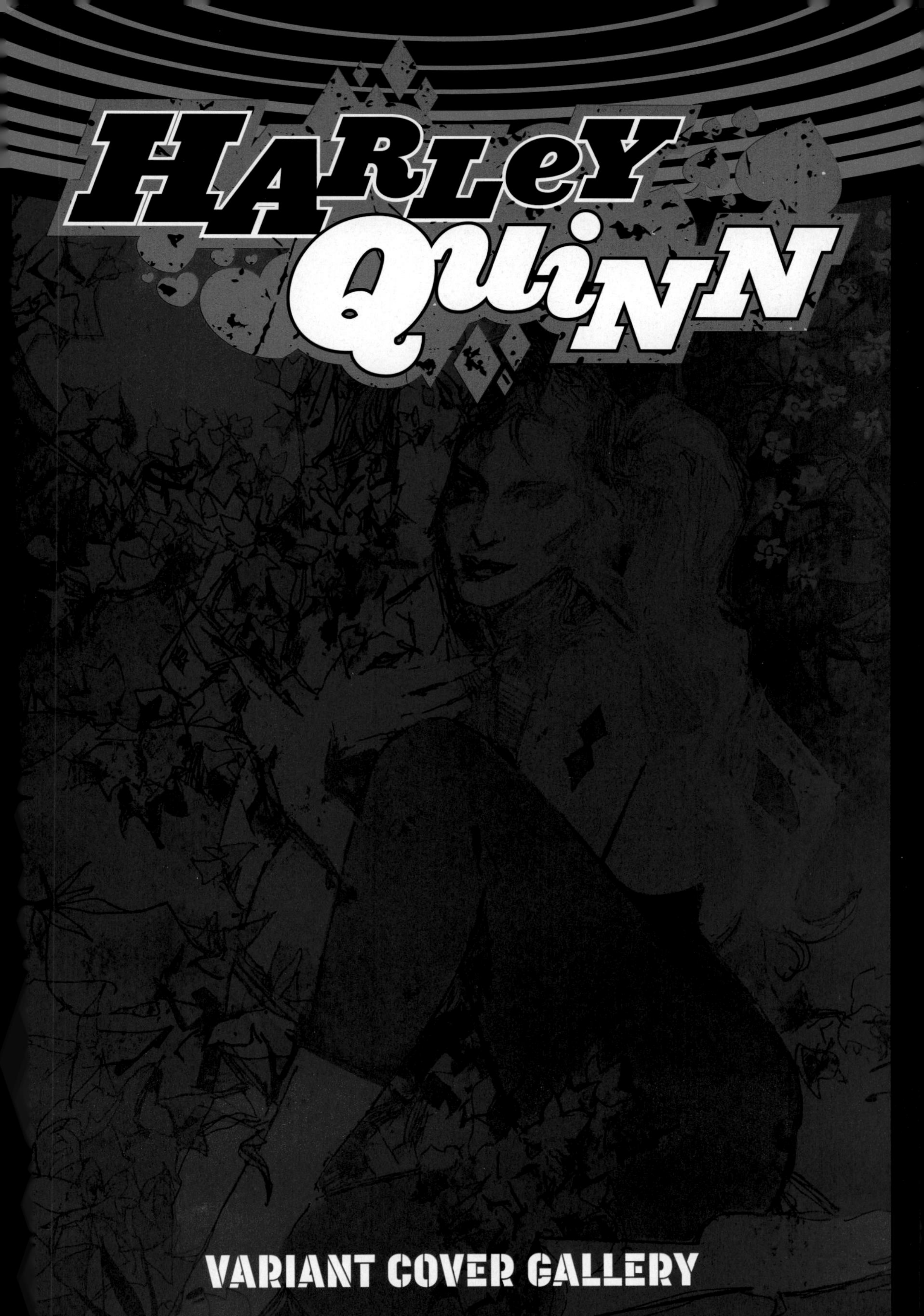
HARLEY
QUINN

VARIANT COVER GALLERY

HARLEY QUINN #1 variant cover by BILL SIENKIEWICZ

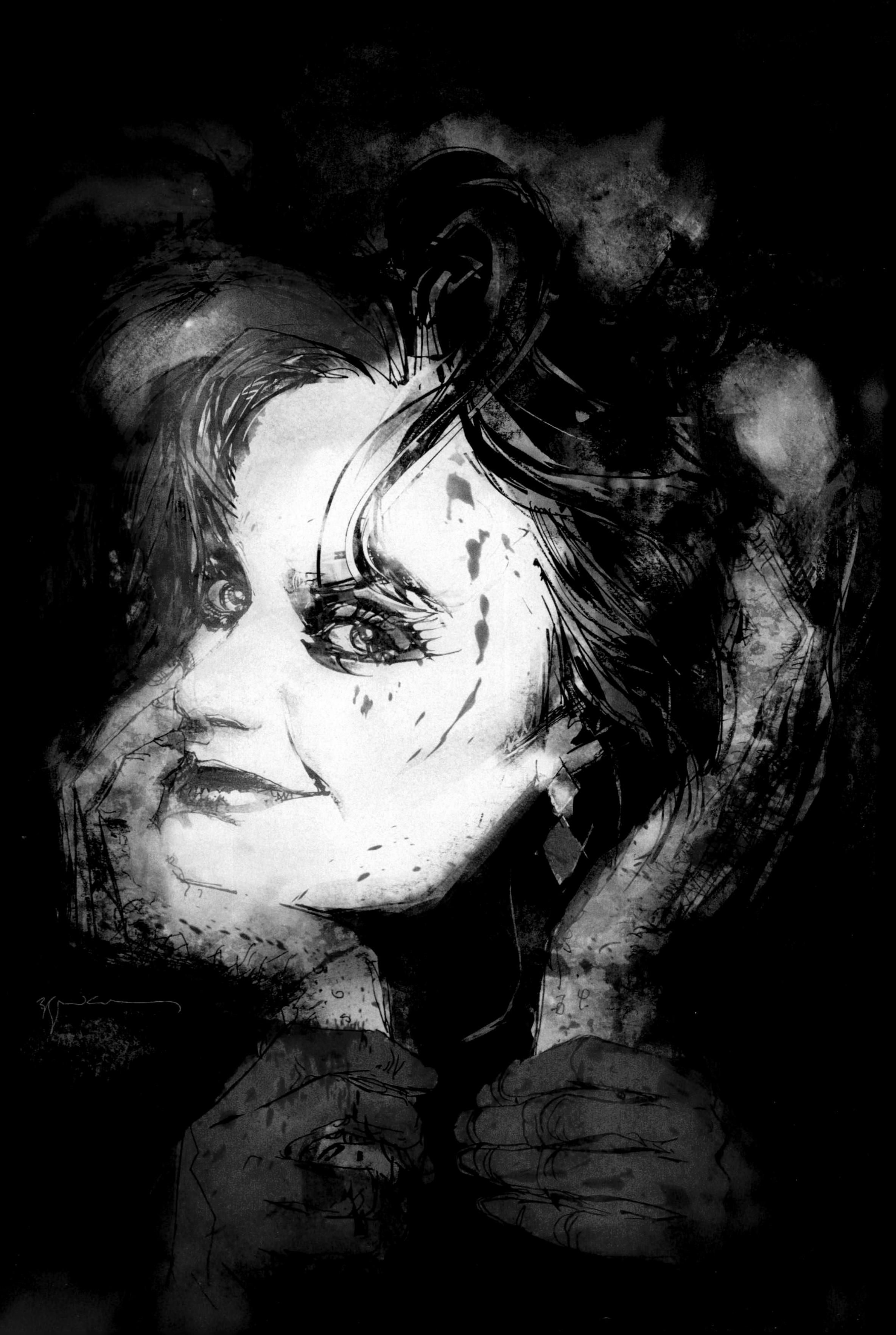

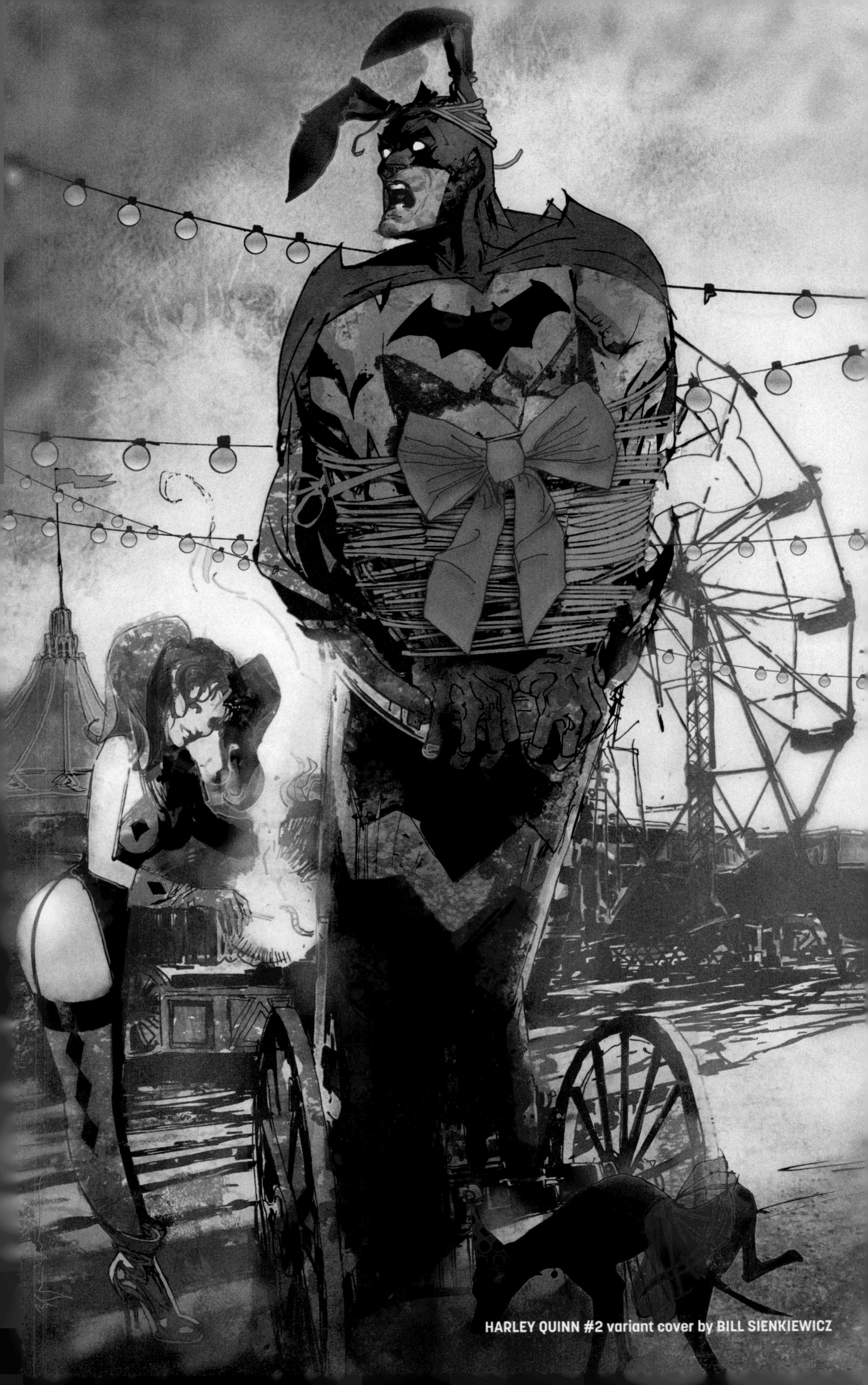

HARLEY QUINN #2 variant cover by BILL SIENKIEWICZ

HARLEY QUINN #3 variant cover by BILL SIENKIEWICZ

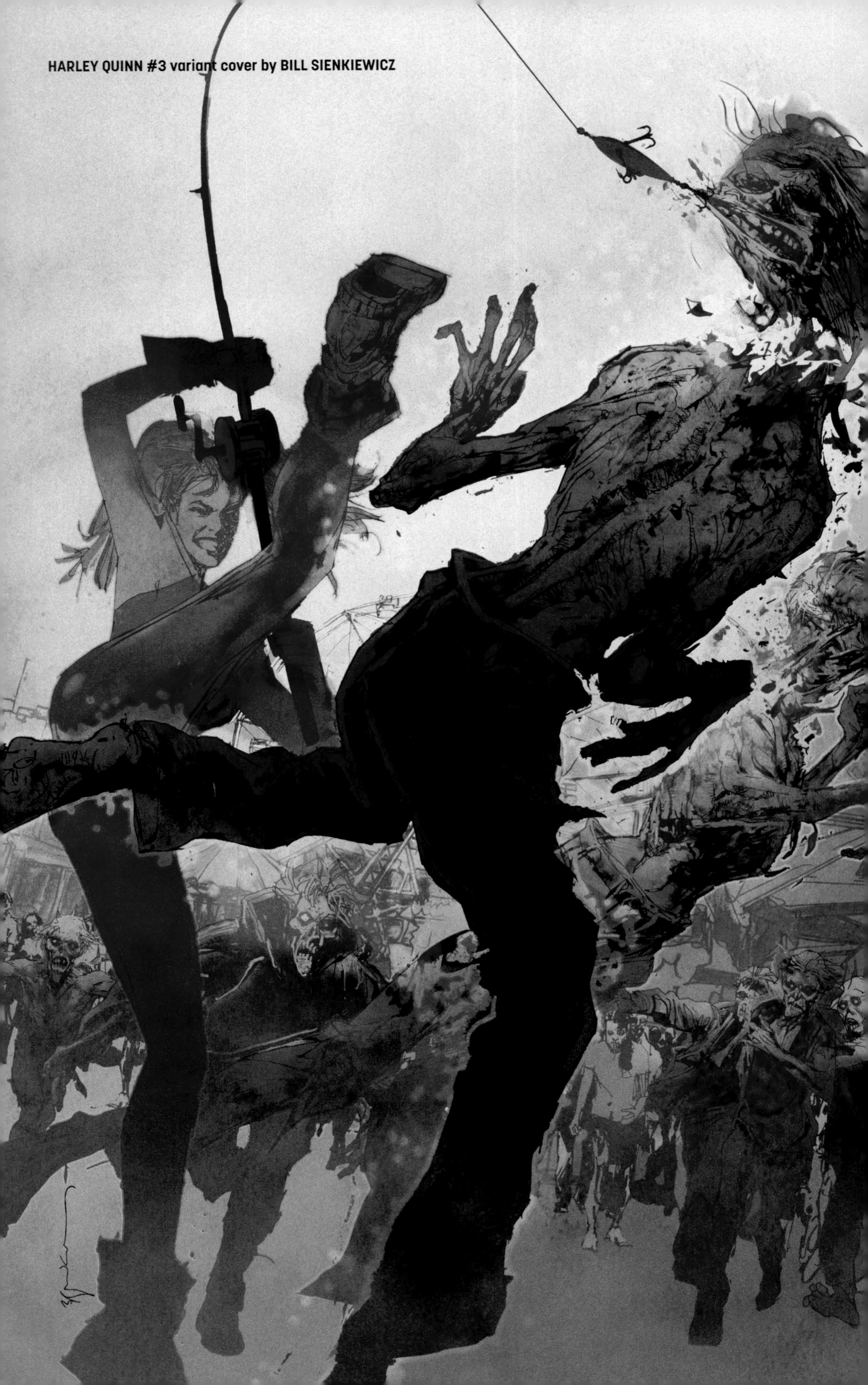

HARLEY QUINN #4 variant cover by BILL SIENKIEWICZ

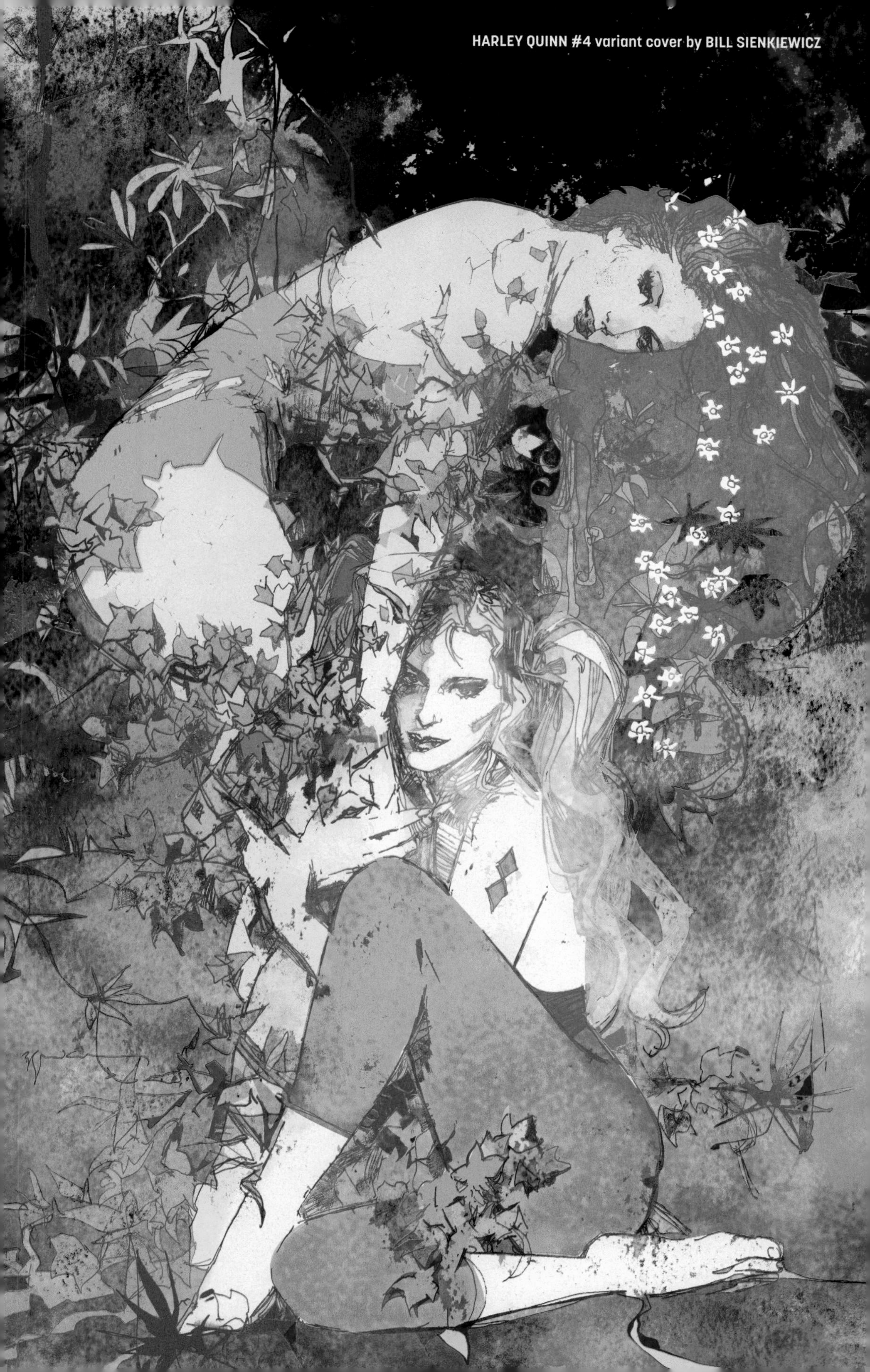

HARLEY QUINN #5 variant cover by BILL SIENKIEWICZ

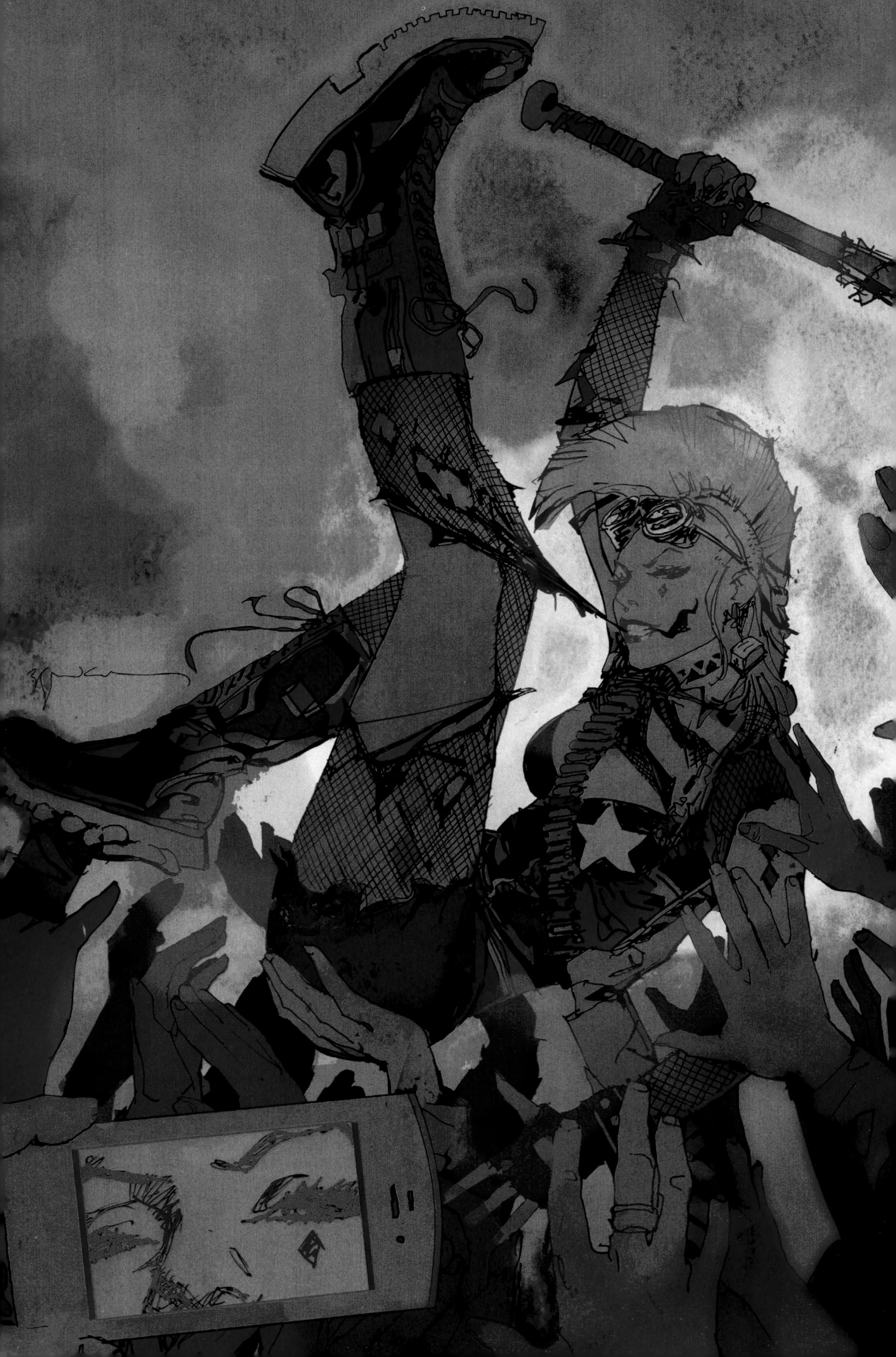

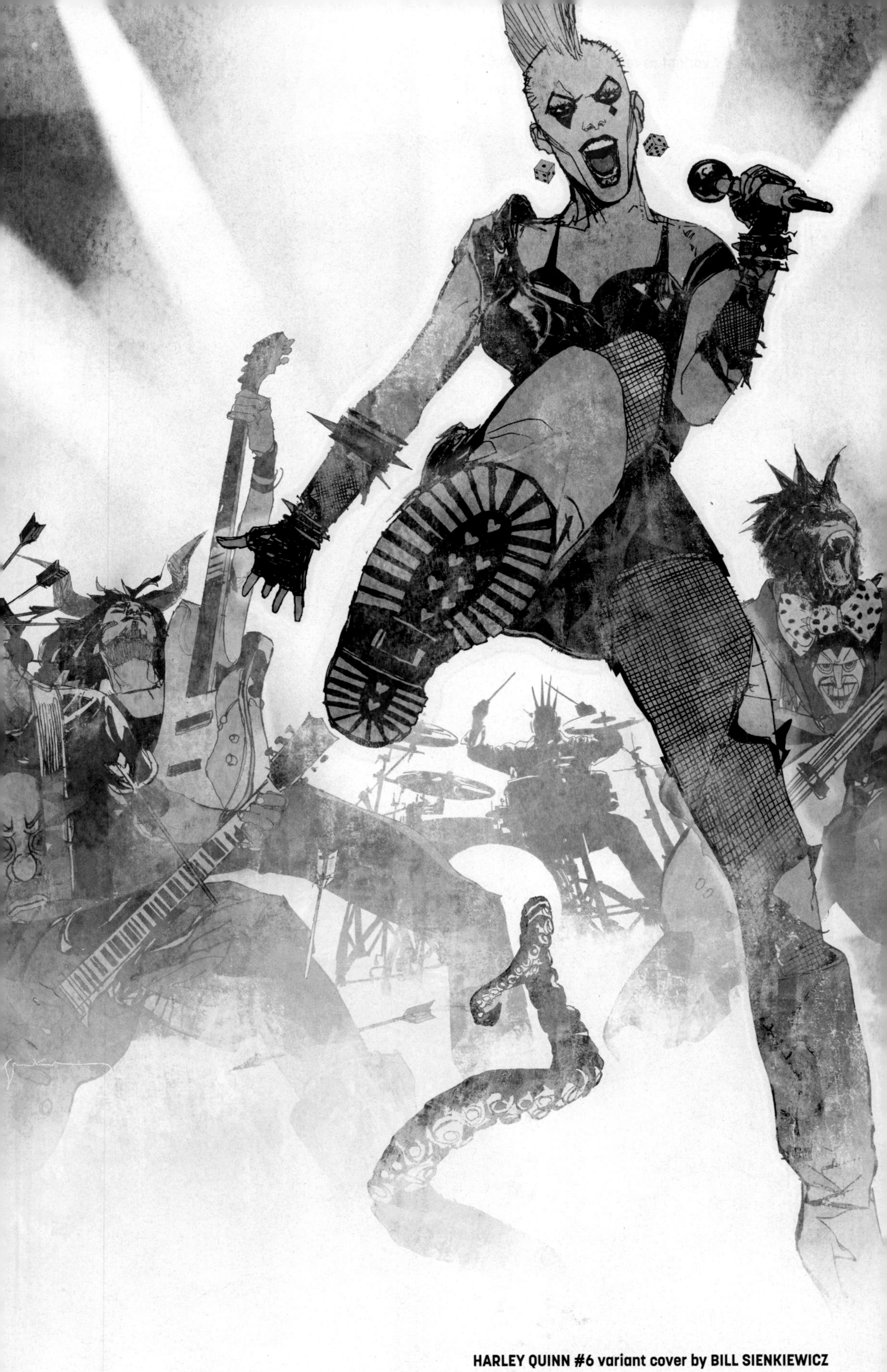

HARLEY QUINN #6 variant cover by BILL SIENKIEWICZ

HARLEY QUINN #7 variant cover by BILL SIENKIEWICZ

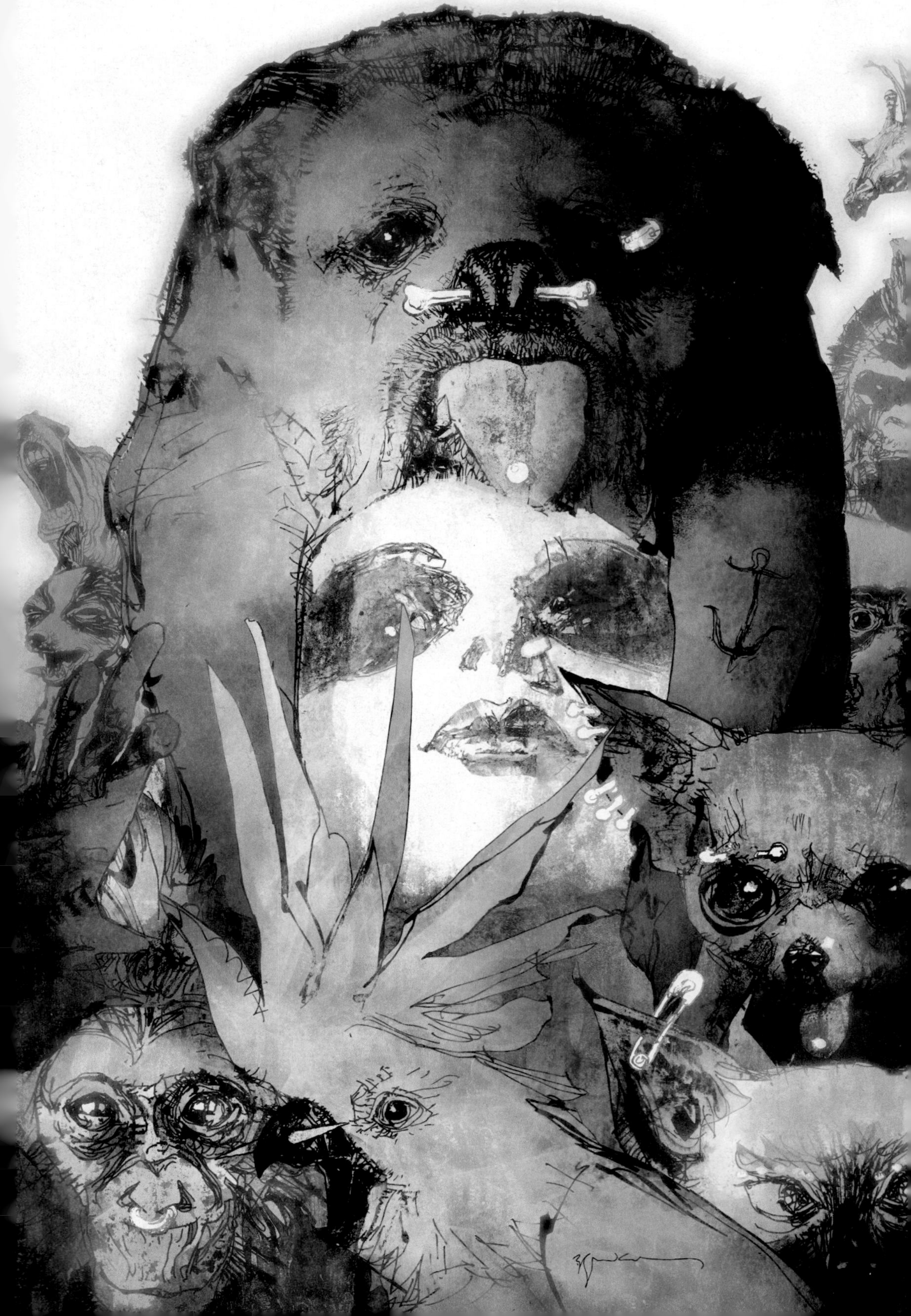

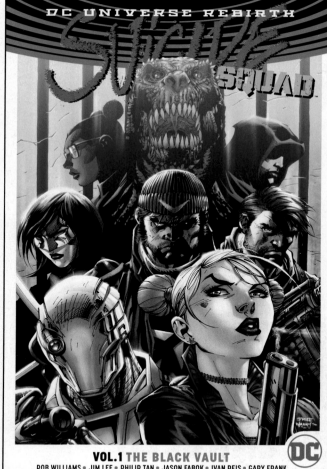

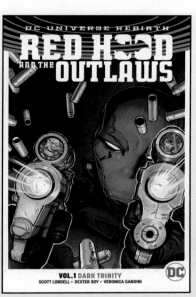

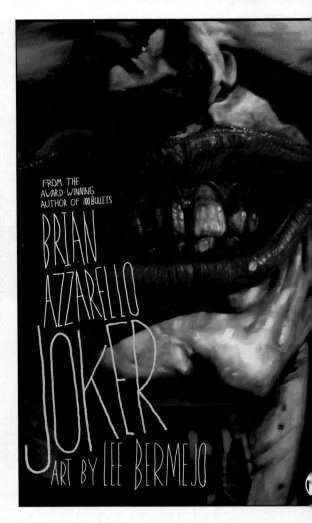